Haida Culture in Custody

Haida Culture in Custody

The Masset Band

Mary Lee Stearns

University of Washington Press
Seattle and London

Douglas & McIntyre
Vancouver

This book was published with the assistance of a grant from
the Andrew W. Mellon Foundation

Library of Congress Cataloging in Publication Data
Stearns, Mary Lee.
   Haida culture in custody.

   Bibliography: p.
   Includes index.
   1. Haida—Indians.   2. Haida Indians—Government
relations.   3. Indians of North America—Canada
—Government relations.   I. Title.
E99.H2S73   970.004'97   80-50862
ISBN 0-295-95763-8

Canadian Cataloguing in Publication Data
Stearns, Mary Lee
   Haida culture in custody
   Bibliography: p.
   ISBN 0-88894-310-5 (pbk); 0-88894-319-9 (cl)
   1. Haida Indians - Social life and customs.
2. Indians of North America - Social life
and customs.   I. Title.
E99.H2S84   970.004'97   C81-091079-9

Cover: Haida Masset in the early 1930s (courtesy of the British
        Columbia Provincial Archives, nos. 13852, 13854)

In Memory of Colleen

Foreword

THIS BOOK is about a group of people with a distinctive culture and history, living on the outskirts of the twentieth century. It attempts to explain what has happened to them in the process of becoming a cultural enclave in Canada. Their experiences are not unique. They are, on the contrary, depressingly familiar to the student of change in tribal societies. The object of this study is not simply to compile another history of depopulation and cultural loss, nor even to record a chapter of this rich human experiment. It is concerned primarily with the *process* of becoming dependent and, more generally, with the processes of change.

What I hoped to achieve when I began field work was the collection of a comprehensive corpus of data for a single society so that I might bring to its analysis the several perspectives that interested me—historical, demographic, cultural, and sociological—though not necessarily in the same volume. My interest was not in ethnographic detail for its own sake. I wanted to pursue the same theoretical issues that occupied social anthropologists working in Africa and elsewhere. I chose to carry on research in North America rather than in Oceania or Africa partly because I wanted to be able to return to my family in an emergency and partly because great sections of the continent were virgin territory for a social anthropologist.

What drew me to the Northwest Coast was the challenge of working in an area which has been described as "the last refuge of the Boasians." Given my primarily sociological orientations, it may seem incongruous that I aspired to admission to this select company. But the influence of British structural-functionalism did not diminish the effects of being steeped in the five sub-fields of the discipline. I still identified strongly with the traditions of North American cultural anthropology.

My selection of Masset was fortuitous. In my first graduate course at

UCLA, Pedro Carrasco assigned me a report on the Haida for his
seminar, which compared the social organization of paired matrilineal
and patrilineal societies around the world. (This was the year before
Schneider and Gough's monumental *Matrilineal Kinship* appeared.)
Finally Wendell Oswalt, having heard that there was still a Haida
population on the Queen Charlotte Islands, suggested that I go and
have a look.

The first major product of this research was my doctoral dissertation
(1973). The present volume builds upon that earlier work incorporating, with some revision, the chapters on habitat, commercial economy,
the family, domestic economy, and ceremonial exchange. I drew upon
more of my field data on demography, ceremony, kinship, and political
history. New chapters on marriage and mating and the administrative
history of the band were written. The introductory and concluding
chapters were rewritten.

The theoretical implications of the data had emerged gradually. I
developed a model of overlapping systems of social relations to
observe the native community in its social contexts during a particular
phase of its history. Papers I read at professional meetings over the
years were designed to test the series of theoretical formulations by
which I hoped to explain aspects of the overall picture. The study,
then, encompasses the total interactional world of the Masset Haida,
examining the articulation of its several social realms.

In addition to its theoretical intentions, the book is an ethnography.
Although I discuss my research methods in the first chapter and in
appropriate contexts throughout the book, this is the point to acknowledge what can only be termed a bias, the only one of those I recognized which I did not try to suppress. This bias was my identification
with the civic-spirited, upwardly mobile "middle ranks" rather than
the haughty "high ranks." I was, moreover, anxious to avoid the
restrictive role of "house ethnographer" even though this provides a
proven method of eliciting rich cultural data. My attitudes were probably conducive to the kind of field research I had undertaken. Because
of my concern with obtaining complete household composition, demographic, economic, educational, and other quantitative data, I
needed to develop a wide base with access to all sectors of the population. It was also necessary to maintain an appearance of neutrality if I
were to study factional alignments and disputes in the community.
Paradoxically, my independent status as a household head, with all the
cultural connotations of that role, enabled me to develop many close
relationships that enriched my knowledge of the Haidas.

In writing this book I have attempted to share that knowledge as well
as to analyze social processes. The "we" who make so many discover-

ies and observe so many developments is not the editorial we or the pontifical we, but the companionable we, the reader and I. When I, as guide, make a decision or recount an experience I will tell you about it in the first person.

Sitting at table all these years with my family, students, friends, and other projects, this book has demanded more than its share. I cannot hope to thank all those who have contributed so much and accepted less. All those debts which I acknowledged in my dissertation, I reaffirm. There I offered my thanks to the people of Masset who not only tolerated "all those questions" but welcomed me into the community, letting me join them at work, at meals, at funerals, and at feasts. This custom of public acknowledgment is one they will consider intelligible and proper.

Among those who took great interest in this work were Peter and Ethel Jones. Not only did they include me in family activities but they arranged invitations to other homes so that I might enjoy maximum exposure to "Haida ways." I remember my "Uncle" Peter Hill with great warmth. Though he now lies in the cemetery at Entry Point along with so many other old friends, I can still hear his mellow voice instructing me in the history and customs of the Haida. I feel a special affection for his daughter and son-in-law, Rose and Alfred Davidson, with whom I shared the role of host at his stone-moving, and treasure the gold medallion they gave me in memory of that occasion. I am grateful to the late Hereditary Chief William Matthews and his wife Emma for many pleasant hours filled with storytelling and reminiscing. I wish to express my thanks to Florence Davidson for invitations to festivities held in her house where I was always warmly received. To all the "old people" who graciously shared their recollections and knowledge with me, a heartfelt "How'a." To all my "mothers," "aunties," and "sisters" with whom I have sipped innumerable cups of tea, again, "How'a."

Several residents of New Masset were particularly helpful. Peter Henson, who was the Indian agent in 1962, introduced me to senior members of the Haida community and obtained permission from his superiors for me to study historical records and vital statistics in the agency office. The hospitality which he and his wife Megan extended to a homesick graduate student was deeply appreciated. When I returned to Masset for the year 1965–66, his successor Wally Easton permitted me to continue my work with the files. Sam Simpson and Gene Simpson, successive managers of the Queen Charlotte Canners, provided information essential to my study of the fishing community. The late Garth Bryans, who was principal of the Masset Elementary and Secondary School during my field year, offered me a part-time teaching job, which provided the opportunity for close association with Indian and white children in the school. I confess to a teacher's pride in seeing so many of those former students emerge as first rate artists. Indeed, this book may be viewed as a study of the social milieu in which the renaissance in Haida art was generated.

In planning my first field trip to the Charlottes I received valuable assistance from the late Wilson Duff who was at that time curator of ethnology at the British Columbia Provincial Museum.

I acknowledge the continuing influence of my teachers at UCLA and, in particular, Walter Goldschmidt. As chairman of my doctoral committee, his careful criticism of draft after draft of my dissertation helped to focus my thinking as I groped toward an understanding of social process. He has not seen this manuscript and cannot be held accountable for its deficiencies. Nonetheless, it was he who first alerted me to some of the themes developed in this book. The manuscript has been read in several drafts by my steadfast friend Jane Underwood whom I first met in Professor Carrasco's seminar. I have relied heavily upon her advice, especially in demographic matters, but, again, she cannot be held responsible for the use I have made of her suggestions. Wayne Suttles, Jay Miller, and Reuben Ware have offered helpful criticisms of the complete work. Steve Harrell read an earlier draft of the chapter on the family system, offering valuable commentary. Several staff members at Simon Fraser University rendered indispensable services, usually at the instigation of Jean Jordan, departmental assistant of Sociology and Anthropology. Sylvia Hadwen Bishop, Bernice Dewick, and Lynn Kumpula typed the manuscript. Jaqui Campbell drew the maps and Lou Crockett the diagrams.

Special recognition is due my colleague, Margaret Blackman. Ever since she came to Masset as a graduate student in 1971, we have shared many stimulating hours, comparing our data on genealogies and lineage membership and discussing our interpretations of Haida history and culture. I am also indebted to my graduate student, Marianne Bölscher, who is in the field at present. Not only has she contributed news of recent events in Masset, but we have exchanged ideas about the meaning of these developments. She will soon be writing her own chapters in Haida studies.

Financial support for my first field trip to Masset in 1962 was provided by the George C. Barker Memorial Fund Award from UCLA. The National Museum of Canada and the University of California supported my field year of 1965–66. Grants to Roberta Hall and me from the University of Victoria Committee on Faculty Research, Leave and Travel for the years 1971–73 enabled me to continue the collection and analysis of demographic data. An award from the Phillips Fund of the

American Philosophical Society in 1973 allowed me to study documents and artifacts of Haida culture in the American Museum of Natural History. Funds provided by R. C. Brown, Dean of Arts of Simon Fraser University, in March 1980 gave me the opportunity to resume field work on the fishing industry in Masset and to prepare the epilogue for this volume.

I am deeply grateful to Richard Stearns for substantial support and encouragement throughout my years at UCLA. Warm thanks are due Francis Dixon for helping in uncounted ways.

I conclude these acknowledgments, which could easily be mistaken for a "thanking speech" at a Haida feast, with reference to my family. The Haidas would think it appropriate for me to make a public statement of appreciation to my parents for their example and instruction, and especially for passing along their own sense of adventure. They would understand my gratitude to my brother Bob whose aid at a critical juncture allowed me to continue working at this task. They would approve this expression of affection for my children who have grown up with this book in their midst . . . for Eileen, my collaborator on the ethnographic film and much else, for Dick, the ideal research assistant but for the foundations' refusal to grant bed and board to a kinsman, and for Michael, a veteran at the age of ten of the discoveries and discomforts of field work, who grew up to become a boatbuilder in Ketchikan.

It is too late now to thank my dearest friend and kindest critic, Dana Morgenson, but his memory lives in everything I do. The volume is dedicated to my sister Colleen, who gave me my first book in anthropology but didn't live to receive this one in exchange.

M.L.S.
Crescent Beach, British Columbia
October 1980

Contents

Haida Culture in Custody

Chapter 1
Introduction

IN MYTHICAL TIMES when the northern Haida Ravens dispersed from their Story Town at Rose Spit, that branch known as the Skidaqao settled just inside Masset Inlet at a place called Uttewas, "White Slope Town." The village prospered, becoming one of the most important Haida centers. After the fateful encounter of the traders Dixon and Portlock at Cloak Bay in 1787, the European tide began to lap at the shores of the Queen Charlotte Islands.

The next century brought more traders and finally, in 1876, the missionary, William H. Collison. He was followed by geologists, surveyors, prospectors, photographers, lumbermen, settlers, cannery operators, even tourists. By this time the northern Haidas, their numbers decimated by disease and migration, had abandoned their isolated north and west coast villages, coming together at Uttewas, now called Masset. Survivors of the southern villages huddled at Skidegate, though a few families still clung to their ancestral sites. In 1876 Parliament approved an "Act to amend and consolidate the laws respecting Indians." The comprehensive new Indian Act had little meaning for the Haidas until 1910 when the Queen Charlotte Agency was established at Masset and the remnants of Haida society passed into the custody of the Dominion of Canada.

For more than half a century a succession of Indian agents, housed first on the Masset reserve and later in the neighboring white settlement of New Masset, exercised broad powers over the lives and affairs of the Haidas. So pervasive was this control that even the activities of keeping house and giving parties were scrutinized. Toward the end of this period, government philosophy began to respond to changes in the climate of opinion in the wider Canadian society and in the world beyond. Integration replaced custodianship as official Indian policy. Then, in 1966, two events occurred which mark a milestone in the social history of the Haidas.

In the spring of that year, the doors of the Queen Charlotte Agency were closed for the last time, its business and personnel transferred to the new consolidated office at Prince Rupert. Although the Department of Indian Affairs still controls the Haidas' business indirectly through native officeholders, the closing of the agency signaled the end of personal paternalism. Later that year the cannery passed from the hands of a local white family to a large Vancouver firm. For decades this company had been the major market for produce and wage labor, fostering the economic interdependence of the Indian village and New Masset. Since the Haidas' relationship with the owners, modeled on that with their Indian agents, had already deteriorated by 1966, the significance of these events was largely symbolic. Nevertheless, the formal termination of these relations, which so profoundly influenced the character of the Masset people and their institutions, offers a vantage point for analyzing the custodial relationship.

What commends this case to our attention is the fact that, despite extensive changes in political, economic, and family relations, the Masset Haidas preserved a flourishing ceremonial life patterned on the old matrilineal model and supporting a modified version of traditional values. This book explores changes in the social realms of the Masset Haida: the protected, inner world of the community and the surrounding, overlapping world of the whites. It shows how these worlds were shaped, how the Haidas see them, and how they have managed to live within their confines.

TRADITIONAL HAIDA SOCIETY

Along with other Northwest Coast tribes, the Haidas are notable in the ethnographic catalogue as one of the few peoples on a fishing-collecting level of economy who were able to maintain sedentary residence and a ranking system based on wealth and hereditary status. Settled in permanent villages along the coasts of the Charlottes, surrounded by the stormy moats of Hecate Strait and Dixon Entrance, the Haidas enjoyed an incomparable ecological advantage. The halibut banks and seasonal salmon runs provided reliable sources of food which could be stored in great quantities. Stands of red cedar yielded inexhaustible supplies of materials for the great plank houses, totem poles, and canoes, as well as clothing and furnishings. With their subsistence needs so amply met, the Haidas enjoyed the opportunity to develop their arts and crafts and the social institutions of ritual, trade, and war.

The social system was based upon autonomous matrilineages, termed "families" by Swanton (1909) and "clans" by Murdock (1934,

1936). The widest kin grouping was the moiety composed of related lineages and symbolized by the Raven and Eagle crests, respectively. The strongest prescriptions of traditional culture governed relations between members of opposite moieties, specifying intermarriage by the rule of exogamy and imposing ceremonial obligations to members of the "other side." Exogamous divisions, which characterized other matrilineal societies of the northern Pacific coast as well, channeled relations of marriage and trade with non-Haidas.

As the corporate group, the lineage controlled economic and symbolic property and performed juridical, political, and ceremonial functions. Internally, this structure consisted of a series of ranked statuses ascribed according to genealogical closeness to the lineage head who was elder brother or mother's brother to other members. Standing outside this system were the slaves, captured in war or purchased from middlemen.

Rarely did the strong authority vested in the head extend beyond his own descent group. Rank entailing political power was attained through hereditary succession to the headship and by competition between heads of segmentary units for recognition in the potlatch. In the absence of any hierarchical organization, the potlatch served the dual functions of integrating lineages of both moieties and of defining boundaries between them by channeling competitiveness and acknowledging rank differentiation. With a premium on wealth and high status. competition also took the form of war. The Haidas terrorized distant villages with their raids for captives and plunder. Their canoes gave them the mobility and striking power of nomads while their own villages were relatively secure from retaliation by mainland tribes. The myths suggest that against other Haidas they waged wars of extermination in pursuit of age-old feuds (Swanton 1908, 1911). No permanent alliances were formed although related lineages were said to "help" each other.

These features of their social life—strong corporate groups under aggressive leadership, the principle of self-help and absence of hierarchical organization, economic self-sufficiency and a seasonal cycle alternating subsistence with other social pursuits—bred those qualities of fierce independence and pride that are often associated with pastoral nomads.[1] Foremost among the changes which this study will attempt to explain is the development of attitudes of dependency and passivity in this competitive society.

1. Goldschmidt attempts to "demonstrate that personality attributes characteristic of a population are in a very large measure to be seen as an aspect of ecological adaptation." The most important element in this adaptation is mobility (Goldschmidt 1971; also see Edgerton 1971).

MODERN SOCIAL ORGANIZATION

At the close of the agency period, Haida society survives as two decapitated communities, stripped of internal autonomy and effective leadership. Their numbers have only partly recovered from the epidemics and migrations of the nineteenth century which reduced the population by 90 percent. In May 1966 fewer than 700 people resided in Masset while the population of Skidegate was half that number. With the establishment of white settlements and industries on the Queen Charlotte Islands, the Haidas lost access to most of the lands and resources they formerly controlled. Many species upon which they depended for their livelihood have been so depleted that government regulation has been imposed. Since they now have an inadequate subsistence base, the people have been drawn into the economy of the larger society as commercial fishermen and wage earners. Only the institutions of kinship, subsistence, hereditary chiefship, and ceremonial exchange can be carried on with the native community.

In listing structural features of modern Haida social organization, then, we are describing an internal field of relations, a microcosm, ignoring for the moment the nature of its articulation with the macrocosm.[2] For, whether this articulation occurs in the economic or political sphere, other areas of social life are segregated from the mainstream by proscriptions against interaction. Our present concern is to identify the structures existing in 1966 behind the "ethnic boundary."[3]

The _nuclear-core family_, consisting of a conjugal pair and their children, with the possible addition of grandchildren and other relatives, has replaced the extended matrilineal household as the basic unit of social life. The conjugal bond has superseded the mother's brother–sister's child tie as the pivotal social relationship.

The bilaterally linked _network of households_ is seen by the people as the nuclear family grown up and settled in separate residences, usually

2. The terms microcosm and macrocosm are used by Bennett (1967). He offers a "games-playing model," which illustrates the possibilities for local people to mold external forces. His focus on individuals in the local setting interacting with individuals in external bureaucracies parallels the approach adopted in this book.

3. The concept of "ethnic boundary" as used here follows Barth: a social boundary entailing a complex organization of behavior and social relations including, in particular, a systematic set of rules governing interethnic social encounters (Barth 1969:15–16). Though the groups that are segregated in the present case are ethnically distinct, I do not follow Barth's usage of "ethnic group," which he defines as "a form of social organization" while deemphasizing "objective" cultural differences (Barth 1969:13–14). My usage is compatible with Keyes' attempt to formulate a concept of ethnic groups based on shared descent, which "take their particular form as a consequence of the structure of inter-group relations" (Keyes 1976:208). In this study, however, I have used the terms "cultural group" and "cultural enclave" rather than "ethnic group," which has other connotations.

not contiguous. This circle of kinsmen incorporates spouses and children, and often parents' and grandparents' siblings and "cousins" as well. While their members do not pool their efforts in subsistence activities, they offer mutual aid in times of crisis, cooperate in providing support for members' ceremonial activities, and sponsor events of community-wide interest. This bilateral circle is not recognized as a formal structure with quasi-political functions, probably because the matrilineal framework survives as a model for ceremonial interaction and as a mechanism integrating the community.

Matrilineal categories include the remnants of 11 lineages of both moieties. Though it has lost its corporate functions, the lineage still serves the senior segment of the population as a reference group. The shift to bilaterality in primary kin groupings does not preclude the retention of matrilineal elements that do not conflict with internal adjustments of the family system. For example, the relationship of father's sister and brother's child is still of crucial importance in the ritual observance of life-cycle events. But the lineage can no longer be mobilized as a group. With its steady decline in numbers, the moiety has increased in importance as a classificatory device which provides a larger pool of relatives on "the opposite side" who may be called upon to fill prescribed ritual roles.

Ranking as a principle of status differentiation is inconsistent with the value the people now place on the economic independence of individuals and nuclear units and on the equality of all village members. Only the symbolic status of hereditary town chief is generally accorded precedence. Nevertheless, descendants of high-ranking chiefs still enjoy considerable prestige and high value is placed upon the passing on of titles in the feasts.

For most purposes, however, the traditional segmentary organization based on descent has been superseded by horizontal groupings based on age. Five cross-cutting *age grades* whose members share special interests and values can be delineated. Children under the age of 14 years comprise 53 percent of the village population, while young adults between the ages of 15 and 29 constitute 21 percent. Persons from 30 to 44 years, who may be referred to as the parental generation, comprise 10 percent of residents. The two senior groups—the middle-aged between 45 and 59 years and the old people between the ages of 60 and 86 years—each account for 8 percent of the population. While not all members of any age category regularly take part in the activities characteristic of their cohort, individuals tend to seek out others of their own age for recreational, religious, community service, and other voluntary activities. The categories reflect discontinuity in socialization, for their members have had different experiences with the outside world and have received a progressively diluted version of traditional culture. As a result, younger people are not systematically enculturated in the "old-fashioned ways" of their elders, but are instead presented with several role models. Consequently, Masset cannot be regarded as culturally homogeneous, although there is strong continuity in behavior as well as in the underlying system of ideas and assumptions.

The terms community, reserve, cultural group, and "the village" (used by the Haidas), refer to the internal field of relations. In modern as in traditional society, the *village* is seen as the largest effective social grouping. The people themselves stress village residence as essential to participation in cultural life. While members of the other surviving village of Skidegate are considered Haidas, social interaction between the two groups is very limited. Nor does the cultural group embrace both communities for, now as in traditional times, there are significant differences in institutions.[4] It is largely in the context of their own village, then, that their identity as Haidas has any meaning or

4. No comparative structural analysis of Skidegate has yet been carried out. Van den Brink reports on the uncordial relations between the two communities (1974:70, 91, 113, 166–69, 265); however, his book must be used with extreme caution. Although he has assembled a great mass of data, he has been uncritical in his selection and utilization of sources; for example, "The description of old Haida culture is based primarily on the picture given by Murdock in . . . *Our Primitive Contemporaries* . . ." (1974:256).

"Library research, investigation of English and Canadian archives, interviews (in 1964 and 1965), and correspondence with informants in Canada supplied the bulk of the material" (256). His gleaning of these sources was certainly thorough. He seemed to receive an extraordinary degree of assistance (ix,x), especially from the Indian Commissioner for British Columbia: "To enable me to Xerox a number of documents, he had almost the entire files of the Masset Agency brought to his [Vancouver] office" (5). Van den Brink's almost total reliance on these sources is responsible for the serious distortions which characterize the entire book.

In fact, his book is most useful when considered not as a study of the Haida, since its author had almost no contact with the people, but as a report on what government officials, clergymen, and a very few other outsiders had to say about the Haida. Their (and his) assessments are biased and in many instances the "evidence" cited is false. Briefly, he purports to compare the processes of culture change as they affected Masset and Skidegate during four periods of contact history. He concludes that the Skidegates are more industrious in preserving and freezing food for winter than the Masset Haidas (151); they drink less (152) and have less illegitimacy (159), but have more telephones and toilets, better water and houses (148–49), and newer cars (170) than in Masset. These comparisons are conveniently summarized at the end of the volume (1974:256–67).

In the period 1900–40, "In contrast to the situation at Skidegate, the Masset council was unable to help the Indians . . . adjust to the economic difficulties; the situation . . . deteriorated rapidly and delinquency increased . . . the population seemed depressed . . . did not make any appreciable effort to find new sources of income. . . . All this gave these Haida a bad reputation among the Europeans and diminished contact with the Skidegates.

"In the 1920s the population of Skidegate was one of the most progressive Indian groups in British Columbia . . . active council . . . excellent reputation as workers and showed initiative in various fields. . . . used the services of banks and profited from the

cultural content. In the intercultural situation as defined by whites, they are categorized simply as Indians. This situation began to change in the late 1970s.

The structural features of the community were shaped by three major factors: changes in technology and economic relations, demographic processes of decline and recovery, and limitations imposed by external political control. Since these factors are related to changes in the external environment of the Haidas, we are not dealing with the consequences of internal technological growth, which is one of five "mechanisms of social evolution" identified by Goldschmidt (1959: 106–44).

Liberally paraphrased, the processes operating in this situation include:

1. Changes in social relations in response to technological and structural changes

2. The development of institutional congruity as changes in crucial institutions are ramified in the social system

3. Selection among available alternatives

4. Cultural continuity, which is not a passive process but depends upon the reinforcement of traditional norms and values

market situation. . . . Independent action based on sound mutual consultation . . ." (1974:262).

Van den Brink's field work consisted of a two-month "orientational visit to the Islands (in 1965), staying in Masset and Skidegate. It was virtually impossible to perform extensive fieldwork at this time. In Masset the situation was extremely tense due to a serious conflict with the managers of the fish cannery . . ." (5). I arrived back in Masset two months later to spend the year in field research. Presumably Van den Brink is referring to me when he writes, "When the band councils opposed the giving of information to outsiders, a Canadian writer [sic] had to terminate her historical research in Massett . . ." (5). I never met Van den Brink, although I was often told in the places I frequented that I had just missed him. Apparently he was never told that he had just missed me.

He continues, ". . . but thanks to my preparatory correspondence I was able to collect information in both Masset and Skidegate on various aspects of the cultural situation of the Indians. In this I was assisted not only by the local governmental official and the minister but also by the Chief Councillor of Masset and a number of Haida who were . . . members of the band council . . ." (5), and he names three men. "At Skidegate the Haida were unwilling to cooperate, with the exception of the Secretary of the band council . . ." (5). Except for Godfrey Kelly, whose letters and remarks are cited frequently, it is difficult to discern the input of Van den Brink's other three Masset Haida informants.

There *are* objective differences between the Masset and Skidegate Haidas, but Van den Brink has contributed nothing to their illumination. His book may be described as journalism, but it cannot be regarded as scholarship. The Masset people were not aware of Van den Brink's work when I visited them in February 1977; however, their rage at another book, which they considered defamatory, was a factor in their decision in 1974 to impose an extremely restrictive contract on all prospective writers, including serious and responsible scholars.

Changes in Economic and Social Relations

The most significant economic changes were stimulated by the introduction of new technological developments and the opening of an external market for produce and wage labor. In an analysis of technological changes introduced during the fur trade period, Joyce Wike
pointed to an important consequence of involvement in the European
market system. "It is inherent in the conditions of constantly 'rebor-
rowing' important elements through the market that the independence
and autonomy of the (so-called) backward economy is lost and its
functioning rapidly and drastically modified" (1958:1089).

Only a small part of the technology of the advanced society was
exported to the Indians. During the fur-trade period this included
firearms and traps, iron tools, textiles, and processed foods (Wike
1947). In the last century the establishment of fish canneries extended
part of the industrial complex to this remote area. Associated elements
such as gas boats, nets, canning equipment, and deep freezers have
been made available for use in traditional subsistence pursuits as well
as in commercially oriented activities. From the standpoint of changes
in complexity of the material culture, however, European tool technology had a limited effect on native society in comparison with the far-
reaching consequences we might expect from internal technological
development (Goldschmidt 1959:115). Even so, the adoption of new
equipment precipitated a reorganization of economic activities as individuals were able to perform their work more efficiently and independently. Kin-group cooperation in productive activities was superseded
by new relationships extending across cultural group boundaries, linking buyer and producer, employer and wage earner. Participation in the
European marketplace, then, permitted and promoted the indi-
vidualization of economic action, undermining traditional forms of resource exploitation based on cooperative labor, breaking the economic
monopolies of chiefs, and weakening their already tenuous authority.

The physical and social mobility offered to individuals by new
sources of wage work had other profound consequences for the social
system. Labor migration, along with disease and warfare, was a major
cause of depopulation. Tribal societies were drained of their most active members, the survivors of decimated lineages regrouping in nucleated villages of which Masset was the largest. Extended matrilineal
households were fragmented and networks of social and ceremonial
interaction disrupted. The systematic socialization of succeeding generations to traditional values was no longer assured.

With the departure of the young and middle-aged for white settlements and the abandonment of the old and very young in native vil-

lages, it would be misleading to say that the matrilineage segmented into its minimal units. Nevertheless, a new form of domestic organization developed. Individual men assisted by their wives earned cash and produced goods for their own consumption. The pattern of seasonal migration in search of employment reinforced the Haidas' perception of the conjugal pair as the most important social and economic unit. In addition, the women's ability to earn cash strengthened their position in the marital relationship. The emergence of the nuclear family, then, may be viewed as a response to economic conditions in which payment for produce or labor is made to the individual rather than the group.

Gough refers to this process as the "disintegration of matrilineal descent groups" (1961). At the heart of her argument is the functionalist proposition that change in a crucial part of a social system is ramified throughout that system. Once radical economic change is set in motion by the opening of market opportunities, the process of restructuring the matrilineal society rolls on to its inexorable conclusion in the disintegration of traditional culture.

She concedes that if the politically dominant society is not interested in absorbing the subordinate population in the market system as producers, consumers, and taxpayers, but is content to confine them on reserves, then traditional institutions may survive (1961:640). Gough illustrates her argument by reference to the Hopi and Navaho societies, which, having comparatively few transactions in the market system, have been able to maintain their cultural coherence. But where pressures such as overpopulation, drought, or crop failure drive the people into the marketplace, she insists, the same symptoms of disintegration may be expected to appear in kinship institutions (1961:641). What she overlooks, however, are the structural factors entailed in "the incorporation of matrilineal descent systems in the market system of an industrialized state." That is, she ignores ethnic boundaries and the mechanisms which maintain them.

Of course, we may expect that changes in economic relations resulting from participation in the marketplace will reverberate in other areas of social life. Nevertheless, we shall see that the full force of these changes does not radiate throughout the dependent social system but is concentrated in economically active groups. With the emergence of the nuclear family, economic activities are carried out almost entirely at this level. Wider kinship networks are not involved except in property exchange, which is conducted in terms of traditional rules. Even exchange between nuclear units of bilaterally linked households follows old rules of formal reciprocity. In this study the shift from the matrilineal to the bilateral mode of interpreting primary kinship obligations is interpreted not as evidence of social disintegration but of adaptation to new conditions. It demonstrates the development of congruity with institutions of the dominant society.

The rights and obligations, norms and expectations attached to roles in the bilateral family differ to some extent from those in the traditional Haida family system. In analyzing modern family structure we do not find a wholesale shift from one form to the other, but rather selection among alternative role definitions. Because of this scope for selection, the bilateral family household can function efficiently in two relational fields, internal and external. The nuclear family is compatible with external economic and social conditions. It is adaptable to and reinforced by the individualized economic action demanded of participants in the Canadian market system. The fact that it is also congruent with the family structure of Canadian society facilitates government provision of welfare, educational, and medical services for its members.

This shift in family organization is reflected in the idea system. Normative statements asserting the independence of the nuclear unit consistent with its external relations are reiterated in the internal social field of the community. Obligations to kinsmen beyond the domestic family are defined by the traditional mechanism of formal reciprocity, which now affirms the identity and separateness of the nuclear unit.

Since the household has become the most important social and economic grouping, its head has replaced the lineage head as the person responsible for the performance of ceremonial functions for his close matrilateral kinsmen. With the emphasis placed on the conjugal bond at the expense of matrilateral affiliations, the provision of feasts is an enterprise of bilateral families, which usually crosscut lineage and moiety boundaries. This interdependence of traditional competitors requires the suppression of the competitive aspect of potlatching as formerly practiced by opposing matrilineages. An uninstitutionalized form of competition has developed between households as their heads vie for prestige in the provision of lavish feasts. In this developing congruity of ceremonial and family relations, traditional social organization is reinterpreted, while much of its distinctive cultural content is preserved. On the other side of the issue, the effects of adaptation to external conditions impinge upon the most traditionally oriented activities even though these are carried on entirely within the community.

Cultural Continuity

Continuity with traditional culture depends upon the reinforcement of old Haida norms and values by several means. Behavior that expresses traditional ideas is practiced by a significant number of village residents. Subsistence activities, exchange of property, observance of life-cycle events, and honoring of matrilateral kinsmen are the most important examples. Not only are cultural patterns kept alive in this way, but social boundaries separating the cultural group from the dominant society are explicitly recognized and reinforced. For example, one speaker at a name-taking feast remarked, "Whites don't give names but Indians should keep on passing names down."

The redefinition of social relations, illustrated by the discussion of shifts in family organization, is an important mechanism for preserving traditional behavior. We noted that the household head has assumed the ceremonial responsibilities formerly assigned to the lineage head, while it is the bilateral network rather than the lineage that provides economic support. We shall examine other instances where responsibility for performing prescribed duties is allocated to substitutes if the individuals or groups originally charged with these obligations are no longer available. For example, the function of witnessing status-validating ceremonies is now performed by the senior age group, which represents the whole community. Formerly witnesses were members of opposing matrilineages who represented the "other side." Similarly, the Women's Auxiliary of the Anglican Church "stands in" for the opposite moiety in life-cycle rites. This realignment of groups has not completely blurred the old social dichotomy, however, for certain ritual roles traditionally assigned to father's sister and male cross-cousins must be performed by an individual of appropriate age and sex in the opposite moiety. If a "real" relative is not available, a surrogate is designated by the host.

We shall see that events as well as relations are often reinterpreted to make them meaningful in terms of the Haidas' cultural assumptions. This process is particularly important where norms of the dominant society are imposed on the people. The application of Canadian law, which is based on unfamiliar principles, will provide several instructive examples of reinterpretation.

Community pressure may be exerted to enforce conformity to group norms, although this is possible only in rare instances where there is consensus among various sectors of the Haida population. "Cultural norms," which relate to Indian status and identity, are supported in this manner. Occasionally when the group itself is threatened, as in cases of homicide, the community mobilizes to impose heavy informal sanctions on the offender.

Underlying this continuity in behavior is a set of traditional percepts that, in 1966, still suffused the Haida view of the world. The Haidas explicitly recognize the authority of these ideas and beliefs, which they refer to as "old Indian ways." The most compelling of these may be noted.

1. Obligations to matrilateral kinsmen involve considerable expense in the performance of life-cycle rituals for the deceased and in the rendering of ceremonial assistance to the living.

2. The use of property as a technique of defining and handling interpersonal relationships and attitudes underlies exchange on the one hand and the prestige system on the other. In the exchange system the circulation of goods reaffirms the mutual interdependence of separate units and reinforces the solidarity of the cultural group. The most prestigious use of property is the provision of feasts, which demonstrates support of the traditional culture. Alternate uses, as in the purchase of boats, houses, automobiles, furnishings, and so on, also earn approval, for the Haidas continue to respect evidence of achievement.

3. Standards of excellence are expected of occupants of or aspirants to high status: generosity in the giving of gifts, payments, and feasts; reliability in fulfilling promises and expectations; willingness to render public service for "the good of the people"; "good behavior," which refers to non-drunkenness and non-promiscuousness. These standards are applied not only to other Haidas but to agents, teachers, nurses, ministers, police, ethnographers, and other members of the dominant sector who presume to intrude on the community.

4. The occupational role of fisherman rests on the conviction that "Haidas have to go fishing. It's in their blood."

5. The idea of rank is still a powerful element of Haida culture although it is no longer supported by the social structure. Descendants of high ranking chiefs continue to claim privileges and precedence while the majority angrily repudiate such claims. Hereditary status is verbally rejected as a basis for instrumental leadership but, until recently, those who offered their services were usually persons of high birth. That the concept of rank continues to form a basic dimension of Haida thought is suggested by their embracing of the union rule of seniority, which offers a finely graded scale of privileges and precedence.

6. Exogamy is a basic rule of traditional culture which continues as a measure of the propriety of a marriage even though it no longer seems to play a recognized part in spouse selection. Among middle-aged and older persons at least, those who "married right" by observing the rule take pride in the fact, while those who "married brothers or sisters" are defensive.

I do not suggest that all Haidas subscribe to these ideas for, as we have noted, members of the different age grades support different interests and values. I do suggest, however, that the outlook of all Haidas is conditioned by this set of attitudes and expectations and that failure to act in terms of these cultural postulates results in guilt feelings of varying intensity. We will find that old people and descendants of the elite are, predictably, far more committed to the performance of traditional obligations than are the young and persons of undistinguished background. Yet even among the latter there is often interest in the "old fashioned ways."

The reinterpretation of these ideas, which we will observe throughout this study, illustrates the gradual erosion of traditional culture as each generation receives a more fragmentary version of old beliefs and values. With the passing of the senior members of the community, a younger generation becomes the new cohort of "old people," bringing its own diminished store of knowledge to the role of custodian of the cultural heritage. With its transition to this new status each generation seems to adopt a more "traditional" orientation than its members had espoused in earlier phases of their own life cycle. The process of reinterpretation, then, expresses both the change and the continuity which are the focus of this study.

External Constraints

A major factor influencing contemporary Haida social organization is external political control. The federal bureaucracy that assumed responsibility for decision-making, administration, social control, education, economic assistance, and medical care of Indians was the Department of Indian Affairs, known at the time of this study as the Indian Affairs Branch of the Department of Citizenship and Immigration. With their incorporation in this hierarchy, Indian communities received the special legal status of a band, a corporate group holding an estate of lands and moneys, replacing the lineages as owners of those ancestral villages which have been assigned to them as reserves.

With the creation of this new structure, the government drew a boundary segregating the cultural groups from the dominant sector, restricting recruitment and interaction. This boundary is delimited by the Indian Act, which defines the status and role of Indian and spells out the duties and powers of the government. These prescriptions are specific in denoting the range of latitude in the provisions and comprehensive in applying to almost every area of Indian life. The boundary has been maintained externally by strict government supervision and internally by collective actions that express cultural traditions. Ironically, the government's designation of native villages as communally owned reserves and of their inhabitants as members of a band, measures intended to facilitate the control and reeducation of

Indians, has instead provided a territorial base for the practice of traditional behavior, fostering a sense of identity which has encouraged a
reevaluation of their heritage and their future.

Colson attributes the survival of the Makah as a group to similar
factors—their political organization in the tribe, their joint ownership
of the reservation, and their status as wards of the government. She
does not, however, find the same conscious efforts to preserve traditional customs (1953:2–3). Epstein concludes that the structural continuity and cultural persistence of the matrilineal Tolai in New Britain
can be accounted for by discrete settlement, continued access to tribal
lands and thus to traditional subsistence activities, and by selective
participation in the cash economy (1962). It will be seen that these
factors are also of crucial importance in the Haida case.

On a more theoretical level, Barth considers the very existence of
basic ethnic categories as a factor encouraging the proliferation of
cultural differences (1969:18). On the other hand, it has been assumed
by administrators and white neighbors of the Haida that as traditional
culture fades with increased Indian-white interaction and the dying off
of old-culture bearers, the social barriers would weaken, leading gradually to assimilation. This has not been happening in Masset, partly
because of the reservoir of hostility which has been simmering in the
Indian community for decades. We shall see that the evidence seems to
support Barth's position. The socially active age groups are now comprised largely of persons who, knowing little of traditional customs,
find new ways of reinforcing the ethnic boundary. Their resentment of
the coercive power used by the dominant sector has been increasingly
expressed in political action during recent years. This study documents
the shifting emphasis in techniques by which boundaries are maintained by external authorities and by the Haidas themselves.[5] Only
time will show how much of old Haida culture will survive the processes of reinterpretation, redefinition of relations, and political confrontation.

THEORETICAL FRAMEWORK

The distinction of internal and external fields of relations requires an
approach that will deal with the native community as a partially closed
social system on the one hand, and as a component of a larger system
on the other. But ethnographic data show the Haidas engaged in trans-

5. Balandier observes that in Kachin, "Leach has revealed an overall correlation
between the two systems: the less cultural integration is developed, the more political
integration is effective, at least through submission to a single mode of political action"
(1970:33).

actions in three spheres—their own village; the local service area, which includes New Masset; and the federal bureaucracy. Each of these spheres is characterized by distinctive patterns of interaction, principles of organization, distribution of powers, and norms and values. As such they comprise three overlapping subsystems of Canadian society.

The native community constitutes a discrete cultural group whose members are related by kinship and bound by coresidence and tradition. To the extent that this group still functions as a community, its members share norms, values, and cultural symbols inculcated in the primary socialization process. Social exchange in this *communal system of relations* is governed by reciprocity and, with the weakening of the ranking system, is essentially symmetrical.

Superimposed on the natural community is the classification of "band," an administrative entity whose boundaries and membership are governed by explicit legal definitions. For the Haida, the "village" and the band are conceptually distinct. The "band-village" is incorporated in the larger social system.

I use the term "boundary structure" for the organizations established to implement the provisions of the Indian Act and to mediate relations between the dominant and subordinate sectors. Boundary structures include the Department of Indian Affairs, the Indian Health Service, and other agencies within the dominant sector, as well as the structures of the band and band council imposed on the dependent group. Boundary structures provide services and regulate interaction between the social levels according to the norms, expectations, and values of the dominant sector. This interaction depends upon mutual acceptance of the implications of the dominant-subordinate relationship. That is, the dependency of the native group, which is a consequence of surrendering control over vital functions, becomes a claim on the dominant group for the performance of those functions. Since these asymmetrical relationships were imposed upon the people without their consent and so rely ultimately upon coercion to achieve the goals of government policy, they may be described as a *compulsory system of relations*. It must be noted, however, that when we analyze actual transactions of Indian agents and other officials with Haida councilors and individuals, we will find much more give and take than the description of this monolithic organization would suggest.

The Haidas interact intensively with other residents of Greater Masset who share the same set of economic and educational facilities and public services. As members of separate political and social units, however, their interdependence is restricted largely to the economic realm. Their interaction is regulated not by shared cultural values but, ostensibly, by instrumental interests in production and exchange. In this situation the adequate role-performance of all participants is ensured, presumably, by their perception of their own self-interest. This patterned interaction may be referred to as a *utilitarian system of relations.*[6]

The compulsory and utilitarian systems comprise the external field of relations for members of the Haida community, but they are not concentric nesting relations. Oriented to different goals which are pursued by different means, they impose conflicting demands upon Indian participants. For example, we learn in chapter 3 that, historically, government officials have required conformity and submissiveness of the Haidas. In chapter 4 we discover that while local whites have often played their roles toward Indians paternalistically, their expectations of Indian performance reflect their own values of independence and achievement. The consequence of these often mutually contradictory approaches has been to weaken the effectiveness of external control over the Haida. By the time the agency office closed in 1966, we find the Haidas attempting to redefine their relationships in the external sphere.

To understand the operation of each of these systems of relations we must examine the crucial role sets, asking what rights and obligations are attached to specific roles, what expectations have been fostered between interacting role-incumbents, and what happens when these expectations are not met. Key relationships are traced through time to show how the ordering of relations and the content of interaction change in response to events and ideas. Structural changes are expressed in the reorganization of social relations, cultural change in the reinterpretation of behavior. My aim has been to depict the social and historical context that delimits the alternatives available to the Haida.

ORGANIZATION OF THE BOOK

In chapter 2 the Haida community of Masset is set in its physical, historical, and social contexts. A sketch of the habitat and history is presented along with a description of the spatial relations and facilities of Haida Masset and New Masset. Chapter 3 deals with the political context, analyzing the Haidas' relationships with Indian agents, nurses, police, teachers, and other participants in the compulsory sys-

---

6. I have adopted the term "utilitarian" from Etzioni's stimulating analysis of organizations as compliance structures (1961). Since I had already identified and explored my compulsory and communal systems of relations before I discovered his study, I saw no advantage in adopting his terms "coercive" and "normative," though there are very intriguing parallels.

tem of relations. In chapter 4 our attention shifts to the local level where economic interdependence has developed between the adjacent communities. The nature and extent of the Haidas' participation in the utilitarian system are investigated.

The remainder of the book focuses on the internal relations of Haida Masset. Chapter 5 examines the structure of the family, which stands at the interface of the internal and external fields. Analysis of household composition yields four forms or phases of family development, which are shown to carry out specialized functions for the communal system of relations. Marriage and mating are aspects of social life which show great sensitivity to changing conditions, as demonstrated in chapter 6 by my analysis of marital and reproductive behavior over the last century. Discussion of the domestic economy in chapter 7 reveals how subsistence activities and exchange uphold traditional values. The persistence of the matrilineal model is considered in chapter 8 where I examine what remains of traditional knowledge and groupings on the one hand and discuss the undermining of authority roles and rules on the other. The continuity of old Haida culture is strongest in the ceremonial exchange system as analyzed in chapter 9. Here we see how bilateral kinsmen are mobilized to support rituals reaffirming the traditional values of matrilineal kinship and rank. The significant findings and implications of the study are summarized in chapter 10.

SOURCES OF DATA

The data upon which this study is based were collected during 31 months of ethnographic fieldwork in Masset, British Columbia. I made a preliminary field trip during the summer of 1962, and returned to Masset in September 1965 with the sponsorship and financial support of the National Museum of Canada, remaining for 12 months. During each summer from 1967 to 1970 I spent three months in the field, and in 1971 collaborated in making an ethnographic film of a Haida feast. Short visits in the summer of 1974 and the winter of 1977 were devoted to updating demographic and other data and to discussing with the people the publication of this work and the film.

During my first summer in Masset I collected as much material as possible for a projected ethnohistory of the Haida. While I attempted to establish cooperative relationships with many persons, the bulk of the material was recorded in intensive interviews or "visits" with seven old people. I collected family genealogies, lineage affiliations, and histories for a majority of village residents and sought autobiographical sketches, reminiscenses, "stories," and other materials. I was given permission by the Assistant Commissioner of Indian Affairs for British Columbia to consult records in the Indian Agency office. These included official birth, death, and marriage registrations of Haidas, and diaries, reports, and correspondence of agents with the Indian Department in Ottawa. Since I was asked not to look into files of police cases, I reconstructed the landmark cases in social control from other reports and from my field notes.

While I was unable to obtain lodging on the reserve that first summer, I paid visits to the village almost every day and entertained friends and informants in the Red Cross Outpost Hospital in New Masset where I boarded for several weeks.

When I returned to the field in 1965 I brought my nine-year-old son and a camper truck, intending to live on the reserve. However, when I accepted a part-time job teaching in the New Masset Elementary and Secondary School, I rented a house in New Masset. I taught social studies and anthropology (under the course title of "Guidance") to an eighth-grade class of 14 Indian and white children. I supervised a correspondence course in home economics for 33 ninth- and tenth-grade girls from both villages. Since there were few facilities for cooking classes and none for sewing, the "live" sessions of this class might be described as a seminar in "Comparative Family Systems" where I, of course, was the most eager student. The school lunch program, initiated by the principal as a project for six 16- and 17-year old Haida girls, was another of my responsibilities. Although this part-time occupation consumed a great deal of time, the small salary enabled me to remain in the field for the entire year.

Teaching offered many opportunities that might not otherwise have been presented. I was able to form close friendships with many of my students and their families, enlisting their cooperation in my work and receiving invitations to social events. I could observe the interaction of white and Indian students in the school and obtain some insight into their attitudes, aspirations, and problems. When people began to think of me as a teacher, I discovered that much of the antagonism directed against me as an ethnographer vanished. Although most of the Haidas had no previous contact with an anthropologist—it was more than 30 years since Murdock's field trip and Drucker visited only briefly while working on his study of the Native Brotherhood—they viewed the role as exploitive. The role of teacher, on the other hand, was considered beneficial by residents of both villages. The Haidas appeared to regard my relationship with them as a transaction in which as an anthropologist I "took" their history from them but as a teacher I "gave" myself.

The friendship that many men extended to my son made my task of studying the fishing industry much simpler; perhaps I should say that it made it possible. Again, the role of working mother made more sense to potential informants than that of ethnographer. Much of the cooperation I received could be traced to a spirit of helpfulness to someone with a rather strange "job."

Because of the importance of demographic factors in understanding change, I made special efforts to obtain complete data on births, deaths, marital and mating histories, reproductive histories of women, migration histories, and genealogies. Much of this data is now being analyzed in preparation for a population history of the Haidas. The first phase of this work, on marriage and reproduction, appears in chapter 6 of this volume. In order to study domestic organization, I collected household composition data for every household in the village at four times during the year, from September 1965 to September 1966. I was assisted in this task by four Haida highschool girls who either had firsthand knowledge of each household or could obtain this information without arousing hostility. Several middle-aged and senior women, who were close friends as well as informants, assisted in collecting and crosschecking these data. Occupational data were obtained as part of this study. For this analysis I selected May 15, 1966 as that point in time when the whereabouts of every person ordinarily resident on the reserve could be determined.

The material on family life, dating, marriage, and childraising was collected primarily by observation and in casual discussions during frequent visits in homes. I usually conducted formal interviews over lunch or afternoon tea in my house in New Masset. Women appeared to regard these occasions as a welcome respite from the incessant demands of large households. Fifteen middle-aged and senior women participated in these discussions at different times. In addition to providing information themselves, close friends took me visiting in households where I had no entree and arranged invitations to parties, feasts, and meetings hosted by others. I reciprocated by making gifts of money or "store goods" from time to time but never at the close of an interview. I provided transportation and meals for informants and made donations for life-cycle events. I attempted to participate in as many activities as possible, going food-fishing and berry-picking, helping to serve at feasts, and joining funeral processions. I also entertained Haida friends when they visited Vancouver and Victoria where I have held teaching positions since 1966.

My methods of analyzing the data are discussed in relevant contexts. I thought it essential to describe the conditions in which all data were collected. A word about tense will be helpful since I have selected 1966 as a vantage point for assessing the impact of government policy on the Indian society. The present tense is used for cultural patterns and structural features in effect at the end of the agency period. Continuing conditions, such as the physical setting and the layout of the community, and continuing relations, such as available services are also described in the present tense. The *events* of 1966, as part of the historical record, are treated in the past tense. To describe them as happening in an ethnographic present would, in many instances, cause great confusion in discussing subsequent changes.

The distinction marked by tense, then, is that between the processual and the historical analyses. The regularities referred to as cultural patterns and structural features are elicited from the analysis of quantitative data and repeated observations. They belong to the realm of the habitual and universal which is implied by the present tense. *Changes* in patterns are, of course, studied in the historical dimension.

My treatment of names of informants and actors in events should be explained. In consulting older works I have found their value greatly enhanced if I could identify their sources. Perspectives differ not only by rank, age, and sex, but also by faction, experience of the outside world, and so on. We all recognize that the analyst's interpretations reflect to some extent the views and situations of that segment of the population with which, by chance or design, he has had most contact. On the other hand, in a small community such as Masset, all visiting researchers seem to hear the same stories from the same people. It is very instructive to read in Dalzell (1968), Van den Brink (1974), and Blackman (1973), not to mention the mimeographed reports of oral history projects and the popular press, the same statements by the hereditary chief on a variety of matters that I have recorded in my own field notes. Even if their source were not identified, there would be no difficulty in attributing them correctly. Not only is there uniformity in the kinds of stories with which, it seems, some of the people rush out to greet us, but persons sharing the anthropological subculture select the same examples to illustrate their points. Thus both Blackman and I (in chapter 8) discuss Chief Sígai's designation of his own son as his heir to the town chiefship of Masset. It is not possible, then, nor even desirable to conceal the sources of the study. The desire to preserve the authenticity of the work is not intended to serve only scholarship. Since all of these studies constitute a kind of history of the Masset Haidas, the record they preserve for the people ought to be as accurate as possible.

Undue invasion of privacy is, of course, to be avoided. To this end, I have distinguished two kinds of data, public and private. In matters of public record and historical significance, persons of prominence are identified by name if there is no risk of damage to their reputations. In speaking of ceremonial matters where public recognition is valued, actual names are used. In analyzing other events, which could not be omitted because of their crucial historical importance but where individuals might be harmed or embarrassed, I reduced the account to its essential features and changed or omitted the names of actors. I did not alter important elements or construct composite characters to confound the reader. Situations that received this minimizing treatment were, for example, legal or criminal proceedings and disputes.

In private matters I have changed all names simply to avoid unnecessary revelations. Very seldom did I have only one account of some behavior I wanted to describe. Here my interest was in representative cases and so, while the details are faithful to the actual event, they could have been provided by any of a number of persons. I have discussed this solution to the problem of confidentiality with various members of the Haida community, native officials as well as friends, and received their approval.

In retrospect, I believe that my continued residence in British Columbia is probably the most important factor in my research. It is relatively easy to keep in touch when one is only an hour's flight from the field situation. In a sense I have never left the field, which I have defined as the interethnic context. I had remained in the area partly in order to study the Canadian scene and partly for personal reasons. With my annual summer sojourns in Masset, I was soon considered a permanent fixture, able to step out of the high-profile roles of fieldworker and teacher. As my friendships deepened and broadened, my knowledge and understanding were immeasurably increased. While I did not deceive anyone about my unabating professional interest in Haida culture and society, I was happy to fade into the low-profile roles of mother, friend, neighbor, and, later, wife. When in 1968 I married Francis Dixon, a white fisherman residing in New Masset, I acquired affines and a stake in harmonious relations between the two villages at a time when those relations were at low ebb. It now became impossible, with my conflicting loyalties, to publish my analyses of the contemporary social situation. In time, the heat went out of these events, but they were soon drowned by new anxieties, for the structure and content of interaction have scarcely changed in intervening years.

My role as an observer during the tense post-agency period was a privileged one and I continued to enjoy "safe passage" across the ethnic boundary. From the viewpoint of the whites, my marriage to a local person gave me the right to be there while my sympathies with the Indians were excusable in a "university teacher." My Haida friends approved of marriage and they approved of my choice. I was never categorized as a New Masset white. In fact, I seemed to be regarded as a useful ally with a seasonal residence in the other camp.

My study of the commercial economy depended upon my access as a fisherman's wife to the male world of fishing. I was able to travel with the fleet as erstwhile cook on a gillnetter and to become familiar not only with the technology but with the attitudes and grievances of the northern fishermen. Part of that experience is drawn upon for this book.

In the summer of 1974 I gave a copy of my doctoral dissertation to Ethel Jones, my closest friend in Masset. I was not concerned so much about the accuracy of my data, which had been painstakingly checked. What I needed to know was whether I had really understood what I had observed, whether my interpretations would ring true to an insider. Ethel must have pored over the heavy "book" all night because the next day she pronounced it "very valuable because it tells how things used to be." While I was disconcerted to find my "contemporary" study so quickly outdated, my object in the present work has not been to catalogue recent events but to develop a more adequate theoretical approach to the analysis of change. It was just as well, for the fieldwork came to an end.

When research became a political issue in Masset in the mid 1970s, I withdrew from active work rather than risk longstanding friendships in a confrontation with the band council. Although some kinds of data continued to be available, it was now difficult to obtain full information on events of the last 14 years during which the band has been governed by its own members under the Indian Act. We would like to know whether changes have occurred that could not have been predicted on the basis of our knowledge of Masset in 1966. We want to know what has happened to the flourishing ceremonial life described in this book now that most of the old people we meet here have made the last journey through the tunnel of trees to the cemetery. We would ask if there is any link between the spectacular media events attending a pole-raising or installation of a "chief" in the 1970s and the life-cycle rituals of the 1960s.

We are curious about the balance of power in the community and about the status of band councilors since the role has been given administrative authority. We wonder whether the long-term trend of marriage to white men, which seemed to be reversed in early returns for girls born in the 1955–59 cohort, has indeed shifted in favor of marriage to other Indians. How has the expansion of the Defense establishment, which brought hundreds of outsiders into New Masset, affected the social and economic life of the area? What are the consequences for the social climate of the school and the education of Indian children? We know that the federal government's salmon license limitation program has beached most of the Haida fleet. What of the men who had to go fishing because "it's in their blood"? And finally, is my hypothesis about the continuity in "internal institutions" upheld? While no definitive answers can be given to these questions at present, we can place the events of the past dozen years in perspective and draw some tentative conclusions in the Epilogue about continuing changes in the social realms of the Masset Haida.

Chapter 2
The Physical and Historical Setting

IN TRADITIONAL TIMES the domain of the Haidas extended over the whole of the Queen Charlotte Islands. This group of more than 150 islands forms a long curved triangle lying off the northern coast of British Columbia between 51°55′ and 54°15′ north latitude and 131° and 133°18′ west longitude. The group, which is about 156 miles long and 53 miles at its widest part, is separated from the mainland by the 50- to 75-mile width of shallow, stormy Hecate Strait. The 30- to 40-mile width of Dixon Entrance separates the islands from the Alaskan archipelago which has been the home of the Kaigani Haida since they migrated from the Charlottes in the eighteenth century. From Cape St. James at the southern extremity of the group it is 150 miles to the northern tip of Vancouver Island.

The backbone of the Charlottes is formed by a range of mountains that rises precipitously out of the sea on the west, reaching heights of more than 3,000 feet. This deeply indented rock wall has been sculptured by continuous Pacific storms. At midpoint these ancient parapets are bisected by narrow Skidegate Channel, which separates Graham Island on the north from Moresby on the south. Moresby Island is about 85 miles long and 38 miles at its widest point. The northeastern sector of the island is lowlying, terminating in the long sandspit at the entrance to Skidegate Channel where the modern airport is located. Most of the remaining 1,060 square miles of land surface is mountainous with deeply indented coastlines.

Graham Island is the largest of the Queen Charlottes, covering 2,485 square miles. From Cape Knox, the most northwesterly point of the Charlottes to the northeastern extremity at Rose Point is 53 miles in a straight line. From north to south the maximum distance is 57 miles. The western and southern sectors of the island are mountainous and forested down to the shores. The northeastern sector is rolling lowland broken by extensive areas of muskeg where vegetation is stunted and comparatively sparse. The heart of the island is occupied by a large salt water "lake" extending for 19 miles in an east-west direction and seven miles from north to south. It is connected with McIntyre Bay on the north by a deep tidal waterway 17 miles long. Both this channel and its large southern expansion are referred to on maps as Masset Inlet. South of the "lake" lies Juskatla Inlet, a body of salt water nine miles long and one to two miles wide. Through the narrow passage connecting these "lakes," the tide rushes with great force, reaching its peak at Juskatla four and a half hours after entering the mouth of Masset Inlet.

In the surrounding mountains are several fresh water lakes that feed small rivers flowing into the inlets. Most important as spawning grounds for salmon are the Yakoun, Mamin, Awun, and Ain. These rivers, choked with fallen timbers and passable only at high water, do not form avenues into the interior. Before the coming of white prospectors and settlers, no overland trails penetrated the dense forest growth. The Indians occupied the shores and islands of the inlets, venturing into the forests infrequently to choose the largest and soundest cedars for canoes and totem poles. The geologist Chittenden, who made an exploratory survey of Graham Island for the provincial government in 1884, described one of his excursions into the interior. "Indian trails were almost invariably found, extending from one to three miles along the water courses, terminating at or near bodies of the finest red cedar, which they had cut for canoes and poles, for carving and building purposes. Upon some of these trails considerable labor had been expended in bridging over ravines, corduroying marshy places, and cutting through the trunks of great fallen trees. Only a few of them showed much use of late years, being obstructed by logs and overgrown with bushes" (Chittenden 1884:58).

On the north shore of Graham Island from Masset Inlet eastward to Rose Spit, sand dunes and forest compete for dominance. Beach-building processes have extended Rose Spit far out into Dixon Entrance where it has constituted a major hazard to modern as well as ancient navigators. Wide sandy beaches continue along most of the exposed east coast from Rose Spit to Skidegate Channel. On this coast there is no safe harbor where boats may shelter during the sudden storms that visit Hecate Strait.

From Masset Inlet westward to Cape Knox, the coast is rocky with many small coves offering sheltered beaches and partial protection from the winds. Aside from Masset harbor, the only large bay on the north coast is Virago Sound about 12 miles west, which opens into landlocked Naden Harbour. At Cape Knox, narrow Parry Passage separates the mainland from Langara Island, which is about five miles long and four miles wide. This island, also known as North Island, is

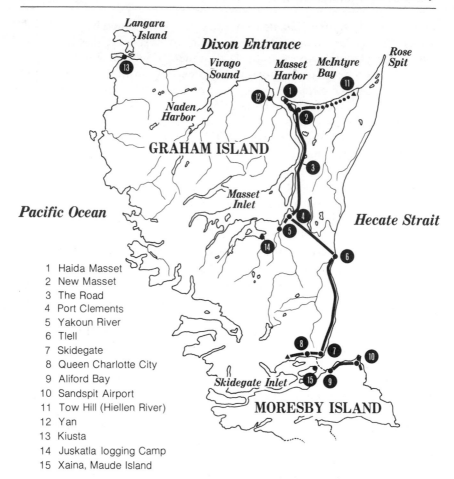

Fig. 1. Northern Queen Charlotte Islands

1   Haida Masset
2   New Masset
3   The Road
4   Port Clements
5   Yakoun River
6   Tlell
7   Skidegate
8   Queen Charlotte City
9   Aliford Bay
10 Sandspit Airport
11 Tow Hill (Hiellen River)
12 Yan
13 Kiusta
14 Juskatla logging Camp
15 Xaina, Maude Island

exposed to storms from the Pacific and from Alaska. It was in 1787 at
Cloak Bay on its southwest coast that European explorers first encountered Haidas on the Queen Charlottes. For the Europeans the event
was made memorable by their obtaining 300 prime sea otter pelts in a
half-hour's trading (Dixon 1789).

The west coast of Graham Island is barren and inhospitable, its
beaches approachable only in calm weather. On the southern margin of
the island, low mountains rise steeply behind the narrow beaches of
Skidegate Inlet. The entire coast of the Charlottes is fringed with islands, many of them little more than stepping stones thickly crowned
with trees.

The climate is of the temperate marine type with mild wet winters and cool summers. The Japanese current exercises a moderating influence. The average January temperature recorded for the Langara Island weather station is 37°F., with an average of 57°F. recorded for August. Averages for Masset, which is located near the mouth of Masset Inlet, differ by only one degree. The average annual temperature for both stations is 46°F. The extreme range recorded for Masset is −2°F. to 84°F. The western mountain slopes receive up to 150 inches of precipitation annually compared with 40 to 60 inches for the lowlands lying in the rain shadow. The average annual snowfall at Masset calculated over a period of 58 years is 29.8 inches, although snow usually does not remain on the ground long before melting and some winters pass with no snowfall at all. Fog in summer and cloudy skies in winter account for low annual totals of sunshine (B.C. Department of Agriculture 1965).

Wind appears to be constant, varying only as to direction. Westerly gales bring clear skies and heavy seas. Even in midwinter there are occasional sunny days when the wind blows from the west. In winter, "southwesters" howl down the inlet, toppling giant trees in the forest and flinging driftwood high on the beaches. "Southeasters" bring rain and calm water, which mean good fishing weather. Another factor with implications for work patterns is the seasonal variation in hours of sunlight. At latitude 54° the time elapsing between sunrise and sunset is 17 hours, 6 minutes at summer solstice, and 7 hours, 22 minutes at the winter solstice.

RESOURCES

As a result of this wet, mild climate, plant growth is lush. Forests of Sitka spruce, giant red cedar, and hemlock clothe most of the land, yielding to marsh and meadow in the lowlands. In the dark forests surrounding Masset Inlet, cedars grow to heights of 200 feet with diameters of four to six feet. Trees are festooned with moss and the floor is covered with thickets of salal and salmonberry bushes, devil's club, and skunk cabbage. Masses of ferns cover fallen tree trunks measuring five to eight feet in diameter, which lie piled upon each other in disarray, making the terrain impassable. Yellow cedar and yew grow dispersed among other trees. Along streams and near the beaches, groves of red alder, willow, and Oregon crabapple fringe the coniferous forests. Although the Haidas utilized many species of the available flora, the red cedar (*Thuja plicata*) was most important, providing material for houses, dugout canoes, and totem poles, while its bark was used for clothing and mats.

In aboriginal times many types of berries grew in profusion on the islands. In addition to salal and salmonberry, the strawberry, elderberry, blackberry, and currant flourished, becoming important items in the diet of the Haidas. Lily roots and a wild tobacco were gathered. The cambium layer of spruce, hemlock, and cedar was eaten fresh or made into cakes. The potato, which was apparently introduced by early explorers, became a staple food in the native diet and was also an item of trade (Dawson 1880:113B–14B; Ells 1906:14B).[1]

Indigenous terrestrial mammal fauna included only the wandering shrew, black bear, marten, short-tailed weasel, white-footed mouse, Sitka white-footed mouse, otter, and Dawson caribou. Land hunting was comparatively unimportant to the Haidas, although furs of black bear, marten, weasel, and land otter were exchanged with white traders when the more valuable sea otter became extinct in the early nineteenth century.

The sea abounds with rich resources that could be harvested by a people with a well-developed marine technology. Mammals of the coast littoral biotic zone, which includes the west coast of the Charlottes, are the harbor seal, northern sea lion, California sea lion, sea otter, harbor porpoise, Baird dolphin, Pacific striped dolphin, Dall porpoise, killer whale, humpback whale, pike whale, and gray whale. Pelagic mammals include fur seal, elephant seal, Scammon blackfish, right whale, blue whale, finback, sei whale, sperm whale, Baird beaked whale, Stejneger beaked whale and Cuvier whale (McTaggart Cowan and Guiguet 1965:28–29). In addition to the prized sea otter, seals and sea lions were hunted.[2]

Fish constituted the major part of the food supply. Most important were the five species of salmon: sockeye (*Oncorhynchus nerka*), coho (*O. kisutch*), pink (*O. gorbuscha*), dog (*O. keta*), and spring salmon (*O. tshawytscha*). Salmon were usually caught when they entered the creeks at spawning time. Halibut and black cod, which were also of great importance, were obtained by deep-sea fishing from canoes. Steelhead and cutthroat trout were taken from inland waters (Carl 1964).

Many species of clams were available including razor, jack-knife, butter, and soft-shell clams. Two species of mussels, *Mytilus califor-*

1. The definitive study of the flora of the Queen Charlotte Islands is that of Calder and Taylor (1968). Turner has included the results of her ethnobotanical studies in the Charlottes in her very useful and interesting handbook on food plants of the British Columbia Indians (1975).

2. Conventional wisdom holds that the Haidas never hunted whales, although those washed ashore were subject to strictly observed property rights. Blackman has collected testimony from old informants, however, which suggests the possibility of whale hunting in the past (Blackman, personal communication; also Duff 1964).

nianus and *Mytilus edulis*, and many types of shellfish including crabs, abalone, sea urchins, and scallops were consumed when available (Carl 1963; Quayle 1960). The eulachon (*Thaleichtys pacificus*) is not found in the waters surrounding the Queen Charlottes, but the livers of herring, dogfish (*Squalus suckleyi*), salmon, and halibut were boiled to produce oil. When possible, eulachon grease was obtained in trade from the Tsimshian. Additional food resources included the eggs of seabirds, migrating waterfowl, and resident species such as Canada geese and blue grouse (Dawson 1880:109B–14B).

TRADITIONAL SOCIAL ORGANIZATION

So rich was this environment that a relatively dense, sedentary population could support itself by a sophisticated fishing and collecting technology. John Work, a Hudson's Bay Company factor at Fort Simpson, estimated a population of 6,593 persons for the Queen Charlotte Islands in the years 1836–41 (Dawson 1880:172B). Dr. C. F. Newcombe's survey of archaeological sites, conducted in 1895 and 1897, shows that the whole coastline had been occupied at one time or another although many of these sites were probably no more than fish camps (Swanton 1909). The earliest fur traders to visit these shores found the people living in villages of from one or two to more than twenty large plank houses. These permanent settlements were often located near good fishing streams or halibut banks. Their large seaworthy canoes gave the people great mobility, however, and villages could be located at some distance from resource areas.

These villages were not corporate units under the headship of a single chief. Rather, they were composed of one or more households of one or more lineages, each of which was an autonomous social, political, and economic unit. The head of the lineage holding title to the town site was recognized as "town master." Although his permission was necessary before newcomers might settle in the town, he had no authority over other groups, which were free to migrate to a new site where their own head would become town master. Boundaries between lineages were maintained by competitive relations, including feud. Principles governing Haida politics at this period were the hereditary succession to the chiefship of units and competition for highest rank among heads of segmentary units.

In this dispersed-village type of organization, forces favoring consolidation of kin groupings are counter-balanced by those encouraging segmentation and migration. Structural features favoring consolidation include lineage exogamy and the combination of matrilineal descent with avunculocal (and an alternative patrilocal) residence. The warlike nature of competition in earlier times placed a premium on numerical strength, thus favoring aggregation. The prestige and power accruing to the head of a numerous and wealthy group prompted an ambitious lineage head to offer inducements to members of weaker groups, who, moreover, were pleased to be identified with a high-ranking protector. At the same time, this very prestige and power motivated younger men to set up households of their own and to compete for the allegiance of kinsmen in founding new lineage towns of which they became chief. Thus we find institutionalized in traditional Haida culture the conflicting values of rank based on hereditary status and the right of individuals to compete for higher statuses, including those of lineage head and town chief (Stearns, forthcoming).

Uttewas, which was one of the most important aboriginal towns, occupied the same general location as the modern Haida village of Masset. During the latter half of the nineteenth century, Uttewas became a nucleating center drawing survivors from isolated north shore and west coast villages. By the 1870s almost half of the estimated 800 surviving members of Haida society were concentrated here (Swanton 1909:106; Dawson 1880:174B). While aboriginal villages of several hundred persons were not uncommon, this crowding together of many small, weak kin groups was a new social and political phenomenon.

In the nucleated-village phase, the lineage continued to function as a corporate group although the economic monopoly of chiefs had been undermined by the intrusion of white commerce and access to a market for wage labor. With opportunities for accumulating wealth outside the Haida social system, it was now possible for individuals of lower rank to raise houses and potlatch in a bid for higher status (Deans 1891:286–87). But although new sources of wealth were available, the ownership of lineage property was not affected by commercial activities until Canadian sovereignty was established nine decades after contact. Economic and domestic activities were carried out by the household group, which continued to perform cooperative labor under the direction of the head even though some of its members had departed.

Nor was there yet any radical change in relations which maintained social boundaries between corporate groups. Moiety exogamy was strictly observed, for example. Indeed, interlineage relations became more complex as lineages with long histories of mutual hostility crowded together in the same village. As blood feud became impractical, new mechanisms for regulating intergroup relations were sought. In these circumstances political competition was transposed from a military to a ceremonial mode, from feud to potlatch. In this ceremonial confrontation of groups within the village, the moiety division was intensified. The dual organization of Ravens and Eagles became more important as a means of channeling aggressiveness, ambition, and tensions.

The aggregation of many small groups in the nucleated village strengthened the position of the town chief who now stood for all the people. But although his political influence had been extended over all lineages in the village, he still had no coercive power. Lineage heads formed a council of subchiefs advising the town chief on matters of community interest. Gradually the village itself emerged as the relevant political unit. Yet, political power could not become hierarchical in relation to the total Haida society or even to this remaining segment unless the narrow particularistic ties of the lineage were so weakened and generalized that their members could act cohesively in other than ceremonial contexts. This step has not been achieved to the present day.

Anglo-Canadian Influences

For more than six decades after contact in 1787, the Haidas' relations with Europeans were centered on the market. Trading vessels visited the Charlottes regularly until the 1830s when the sea otter became extinct. In 1834 the Hudson's Bay Company established Fort Simpson on the mainland to carry on trade with all the northern tribes. In 1852 the Haidas began visiting Fort Victoria on southern Vancouver Island where they sought wage work and the excitement of the white man's settlements. But the presence of whites in the Haidas' homeland was only gradually established. In the early 1850s a trading post, later taken over by the Hudson's Bay Company, was founded in Masset (Dalzell 1968). The first missionary, William H. Collison, who had arrived in 1876, established the Anglican Church (Collison 1915).

Governor James Douglas of British Columbia had proclaimed the islands a Crown Colony in 1852 after the discovery of gold raised the fear of an incursion of American prospectors such as occurred when gold was found in the Cariboo area. But aside from a rare visit to show the flag by vessels of the Royal Navy (Gough 1971:132–34, 146), no political authority was exercised over the islands until 1871 when British Columbia entered Confederation. The extension of Canadian jurisdiction to the Charlottes was an aspect of its assertion of sovereignty over this section of the Northwest Coast.

In 1882 the Indian Department sent Reserve Commissioner Peter O'Reilly to lay out reserves for the newly created Masset band. When asked to select areas to be set aside for their exclusive use, the Masset Haidas asked only for title to sixteen ancient village sites and fishing stations that had been the private property of various lineages. These reserves, with six others added later, were designated as the communal estate of the Masset band. No tribal lands passed into the hands of individual Indians who might use them for personal gain or dispose of them to outsiders. All other lands and resources on the Queen Charlotte Islands were claimed by the Crown.

During the early years of the twentieth century, two kinds of economic interests drew whites to the area. Businessmen—miners, lumbermen, land speculators—were attracted by the natural resources and unoccupied tracts of the islands. Homesteaders were lured by promises of unlimited opportunity on "the real last frontier" (Dalzell 1968). In 1908 developers laid out the townsite of Graham City, later renamed New Masset, three miles up the inlet from the Haida village of Masset. The Haidas, however, were not confronted by masses of land-hungry settlers. Indeed, the provincial government's practice of leasing large tracts to timber and mining companies worked greater hardship on prospective homesteaders than on the native inhabitants. In any event, these mountainous islands with lowlands covered by muskeg are unsuited to agriculture, a fact, incidentally, which did not deter the Indian Department from attempting to teach farming to Haida fishermen. Environmental conditions are somewhat more favorable to ranching but, with infrequent steamship service, the difficulty of shipping meat to market made this enterprise economically unfeasible. Many homesteaders, unable to make a living on their preemptions, left the Charlottes during and after the First World War. Others moved into the settlements of New Masset, Port Clements, and Queen Charlotte City.[3]

The settlers had not been able to establish large farms or ranches requiring a steady supply of cheap labor. Nor were lumbering and mining companies forced to recruit Indians, for an unlimited supply of transient white and Oriental workers was available in job-hungry British Columbia. Only the fish canneries, which began to appear on the coast in the last two decades of the nineteenth century, depended to any extent upon Indian labor.[4]

With the construction of the residence and office of the Queen Charlotte Agency on the Masset reserve in 1910, the Haidas came under close government supervision. From that time, contact between the two populations was mediated by the Indian agent. The conditions and

3. A history of white settlement of the Queen Charlotte Islands, told by the daughter of homesteaders at Port Clements, is presented in Dalzell (1968). Her account of Haida culture is, however, much less informed.
4. A monumental compilation of data on the salmon fishing and canning industry in British Columbia has been made by Cicely Lyons who was for many years secretary to executives of British Columbia Packers Ltd. (1969). Also see Rolf Knight 1978.

consequences of the Haidas' relationship with government officials on the one hand and local whites on the other are examined at length in the next two chapters.[5]

The Village

Uttewas, "White Slope Town," lay on the inner flank of the peninsula that forms the eastern portal of Masset harbor. Pointing in a northwesterly direction toward the sheltered western side of McIntyre Bay, which is an indentation of Dixon Entrance, this densely wooded finger of land protects the mouth of the harbor from the storms of the open sea. From Entry Point on the inside of its rounded tip to the southern side of Delkatla Slough where it joins higher ground, the peninsula is three and one-half miles in length. In its center are the "flats," about 900 acres of lowlying meadowland cut by the slough, which overflows at high tide. The seaward side of the peninsula, known as the "north beach," forms the western end of the long concave shoreline extending for about 20 miles to Rose Spit. It appears as if the low marshy ground were shored up at its margins by sandbars that have stabilized and grown over with forests, leaving low ground in the center.

A description of Uttewas as it appeared in September of 1817, during what I have termed the dispersed-village period, was recorded by the explorer Roquefeuil.

> Early on the 26th we entered the port, or rather arm of the sea, at Massett under the guidance of an Indian named Tayan. . . . At eight o'clock we passed the southeast point, and soon after, being opposite to a large village, we were surrounded by canoes. . . . As far as we could judge, the huts composing the four villages on the two sides of the entrance are better built, and in better order than those to the north. There is something picturesque in the whole appearance of this large village. It is particularly remarkable for the monstrous and colossal figures which decorate the houses of the principal inhabitants, and the wide gaping mouths of which serve as a door. . . . Ascending the arm of the sea, there is, on the north side, above the largest village, a fort, the parapet of which is covered with beautiful turf, and surrounded by a palisade in good condition. [Roquefeuil 1823:87–88]

The appearance of these settlements during the nucleated-village period is described by the geologist Dawson.

> About the entrance to Massett Inlet there are three villages, two on the east side and one on the west. The latter is called Yan, and shows about twenty houses new and old, with thirty carved posts. The outer of these, on the east side, at which the Hudson Bay Post is situated is named Ut-te-was, the inner

5. A history of Indian-white contact and conflict in British Columbia appears in Fisher 1977. A somewhat different view is provided by La Violette 1961.

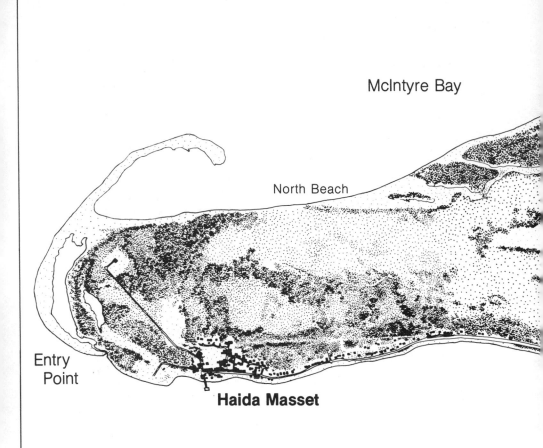

Fig. 2. Masset villages, 1966

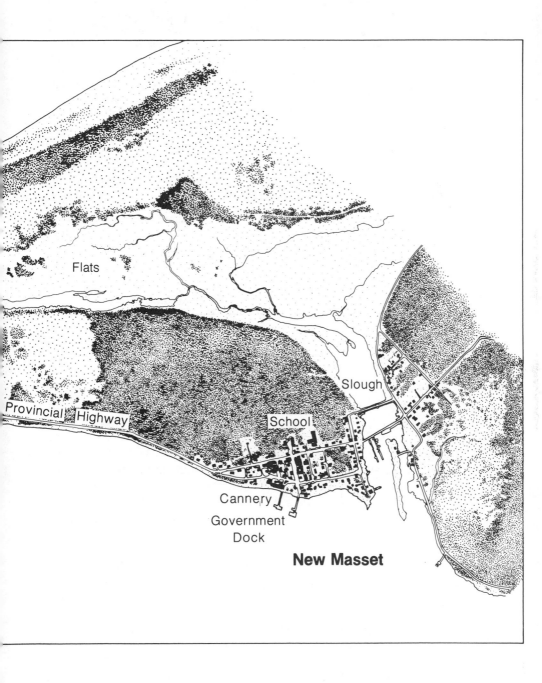

Flats

Slough

Provincial Highway

School

Cannery

Government
Dock

New Masset

Kay-yung. The Ut-te-was village is now the most populous, and there are in it about twenty houses, counting both large and small, with some from which the split cedar planks have been carried away, leaving only the massive frames standing. Of carved posts there are over forty in all. . . . At the south end of the Ut-te-was village is a little hill, the houses on and beyond which appear to be considered as properly forming a distinct village, though generally included in the former. The remaining Masset village (Ka-yung) is smaller than this one, and was not particularly examined. [Dawson 1880:163–64B]

The account of another geologist, Chittenden, who visited the area six years later, differs in certain details, such as the number of occupied houses, but adds further information. By 1884 the villages of Yan and Ka-yung had been abandoned.

There are three villages near the entrance to Massett Inlet: Yan—abandoned—with 20 houses and 25 carved poles, on the west side, and Utte-was—now Massett—and Ka-yung, situated about a mile below, on the east. Massett is the principal village of the Hyda nation, now containing a population of about three hundred and fifty Indians, 40 occupied houses, 50 carved poles, and the ruins of many ancient lodges. The Hudson Bay Company have had a Trading Post here since 1855, Mr. Alexander McKenzie having been their agent for the last six years. He is the extreme north-western resident White man on the soil of the Dominion of Canada. The Episcopal Church of England established a mission at Massett in 1877, now under the excellent charge of Rev. Chas. Harrison and wife. At Ka-yung we found only the ruins of a few houses and carved poles. [1884:23]

In 1966 a visitor strolling down the streets of the village could not find a single cultural object to identify Masset as an Indian settlement. The last of the old totem poles was cut down in 1962 to prevent its falling against the power lines in a storm; the new pole carved by young Robert Davidson was not erected until August 1969. At Kayung, which had been reclaimed by the forest, even the ruins are gone. But in the cemetery near Entry Point, behind the electric range light for marine navigation and the fuel tanks of the Department of Transport, a few relics of the missionary period remain. Crest figures sculptured in the round in marble and carved on flat headstones mark some of the graves in the older section.

To the boat passenger following Roquefeuil's path down Masset Inlet from the sea, the village appears in 1966 as an unbroken row of houses extending for a mile and a half along the shore, past Ídjao, the grassy hill where stood the fort, on along the beach and past the ancient site of Kayung. Public and industrial buildings are located on the beach. At the north end is a wharf of a size to accommodate sea-going vessels. A large boathouse with a sign identifying the premises as those of the Haida Boat Works and an old store building occupy prominent positions on the shore. Four or five fishing boats are moored near the dock and a dozen or so outboard motor boats are drawn up on the beach. Three hundred yards along the beach from the dock stands the large community hall and beside it, the small red firehall. Some distance further along the beach, just below the site of Kayung, is a sawmill.

On going ashore the traveler finds that a road runs along the beach paralleled by a plank sidewalk that appears to prevent the houses from encroaching on the beach. The old part of town occupies a basin bounded on the north by the slough near Entry Point, on the east by a bluff about 20 feet high and on the south by Īdjao, called Mission Hill on the charts, where no trace remains of the ancient fort. In this section, a row of 21 houses is lined up along the main road with a second row of 15 behind them. In the south half near Mission Hill a dirt road separates the second row from a third on higher ground where six houses are located. In the northern half of the basin a large area of low ground, which may have been flooded by tidal overflow in earlier times, lies behind the second row of houses. Now dry for most of the year, this area is used as a school playground and soccer field.

On a small knoll to the north of the field, the Indian Day School stands on the site formerly occupied by the Hudson's Bay Company trading post. On the bluff behind the field about a quarter mile from the beach are located four modern Indian houses as well as the buildings serving the institutions of white society: St. John's Anglican Church, the rectory, a teacherage occupied by the principal of the day school and his family, and the Indian Health Service clinic and residence.

Nine more houses are widely scattered along two side streets, making a total of 55 houses in the old section of town. Another 44 houses, many of them new, are strung out in a single line south of Mission Hill along the road to the neighboring white settlement of New Masset. With the accelerated building program that has been carried out since 1966, the single row has become a double and triple one as new building sites are cut out of the bush. Even so, the rows of houses march steadily toward New Masset as though they meant to merge.

Houses in the old part of town generally represent the second generation of European-style buildings. Traditional planked cedar houses with excavated stages were replaced in the 1890s and early 1900s by rectangular frame structures usually raised one or two feet off the ground on posts. These houses, neatly shingled and painted, stood among the ruins of old lodges and aging totem poles. Many of these new buildings were one-storied with hip roofs, a door in the center, and pane glass windows on each side. Another popular style was two-storied and gable-roofed with glass windows at each end. A more elaborate style featured bay windows and gabled dormers in the

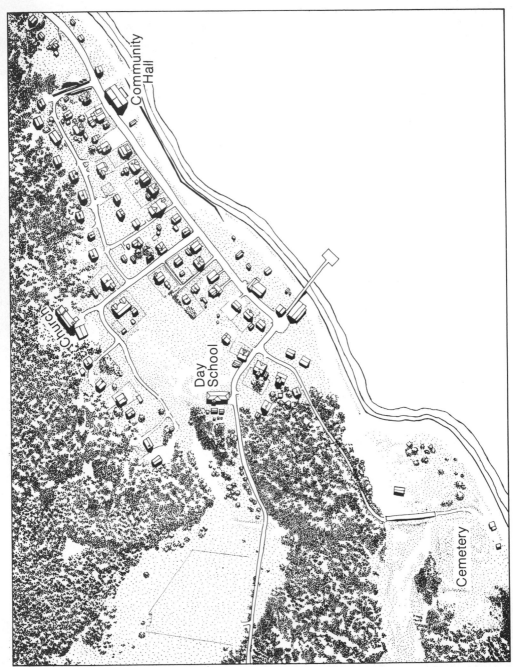

Fig. 3 Haida Masset 1966

fashion of contemporary houses in Victoria. Several of these old houses were still standing in 1962, but since then most have burnt down or been razed to make room for new construction.

The second-generation houses financed and built by their owners between the 1930s and 1950s tended to be large bungalows with porches. Indian Branch architecture of the 1950s displays red and green asphalt shingles applied to the exterior of the same type of house. In the early 1960s materials for smaller wooden houses were supplied to householders by the Indian Branch. The house type of the late 1960s was a two- or three-bedroom ranch house with poured concrete basement and indoor bathroom, much like an inexpensive suburban tract house. By 1970 this type was being constructed with a high basement, providing additional rooms at ground level. These two latter forms predominate in the newer area built up along the road to New Masset.

Despite the differences in age and exterior appearance of houses in the village, their interior arrangements are remarkably similar. Rooms tend to be larger and fewer than in "white" houses of comparable size. Often they have a cluttered appearance, for closets and storage chests are few and unable to hold the accumulated possessions of people who move infrequently. Fairly typical of the second-generation houses in the old part of town is the home of William Barnes and his family. Built in 1961 with $2,000 worth of materials supplied by the Indian Affairs Branch, the house is set well back on a lot facing the inlet. William's kinsman, a skilled carpenter, drew up the plans and supervised the construction of the framework and exterior, while another kinsman helped him to finish the inside. Before moving into their new house in December 1961, William and Mary Ellen and their six children had lived with her mother in a bay-windowed Victorian house that stood at the front of the lot. When the new house was built Mary Ellen's mother transferred title to the lot to her daughter. Shortly thereafter the old house was razed.

The layout of the Barnes's house, which is common to many others in the village in 1966, reveals and structures the life carried on within it. The house is approximately 30-by-30 feet with a small indentation for a porch on which is hung a rack for drying either laundry or fish. The front door opens into a vestibule studded with a score of wooden coat pegs. Beyond is the small master bedroom, the bed surrounded by bulging cupboards and closets. A stairway ascends from the vestibule to the attic dormitory furnished with iron cots which are used by other members of this large family. On the left as one enters the front door is the main room of the house, 15-by-30 feet. A slight partition at midpoint suggests a functional division into living and dining rooms, but in practice the whole area is used for whatever activity is in progress.

The large windows overlooking the inlet are curtained with blue and white floral fiberglass drapes. An overstuffed sofa and chair are backed up against the windows to face a portable TV set mounted on a high shelf on the side wall. Although but one channel can be received, and that very poorly, the set is turned on most of the time. A small cast iron wood stove warms the room. Against the rear wall is a large deep freezer and beside it an upright piano and a treadle sewing machine. A new chrome dining room table and ten chairs occupy the central floor space. Here the girls do the ironing and watch over the infants asleep in baby carriages during the day. When a feast is given, the furniture is pushed back or removed and the room becomes a banquet hall. Long sheets of plywood are placed on sawhorses to make two tables seating 22 persons each. Meetings of the various clubs and committees, band council sessions, Pentecostal prayer meetings, union meetings and other semi-public activities are frequently held here. Straight chairs and benches brought in to increase the seating capacity are lined up along the walls of the combined rooms.

In the right rear quarter of the house is the kitchen. In the cupboards along one whole wall are the utensils and china. Almost every family has "feast china" in many settings. There is a long work counter but as yet no sink. Meals are cooked and water heated in large kettles on the oil stove. A large, almost new refrigerator stands near the back door. Against the window is a large round oak table covered with oilcloth where family meals are served; in the evenings members of the family and close friends sit here over mugs of coffee and plates of warm homemade bread. Opening off the kitchen is the pantry whose shelves are stacked high with cans of meat and fish and jars of preserves and jellies. Here stands the new electric wringer washing machine and the wash boilers used for laundry and baths. Later, when the water system was installed in the village, this room became the bathroom. Meanwhile, an inside tap permits water for drinking and cooking to be drawn from the rain barrel outside.

Although much of the social life of the village is carried out in the homes, any event attended by large numbers of people is held in the community hall, which stands on the beach below Mission Hill. Built by volunteer labor during the early 1930s, this large building resembles a gymnasium with an elevated stage at one end, a kitchen at the other, and a gallery for spectators. Public meetings of the band council, union meetings, dances, and dinners given by associations to raise funds for their projects are regularly held here. When the Masset Athletic Club was an active organization, basketball games were held weekly and intervillage tournaments drew large crowds. Before television was available, movies were shown twice a week. Special events such as a luncheon for the lieutenant governor, the Canada Centennial birthday party, and a convention of the Native Brotherhood have been held in the hall. Individuals also rent the building for wedding feasts and dances, anniversary parties, and other large gatherings.

In 1966 community services are few. There is no running water in the houses, although many of the older homes have rainbarrels that supply drinking water through all but the summer months. The large water tank on Mission Hill feeds standpipes placed along the streets at a ratio of one to every three houses. Occasionally this supply fails, as, for example, when the pump broke down and spare parts could not be obtained locally. At such times individuals are forced to travel by taxi or borrowed car to a spring located about five miles away on the road south of New Masset. Before 1964 the only source of electrical power available to villagers was the small generators used in half a dozen houses to operate a few light bulbs. Government buildings on the reserve were supplied by the Defense Department's generator in New Masset. In 1963 the sale of timber holdings on the peninsula behind the village swelled the band's capital fund. With permission of the Minister of Indian Affairs, who makes the ultimate decision on expenditures from band funds, the wiring of houses in the village was financed from this source. When the limited telephone service available in New Masset was extended by a dial system in 1964, party phones were installed in many Indian houses, linking the reserve directly to the outside world.

This, then, is the home of the Masset Haidas whose dominion over the entire northern half of Graham Island has dwindled to 22 ancient village sites and fishing stations. This is the beach that could launch two-score war canoes on voyages of trade or plunder. This graveled shore was the workshop that resounded with the thud of adzes chipping at cedar, that was crowded with men fleshing pelts of sea and land mammals, with women drying halibut, with children playing. Here stood that transplanted forest of "colossal figures" that marked the houses of the greatest men. Here was the front yard of the village, cluttered with drying racks and with canoes pulled up beyond high-water line and covered with mats and blankets. Here lay the hollowed logs and roughed-out canoes waiting to be finished. Even in 1884 Chittenden could write, "Massett is the shipyard of the Hydas, the best canoe makers on the continent, who supply them to the other coast tribes. Here may be seen in all stages of construction these canoes which, when completed, are such perfect models for service and of beauty." [Chittenden 1884:57]

In 1966 the beach is idle. The only sound is the whine of a power saw cutting up driftwood. Old men sit on blocks of stove wood, talking in the sun. Children in rubber gum boots play in the beached motor boats or wade along the shore. A man caulks an overturned skiff. Laundry flaps on a line attached at one end to a power pole and at the other to an old smokehouse.

The boathouse is empty. Although several large seine boats were built here during the 1950s, the economics of fishing and financing made such construction impractical in the 1960s and 1970s. The village wharf has long since fallen into disrepair. When the *Skeena Prince*, now departed from northern waters, still brought its weekly cargo of food, mail, and other goods, it tied up at the government dock in New Masset.

The old store building is vacant. Here the Masset cannery, the Masset Co-op, and various individuals have successively operated a general store, but these enterprises have long since died or moved to New Masset. In 1962 the premises were used for a pool hall, but three years later the people were patronizing the new pool hall and bowling alley owned by a Chinese in New Masset. In 1966 there are no stores or "coffee houses" in the village, although from time to time people have opened little shops in their homes selling candy, cigarettes, soft drinks, and a miscellany of other staples. A few householders occasionally sell firewood or the surplus of their own baking to their neighbors. Some women make "popsicles" in their home freezers for sale to neighborhood children.

The small red firehall with a tower at one end for drying hoses is used to house a jeep. Because no one in the village is able to maintain this vehicle and its equipment, it has been turned over to the volunteer fire department of New Masset with the understanding that the latter would fight fires in both villages. The agreement has been faithfully observed.

The sawmill on the beach near Kayung has stood idle for years. It had been inherited by a successful fisherman who found it financially unnecessary to operate two businesses. Consequently, in a forested habitat, there has been no source of milled lumber for housebuilding or any other construction. The abandoning of facilities that once supported the economic life of the village reflects the growing dependence of the people on the physical plant and social services of the larger society.

There is symbolic significance in the location of buildings housing government agencies in 1966. The Indian Day School occupies a small knoll, while the nurse's residence and the teacherage are built on the bluff behind the village. The Anglican Church and rectory are ranged along the same shelf where they may be seen from all parts of the old section of town. To the white observer, the elevated positions occupied by representatives of the dominant society connote social distance, but it seems that the Indians formerly interpreted this arrangement as evidence of protectiveness and benevolent concern. The symbolism was most explicit in the case of the nurse. When she was away and there was no light in the house on the bluff, people were uneasy. They would say that if something should happen they would not know where to turn.

In 1966 the Queen Charlotte Agency was merged in the North Coast Agency with offices in Prince Rupert, and the New Masset office was closed. The agency residence was then occupied by a field officer with less comprehensive duties who reported to the agent. At about the same time a new band office, providing meeting rooms for the council and general office space, was built on the reserve. This building was located in the newer part of town in response to complaints that all facilities were in the old section where they were inconvenient for many people. Much of the business carried on in the band office has been concerned not with the exercise of self-government, but with the provision of those social services on which the community has come to depend. This dependence on the larger society is manifested in the turning away from the beach. Although the village faces the inlet it is now oriented to the road connecting it with New Masset and the world beyond.

The Road

Beginning at the foot of the dock in Old Masset, the road is the northern extremity of the provincial highway that traverses the length of Graham Island, linking its settlements. From Haida Masset the road runs through New Masset to Port Clements, passing close by the Nadu River where a peat moss processing plant employing about 30 Haidas operated during 1967–68. Port Clements is on the expanded "lake" of Masset Inlet where many Haidas formerly found employment in the sawmill and refreshment in the beer parlor. At "Port" a private road branches off to the west to Juskatla, where a large logging camp is located. The main highway turns east, crossing the muskeg between the inlet and the shores of Hecate Strait, emerging at Tlell, a sport fishing and ranching area. It continues down the east coast of Graham Island, through Skidegate Indian reserve, and on through Skidegate Landing to Queen Charlotte City. At Skidegate Landing a water taxi provides transportation to Moresby Island and the airport at Sandspit where planes depart for Vancouver and Prince Rupert. At Queen Charlotte City are located the United Church Hospital and the only government liquor store on the islands until the spring of 1971 when a liquor store opened in Masset.

Although the Haidas travel this road frequently by private car, bus, and cab for many purposes, their most intensive relationships with white society involve the residents of New Masset.

NEW MASSET

The village of New Masset has a population of 547 in 1966, but the area served by its physical plant includes about 1,300 persons. Three distinct groups interact in the social field we may designate as "Greater Masset": almost 700 Haida band members living on the reserve, residents of New Masset, and transient Navy personnel and their dependents.

The only important local industry is the Queen Charlotte Canners, which is the major market for the produce of fishermen and the largest employer of wage labor. One outside organization, which has been represented in Masset since the Second World War, is the Royal Canadian Navy. A small base staffed by about 25 men is located outside of town about three miles along the road to north beach. A canteen and barracks for single men is maintained on the base, while some of the married men and their families occupy a compound of six houses in town. In the years since 1966 the Defense Department has expanded its facilities in Masset and greatly increased its staff. As a result, the physical aspects and social relationships described in this study have been drastically altered.

The original surveyor's map of New Masset shows a neat grid of three broad avenues paralleling the inlet, intersected by eight cross-streets. In 1966 half of this area is still in bush. One of these broad avenues is the provincial highway, called Collison Avenue for that portion that lies within the town limits. Near its intersection with Main Street are the credit union, a gas station and auto repair shop, the Canadian Legion clubhouse, a dry goods store, and the hotel. Farther along this road is the community hall, a shabby building occasionally used for town meetings, movies, a traveling road show, a trial, political rally, or basketball game. Across the street is the eleven-room school attended by about 200 Indian and white students.

At the edge of the school grounds stands the small Anglican Church built by the first settlers. With a minister residing in the old rectory on the waterfront, the Anglican Church is still active in Masset. The tiny Catholic Church, on the other hand, is used only on the rare occasions when a visiting priest says Mass for half a dozen of the faithful. Beside this church is a trailer housing the phone company equipment and a concrete building where spruce cones were formerly processed for seed.

The business district of New Masset centers on Main Street, a wide graveled road, which runs at right angles to the inlet for two blocks, terminating at the edge of the forest in the east and at the government wharf in the west. Actually the wharf is an extension of Main Street and may be considered as the terminus of a marine highway connecting Masset with Vancouver 500 miles away. In 1966 the freighter bringing food, mail order purchases and other goods, and taking to market the canned and frozen fish pack, arrived every week. This frequent service is a recent development, for in 1962 the boat visited Masset only twice a month. The oil tanker stops here periodically to refill the huge storage tanks that supply stove oil and fuel for boats and motor vehicles. The dredger, which maintains the channels, and the tender, which services the navigational signals of this highway, pay annual visits to Masset.

The waterfront is dominated by the large corrugated aluminum buildings of the cannery. At the end of its long dock is the shed housing the fish-buying station, ice plant, and net loft. Here also are facilities for cleaning fish before quick-freezing or canning them. Fishing boats dock at the wharf to unload their catches and take on ice and water. Trucks and large carts trundle the fish from the dock shed to the large processing plant on the shore.

On the corner of Main Street near the government dock stands the old-fashioned general store, whose proprietor has been in business for over 40 years. Some distance up Main Street is the Red Cross Outpost Hospital, opened in 1956. In 1966 the Red Cross Hospital, staffed by a nurse but no resident doctor, is used only for emergencies and clinic twice a month.

Across the street is the Co-op store, which handles foodstuffs and an assortment of housewares, hardware, and clothing. Next door is the small post office where most of the population of Greater Masset gravitates on mail days. In 1966 mail, flown in to Sandspit from Vancouver, is brought to Masset by bus twice a week. The postmaster also operates the oil business and the electric generators that supply electricity to both villages.

The "Avon lady" lives next to the post office where she uses a small room as a shop for her cosmetic business, patronized by women of both villages. A few doors down is the Dragon Bowling Alley, with snack shop and pool hall, a favorite "hangout" for Indian and white males. Bowling leagues, in which residents of the whole northern area participate, keep the alleys busy on most evenings. The Masset Cafe next door was a favorite haunt of Indians until it was closed down. A machine shop, water tower, and garage are also located in this block.

At the eastern end of Main Street is the large brick building occupied by the Royal Canadian Mounted Police (RCMP). An office, jail, and residence are provided for the corporal and constable in charge of the whole northern area. Beside the police station is the village office and residence of the village clerk. The fire engine and jeep are kept in a shed at the end of the road. The office of the Indian Agency is, in 1966, located in this area.

Just south of the village lies Delkatla Slough which runs into Masset Inlet. In this small protected harbor the federal government maintains floats where fishing boats tie up. During the fishing season from April through October the floats are the center of activity for fishermen of both villages. The high sandbar on the south side of the slough is used as a parking and loading area for seaplanes, which provide service to Prince Rupert on the mainland and to other points on the Charlottes.

Aside from the businesses mentioned, few services of a professional or skilled nature were available to residents in 1966. An electrician who wired houses and repaired electronic equipment on boats also operated a radio and television shop. One man ran a taxi and occasionally gave haircuts until he quit to go fishing. Persons requiring skilled tradesmen such as plumbers had to bring them in, paying their expenses as well as wages. There was no barber shop or beauty salon, no resident doctor, dentist, or optometrist. Although a doctor from the Queen Charlotte Hospital held clinic in Masset every two weeks, persons needing hospital care had to go to the other end of the island or to the mainland. And, of course, most of the food, clothing, building materials, machinery, household goods, and many other articles were transported to the island on order. Not only did residents of the Indian village and the neighboring white settlement share a single physical plant, but both were heavily dependent on the metropolitan areas of the province for the necessities of life.

Chapter 3
The Political Context

By THE 1960s it would have been unfashionable, if not perilous, to suggest that the paternalism of the Indian Department was anything but an unmitigated evil. Indeed, this study documents the devastating consequences for one Indian society of the total control exercised by the federal bureaucracy. In many respects that control persists, divested of its single redeeming feature—the intense, caring relationship that occasionally developed between Indians and their agent. In tracing the administrative history of Masset, we shall learn how a strong affective bond was established between the Haidas and their first permanent agent, Thomas Deasy.

In the early reserve period the agent was expected to oversee the whole of community life, supervising the home, education, economic activities, moral behavior, health care, and governance. With departmental reorganization, the role was redefined. The agent was removed from personal, intimate association with the people and relegated to an office where he was occupied with paper work. His duties were distributed among a corps of civil servants who tended toward impersonality in their relations with Indians and neglected the nurturant aspects of their roles. But from the Indians' point of view, relations with government were still focused on the agent. To some extent he continued to mediate their contacts with agents of other boundary structures. The amorphous bureaucracy to which all their concerns were referred and from which all decisions descended was simply "Ottawa."

THE COMPULSORY SYSTEM OF RELATIONS

Boundary structures (we recall from our discussion on pp. 15, 17), are those organizations which bridge the social and jural boundary segregating the cultural group from mainstream Canadian society. These organizations, taken together, constitute the compulsory system

of relations. Their present structure reflects the shift toward depersonalization and professionalism in providing services to Indians.

The major boundary structure is the Department of Indian Affairs
and Northern Development, known in 1966 as the Indian Affairs
Branch of the Department of Citizenship and Immigration. Its highest
official is the Minister of Indian Affairs. The sweeping powers assigned
to him by the Indian Act are, of course, exercised in his name by
officials on lower levels. By the time of this study, much of the authority formerly concentrated in "Ottawa" had been delegated to nine
regional supervisors. Each supervisor presides over a regional head-
quarters which includes specialized divisions concerned with administration, welfare, economic development, reserves and trusts, the operation of agencies, education, engineering and construction, and enfranchisement (Canada 1961:279 *passim*).

The Department retains control of the political functions of policy-
making and administration, maintaining a liaison with other branches
of government which provide special services such as medical care.
Educational responsibilities are shared with provincial departments of
education. Since in criminal matters the Indian Act is superseded by
the Criminal Code of Canada, legal sanctions are enforced by the
police and courts.[1]

Though education and law enforcement are tasks of the state, they
are carried out on the ground by individuals—teachers, police, magistrates—living in New Masset. This means that the police and magistrates constitute a secondary system of authority relationships which is
superimposed on the local utilitarian system, distorting its operation.
Unlike teachers, Indian agents, and nurses, the police and magistrates
are not integrated into reciprocal relationships with the native people
nor bound to them by any common interests or values. They are not
responsible, nor often responsive, to the people. Their exercise of
power is considered arbitrary, unpredictable, uncontrollable, and,
therefore, illegitimate in native eyes. It generates hostility and resistance to all whites, throwing up barriers to interaction in the economic
sphere, leading eventually to the politicization of utilitarian relations
(see chap. 4).

Returning for the present to the structure of the compulsory system,
the Minister is represented on the local level by the Indian agent or
superintendent who is in charge of the agency, a unit formerly based on
a cultural group and comprised of two or more Indian bands. Until 1966
when seven Tsimshian and Haida bands were amalgamated in the

1. A survey, *Indians and the Law*, prepared for the Minister of Indian Affairs and
Northern Development provides a useful overview of problems of native peoples and
justice (Canadian Corrections Association 1967).

North Coast Agency, the Masset and Skidegate bands made up the Queen Charlotte Agency.

The band, of course, belongs to the dependent sector of the compulsory system. All registered Indians are enrolled on the membership list of this corporate group. Membership in the band, as distinguished from membership in "the village," is restricted to males descended in the male line from persons entitled to use Indian lands in May 1874, the legitimate children of such persons, illegitimate children of women so descended, and wives and widows of members. Unless they become enfranchised or, in the case of women, marry non-Indians, band members retain their legal status as Indians and their band membership even though they reside permanently away from the reserve (Canada 1951:Indian Act, Sections 11, 12).

In 1966 the Masset band numbered 967 members, including 509 males and 458 females. Two thirds of these members were resident on the reserve at that time. (For a description of non-resident members, see Stearns 1973:50–51.)

The band estate consists of 26 reserves with a total area of 2,214.16 acres. In 1966 only 60 acres of one village site, Masset Reserve No. 1, were used or occupied. The band held capital funds of $83,803 and revenue funds of $2,529.

Some limited power over their own affairs is vested in the band council, located on the lowest level of the administrative hierarchy. Its members are nominated every two years at a public meeting of the band and elected by a majority of votes cast. The electors are members of a band who are 21 years old and ordinarily resident on a reserve. Results of these elections are scrutinized by officials in Ottawa and the councilors confirmed in office if they are acceptable to the Branch.

A summary of the provisions of the Indian Act, outlining the allocation of responsibilities, will show how powers are distributed in the compulsory system. The power to constitute, amalgamate, or dissolve bands and to authorize the use of reserve land is vested in the Minister. He has jurisdiction and authority over the testamentary affairs of deceased Indians and the property of mentally incompetent Indians. He is charged with the management of reserves and surrendered lands. He controls the band's capital and revenue funds although in this instance the band must consent to his expenditure of its moneys for purposes specified in the Act. He may make loans to Indians and operate farms on reserves. It is his duty to supervise the election of band councilors.

The band council is empowered to protest entries or omissions in the band list, approve or disapprove applications for band membership, allot reserve land to members and approve transfers of land, determine priorities for allocation of new housing and dispose of resources such as timber, gravel, and so on. These prerogatives give councilors some control over the affairs of other villagers and leave them open to charges of abuse and favoritism.

The Indian Act specifies a limited number of activities concerning which councilors may pass by-laws drawn up according to a model circulated by Ottawa and subject, of course, to approval of the Minister. Under Section 80 of the Act the council may make by-laws governing matters of health, such as quarantines, the regulation of traffic, water supplies, public amusement, and peddlers. It may prescribe control of domestic animals and weeds, designate building codes and zones, and carry out the construction and maintenance of public works. It may authorize removal of trespassers. Fines not exceeding $100 or imprisonment for not longer than 30 days may be specified for infractions of these by-laws. It is important to note that the council has no authority to enforce its decisions or to act in a judicial capacity. Nor does it enjoy any autonomy even in the limited area of action permitted by the Act, for as indicated above, all proposed bylaws are subject to review by the Minister. Unless nullified by him, they come into force 40 days after their enactment.

When a band has reached "an advanced stage of development" the council may, with consent of the Minister, pass money by-laws levying taxes for use of reserve land and issuing business licenses. Such moneys may be used to pay officials for conducting band business and for supporting band projects. Control of capital and revenue funds, however, remains with the Minister.

On the level of the reserve-community, this formula envisions a pattern of instrumental leadership shared between the agent and the band councilors. With the agent acting as tutor and "watchdog of Ottawa," the councilors are expected to make decisions and allocate benefits provided by the federal government. Native officials hold only the statutory powers vested in their office, which do not endow them with any "personal power" in addition to whatever prestige and influence they enjoy as persons.[2]

In "the village," which is how the Haidas refer to the communal system, the agent and his "yes men" or "tools of the government" are irrelevant. Here, in 1966, the only formally recognized leader is the hereditary chief, William Matthews, who occupies a status handed

2. My analysis of leadership and the kinds of power available to elites in the compulsory and communal systems is greatly influenced by Etzioni, especially chapter 5 (1961:89–126). He distinguishes "officers" (or officials) whose power is derived mainly from their position in an organization and "leaders" whose power is normative and derived from personal characteristics. "Formal leaders" occupy organizational positions and also exercise personal power over subordinates. "Informal leaders" are those without offices whose only power is personal (1961:90).

down from traditional society. His leadership, which derives from the strong personal qualities he brings to his position as head of the lineage "owning" the town, is limited to the expressive sphere. He does not attempt nor would he be permitted to assume any instrumental functions. Informal leaders, who have personal influence but no institutionalized roles, occasionally emerge in competition with the chief on specific issues. They may head a faction and become "community leaders," but their support is often tenuous. We shall observe in chapters 4 and 8 how leaders of the militant faction are able to galvanize public opinion when it is running against establishment leaders, only to find their momentary power subsiding when the crisis passes.

Together, the formal and informal leaders act as spokesmen for the Haida in opposition to the government interest represented by the agent and band councilors. In Masset the conflict between these elements has intensified over the years, reflecting the strains generated in the native community by shifting government policies.

This pattern of leadership divided between government representatives and the hereditary elite demonstrates the segregation of instrumental and expressive roles which has resulted from the undermining of the native authority system. In pre-reserve society, leadership in both expressive and instrumental activities was exercised by lineage heads who combined a validated position with personal power. In the early reserve period the agent was careful to consult with the chiefs in order to gain their support for whatever measures Ottawa instructed him to take. Because the relationship between the agent and the Haidas was based on a strong affective bond, he was able to gain enough cooperation from the people to exert personal influence in instrumental spheres. This pattern was still strong in 1966 even though decreasing commitment on both sides had eroded the bonds between the people and their agent.

Band councilors, on the other hand, are dismissed by the people as ineffectual and problems are taken directly to the agent. Their ineffectiveness is due largely to the ambiguity of their role as powerless lower participants in the Indian Branch hierarchy, a condition recognized by the epithet, "tools of the government." It cannot be assumed, in the absence of evidence, that more power and prestige have been associated with the role since 1966 when the agency office was moved to the mainland.

The concentration of power on the federal level has had other serious consequences for the conduct of community life. No longer is the cultural group a coherent community providing a full set of services for its members. Not only has there been a loss of functions, which has destroyed the self-sufficiency of the native society, but there has been a separation of "operative" and "regulative" institutions (Nadel 1951:135, 141). Only kinship and marriage, the subsistence economy, hereditary chiefship, and ritual are "internal institutions" carried on within the Haida village. All of these are either operative or self-regulating in that they are governed by normative rules of behavior. Operative institutions such as those concerned with domestic activities and recreation fulfill their purposes directly without external regulation. Kinship institutions are self-regulating in that carrying out their tasks maintains the group that practices them, again without external regulation. Chiefship and ritual may be considered informally regulative in that they develop and express normative standards for the group. There are no formally regulative institutions or roles charged with the interpretation of norms or the administration of sanctions within the community. This segregation of operative and regulative institutions, which I shall refer to as "structural discontinuity," prevents the reinforcement of norms by overlapping institutions, creating serious problems for socialization and social control. Stripped of the coercive power vested in political and legal institutions, the only goals which the community can carry out independently are those oriented to cultural definition.

The construction of this compulsory system of relations spans a century in which Canada itself has undergone considerable social and political evolution. It seems that in the early years of Canadian jurisdiction, all sectors of society accepted the premise that Indians were wards of the government. This general consensus justified the segregation on reserves and the assignment of a special legal status to Indian people. Indians themselves have resented the disadvantages and defended the privileges of their status, while comparatively few renounced it by becoming enfranchised.[3]

We may describe the goals of the original compulsory system as primarily custodial with a secondary aim of socializing native peoples

3. National figures of Indian enfranchisement for 1955–75 are given in Perspective II, Table 14.9, p. 285 (Statistics Canada 1977). During 1960–61 to 1964–65, 401 adults and 239 children were enfranchised by application (compared to 2,198 women and 694 children enfranchised by marriage to a non-Indian). From 1970–71 to 1974–75 the total of applications was 54 adults and 20 children. In contrast 1,823 women and 117 children were enfranchised by marriage. For British Columbia, Hawthorn, Belshaw, and Jamieson (1958) found only 174 persons enfranchised in 1954. Enfranchisement here refers only to loss of rights under the Indian Act. It has no connection with voting rights, which were guaranteed to all Indians in 1960.

"Prior to 1972–1973 minor, unmarried children were automatically enfranchised with their parent(s). Since 1972–1973 minor, unmarried children have been enfranchised only when it is requested by the parent(s) and when the application is approved by the Dept. of Indian and Northern Affairs" (Statistics Canada 1977:285, note 2). For a more detailed discussion, see Hawthorn, Belshaw, and Jamieson 1958:385, 481–84).

to the norms of the dominant society. The Indian Department attempted to control and set norms for all activities in which Indians were engaged. Economic self-sufficiency was encouraged but no attempts were made to incorporate Indians into Canadian society either as labor force, taxpayers, or consumers. On the contrary, government policy aimed at protecting native peoples from corruption and exploitation by isolating them on reserves under the watchful eyes of agent and constable. Coercive means such as constant surveillance and forcible restraints were employed to enforce the norms of cleanliness, sobriety, chastity for the unmarried, and orderliness.

But government philosophy is sensitive to changes in the total social system and the world beyond. Since 1945 the world-wide ferment over civil rights and the nationalistic aspirations of former colonial peoples have greatly affected Canadian attitudes toward its own dependent groups. The authors of the "Hawthorn Report" compare the "paternalistic ideology" that dominated policy-making from 1867 to 1945 with the "democratic ideology" that has pervaded administrative planning since the Second World War (Hawthorn 1967:22–23). In contrast to the custodial orientation of the early decades, the postwar trend emphasized the opening up of the reserves and the eventual integration of Indians into the mainstream. Consistent with this new orientation, the Indian Branch no longer set standards of behavior for private areas of life. The oppressive surveillance to which Indians were subjected for so many years was lifted. The norms to which they are now expected to conform are those codified in Canadian law and in the revised Indian Act (Canada 1951).

The shift to integrational goals was intensified during the 1960s. The encouragement of integrated education, fostering of community development, and provision of capital to enable Indians to "compete" in the wider economy are conspicuous examples of Branch policy during this period. Two symbolic gestures, extending to Indians the rights of citizenship, were made in those years. Indians were empowered to vote in federal elections in 1960, and in 1965 actually exercised this right. During this period they received their "liquor rights" in British Columbia enabling them to buy liquor and to drink in public places. In 1967 the Branch sent a questionnaire concerning a proposed new Indian Act to all Indians over 18 years, asking their assistance in redefining their status and role in society. At public meetings held on reserves, Indians were invited to make suggestions, to tell officials "what they wanted." According to Arthur Laing, then Minister of Indian Affairs, the new Act would give more self-determination to Indians and more local autonomy and easier access to capital to bands. New achievement goals were set for the Indians. Public statements by government officials during this period stressed that Indians were expected to "show some initiative," to get to work, to capitalize on the economic resources of their reserves.

Any illusions the people might have cherished about the outcome of these "consultations" were shattered in June 1969 when a White Paper, denouncing the old policy as bankrupt, was tabled in Parliament. The Indian Act was not to be amended, it was to be repealed and the Indian Affairs Branch abolished within five years. Indians were to occupy "a full role in Canadian society and in the economy while retaining, strengthening and developing an Indian identity which preserves the good things of the past and helps Indian people to prosper and thrive" (Canada 1969:8–9). The ethnic boundary was to be struck down, but at the same time special assistance to Indians would continue. Federal moneys for support of Indian education and other special programs were to be turned over to the provinces. Indians were to be helped to "catch up" by vocational counseling and training, grants to establish businesses, and other unspecified aid. While Indians were being welcomed into Canadian society, "Indian culture" was to be encouraged and other Canadians were asked to "appreciate" the Indians' contribution.

Thus, the government had pushed the concept of integration to its logical conclusion, completely reversing its original policies. With this stroke the general consensus under which Indian Affairs had been administered was destroyed. The passive acceptance that the people gave to the concept of wardship was replaced by active opposition which prevented implementation of the new policy. Of course, this was not the first outburst of Indian anger nor are the events that spark such responses everywhere the same.

In writing of earlier reaction to the land-title question La Violette observes, "A provincial government replaced colonial rule, and almost immediately *Imperial policy was reversed* with respect to land for natives. It is not hard to comprehend how the experiences of the natives gave rise to a resentment that developed into open hostility and hatred, and to feelings of inadequacy in coping with the problems of becoming a displaced population" (1961:141, emphasis mine). Describing the active role of the Allied Tribes, he continues, "The most distinguishable and most inexplicable development was the change from mere feelings of resentment and hostility owing to specific incidents, to a persistent, sustained, and concerted effort which by 1917 had become a well-directed demand based upon a literature of injustice" (p. 141).

The Haidas were only peripherally concerned in the land-claims litigation spearheaded by the Nishga (La Violette 1961:98–144; Drucker 1958:86–103) and did not adopt an aggressive posture toward whites until much later. The specific incidents that triggered a more active expression of alienation in Masset will be identified in this and the following chapters. More general processes will be examined by analyzing the foundations of the special relationship between Indians and the federal government.

The terms of this relationship are precisely defined in the Indian Act. This set of rules is specific in denoting the range of latitude in its provisions and comprehensive in applying to almost every area of Indian life. The content of the interaction as recorded in reports and other documents is constantly reviewed by "Ottawa." Role definitions are universalistic, affecting all Indians in Canada. They are ascriptive in that eligibility for band membership is determined by descent from a person entitled to use Indian lands in 1874 or marriage of a woman to such a person. The government's orientation is instrumental; the prescriptions are directed toward meeting certain functional obligations to dependent populations. But the implementation of the relationship requires receptivity, or what we will refer to as complementary role behavior, on the part of the Indians. According to Parsons, complementary interaction can only occur where some common value orientation or standard is held by both sides (1951:36–39). To say that a universalistic–achievement-oriented society administers a particularistic-ascriptive subsystem gives some insight into the conflicts that may be expected.

On the ground, Canadian society was represented, as has already been indicated, by the Indian agent. His relationship with the native people may be described as one of an actor-public type in which he functions independently with respect to an undifferentiated constituency (Nadel 1957:80–82). In this setting, his value orientation is ideally universalistic and affectively neutral; however, this does not preclude the development of affective attitudes which are expressed as concern. While the role of agent is defined by specific obligations, a genuine concern for the Indians' welfare creates a diffuse relationship with strong moral overtones. As a result, his custodial responsibilities may be carried out with zealous protectiveness toward his charges. These attitudes on the part of early agents encouraged, perhaps even required, passivity and submissiveness on the part of the Indians.

The Haidas' value orientations stress affectivity, diffuseness, and particularism in social relations along with strong expressive interests. They related to the roles of Indian agent, teacher, nurse, and minister by giving esteem to their incumbents without necessarily internalizing the values which these persons tried to instill in them. What they prized in the relationships was the concern expressed for their welfare.

Given the almost complete control of Indian affairs exercised by the agent, it was perhaps inevitable that his role should become paternalistic. The strong dependency needs of Indian groups were fostered under this system. Parsons points out that in societies with strong expressive orientations the primary focus of the total reward system is to be sought on the level of love and responsiveness (1951:131). This would explain the great value placed by the Haida on solicitude and paternalistic concern when expressed by outsiders in authority roles. In the case of Indian agents, their very interference and supervision were symbolic of that concern. The Haidas responded with submissiveness and passivity in exchange for affective rewards. Most agents, however, recognized that the Indians' docility was role-playing behavior.

We must remember that this dependency was fostered in members of a society which had, in aboriginal times, been fiercely competitive. The establishment of this new value pattern was greatly facilitated by the fact that Haida society suffered an 80 to 90 percent population loss after contact. The weakening of traditional institutions and groups resulted in discontinuity in socialization to old Haida culture at the same time that alien authority was being imposed upon them. The new forms of social organization restored orderly relations, but on a basis that deprived the subordinate group of effective internal leadership and control of its own affairs.

Socialization

Coercive control was reinforced by an extensive program of socialization. The essential feature of socialization, according to Parsons, is the inculcation of common values and norms in ego through incorporating him into a complementary role relationship where his behavior is sanctioned by the attitudes of an alter. Ego internalizes the desired norms and values only when certain conditions are met. First, alter must control the interactive situation so that he may reward or punish ego's behavior. Second, alter serves as a model for imitation and instructs ego in the desired behavior. Third, a reciprocal attachment involving attitudes of loyalty and love, approval and esteem is established which ego seeks to maintain by conformity to alter's expectations. When these attitudes of esteem, loyalty, and so on are expressed by ego, the implication is that he has formed a personal attachment to alter or has internalized the norms the latter is enforcing, or both (Parsons 1951:211–14). We may then conceive of alter as exercising normative power and expressive leadership. Furthermore, once established, the tendency is for these relationships to be maintained (Parsons 1951:204–5, 213).

Application of Parsons' model to the Masset data shows that in the early reserve period all three conditions necessary to successful socialization were met. The Indian agent controlled the total interactive situation, dispensing rewards and punishments according to official policy and his own rigid standards. He instructed and inspected and strove continually to set a good example by his own behavior. And, certainly, a strong reciprocal attachment developed between the Masset Haidas and their agent. But although the agent-Indian relationship had a strong normative component, it did not result in the internalization of many of the desired norms of Canadian society. On the contrary, in this restricted situation where the agent exercised an iron control over community life, the alienation provoked by his coercive measures took the passive forms of submissiveness and dependency. The Indians' behavior barely masked a smouldering resentment that was perceived by their white benefactors as ingratitude. These are the patterns, then, to which the Indians were socialized as unwilling participants in the compulsory system. This dependency is the unintended consequence of a relationship in which coercive means were used to ensure conformity to externally imposed norms and values. By submitting to the domination of the Indian agent, hiding their alienation by passive withdrawal, the people did not jeopardize the prized affective rewards.

The process by which stable interactive relationships between Indians and administrators were established is vividly documented in the agents' diaries, office memos, monthly and annual reports, and official correspondence with "Ottawa." In citing these data it is not suggested that the course of Haida history was determined by the personalities of the white agents of change. Agent Deasy and "Nurse Chapman," who have unwittingly served as informants about the role and attitudes of the paternalistic civil servant, seem almost like stock characters, manipulated by the heavy hand of the federal bureaucracy. Surely they cannot have been unique in the experience of native peoples.[4]

It must be acknowledged, however, that Thomas Deasy left an indelible imprint on Haida culture. Born in 1857 in Portsmouth, England, he was the son of a member of the Royal Engineers and veteran of the Crimean War. In 1859 his father's detachment was sent to New Westminster, capital of British Columbia, to build roads and bridges and to assist in establishing law and order in the new colony. Ten years later

4. The point is important. We may expect to see more suits like that brought by the Musqueam band against the federal government, alleging fraud in leasing 162 acres of reserve land to the Shaughnessy Golf and Country Club for 75 years (1958–2033) at a rent far below market value. In that case, much blame was attached to the former Indian agent. In holding the government accountable for past management—or mismanagement—of their affairs, it will be unfortunate if the Indians' attention is diverted from policy to individuals (*Vancouver Sun*, September 19 and 22, 1979).

the family moved to the new capital of Victoria, settling near the legislative buildings. Thomas went to work early, serving as a page in the Legislature. In 1871 he became a printing apprentice in the composing room of the British *Colonist*. He pursued two occupations: at the Legislature as messenger and, later, sergeant-at-arms; and at the Government Printing Office as a printer. Subsequently, he worked for Joseph Trutch at the Canadian Pacific Railway and then as a printer at the *Times*.

It was through his association with the Victoria fire department that he achieved eminence. He joined the volunteer department as lantern boy at the age of 13, advanced to the bucket brigade at 16, and became a regular member of a hook and ladder company at 18. His energy and ability earned him rapid promotion. According to the *Colonist*:

> During the lively times of the seventies and eighties, when the three companies here used to race to reach a fire first, Mr. Deasy held the offices of second and first assistant foreman, and foreman of the hook and ladder company. As a volunteer fireman he also held the position of assistant chief engineer.
> When the fire department was taken over by the city as a civic responsibility [1886] and the entire organization made into a paid department, Mr. Deasy was elected assistant engineer by the ratepayers. He served in that capacity for two years and was a candidate for the position of chief engineer against the late Chief Phillips and the late H. Rudge. He received more votes than both the other candidates combined. [*Colonist*, April 10, 1936]

Deasy was then thirty years old. The department over which he presided included both volunteers and a paid force of 26 men, three of whom received salaries of $60.00, three, $16.25, and eighteen, $14.00 per month. The job was demanding: "firemen were expected to be on duty 24 hours a day, seven days a week with time off for meals" (Gregson 1970:162). The prospect of building an efficient, disciplined firefighting force was not encouraging.[5] Deasy's accomplishments as

5. In his sprightly history of Victoria, Harry Gregson described the previous, volunteer department as inefficient, hampered not only by bad roads and poor water supplies but by rivalry. The first volunteer group was the Union Hook and Ladder Company formed in 1860, but "two rival companies speedily came into being, namely the Deluge Company chiefly composed of Britishers and the Tiger Company, chiefly Americans. National pride and firefighting zeal often vented themselves in the sabotaging of the efforts of the rivals, a favourite method being to disconnect the rivals' hoses" (1970:161).

The volunteers were "enthusiastic and bibulous" in their "gorgeous uniforms . . . scarlet shirts trimmed with black velvet, silver helmets, shining belts and black pants." On Firefighters' Day (May Day) "the firemen assembled first outside the homes of the mayor, aldermen, lieutenant-governor and other benefactors to receive verbal and liquid homage to their good citizenship. Then they paraded downtown. Most saloons along Government Street felt custom-bound to help quench the seemingly insatiable thirst of the volunteers, some even installing barrels on the sidewalk. Many saloon keepers must have thought eventually that fires would be less expensive than fire brigades because there were 70 thirsty firefighters in the Deluge Company, 65 in the Tiger Company and

fire chief, reviewed in an editorial in the *Times* at his death, provide a
glimpse of the qualities he would bring to his career as an Indian agent.

> There was a time when Thomas Deasy . . . was one of the most promi-
> nent figures in this community. He was a man of many activities, but the
> sphere in which his vivid personality reached its most arresting proportions
> was the fire department, of which he was chief for many years. In that
> capacity he was known all over the Pacific Coast as an exceptionally able
> executive who with limited facilities and small expenditures developed an
> efficient fire-fighting service.
> In those days Victoria's fire department was largely a volunteer service,
> the permanent part of it comprising chiefly those who had the direct supervi-
> sion of the mechanical equipment. In spite of this anomalous condition Chief
> Deasy maintained the strictest discipline, the volunteers readily accepting
> his leadership. He was familiar with every building in the city from roof to
> basement and knew precisely where to go when a fire broke out and how to
> tackle it. Victoria was a very inflammable community then, particularly the
> Chinese section of it.
> Mr. Deasy was a man of wide information, and there was scarcely a limit
> to the interests which intrigued his alert intelligence. No public celebration
> or ceremonial was complete without his dominant personality. He was a
> capable writer and often contributed to the press interesting articles on many
> subjects. . . . [*Times*, April 11, 1936]

A former subordinate wrote of him, "I served under him for twenty
years, and always found him at heart wrapped up in the skillful administration of his official duties, a strict disciplinarian, a genial friend,
always keenly observant of the protection of the lives and property of
his public. He was keenly interested in all brands of sport and always
easy of approach. He was also a prolific writer and always a loyal and
faithful citizen" (*Colonist*, April 17, 1936). In 1901 Deasy resigned as
fire chief to join the Dominion police. After several years in that service
he received an appointment in the Indian Department.

Thomas Deasy was 53 years old when he took up his post at Masset
as the first permanent Indian agent. His tenure from 1910 to 1924
defines the early reserve period on the Queen Charlotte Islands. In the
records he appears as the archetype of the paternalistic administrator—gruff, untiring in pursuit of his duty, a man of strong Christian
principles. Old informants recall that "he was always full of arguments." In addition to the legitimate authority vested in him as an
official of the Department of Indian Affairs, Deasy had considerable
personal influence owing to his forceful personality and obvious com-

---

another 60 in the Hook & Ladder crew and they drank not only on Firefighters' Day but
during the rehearsals for several days prior to it.
  "The post of fireman, not surprisingly, was much coveted. There was no pay . . . a
member even paid to join . . . but the liquid and other fringe benefits such as periodic
benefit concerts were substantial." [Gregson 1970:161–62]

mitment to the welfare of the people. He was, in Etzioni's terms, a
formal leader (1961:90). He cultivated two-way communication with
the people by consulting continuously with recognized chiefs and
elders. Deasy was assisted in carrying out his many responsibilities by
a field matron, school teachers, and a special constable. He was able to
displace onto the constable some of the hostility provoked by the
strong coercive measures he ordered. Deasy understood his duties to
include the socialization, protection, and correction of his charges.
After 12 years' service in the Queen Charlotte Agency, he set forth his
interpretation of his role in his annual report for the year ending March
31, 1922.

> They (the Indians) must have a guiding hand with them. The duties of an
> Indian agent shows that they cannot progress unless under the strictest of
> discipline. The whites and others must be kept off their reserves as they
> have been during the last twelve years. They must be taught many lessons in
> thrift and morals. Their bodily health must be conserved. Advanced as they
> are in the eyes of the outer world, they have many customs that it will be hard
> to eradicate. The environment of the Indian home is not yet all it should be.
> We have been endeavoring to raise the standard of cleanliness and good
> living conditions and it will take time to prove to the younger generation that
> the ways of their forebears is not correct. We had the older Indians to
> educate as well as those coming from the schools. Diametrically opposite, it
> has been difficult to show the young man and woman that "civilization"
> with all its trials and tribulations is better than the easy mode of life of the
> aborigine. We took them from heathenism to the light of Christianity which
> is hard to follow.

Elsewhere in the report Deasy refers to the Indians' response to
these ministrations. "The Indian is far from being the childish ward
ascribed to him by many. He may be reported as docile and *all that is
required from a ward of government* but beneath the surface is the
bitterness of restraint and the complaint that the white man has in-
vaded his territory abolishing his old customs and habits" (emphasis
mine).

Deasy's diaries show him in almost daily consultation with the constable, field matron, reserve teachers—Indian and white, the elected
chief councilor, hereditary chief, and any Indians who called at the
office on business. He met frequently with church ministers, the
medical officer when one was available, the magistrate and provincial
constable at New Masset, the captain of the steamer that called bi-
weekly, and anyone else who had business on the island. He attended
church services on the reserve as well as weddings and funerals. He
visited the sick and dispensed fencing, seeds, and other materials. He
inspected the school, gardens, water works, and construction projects.
His work day began at 8:00 A.M. and he frequently remained in his

office until 9 at night. He made inspection trips to other reserves and to camps where Indians were working. He traveled to Skidegate as often as possible to supervise that band's business.

In those days it was necessary to take the steamer from Masset to the mainland and thence back to the south end of Graham Island. Because of the length and expense of the journey, the Skidegate band escaped the unrelenting surveillance that was the lot of the Masset Haidas. Even so, the agent kept in constant touch by telephone and telegraph.

Special constables were appointed from among white men resident in New Masset. Most of these were settlers who had preempted land for a homestead and found the salary of $75 per month attractive. The duties of the office were strenuous, however, and turnover was rapid. Deasy instructed his recruits in their responsibilities by letter. The constable was expected to "be on duty at all times." He should be present at the wharf "where hundreds of fishermen dock to prevent the landing of drunken men or intoxicants." He was to act as truant officer and compel parents to send children to school. He was to keep watch on stores where patent medicines might be sold, to act as public health officer, to inspect houses, and to warn Indians about epidemics. He was to instruct the Indian council concerning the by-laws, carry out patrols of the reserve, and cooperate with provincial authorities in enforcing the Prohibition Act. Occasionally he made the long journey to Skidegate in the agent's place.

Deasy attempted to secure the cooperation of provincial and dominion police in protecting the Indians from rum peddlers and other undesirable characters, but these officers were not continuously available. Band members were appointed annually by the council to act as constables but in the absence of Indian Department recognition, the role was not respected by other Indians and its occupants were ineffective.

Educational needs were to be met by the construction of an Indian day school on a large plot of reserve land where a "demonstration farm" could be developed. In the early days before the establishment of the local agency, Anglican Church missionaries provided classroom instruction for the village children. The church also maintained an industrial boarding school at Metlakatla, which many Masset people attended before it was closed in 1908. The Indian Day School opened in 1912 with a white teacher in charge. Since it was difficult to retain white teachers because of the low pay and isolation, Deasy persuaded the Indian Department to allow him to hire native teachers. Attendance at the day school was very irregular. Indeed, the Haidas actively resisted the school programs forced upon them, and with good reason.

The educational process envisioned by their administrators meant the complete reorientation of native life. Not only were the basic skills of reading, writing, and arithmetic to be taught to the children in class-rooms, but the "civilizing pursuits" of farming and ranching were to be substituted for the "unsettling" occupation of fishing.

In his capacity as truant officer, the special constable checked the daily attendance. In April of 1916 he reported that there was "no trouble on the reserve and the taking of children to school occupied more of my time than anything else." The following April his successor wrote in his monthly report, "I endeavored by calling on the parents of those children persistently absent from day school to get them to cooperate in seeing that the children attend school regularly." Under the band by-laws the council was empowered to impose fines on the parents, but the councilors were scattered over the island and could not be called together to take action. The only Indian constable was employed on a steamer and was not available to lend assistance. The most effective solution to the problem of absenteeism was to send the children to residential schools where the "distracting influence" of the home environment might be eliminated and the norms of white society more efficiently inculcated.

Plans for education in farming were poorly received. The Indians were encouraged to maintain the potato gardens they cultivated in the fertile soil of old village sites. Investigating complaints of damage to their crops by deer, the constable found that while unfenced gardens had suffered extensive destruction, fenced gardens were undamaged. As deer and cattle multiplied the people responded, not by adopting fencing, but by abandoning their gardens.

The Indian Department's agricultural program included the introduction of cattle raising. Accordingly, the Department purchased a bull for the Masset Indians. In a report to Ottawa of February 1924, Deasy enclosed a voucher for $18.64 for fodder, explaining his difficulties in trying to make the Indians care for their cattle. This report throws light on the results of these educational efforts as well as on the relationship between Indians and agent:

> The Indian Department purchased a bull for the Indians of the Masset band and I was instructed to ask them to feed the animal during the winter months. I found that the animal was starving to death and although I begged the Indians and whites in the neighborhood to look after the animal, all the return I received was complaints that the bull was here and there starving. I sent two Indians after the animal and put it in a field attached to the resi-dence of the teacher and ordered food at once from Prince Rupert. The Indian Council had a small amount of funds on hand which they turned over to me and I paid for the food.
>
> The Indians are engaged in Revival Meetings at night and playing football

during the daytime. They are even allowing their own cattle to starve to death. I telegraphed Prince Rupert and Victoria to send me food. As usual with the Indians many of them have given up the occupations they had in logging camps and at the sawmill and are "hiving" on the reserve during the winter months. They are holding meetings, socials and basket parties nightly under no white clergy man and appear to care for little but sport and gatherings where they talk intermittently [sic]. With the whooping cough in almost all of the homes they are inviting others from outside to visit them but we would not allow others to come which appears to meet with their disapproval. . . .

I am caring for the animal personally. The Indians are as a rule cruel with the lower animals. They let them run around until many fall down and die. I would propose selling the bull in the spring and not giving any assistance in future towards cattle raising. The Indians are fishermen and care little for their cattle, being away during the summer and neglecting their cattle during the winter. Where the Indians have gardens, they are continually complaining of cattle breaking in and destroying their vegetables. The few have cattle. The many have gardens. The cruelty to the animals in allowing them to starve and to run around without care does not appear to have any effect on the Indian.

The agent's own frustration is vividly expressed in his conclusion. "When the Department does things for them they appear to think we should care for their own sick, to make all improvements, to care for their cattle and to treat grown men and women as children. They have no gratitude and are continually reciting their grievances against church and state. If one is aided, the whole consider themselves neglected. When we endeavor to make them send their children to school, they take the children away to some outlying settlement. When they return from industrial school they claim they were mistreated there. When the children come home for vacation during the summer many do not return. . . ."

The pattern of dependence in relations with the agent was fully established without the latter realizing how completely his own behavior reinforced it. But within the sphere of family and ceremonial life the Indians carried on neotraditional cultural patterns with great indifference to the white model located among them. Undaunted, Deasy continued to concern himself with the health, morals, sobriety, and correction of the Haidas.

Health Care

Responsibility for health care of the Indians, as for education, had been assumed by the missionaries and their wives as an expression of their concern for the welfare of their flock. Reverend Collison, the first missionary to serve the Haidas, described his ministrations to the people (1915). In his annual report of 1912, Deasy commended the wife of

Reverend Hogan for her voluntary medical services to the Indians. The Medical Marine Mission was also active in this field (Peake 1959). Among the settlers who came to Masset in the early decades of the century were physicians and nurses who were called upon to care for the Indians as well as neighboring whites. These practitioners received a small stipend for their services, but they were not available on a regular basis.

During Agent Deasy's tenure, his wife served as field matron of the reserve. She delivered babies, treated injuries and disease, dispensed medicines, and inspected houses. She visited the school and lectured both students and mothers on sanitation and hygiene. When no medical officer was at hand, she remained on duty day and night. When the Deasys retired, Mrs. Grace Frost, a white nurse from New Masset, carried out the duties of field matron for 35 years. Whenever she was called she made the three-mile journey to the reserve on foot or horseback at all times of day and in all weathers, or so say the local traditions.

The part-time role of public health officer was performed by the special constable. On one of his inspection trips to fish camps where Indians were smoking salmon for the winter, the constable serving in 1917 wrote, "I found the camp fairly clean and every one well excepting an old man. The camp was alive with thousands of gulls which doubtless accounts for the lack of refuse. I conferred with the leading men regarding the desirability of keeping the houses and everything about them clean."

Visiting the sick and inspecting dwellings continued to be an important responsibility for many years. The agent's report for April 1940 stated that "the field matron paid a visit to the cannery and reports that the Indians are all well and their huts very well kept and clean." The approval with which the people were rewarded for such efforts was a very important factor in securing their conformity to the norms of cleanliness. In 1962 an old woman mentioned these inspections: "Now they just don't care about us anymore. The nurse never comes to look at our houses now." Even better-educated older people interpreted the change of attitude and behavior by agents, nurses, and others as evidence of indifference to their welfare.

Social Control

Despite the considerable resources devoted to socialization it continued to be a secondary goal of the compulsory system. In keeping with its primary orientation to custodial goals, the Indian Department committed its major efforts to the maintenance of order and the prevention of deviance.

The agent manipulated a formal sanction system embodied in the Indian Act, which specified proscribed behaviors and penalties for infractions. Under the Act, intoxication, prostitution, stealing, potlatching, and trespassing on the reserve by unauthorized persons were offenses. In the earliest years the agent, in his capacity of justice of the peace, dealt with cases brought before him by the special police constable. In cases involving the use of intoxicants the usual penalty was a fine of $5 to $25. An Indian convicted of supplying intoxicants was fined $30. Jail terms of 20 days or so were imposed for default or repeated offenses. Suspended sentences were sometimes given for theft and assault.

When provisions of the Criminal Code were violated and where whites were involved, cases were heard by the stipendiary magistrate in New Masset, with the agent serving in an advisory capacity. Relatives sometimes acted as legal counsel for the accused. In the case of a man arrested and charged with maiming a cow belonging to another band member, his brother and brother-in-law sought to "obtain evidences in his defense." The charge was reduced to one of ill-treating a cow, and the case was tried summarily. The defendant pleaded guilty and was sentenced to 30 days of hard labor in the New Masset jail. It appears that such sentences were actually served on the magistrate's nearby ranch (Dalzell 1968:78). The most serious case involved a Masset Indian who assaulted a Skidegate Haida during a quarrel on the fishing grounds. The charge was changed from one of assault to that of assault occasioning grievous bodily harm. The man pleaded guilty and was sentenced to six months of hard labor at Oakalla Prison farm on British Columbia's southern mainland.

Deasy sought to protect the Indians from what he considered unjust treatment in the courts. He protested to the Indian agent at Prince Rupert about the continual fining of Haidas in police court. In writing to his superiors in Ottawa about the need for closer supervision of Indians off the reserve, he stated, "The authorities in the cities and towns take little notice of the Indian unless fines are in sight." He also attempted, though with little success, to obtain redress for Indians through court action against whites. In February 1916 he wrote to the Secretary of the Department of Indian Affairs about the status and powers of an Indian agent with respect to cases under the Criminal Code and not specifically mentioned in the Indian Act:

Where we have white settlements adjacent to Indian reserves and cases come up in which Indians are directly or indirectly concerned, the stipendiary magistrate when we sit with him has the power, according to his own statement, to have us with him only in an advisory capacity. In a case held here (Masset) the magistrate committed a white man for trial on a charge of wounding an Indian woman. The case was quashed by the grand jury and no true bill found. All of the testimony was written by the magistrate, signed by the witnesses and submitted by the magistrate without consulting another member of the court, a justice of the peace, or myself although we sat on the case with him. In almost all such cases appealed or sent to the Supreme Court, the convictions have been quashed on appeal or thrown out by petty and grand juries.

Throughout the first three decades of the reserve period there seem to have been few problems in enforcing the law. Cases of drunkenness, assault, and immorality were not numerous. In 1920 Deasy wrote to Ottawa, "I cannot state that the Indians are behaving out of the ordinary. The majority are sober and law abiding but a few of the younger men and a number of the girls and women are misbehaving." He believed that continued good behavior of the majority could be guaranteed by close supervision and instruction by himself and the constable. Equally important was the protection of the Indians from exploitation by outsiders, particularly those bent on supplying liquor or seducing the women. In 1916 a constable reported, "We only hear of indulgence in intoxicating liquor when the Indians visit outside towns." In an undated report of the same period Deasy wrote,

> With regard to the manufacture and sale of intoxicants: I cannot state that our Indians are either manufacturing or dealing in spiritous liquors. The unrestricted sale of intoxicants in stores and other places without license is not encouraging for those endeavoring to suppress the traffic. Indians must go to stores for food. The stores also keep "near beer," "invalid's port wine," and "essences." The mill towns, canneries, post offices and other places also have stores. They also sell patent medicines containing alcohol. We have few cases of drunkenness on our reserves. But the temptation in outside places, where we have no doctors, to obtain patent medicines containing alcohol is before the Indian.

Instructions forwarded by the Department of Indian Affairs reveal little knowledge of local conditions. "It is thought," states a letter from the office of the assistant deputy on August 26, 1920, "that with two constables at Masset and the RCMP there should be little difficulty in enforcing the law in regard to the supplying of intoxicants. . . . You should report any information which you may have to the officer in command of the RCMP for action."

Deasy replied, "We have no RCMP on these islands. We had one visit from that force some months ago. . . . With several hundred loggers, a large number of fishermen, several hundreds of Indians and the opportunities for illicit traffic in intoxicants we are sadly lacking in police protection. The Provincial constable went out on 20 days of vacation, we have no dominion officer and are entirely dependent on a special police officer to cover the large territory.''

The prevention of sexual misbehavior was seen as a major responsibility. Periodically the constable was despatched to the sawmills and fishing grounds to check on the behavior of Indians who were away working. In September 1917 the constable reported to Deasy, ''There have been quite a number of Indians up at New Masset every day picking berries and I have made it a point to watch them closely for reports reached me that they were not conducting themselves as might be wished.'' During the following month Deasy notified the constable that ''an Indian of Masset band . . . is illegally cohabiting with an Indian woman of said band. . . . Kindly investigate and report in writing full particulars on both parties and evidence that may be adduced regarding these two Indians.'' In December of 1919 Deasy instructed a new constable that the same man, ''an Indian under suspended sentence is reported to be living with a crippled and diseased Indian woman, both unmarried. This should be stopped. It is also stated that an Indian woman . . . is living with a white man contrary to the provisions of the Criminal Code.''

A constable reported in February of 1915 that he had ''looked into'' the condition of the Indian women of Queen Charlotte Island in Prince Rupert. ''Some of them are living in cabins and in two lodging houses that are not proper places for Indian women. The few women away from the reserves are not good characters and some place should be found for them and for Indians that visit Prince Rupert. Many are arrested of the Indians visiting that city and are usually mulcted in fines.'' At least two such women were sentenced to the Oakalla Prison farm for six months for vagrancy after repeated fines. Upon their release the Indian Department in Ottawa instructed Deasy to ''look into their future behavior.'' He in turn directed the constable to write to the authorities in Prince Rupert or go there himself to investigate the case: ''The parents and relatives do not appear to have any control over them and it is necessary that action should be taken to prevent them from further infraction of the law.''

While many persons clearly resented this interference, there is evidence that others turned to the agent for protection and mediation in internal village affairs. In the agency files was a letter in a fine hand, dated December 1916 and signed, ''From a young girl.'' The women referred to in this letter were employed at the Skidegate Oil Works, processing dogfish livers.

> Dear Sir, I am writing you this letter to ask you if you can do anything to send . . . and her daughter away from the oil works. For there [sic] making a lot of trouble among the people here by telling disgraceful stories about

them and lowering nearly all the young girls of this place as low as themselves and quite a few have asked me to write to you about it and ask your
help to try to drive them away from here. Both her and her daughter made
trouble at Aliford Bay last summer amongst the women by carrying lies
between them and started quarrels there. Her daughter is worse and she is a
disgrace to us young girls here. She was acting disgracefully at the Bay and
white people naturally thought we are all of the same kind. I am sending you
this letter with the assurance of your help. So kindly give it your special
attention and trusting you will act immediately try your best to get the
daughter away if you can't get the mother to go. You are our agent and I am
sure you will help us in this matter for you always want us to have peace in
our village.

There is no indication what action, if any, was taken by the agent.

While the Indian Act had seriously undermined the native authority
structure, the Indians were initially permitted to share responsibility
with the agent in certain internal affairs. Section 194 of the Indian Act
of 1906 and Section 185 of the Act of 1927 were interpreted so as to
allow the participation of band councilors in judicial proceedings of
various kinds. Under Section 4 of the Masset Indian Reserve by-laws
the council, with the approval of the Indian agent, had power to arrest
or summon "any person or persons, members of the band, charged
with breach of the peace, profligacy, intemperance, or offence against
morality. With the Indian agent the person or persons so arrested may
be tried by said Council under Section 194 of the Indian Act."

In the context of band-council hearings, then, the agent developed a
close working relationship with the councilors who were recruited
from among the respected elders of the village. This cooperation
reflected a congruence of interests in maintaining order and resolving
interpersonal disputes. It did not require or imply a foundation of
shared norms or values. In describing a similar collaboration of elites
and inmates of coercive organizations, Etzioni makes a point that has
particular relevance for this analysis: "Any change in the situation may
cause this limited area of concurrent interests to disappear" (1961:97).
As long as the interactive relationship of agent and Indians remained
stable, however, it appears that the people accepted his leadership in
matters of social control.

Many of the matters dealt with by the band council and recorded by
agents and constables seem rather trivial. Three cases involved
assault. A man who struck another against whom he nursed a grudge
was bound over to keep the peace and charged $4 in court costs. Three
young men were brought before the council for a fight that began with
throwing snowballs; they were reprimanded and warned to keep the
peace. Another man was fined $12 for interfering with one of the con-
stables in the execution of his duties. The council held two sessions to

deal with a case of "immorality," finally imposing fines of $10 on the young man and $7 on the girl.

The unwillingness of councilors to pass judgment on their own kinsmen is familiar and predictable. In 1924 Deasy wrote to the Department recommending that Section 4 of the by-laws be eliminated. "Almost all of the Indians of a Band are closely related and a council will not carry out such a section satisfactorily. I find that Indian councillors and Indian police officers will not arrest or convict their fellows of a band unless it is some Indian without friends or relatives."

An instance of the council singling out such a person is recorded in a letter of February 1925 addressed by members of the band council to the "Indian agent or higher authority." They asked whether they had the power to regulate traffic on a reserve road maintained by voluntary labor. Since the road was "suitable only for pedestrians and light horse vehicles," they asked whether they had the "right to stop *any* owner of an automobile from crossing the reserve boundary and running the car along the reserve road."

In forwarding the letter to his superiors, the new agent who replaced Deasy at Masset explained,

At present there are two autos in the village. One of these belongs to a member of the band but as it is in my opinion irretrievably damaged it is unlikely to cause any trouble. The other belongs to . . . who is not a member of the band but resides in the village. He is an Alaskan Indian who has resided here for several years now. He is not very popular with most of the Masset band whether on account of the fact that he has never given up his citizenship of the U.S.A. and joined this band or not I cannot state, but the fact remains that there is a good deal of ill feeling which may to some extent be at the bottom of this statement. [This man was the son-in-law of a very high-ranking lineage head, but these were *affinal* relatives.]

Nevertheless, the agent recommended that the council be given power to regulate traffic. "The men of the village have given up quite a bit of time lately to improving the road running through the village, and have done this willingly without remuneration. Obviously they resent anyone ruining their work and have made up their minds to prevent this destruction. There is no doubt that if the road put in order cannot be controlled by the villagers and heavy traffic kept off, that this piece of work will be the last that will be done voluntarily, which in my opinion would be one of the worst things that could happen." There is no information on the disposition of this case, but later the band council exercised the power to regulate traffic.

The council proceeded against this same man on another occasion for the "nonpayment of taxes and the taking of water from the village taps without having asked the council." The chief councilor felt that charges against . . . should be dropped because he had "given a good donation toward the water supply on the night of the pie party in aid of the water system." The defendant agreed to pay the $10 tax on the sawmill he operated on reserve land. Here the Indian Department took a hand, proposing that the band admit . . . as a member and arrange for him to pay some compensation to the band as rent for the land where the sawmill is located.

In passing by-laws that imposed curfews and prohibited trespassing, the council attempted to use its limited authority to control the behavior of the young. Section 5 of the by-laws states that "the council may fix the time when all members under 18 years of age may be in their homes at night, which is sundown, and may fine or imprison children who refuse or neglect to comply with this regulation." While it is difficult to believe that the Minister approved the by-law in this form, this version is found in the files. The reference to imprisonment of children who ignore the curfew suggests another aspect of the Minister's power of review.

One of the band members agreed to blow his bugle to signal the curfew hour each night. The council, having no money of its own, resolved that the bugler be paid $25 per year from the trust fund of the band. The question of payment for this service is bandied about in official correspondence year after year. The Department refused to permit the council to assume any such fixed expenditure when its band funds amounted to only a few hundred dollars. The same consideration governed the Department's refusal to approve payment of $25 per year to each of the native constables. Agents believed that a token salary and an official badge would give the constables badly needed prestige and increase their effectiveness. With its refusal, the Department threw away a valuable opportunity to institutionalize the role in native society.

Section 8 of the by-laws provides that any "Indian constable may order a trespasser to leave the reserve and such order shall be carried out without delay." These orders would have applied, of course, to non-Indians to whom the authority of the provincial constable was more acceptable. The latter also had the authority to arrest any native for being off the reserve after sundown "unless a good legitimate explanation" was given. The problem of trespass became acute during the years of the Second World War with the construction of an airstrip on the north beach. Air Force and construction crews entered the reserve after sundown with a truck and carried off some of the girls to their camp for all-night parties. When the councilors protested, the agent conferred with the commanding officer, who promised to put the reserve out of bounds for military personnel. The rule does not seem to have been observed, for the complaints continued.

Taxi traffic between the Masset villages was another subject that vexed the councilors. Though it was recognized as useful, it was regarded at the same time as a kind of trespass. Resolutions were passed from time to time prohibiting taxis from entering the reserve after 9 o'clock in the evening "on account of the considerable traffic by young people between the village and New Masset."

Over the years the people's abiding concern with the behavior of the young is expressed in their attempts to take formal action whenever possible, not only in the passing of by-laws, but in the conduct of judicial hearings. In January of 1942 the Masset Cannery store on the reserve was broken into and some goods stolen. Four boys were arrested and brought before a council meeting attended by the agent. Sentences were determined by the councilors and the agent sent letters to the parents informing them of the action taken. In one case the letter read, "In consideration of his age, the council took a very lenient view, considering your circumstances and instead of going through the police court, it was tried by the Council and myself and it was agreed that he pay to the Treasurer of the Council the sum of $15 for damages and stolen goods, to be paid within 30 days and that he be of good behavior for four months." The agent suggested that this boy be sent out to the residential school where he would receive more adequate supervision than his widowed mother could provide. The leader of the group was fined $20 while two other boys received lesser fines of $5. All were advised that they must not carry or use a gun for any purpose until they reached the proper age.

In December of 1943, nine juvenile boys, not including any of the four charged above, were arrested for stealing cases of beer from the dock. They appeared before the council and were released "on probation of good conduct for an indefinite period of time."

There is reason to believe that such action was effective as a deterrent to repeated misbehavior by juveniles. Nevertheless, the council's limited authority to participate in processes of social control was soon to be revoked. In 1955 after the new Indian Act of 1951 had come into effect, a Department official wrote to the agent regarding proposed by-laws submitted by the Skidegate band. He stated that the conduct of court by the band council "falls within the field of judicial proceedings and does not appear to be covered under Section 80 of the Indian Act. The courts, which usually hear Indian Act and other cases, are the properly constituted authority and it would not appear to be within the power of band councils to act in a judicial capacity." The people's elected representatives were thus denied the power to adjudicate local disputes and to sanction the behavior of juveniles. The working relationship with the agent in this important area of community action was dissolved, to be replaced by impersonal, often indifferent, sometimes hostile contacts with white police and magistrates.

Realization that band-council by-laws were poorly enforced led to a further change in policy. In February of 1961 the Indian commissioner for British Columbia announced that the Royal Canadian Mounted Police would henceforth enforce band by-laws dealing with the regulation of traffic, observance of law and order, prevention of disorderly conduct, regulation of hawkers, and protection of fish and game. These duties fell upon two RCMP officers stationed at New Masset. Since they were responsible for law enforcement in all the communities of northern Graham Island, their attention to the internal affairs of the Haida village was necessarily limited. In theoretical terms, the police did not have the resources to control the total field of social interaction by coercive means. Nor, as agents of a secondary authority structure, did they have access to normative power, which draws upon the consensus of the people.

We have referred to the segregation of regulative and normative powers as structural discontinuity. As police and legal functions have been increasingly exercised by separate institutions in the dominant society, they have been less effectively exercised on behalf of the dependent group. For example, much of the disruptive behavior with which the council was formerly able to deal involved minor offenses and neighborhood disputes. Under the new system such matters are often not dealt with at all, but contribute to an atmosphere of tension and suppressed hostility. Further, many serious offenses which do warrant legal action are suppressed because the intervention of police in community affairs exposes the villagers to the retribution of "white man's law" (also Bölscher 1977:7.2.2). Finally, when the limited judicial responsibilities which the band council exercised in earlier decades were stripped away, the community's respect for its elected officials was diminished.

The depersonalization of relations which we have traced in the field of social control was echoed in other areas of administration as the government redefined its goals and reversed its expectations. In repudiating its paternalistic orientation, the government expected the Indians to reject dependency and adopt an achievement orientation. But the Indians had been successfully socialized to Canadian society by missionaries and agents who guided them through a difficult transition without serious upheavals. During their prototypal relationship with agent Deasy over a period of 15 years, expectations of a high order of solicitude and patience from their governors were fostered. The Indians might resent and passively resist coercive control, but such relationships, which clearly had a strong affective component, were stable. When Deasy passed from the scene, however, it became apparent that few of the norms he supported had been internalized.

Study of agents' reports and other documents in agency files suggests that the men who succeeded Deasy at Masset were less dominating personalities. On the other hand, their attitudes toward and transactions with the Indians probably reflect the shift in government aims. Throughout the 1930s and 1940s the overwhelming emphasis on protection and compulsion diminished and efforts were directed toward improving the Indians' living conditions. From their own testimony, the people seem to have been disillusioned with the performance of later agents. Until recently they tended to idealize persons who occupied authority roles, an attitude which seems to be connected with permissiveness in their own behavior (Parsons 1951:317). When their expectations of total selflessness and purity were disappointed, they sought to punish the offending persons, typically by removing them from their posts. An example of such action is found in two undated petitions referring to incidents which probably occurred in the mid-1940s.

In almost identical wording, the petitions demand that the band council remove the doctor and field matron from their posts "for the following reasons: Our people have lost confidence in him (her). We realize that he (she) has no interest in our welfare. We feel he (she) neglects his duties towards our people because he (she) does not know our conditions." The petitions, demanding that the doctor be replaced "with a licensed doctor" and the nurse "with a real nurse," bore 65 signatures. Neither of these persons was replaced, but one might speculate that their work was made more difficult by the hostility they encountered.

Most teachers, nurses, agents, and others who take up service with the Haidas are unaware of the model with which their performance is compared. With the ideological shift away from paternalism, few civil servants now develop close attachments to their clients. An exception was the Indian Health Service nurse stationed on the reserve at the time of my first field trip in 1962. "Miss Chapman," a woman in her mid-thirties, had earned the complete trust of the Indians. Examination of the terms under which her relationship with them was conducted will demonstrate how strongly internalized is the value pattern in which the Haidas exchanged their passive conforming behavior for their agents' solicitude.

The Haidas had made great demands on previous nurses, calling for "emergency" care at all hours of the day and night. Miss Chapman, recognizing this behavior as a "testing process," established regular hours for clinic and house calls, attempting to preserve her dinner hour and days off from unnecessary interruptions. The people respected this schedule though they seemed to show no hesitation in calling her when problems arose. For her part, she was scrupulous about returning when promised and leaving word where she could be reached in an emergency. A nurse was available at the Red Cross Outpost Hospital in New Masset, but the people were diffident about calling on her as it was understood that this facility was "for the whites."

Miss Chapman understood the expectations which the Indians attached to her role. As she explained, they expected her to be pure and above reproach. They didn't think it was "normal" for her to live alone and would have liked to see her marry. But, living in the clinic-residence on the bluff, she was under constant surveillance. She was careful not to entertain late callers or to behave in an unseemly way. She maintained a calm, friendly but aloof attitude, which was as reassuring as the lighted window in the clinic overlooking the village.

Miss Chapman was very protective toward the people and an apologist for their behavior. She thought that the Indians' hostile, resentful attitudes toward whites in general were a sign of development, that they were throwing off the yoke they wore as wards of the government and daring to have "unapproved" attitudes and behave in unapproved ways. They were testing their ability to defy authority. She thought that the various types of bad behavior—drunkenness, rowdiness, assault and so on—were "regrettable but only to be expected, all things considered." She described a few examples of inappropriate behavior by young people and said, "When you let them know that this isn't done, they are embarrassed and grateful to be set straight." The point was that, "it is our duty to show the people by example, and instruction when necessary, what to do." Seeing herself as one of the few whites who really understood and knew what went on, she felt it was her place to protect the Indians from white culture and to interpret that culture to them.

On one occasion an adolescent boy assaulted a young RCMP constable at a dance. Since he had received a slight cut, he was brought to the clinic for treatment before being taken to jail. When the nurse was alone with him she said that he was too nice a boy to get into this kind of mess and that he owed it to his people not to disgrace them or the whites would think that all the bad things that were said about the Indians were true. As she told me of this incident, I understood that the boy had been chastened. Apparently old people use the same pleas with youngsters—not to disgrace the Indians. She said that it was unusual for her to discuss such matters with them. She didn't want to know about their fights with each other or the police. An eleborate game went on between them. She pretended not to see them misbehaving or to know how they got hurt when they came to her for treatment after a brawl. For their part, they usually didn't come because they were ashamed to let her know that they had been brawling. And while she pretended not to see them drunk, they pretended she didn't see them. On their next encounter there was no embarrassment and no mechanisms for bridging it and reestablishing the relationship were necessary. While this game enabled them to save face, she maintained her aloofness from the disputes, troubles, and rivalries of the village.

Since Miss Chapman has gone on to other stations, the symbolism of the lighted window seems to have been forgotten. Or perhaps the people have become resigned to the impersonality which by 1966 characterizes almost all of their relationships with the dominant society.

EDUCATION

In one boundary structure the people still found the last vestiges of that special relationship in which conformity is exchanged for concern. The school, as the institution where socialization to the norms and values of the dominant society is the primary objective, would seem to be the ideal instrument for achieving integrative goals. In recent years, as the social and economic self-sufficiency of the reserves has broken down, Indian parents have developed more favorable attitudes toward the school. Indeed, many cherish an exaggerated faith that education will open the doors of white society to their children. This hope is clearly shared by the Indian Department, which in 1966–67 allocated $9.9 million (or 53 percent of its total expenditures in British Columbia) to education (Fields and Stanbury 1970:10, 15, 16).

By the 1960s the pattern of segregated education typical of earlier decades had given way with the shift to integrational policies. Indian day schools and residential schools were gradually being phased out. The federal government negotiated with provinces, as it had earlier negotiated with denominational groups, to carry out the actual processes of education in return for financial support. According to agreements with local school boards, monthly tuition of $25 per capita was paid for each band member attending provincial schools.[6] In addition, the federal government helped finance the costs of school construction

6. The annual tuition of $250 paid by the federal government in 1966 for each Indian student in provincial schools was raised to $533 in 1968 and to $580 in 1970 (Fields and Stanbury 1970:20–21, Ed. note).

to accommodate the enlarged student population. The cost of bus transportation for students from the reserve to school was also supported by federal funds.

These arrangements would seem to meet the government's responsibility for Indian education. In their analysis of the total cost of education in British Columbia, however, Fields and Stanbury observe that in 1966 the federal government paid to local school districts only 37 to 58 percent of the total annual expenditure per student. "In terms of the Provincial average the Federal grant amounted to *one-half* the total expenditure per enrolled pupil in B.C. in 1966" (1970:25). They raise the further point that, contrary to widespread belief, it is not certain that the federal government *is* financially responsible for the total cost of Indian education (1970:23, 25). It is likely that the deficits incurred by the school boards as a result of integrational policies may account for much of the hostility expressed toward these schools by local people. In the next chapter we shall find more clearcut evidence that economic and political competition plays as large a part as freefloating bigotry and racism in feeding the tensions between the villages.

The Masset School

During 1965–66 approximately 70 children of the Masset band were enrolled in the three primary grades of the reserve day school, while three older children were "away" at residential school. The great majority, 129 children, attended the New Masset Elementary and Secondary School where they comprised 48 percent of the student body.[7]

Ten grades of academic instruction were offered in the New Masset school in 1965–66. In addition, there was a special primary class of 13 children who were incapable of performing any kind of academic work in a regular class situation. These children, 85 percent of whom were Indian, were given special training in muscular coordination and

7. For the total band of 986 persons, the Indian Department lists 260 schoolaged children as of January 1, 1967. Of 265 persons enrolled in various types of schools, 74 are in Indian day schools, 10 in Indian residential schools, 169 in provincial schools, and 12 in vocational schools. None were in university (Department of Indian Affairs and Northern Development, January 1, 1967). "Schoolage children" obviously applies only to those 5–16 while the tabulation would include all band members enrolled in any educational institution. My figures pertain only to the band members residing on the reserve and in New Masset. Although the discrepancy is probably slight, it should be noted that my data pertain to the academic year of 1965–66, while the report refers to the midpoint of the next school year. It is also important to note that not all schoolage children are actually attending school. Fields and Stanbury state, "By 1966–67 we estimate that of the Indian population (on reserves in B.C.) aged 5–24 years about 61% were attending school. This compares to 56.8% in 1961" (1970:13).

speech skills. On the secondary level, an "occupational program" was conducted for 11 students who showed no interest or aptitude in academic studies. In this all-Indian group, girls were assigned the preparation of hot lunches for sale to the children, while the boys occupied their time with woodworking and tinkering with old machinery.

There was no provision at that time for the teaching of eleventh and twelfth grades in any school of the Queen Charlotte School District. Non-Indians who completed the tenth grade qualified for an allowance from the province to finish high school on the mainland, while Indians who wished to undertake further study in high school, technical institute, or university were guaranteed support by the Indian Branch (Fields and Stanbury 1970:28–33). Up to that time only one Haida student had registered in a university, but when the social environment overwhelmed him, he dropped out without completing the first year.[8] Many other students competed successfully in outside schools, earning better grades than they had in Masset.

The content of the curriculum is regulated by the provincial Department of Education, but providing equipment and facilities is the responsibility of the local school board. Pupils are able to study the basic subjects of arithmetic, reading, and English composition, as well as science, art, and French. Facilities for training in so-called vocational subjects, however, were often inadequate or entirely lacking. Particularly was this true of home economics and shop courses, the programs of greatest immediate value to Indian students. For example, the small kitchen opening off the "activity room," or gymnasium, was equipped with a propane gas stove, an electric refrigerator, and cupboards. It served its original purpose as a place to prepare refreshments for social occasions held in the gym. Though inconvenient, it was possible for five girls to prepare 60 hot lunches in this room. But to conduct cooking classes for 30 tenth-grade girls in this area was an impossibility, given the limitations on class time and teachers' resources. There was no sewing machine or other dress-making equipment with which to teach the prescribed course "Clothing and Textiles." Since very little sewing was being done at this time by village women, girls had little opportunity to learn this useful skill.

On the other hand, the school was well supplied with electric typewriters for instruction in business and commerce classes. Since the local economy provided few jobs in these categories, neither Indian nor white students were highly motivated to learn typing and other secretarial skills. This unbalanced program has been remedied since

8. During 1965–66 only 21 B.C. Indians attended a university. In 1966–67 the number increased to 36 students (Fields and Stanbury 1970:31). The numbers have increased sharply in recent years.

1966 by a massive expansion of school facilities, reflecting changes in the community, which have, in turn, radically altered the social climate of the school (Bölscher 1977:8, 8.1, 8.2).

In 1966 that climate was a favorable one for Indian children, a condition that may be attributed to four factors:

1. The composition of the student body with its high proportion of Indians

2. The absence of any real differences in preparation and goals between Indian and white students

3. The sympathetic attitudes of the teaching staff, most of whom were committed to integration

4. The success of the principal in insulating the school from the tensions and pressures of the community

During the year, 266 students were enrolled in the New Masset school. In addition to the 129 band members living on the reserve, who made up 48 percent of the student population, another 72 children (27 percent) living in New Masset had one or both parents of Indian background. In these latter families, attitudes toward Indian identity and values ranged from complete acceptance to complete rejection. Between many of the New Masset Indians and their kinsmen on the reserve, close interaction was maintained. Even those who considered themselves "white" did not express open hostility to reserve Indians in the school context. Thus, an overwhelming 75 percent of the student body could be viewed in at least some respects as sharing an Indian background and prospects.

Of the remaining students, 44, or 18 percent, were children of white parents permanently residing in New Masset. Grouped with these "local whites" were three Chinese children whose parents operated the bowling alley and restaurant. Eighteen children of transient Navy personnel and teachers were classified as non-local whites because they had received part of their schooling "outside." Many of the local whites aspired to the middle class model represented by the Navy families and other civil servants such as the police and Indian agent. The educational backgrounds and life experiences of children of local and non-local whites, however, are so dissimilar that this 25 percent of the student body did not form a solidary group.

Relationships between Indian and white children at school were friendly. There was no noticeable tendency to form exclusive cliques based on cultural group membership. Children of the same family spent the lunch hour together, for older children were expected by their mothers to look after siblings. In home economics classes sisters usually paired off to carry out cooking and cleaning chores. But in choosing teams for sports or classwork, there was no alignment of Indian versus white. Other teachers agreed that relationships between students of Indian and non-Indian status were unmarred by discrimination although discriminatory attitudes prevailed in the community at large. This internal harmony of the school reflected the relative homogeneity of the student population.

One method I used to probe for significant differences was a questionnaire administered to all students from grades five to ten and to the occupational class. Since the results were to be discussed in a teachers' workshop, the principal gave his consent for this project. My status as a part-time teacher enabled me to enlist the cooperation of other teachers in administering the questionnaire during class time and in interpreting the results. Responses were received from 78 band members, 31 New Masset Indians, 24 local whites and 5 non-local whites, or 95 percent of students enrolled in those grades.

The data may be briefly summarized. One set of questions dealt with family organization—household composition, occupations of parents, and chores of children. In contrast to the large, complex households of Haida Masset, New Masset households were usually composed only of parents and children. Aside from seasonal work in the cannery, few mothers in either village worked outside the home. Occupations of fathers were very similar, although residents of New Masset earned higher incomes, as I verified from other data. Kinship ties between households were much more intensive in the Haida village. Children had the same kind of family chores, regardless of residence. Material objects that affect behavior and relationships, such as radio, television, deep freezers, and cars, had been available longer in New Masset, but were becoming common in the Haida village.

Information was elicited about languages spoken in the home, aspirations for further education and occupational preferences, study facilities in the home, kinds of social activities carried on in the home, and "horizons." Horizon refers to contacts with and knowledge of the outside world—travel experiences, vicarious knowledge acquired through magazines, books, newspapers, television, radio, and so on. On most of these points there were surprisingly few differences between local children, Indian and white, especially when compared to the five students who had lived and attended school "outside." Few of the local children had ever been away from the Queen Charlotte Islands. This isolation seemed to be far more significant than cultural differences, which were expressed mainly in the kinds of social activities carried on in the home.

In New Masset there was no parallel to the Haidas' life-cycle rituals and feasting complex. As we shall see in later chapters, however, activities oriented to traditional Haida culture were, by and large, confined to the old people. The principal of the integrated school in Queen Charlotte City, which is attended by members of the Skidegate band, had reached similar conclusions about the homogeneity of the student population in that area. It could not be said that there was a specifically "Indian problem" in education at Masset in 1966.

Responses to the questionnaire shed some light on students' orientations to school and on their achievement motivations. In replying to questions concerning their hopes and plans for the future most students, Indian and white, expressed a vehement wish to "get out of Masset." Few were committed to any specific plan of action, although most white students expected to finish high school on the mainland. All expressed a desire to "look around" at the world. For Indian girls, marriage to a "Navy guy" or logger offered the prospect of escape. Indian boys, for the most part, expected to "end up" fishing or logging on the Charlottes.

Teachers and school administrators were acutely aware that the educational system was irrelevant to the economic opportunities existing on the Queen Charlotte Islands. As the principal of the Queen Charlotte City school phrased the problem in the teachers' workshop, "When a young fellow can go out and make $1,000 a month in summer as a fisherman or $600 a month year round as a logger, how do you motivate him to stay in school?"[9] Though the expectation of big money was no longer realistic for either whites or Indians, it was reflected in their stated aspirations. The Indian agent stationed at Masset felt that integration was the solution. He actively encouraged Indian boys and girls to go out to school on the mainland where they might have more diversified experiences and perhaps relocate themselves eventually. The Masset principal, on the other hand, was concerned about losing the best athletes and scholars to outside schools, thus lowering the quality of education in the local school. Both agreed on the necessity for raising the aspiration levels of all students.

Standing between the students and these two kinds of administrator—the agent and the principal—were the teachers. Categorized by local residents as a clique of transient specialists, they were not fitted into the local status system. The lack of acceptance by the community limited most of their social contacts to other members of their own group. Of 12 faculty members employed in the Masset school in 1965–66, only one considered herself a local resident. Most of these persons received their training in the universities of the lower main-

9. Fields and Stanbury estimate that in 1966–67 only 26.5 percent of all B.C. Indian children in school were enrolled in grade 7 or higher (1970:13). Of 253 students in the Masset band, exclusive of those in "vocational" classes, only 16.9 percent were enrolled in grade 7 or higher.

land. Those who were not fully certified at the time of their employment attended summer school to meet increasingly stringent requirements for teachers in British Columbia. This seasonal outflow of teaching personnel supported the local definition of teachers as transients and reinforced their own identification with the larger society. Thus the value orientations they brought to their work differed sharply from those of the community. Committed to the universalistic achievement standards of Canadian society, they were enthusiastic about the opportunities and responsibilities of their role. Many teachers, particularly the young and unmarried, were drawn to the Charlottes by an interest in Indians and Indian culture. Their concern for their students was expressed in their efforts to maintain an open social environment and to encourage active participation by all class members.

The Indian children in Masset responded very favorably to this treatment. Many values are inculcated in the school situation. In addition to scholastic excellence the demand for achievement may be met in several ways. In sports competition Indian children were often outstanding. Many others could take pride in perfect attendance and in their punctuality; "helping the teacher" after school was a means of winning approval. The school lunch program gave the Indian girls who had failed academic subjects a chance to feel useful and productive.

In contrast to the affective rewards for conformity, sanctions for disapproved behavior tended to rely on physical force. Detention after school might have been effective, but was not employed. Corporal punishment, chiefly in the form of strapping the palm of the hand, was recognized and practiced in British Columbia schools at that time, carried out by the principal in the presence of witnesses. Such measures were infrequently required and none of the pupils who remained in the school could be described as alienated or as "problem students."

In addition to his administrative duties the principal had limited power to make policy regarding internal school affairs. He used this power to adapt the educational program more effectively to the needs of the students. For example, he devised the school lunch program as a meaningful project for the girls' occupational class as well as a means of improving the nutritional quality of children's lunches. More important perhaps, he insulated the school from some of the destructive pressures of the white community. He was constrained, of course, by his responsibility to the school board, which represented white opinion on the local level. This opinion was overwhelmingly opposed to the "Indian invasion" of the school. One individual who was serving on the school board when the Indian Affairs Branch proposed integration recalled that "the offer of tuition and capital grants seemed like a

godsend." Faced with local ratepayers' resentment of any tax in-
creases for school bond issues, the board members had been unable to
undertake improvements in school facilities.[10] The Indian Branch
proposal thus made possible wider course offerings and more grade
levels than the small number of white students was entitled to. The
resulting "flood" of Indians into the school system seemed to come as
a great shock to many white residents of New Masset. It has already
been suggested that their anger may be traced, at least in part, to the
unpleasant realization that the federal government was not prepared to
underwrite the total cost of Indian education. Their resentment was
expressed in steady harassment, which may be understood in the context of intervillage competition. The involvement of the school in the
political competition between the communities demonstrates the
limitations of that institution as an agency for improvement and integration. Nevertheless, the principal, by resisting interference in the
internal functioning of the school, was able to protect the special relationship of teachers and students.

At first glance the content of this relationship contrasts sharply with
the paternalism of Agent Deasy and Nurse Chapman. In different ways
each of these dedicated civil servants sought to shield the Haidas from
the destructive effects of white society. For Deasy, exploitation and
corruption in the forms of drunkenness and "immorality" were the
great evils to be kept at bay by constant vigilance. For Miss Chapman,
shaking off their shackled status as wards of the government and learn-
ing to behave in "unapproved" ways were the necessary steps to
maturity for the Indian. Each accepted the role of sympathetic in-
termediary with the threatening society. And each was rewarded by
the passive, conforming, yet deeply affective responses of the people
they served.

By the 1960s the role of the self-recruited friend of the Indian was to
fight for his place in the integrated scheme, to disarm those who would
stand in the way of the Indians' full participation in Canadian life. The
idealism and commitment of teachers, along with principals and the
"new breed" of Indian agent, were matched by the supportive attitudes of the Haidas. The majority of Indian parents, for example,
professed great interest in the school, expressing a strong desire to help
their children as much as possible "in getting an education." They
attended school programs, concerts, and sports events and supported
fund-raising projects, such as cake and candy sales. These attitudes

10. Local governments were responsible for financing 55 percent of the total expenditure on public schools in 1965–66 and 56 percent in 1966–67. The remaining portion was
financed by the provincial government (Fields and Stanbury 1970:25).

were not always matched by performance in providing facilities and time for study. Nor did all parents insist on regular school attendance by their children, occasionally keeping them home to help with chores.

As an institution presumably intended to foster intellectual development and carry out vocational training, the school is hardly adequate. Its great importance in the socialization of the Indians lies in the establishment of stable interactive relationships between white and Indian children and between the latter and white adults who take a friendly interest in them. Here they are exposed to the values of Canadian society although few find paths leading to fuller participation in that wider sphere. As a boundary structure administered by the Department of Education in Victoria, the school does not mesh smoothly with other institutions in which Indians are expected to participate.

From the standpoint of the individual, it may be said that the life cycle is poorly structured. Children are fed into the school system automatically now that their parents or surrogate parents have, in principle, accepted the compulsory rules regarding attendance. But many children have a makeshift family life and fail to receive the necessary physical care and emotional support to enable them to succeed in school. Most children attend at least until they are 16, the legal age for leaving. Girls drop out if they become pregnant. When students eventually leave, with or without a diploma, they rarely find immediate employment. Fishing and cannery work, which are the mainstay of the local economy, are seasonal occupations and there is great competition among adults for available positions. Even those who succeed in finding work in this industry face years of seasonal idleness. Some boys try to get work at the logging camps, but older and experienced men are preferred. The opportunity to undertake specialized occupational training on the mainland is open to Indian people, but until recently this option entailed resettlement away from the reserve in order to practice new skills.

There is a breakdown of institutions at the point where the individual should be moved from childhood and adolescent roles into adult roles. He is not introduced to the community in an occupational role which would capitalize on the achievement orientations stressed in the school. In the absence of meaningful achievement goals in Indian society, there is no measure of the degree to which these orientations have been internalized by the students. The successful adjustments made by many of those continuing their education outside suggest that the school has not failed completely in this aspect of its functions. Yet, without some reinforcement of these orientations, it is likely that they are soon extinguished. But this is an instrumentally oriented view, reflecting the attitudes of the observer. For most of the Haidas the school was a boundary structure that still worked.

In other areas of social life we have traced a decrease in commitment by both Indians and administrators as affective, particularistic ties were replaced by impersonal, specialized relations. The Haidas view these changes as a breach of faith. The reversal of attitudes by elites in the compulsory structure has led to disillusionment, disruption of established expectations, and the need to adjust to the new situation.

Very early the Haidas had developed an ambivalent orientation to whites. Their attitudes are precisely described by the term "ressentiment." "This complex sentiment has three interlocking elements. First, diffuse feelings of hate, envy and hostility; second, a sense of being powerless to express those feelings actively against the person or social stratum evoking them; and third, a continual re-experiencing of this impotent hostility" (Merton 1957:155–56). The qualifying term here is "actively" express.

On the one hand, their great dependency, deeply ingrained by long socialization, was expressed in passive, conforming behavior. On the other, dependency was offset by resentment at the massive interference in Indian life, at the loss of dignity and autonomy. "The middle and older generations still harbour their resentment and it may continue as part of the Indian personality in British Columbia and of the pattern of interactions between whites and Indians"[11] (LaViolette 1961:101). Parsons suggests two possibilities for handling such strains: the repression of one side of the ambivalence, or the gratification of both sides by fixing on alternative objects (1951:252–54). The Haidas eventually chose the second alternative, venting their negative behavior on the local whites, the safer outlet, while maintaining for the time being a more or less conforming orientation to agents of the federal government.

11. The Haidas have never engaged in the kind of manipulation of whites which Braroe analyzes so perceptively for the Short Grass Cree (Braroe 1965, 1975). This is undoubtedly why local observers describe them as "a proud people."

Chapter 4
The Economic Sphere

THE ECONOMIC interdependence of the two Masset villages has tended to undermine the social segregation of their members. Indeed, New Masset may be considered as an extension of the Haida sphere of action. Roles occupied by Haidas are those of customer, wage-earner, and self-employed fisherman. Since whites also play these roles, Indian status is secondary. The complementary roles of merchant, employer, and fish-buyer are played by whites. Since these role-categories cut across the ethnic boundary, a single set of norms and expectations is imposed on all participants. In this instrumentally oriented or "utilitarian" system of relations, role performance is, ideally, governed by self-interest. Shared interests, even instrumental interests, tend to override some of the barriers between culturally distinct sections. In this chapter we shall see, for example, that successful Indian and white fishermen regard each other with respect and subscribe to an ethic of mutual aid.

But if the ethnic boundary is weakened by cooperation in the economic realm on the one hand, it is reinforced on the other by continuing contention between the villages. For while the Haidas' interests in New Masset are oriented primarily toward earning a living and obtaining goods and services, they also pursue other goals in this setting. Participation in the commercial economy provides opportunities for validating status and earning prestige. Ambitious persons are occasionally able to mobilize support and assert leadership. Acting as a solidary group, the Haidas have been able not only to control their deviant members but to exert pressure on the local whites. The pursuit of political goals serving the expressive needs of the Haida population reinforces the ethnic boundary from within.

OCCUPATIONS

Analysis of the Haidas' occupations indicates the nature and extent of their participation in the commercial economy in 1965–66 (Table 1). The data were collected during the spring and summer of 1966 in connection with my census of households. Employment and income data for the fishing season of 1965 were made available to me by the manager of the Queen Charlotte Canners. Other sources of information were Indian Agency files and the voters' registration list of 1965.

Of 158 males between the ages of 15 and 69 who were residing in the village in May 1966, 122 were employed. Of 128 female residents between the ages of 15 and 64, 59 were employed. According to Table 1, 68 percent of employed men were identified by themselves or members of their families as fishermen. Another 5 percent combined fishing with winter employment in logging. In addition to this 73 percent of male adults who fished for a living, 11 percent were employed in the cannery as shoreworkers. Full-time loggers accounted for 4 percent of the male labor force, while 8 percent were employed as laborers in slashing bush for highway construction. The 4 percent of men classified in the job category "other" were engaged in providing services. They include a lighthouse keeper, silversmith, janitor, carpenter, and taxi driver. For women the only available jobs have been in cannery work, although in 1966 one young woman obtained a job as clerk in the Co-op in New Masset. The other 58 employed women, or 98 percent, were shoreworkers. Of 181 employed Haidas, only three—the lighthouse keeper, silversmith, and janitor—were not involved directly in the New Masset economy. Wage work accounted for about half of all employed Haidas, while the remainder were "independent" fishermen. But 89 percent of all Haida workers living on the reserve in the spring of 1966 had earned at least part of their income during the previous year in the fishing industry. This employment pattern reveals strong continuity in the nature of economic activity, in seasonal work rhythms, and in exploitation of traditional resource areas.[1]

THE FISHING INDUSTRY

In 1965 the Queen Charlotte Canners expended a total of $597,932 for fish sales, shoreworkers' wages, crew shares, and clam hauling.[2] This market was served by three categories of persons:

1. Bölscher (1977:5.1–5.1.3) provides employment data for 1976. An important recent book on the labor history of B.C. Indians is Knight 1978. Writing in a lively, sometimes contentious style, Knight challenges many conventional views of the subject, particularly the continuity of traditional attitudes toward work. He also provides a comprehensive, detailed treatment of Indian work history not available elsewhere.

2. The property values, incomes, and prices quoted here and in chapter 7 are those of 1965–66.

TABLE 1
PRINCIPAL OCCUPATIONS OF MASSET RESIDENTS, 1965

Occupations	Male		Female	
Fishing	83	68%		
Fishing-Logging	6	5%		
Shorework	14	11%	58	98%
Logging	5	4%		
Laboring	9	8%		
Other	5	4%	1	2%
Total Persons Employed	122	100%	59	100%

1. Members of the Masset band living on and off the reserve
2. Residents of New Masset including whites and persons of Indian background who are not band members
3. Non-local persons including transient fishermen and Navy personnel who "moonlight" as producers and cannery workers

Table 2, which summarizes earnings in the fishing industry, indicates that the total sum was divided among these three categories in roughly equal amounts. The nature of their participation varies, however: non-local fishermen (col. C) account for almost half of all fish sales, while Haida band members (col. A) earn almost two-thirds of all funds paid to shoreworkers.

The largest proportion of the cannery's expenditures, 64 percent, was made for the purchase of salmon, halibut, crabs, and clams (col. D). About half of the total sum was earned by commercial fishermen from other ports who spent part of the fishing season in the waters surrounding the Queen Charlottes (col. C). The other half was divided between residents of the Masset villages (cols. A, B), with the Haidas earning less than a quarter of the total.

Band members played a more dominant role in other aspects of the fishing industry. The processing of sea foods by freezing or canning entailed the payment of $142,822 in wages, or 24 percent of the total expenditure (col. D). Of this sum, Haida shoreworkers took home 60 percent as compared with 34 percent paid to New Masset residents and 6 percent to non-local persons. The latter category is comprised of Navy personnel who work part-time as fish buyers or clerks. Band members who worked as crewmen on seine or crab boats received 39 percent of all crew shares while 55 percent was paid to residents of New Masset. Clam hauling was a relatively unimportant part-time activity for both groups.

Not only do the three categories dominate in different aspects of the fishing industry, but the relative importance of the various productive

TABLE 2
DISTRIBUTION OF INCOME IN THE FISHING INDUSTRY, 1965

Source of Earnings	Haida Band A	Local Non-band B	Non-local C	Total D
Fish Sales	$ 91,400	$103,074	$191,548	$386,022
	24%	27%	49%	100%
	45%	54%	93%	64%
Shorework	$ 84,279	$ 49,018	$ 9,525	$142,822
	60%	34%	6%	100%
	41%	26%	5%	24%
Crew Shares	$ 25,197	$ 35,619	$ 3,674	$ 64,490
	39%	55%	6%	100%
	12%	19%	2%	11%
Clam Haul	$ 3,210	$ 1,388	. . .	$ 4,598
	70%	30%	. . .	100%
	2%	1%	. . .	1%
Total	$204,086	$189,099	$204,747	$597,932
	34%	32%	34%	100%

NOTE: First row percentages represent source of earnings; second row percentages represent proportion of cultural group so engaged.

activities varies from group to group. By combining the incomes of self-employed fishermen and men who serve as crews, we find that 57 percent of the Haidas' earnings are derived from fish production as compared with 73 percent for New Masset fishermen and 95 percént for transients. Cannery work accounts for 41 percent of the Haidas' income, but only 26 percent of the total fishing-related income for other local people.

One further point may be made in anticipation of discussion later in this chapter about the value placed upon independence of action in fishing: of the total fishing income of $116,597 received by Haidas, 78 percent was earned by own-account fishermen as compared with 22 percent earned by crewmen.

With regard to the relative earnings of fish producers as summarized in Table 2, we note that these differences in income are related to differences in size of these loose groupings, in patterns of exploitation, and in technology. In 1965 fish sales were made by 183 band members, 44 New Masset residents, and 182 non-local persons. Before comparing *per capita* incomes it is necessary to distinguish between full-time and part-time producers. A full-time producer is defined as anyone who sold a minimum of $100 worth of fish, clams, or crabs to the cannery. This criterion is not entirely satisfactory since a few part-time producers exceeded this amount. On the other hand, earnings of several older Indian men who had no other employment during the year barely surpassed this figure. Part-time producers include children, women, and men with other employment who dig clams or borrow a boat on weekends to go fishing.

As shown in Table 3, which summarizes total sales and average earnings of part- and full-time fishermen, a high percentage of persons in all three categories sold less than $100 worth of fish. Almost half of all Haida and New Masset producers are part-time fishermen (col. A), accounting for a very small proportion of total fish sales (col. C). More than a quarter of all "outside" fishermen find the fishing poor, sell their catches worth an average of $47, and move on (col. E).

Omitted from Table 3 are two local non-band fishermen, owner-operators of three seine-crab boats. These men received payments totalling $50,132 after the deduction of crew shares. The inclusion of these payments, representing about 49 percent of all purchases from local fishermen would seriously distort the average earnings of New Masset producers. This sum is included in Table 2 (col. B), however, under fish sales by local non-band fishermen. Included in Table 3 are the earnings of the other 21 local non-band producers, which represent 50.6 percent of the income of this category (col. D).

The average earnings of full-time fishermen, as presented in Table 3 (col. F), are unrealistically low as a result of setting the minimal value of fish sales at $100. The chief advantage of this procedure, as noted above, is the segregation of occasional fishermen who comprise such a large proportion of producers. A more accurate picture of the incomes of full-time fishermen is presented in the analysis of the various specialized fleets; however, Table 3 faithfully reflects the *relative* incomes of Haida, New Masset, and transient fishermen.[3] The discrepancy between incomes of Haida and local non-band producers is paralleled by the difference between the latter and non-local fishermen. This disparity widens when it is pointed out that while local fishermen rarely exploit fishing grounds away from the Charlottes, transient fishermen regularly spend part of the season at other points on the coast, earning funds not included in these figures. With respect to mobility, then, New Masset Indians and whites have adopted behavior which Hawthorn and his collaborators find characteristic of Indian fishermen:

3. Reference to broader studies of the Indians' position in the fishing industry helps to explain the Haidas' comparatively low standing (Drucker 1958:122–26; Gladstone 1953; Gladstone and Jamieson 1950; Hawthorn, Belshaw, and Jamieson 1958:107–23; also Knight 1978:78–100).

". . . they have tended to confine their fishing to an area around their home reservations, or around the canneries that employ them, thus keeping their operations close to shore, in protected inlets and river mouths" (Hawthorn, Belshaw, and Jamieson 1958:117). With respect to technology, however, we will observe considerable differences between Haidas and other fishermen, for local non-band producers emulate outsiders in this matter.

To evaluate the Haidas' participation in sociological as well as economic terms we will analyze their occupational roles in the fishing industry. These fall into the major categories of producers and processors. We shall consider these activities in turn, examining the various methods of fish production in the next section, then taking up cannery organization and the role of the shoreworker. Our analysis focuses on the permanent population of northern Graham Island: Haida band members, New Masset residents of Indian background, and whites. Since they do not participate in the local community, transient fishermen are excluded.

Fish Production

While the fishing industry is commonly described as "seasonal," it is actually based on a succession of seasonal cycles of several species, which permit a continuous harvest from early spring to late autumn. Five species of salmon are caught in offshore and inland waters in a succession of "runs." The spring salmon run begins in late March and

TABLE 3

EARNINGS OF FISH PRODUCERS, 1965

Category	Number		Sales		Average Earnings	
	Part-Time A	Full-Time B	Part-Time C	Full-Time D	Part-Time E	Full-Time F
Band Members	85 46%	98 54%	$2,843 3%	$ 88,557 97%	$33	$ 903
Local Non-band*	21 48%	21* 48%	$ 450 .04%	$ 52,492* 50.6%	$21	$ 1,280
Non-Local	50 28%	132 72%	$2,326 .01%	$189,222 99%	$47	$ 1,433

*Not included are the earnings of 2 owner-operators of seine-crab boats totalling $50,132.00, or 49%, of the total income of this group.

continues through the summer. The sockeye run in early summer is followed by coho in July, pinks in August, and dog salmon in early autumn. Halibut are fished on the rich banks off the coasts of the Charlottes beginning in the spring. Dungeness crabs are caught in Dixon Entrance in early April, with activity shifting to Hecate Strait later in the season.

To harvest these resources, local people engage in several different types of fishing—seining, gillnetting, trolling, and jigging. Each type is distinctive in technology, size of capital investment, manpower requirements, and external regulation. These characteristics entail differences in work patterns, entrepreneurial ability, and norms and values.

Another type of fish production is the digging of razor clams on north shore beaches during the spring and summer. In 1965 clam digging, which was carried on mostly by Indian women and children, was comparatively unimportant. Because clam sales are subsumed under fish sales in cannery records, it is not possible to calculate the exact sum paid to persons who engage in this activity.

All types of fishing are open to Indians in the sense that recruitment to the various "fleets" takes no account of cultural group membership of participants. Table 4 shows the distribution of seining, "mosquito," trolling, and gillnetting boats among residents of northern Graham Island. Seventy-seven boats are owned by 74 "persons." The cannery

TABLE 4
CULTURAL GROUP MEMBERSHIP OF MASSET BOAT OWNERS, 1965

Boat Type	Haida A	White B	New Masset Indians C	Queen Charlotte Canners D	Total E
Seine-Crab		2 (3 boats) 67%		1 (3 boats) 33%	3 (6 boats)
Mosquito	35 88%	5 12%			40
Troller	10 59%	7 41%			17
Gillnetter	3 21%	7 50%	4 29%		14
Total	48 62%	22 28%	4 6%	3 4%	77 100%

owns three seine-crab boats (col. D), while one white man owns two and another owns one (col. B). Of local boats engaged in commercial fishing, 62 percent are owned by band members (col. A) as compared to 28 percent by whites (col. B) and 6 percent by persons of Indian background (col. C) living in New Masset. The Haidas' ownership is heavily concentrated in the outboard "mosquito boats," which require minimal capital investment and reflect their adaptation to the commercial economy. To understand the conditions and effects of this adaptation, we will examine the types of fishing in which Haidas are engaged.

Data for this analysis are provided by a census of all boats in the northern Graham Island area carried out independently by three workers. Two were eighth-grade students, one Indian and one white, both sons of fishermen. They received the cooperation of their fathers and other men. I completed the third set of forms with the assistance of my own two sons and local fishermen. On the forms were recorded the type, size, age, horsepower, owner's valuation, skipper, crew, and builder of all boats. These data are the basis for comparison of capital investment,[4] specialization in types of fishing, and so on. Records from the cannery make possible comparisons of productivity, although the data are not complete for all fishermen. Some of the trollers, for example, are members of the Prince Rupert Fishermen's Cooperative Association and their earnings were not available to me. I have indicated in the discussion where data are incomplete.

Seining. Purse seining is an effective method of catching schooling fish such as salmon and consequently it is widely employed on the British Columbia coast. Few individuals, however, can afford the investment required for a boat equipped with radar, sonar, and hydraulic gear in addition to fish-catching gear. In Masset, we noted, two seine boats and a crab boat of comparable size are owned by two white men; the cannery owns three (Table 4).

In 1966 no seiners were owned by band members, although the Haida Boat Works was a center for construction of these 50-foot planked boats during the 1950s (Gladstone 1953:34). The largest fishing companies financed their construction by Indians who operated them under an agreement to deliver their catches to the company at the of-

4. The value of those vessels remaining in the fishing fleets has tripled and quadrupled in the years since this study was made. The increase is not due solely to the inflationary spiral of the 1970s, which has had such grave consequences for all sectors of British Columbia's economy. Even more crucial for the fishing industry is the federal government's salmon license limitation program activated in 1968. Under this plan no new salmon licenses are issued. The owner or prospective owner of a new boat must acquire an existing fishboat, retire it, and retain the license. This has driven the value of a licensed boat to about $1,000 per foot. To this is added, of course, the value of new equipment, especially electronic devices, not available or common in 1966.

ferred price. As company employees, the skippers were set production quotas and dispatched to areas where large fish runs were expected. In the recollection of many persons now in their fifties and sixties, these were happy days. Many Indian women were cooks when the boats skippered by their husbands ranged along the entire coastline of British Columbia. Often several of the Masset boats with wives and children aboard journeyed to the fishing grounds together. The fleets visited the villages of other coastal tribes along the way, enjoying great hospitality and sociability. All of these boats were later repossessed by the companies. Their loss is attributed both to the exploitiveness of the fishing companies and to the fact that good fishermen are not always shrewd businessmen.

There is no doubt that many native boat operators fell victim to sharp practice. On the other hand, there is often an element of flamboyance in economic behavior. The story is told by both Indians and whites—and good naturedly acknowledged by the hero of the piece—of a native skipper who received a check for $47,000 from the local cannery. Off he went to Vancouver without paying the $500 installment on his loan against the boat. He rented an entire floor of one of that city's best hotels, stocked the rooms with liquor, and held open house in a display of hospitality quite consistent with the value placed on generosity by high ranking Haidas. Only when his money was gone did he go home. Since he was unable to meet the now overdue payment and succeeding installments, the boat was eventually repossessed by the local cannery, which was probably the least exploitive company on the coast. Though this story is sometimes told by whites as an illustration of the Indians' improvidence, the listener is also informed that this man had made half a million dollars in fishing, an accomplishment that any fisherman, or businessman, respects.

The boat in question is still referred to as an "Indian boat" although it has served the cannery as seiner and packer for more than a dozen years. The job of skipper has been held by the builder, his brother, and other Indians. During the season of 1965 her crew included the Indian skipper, two band members, two whites, and two New Masset Indians. Crews of mixed cultural group membership are characteristic of privately owned vessels as well as of cannery boats. As Table 5 shows, 14 of 36 persons engaged in seining on six boats during 1965 were band members, 12 were whites, and 10 were New Masset Indians. Two of the six skippers were also band members.

While Haidas formerly predominated in seine fishing, both as skippers and crews, by 1965 their representation in this branch of the industry had declined to a still significant 38 percent of the local work force. Two factors are responsible for this decrease. First, as the Masset-built seine boats have been repossessed by the companies, the center of seining has shifted away from the Charlottes, with mainlanders replacing Haida crews. Second, those boats remaining in private hands have tended to specialize in the very lucrative crab fishery for as much of the season as possible. Since a crabber requires a crew of three including the skipper, as compared to a crew of seven for seining, the number of available jobs is reduced.

TABLE 5
CULTURAL GROUP MEMBERSHIP OF SEINE CREWS, 1965

Cultural Group	No.	Percentage of Total
Band Members	14	39
Whites	12	33
New Masset Indians	10	28
Total	36	100

The technology of seining requires a high degree of skill. On the square stern of these broad-beamed 50-foot boats is mounted a drum resembling a huge spool upon which the seine net is reeled. One edge of this net is attached to a line of corks which keep it afloat in the water, while the other edge is weighted so that it will drop, forming a wall around the school of fish. When the skipper spots a school he runs the boat around it in a wide circle, paying out the net. One end of the net is held by two men in a skiff. When the seiner has completed its circle, the ends of the net are joined and a drawstring around the bottom edge of the seine is pulled tight by power winches. When the bottom has been closed, the fish are caught in the purse and the work of scooping them into the hold of the boat with a power-operated dip net begins. This kind of fishing calls for swift action and coordination. The crews average seven men, all of whom share the profit or loss of the enterprise. Since the only capital required of a crewman is a pair of gum boots and a slicker, most young men in Masset, white and Indian, have traditionally begun their fishing careers as crewmen on a seiner or crabber.

The five locally owned seiners are converted to crab boats by removing the drum and net. On the north coast, the crab season opens on the first of April. Two or three weeks later when the area is fished out, the boats move to Hecate Strait on the east coast, each boat setting about 300 pots. When fishing is good there may be up to 50 crabs worth 20 cents each in every pot. After spring crab fishing, the net drum is again installed on the boats so that they may participate in the pink run in mainland rivers. Fall crab fishing is resumed after the pink run in Masset Inlet in August.

During the 1965 season, the average crew share for men working on a combination seiner-crab boat was $1,640. The average figure masks a range of from $100 for men who made only one or two trips to $3,000 for steady hands. Income records were not available for the very profitable season of 1966. Unfortunately, the poor season of 1965 is more typical of the fishing industry on the north coast in recent years.

The great attraction of seining in past years was the possibility of quick riches for owner and crew. The efficiency of the seiner in harvesting salmon meant that crew shares were large, while almost no expenditure was required. This very efficiency caused the Department of Fisheries to impose strict regulations on the operations of seine boats. At the same time, an alternative type of fishing boat offering the advantages of low capital requirements and relative independence of action has been widely adopted by the Haidas.

The Mosquito Fleet. Small outboard-motor boats are particularly suited to the needs of the majority of Indian fishermen who use them not only for commercial fishing but for subsistence fishing, for transportation, and, in one or two cases, for seal hunting. Since materials are provided by the Indian Affairs Branch, the boats can be built with little capital investment on the owner's part. Outboard motors were purchased at cost through the Indian Branch and paid for by deduction of a percentage of the owner's sales to the cannery. Inspection of the boats reveals great variation in the degree of skill brought to their construction. While some of these small boats demonstrate the meticulous craftsmanship of practiced boat builders, others are crude floating boxes, windowless, unpainted, and ill-equipped.

The mosquito fleet, as it is called, included 35 boats in the spring of 1966, while five part-time fishermen in New Masset built similar craft (Table 4, cols. A, B). After analyzing size, horsepower, age, and owner's valuation for the 35 Indian boats, we may describe the typical mosquito as 16 feet in length with a small cabin, an 18-horsepower motor, two years old, and having a mean value of $800. The mosquito is rigged with two poles for trolling for spring salmon and coho. It may be fitted with rollers but no drum for use with a half length of gill net for sockeye fishing. In this case, the net is payed out and hauled aboard manually. Fishermen jig for halibut, but may also set out a skate of gear that lies on the sea floor. Although these small boats are quite seaworthy, their operators always go out to sea in pairs or groups and take up positions within range of each other where they will be able to render aid if necessary.

A second advantage offered by the mosquito is economic independence. Since the boats are easily operated by one man, their owners enjoy great freedom of action. Young sons between the ages of 9 and 16 often go fishing with their fathers in order to learn the skills. Older sons strike out on their own, either by acquiring a mosquito, joining a seine or crab boat crew or helping on a troller owned by an Indian relative or a white man. Since the mid-1960s young men have tended to seek wage work as laborers rather than becoming apprentices in the fishing industry. Older sons who find themselves between jobs may fill in their time by helping their fathers to fish, but in only two cases did a son become his father's partner. In both instances the boats were not mosquitos, but trollers. Wives often accompany husbands to the fishing grounds to cook for them, but do not actively participate in the work of fishing.

Many of the mosquito boat operators are older men who spent their most productive years as skippers or crewmen of company fishing boats. Others are former trollers who are semi-retired but who use their mosquitos to earn cash and to fish for household consumption. Boats seem to be lent freely within the linked households of a man and his sons or sons-in-law. Many persons who depend upon some other employment for the major part of their income sell a few pounds of fish caught incidentally. Boats are commonly borrowed for subsistence fishing. There seems to be no formal compensation for this use within the family or restitution in case of damage.

Men of all ages—single, young fathers, heads of three-generation households, and pensioners—engage in fishing with mosquitos as is indicated in Table 6 (col. A). Twenty-five of these small boats are owned by household heads while ten belong to sons living at home. Of the latter, three belong to adolescents who have been given a cast-off boat when their fathers built better ones for their own use, but none of these boys engaged in commercial fishing during 1965.

The age distribution of Indian owners of the three types of boat is shown in Table 6. An overwhelming 73 percent of all Haida boat owners representing all age groups use the mosquito in commercial fishing (col. B). Their earnings are presented in Table 7. Cannery payments ranging from $38 to $4,373 were made to 32 band members in 1965. Average income from this source was $1,287. It should be noted that 56 percent of all mosquito fishermen earned $1,000 or less, while only 18 percent earned more than $2,000. Two New Masset men using similar gear earned $253 and $1,696 respectively.

Trolling. For those Haidas who consider themselves professional fishermen, the mosquito is completely inadequate. These men prefer trollers, the deep-hulled, narrow-beamed vessels with small wheelhouses. Many of these boats were built in the village years ago and

TABLE 6
AGES OF HAIDA BOAT OWNERS, 1965

Age	Mosquitos A	B	Trollers C	D	Gillnetters E	F	Total G	
15–29	12	34%	1	10%	1	33%	14	
30–44	6	17%	4	40%	2	67%	12	
45–59	10	29%	2	20%			12	
60–74	6	17%	3	30%			9	
75–79	1	3%					1	
Total	35	73%	10	21%	3	6%	48	100%

TABLE 7
INCOMES OF MOSQUITO FISHERMEN, 1965

Income	No.	Percentage of Total
$ 10–1,000	18	56
1,001–2,000	8	26
2,001–3,000	3	9
3,001–4,000	2	6
4,001–5,000	1	3
Total	32	100

passed down from father to son. Trollers are operated by one or two men. The boats are fitted with two or four long poles, which are lowered at different angles to the water so that the trailing lines cannot tangle. Spoons and hooks are attached to the lines, each of which may be pulled in and payed out independently of the others. Winches controlling the spools of line are driven by the engine. As the boat passes slowly over the fishing grounds, one of the men pulls in the lines to remove the fish and sets them out again.

When compared with net fishermen who may scoop up whole schools of fish in one set, the troller works long and arduous hours; however, his comparative inefficiency in mining the seas has compensations. The north coast of the island, particularly around North Island, is rich in spring salmon and coho, two species that may be caught on hook and line. Since they do not suffer ugly net gashes, troll-caught fish command high prices.

Another advantage enjoyed by the troller is his relative freedom. Trollers are not subject to the rigid restrictions on times and places for fishing that govern other types of fishermen. Their season begins in April and lasts until October, with no weekend closures. They fish in daylight, which in these northern latitudes lasts for 17 hours in June. Consequently, they spend more time on the fishing grounds than other fishermen, particularly if they carry ice in their holds with which to refrigerate the catch. At night they drop anchor in a sheltered place or head for one of the fish camps maintained by the Fishermen's Co-op at Seven Mile or North Island. Here they may sell their fish and obtain fuel, water, and food supplies.

There is a solidarity among trollers regardless of cultural group membership, which is reinforced by their hostility to gillnetters. Of the local fleet of 17 boats, 10 are owned by Haidas. Troller operators are older than other types of fishermen as shown in Table 6 (col. C). Nine of the men are household heads, while in the tenth case, two old bachelors share a house owned by one and a boat owned by the other. In two cases, a son acts as crewman for his father.

Indian boats tend to be somewhat older, smaller, and have less powerful engines than those owned by whites. They range from 25 to 39 feet, compared with the range of 32 to 38 feet for local white boats. They are equipped with engines of from 25 to 110 horsepower, although one is equipped with a 16-horsepower engine. Indian boats are from 10 to 36 years old and valued at from $600 to $12,000, with an average of $6,130. They are not equipped with radar, sonar, and other electronic gadgetry, nor do all of them have two-way radios. Most of these boats are owned outright by their operators. Trollers owned by whites, on the other hand, are seldom built by their owners and are usually heavily mortgaged. Three of the seven boats are new with completely up-to-date equipment. Their values range from $5,000 to $25,000, with an average of $11,500. These boats resemble those of "outside" fishermen in every respect.

Earnings for Indian trollers fishing for the cannery in 1965 are shown in Table 8. Income from trolling ranged from $226 to $5,361, averaging $2,493. Incomes for two white trollers for whom figures were available were $3,434 and $7,315, averaging $5,375.

Gillnetting. Gillnetting is the type of fishing that most appeals to the more independent, aggressive, and competitive men. They can make more money in less time than trollers and they enjoy a freedom of action that is denied to the seiner skipper and crew. It is in this type of fishing that Haidas are underrepresented, owning only 21 percent, or 3 out of 14 gillnetters (Table 4, col. A).

In addition to 3 gillnetters owned by band members in 1966, 4 boats are owned by New Masset Indians and 7 by whites (Table 4). Boats range in age from 1 to 31 years and in value from $4,500 for the oldest boat to $20,000 for a new 31-foot fiberglass craft. Average value is $9,727. Six gillnetters have engines of about 100 horsepower, 2 have

TABLE 8
INCOMES OF HAIDA TROLLERS, 1965

Income	No.	Percentage of Total
$ 10–1,000	2	20
1,001–2,000	1	10
2,001–3,000	4	40
3,001–4,000	1	10
4,001–5,000	1	10
5,001–6,000	1	10
Total	10	100

150 horsepower, and 3 have 280-horsepower engines. Relative horse-power is significant because it determines the pairing off of fishermen. Boats of similar speeds travel together to and from the fishing grounds.

One band member operates a comparable boat—a 38-foot, 100 horsepower, 6-year-old boat valued at $12,000, which he is purchasing from the cannery. Two other band members, brothers, built a 29-foot and a 21-foot boat, each with 75-horsepower engine and a value of $4,000. The latter two men gillnet but are not members of the gillnetting fleet. That is, they do not share the achievement orientations, the common lore, the common problems, that make the gillnet fleet a solidary group. The first mentioned man is a full and respected member of this group. In 1967 another Indian from a mainland band acquired a typical gillnetting vessel and joined the fleet as a full member.

Earnings of the 11 gillnetters who operated their own boats during the 1965 season ranged from $2,353 to $10,912. The low figure refers to the earnings of a band member mentioned above as applying the technology but not the orientations of the gillnet fisherman. The second highest income, $7,861, was earned by the band member who is buying a boat from the cannery. The average earnings of gillnetters for 1965 were $5,434.

Value Orientations

Full-time fishing requires that a man spend a great deal of time away from home during the season. Seiners and trollers are gone for days and weeks at a time. Gillnetters commute to their local fishing grounds four nights a week, weather permitting, but although they return to the floats in the morning, their days are taken up with sleep, net mending, boat maintenance, and gossip. In an occupation where a man's produc-tivity depends upon his own initiative, gossip substitutes for the coercive pressures of time clock, assembly line, and supervisory personnel. All matters of technical or personal interest to the fishermen are discussed on the government floats at New Masset where the majority moor their boats. The comradeship and competition between men and the social control provided by gossip and ridicule support an achievement orientation to fishing. A man's desire to enjoy the esteem of his fellows motivates him to observe the disciplines imposed by the group.[5]

The basic rule observed by white fishermen of New Masset is the separation of occupational and domestic activities. In New Masset, "Fishing is man's work," and "Women don't belong on boats." If a man takes his wife along it is generally felt that he spends less time fishing than he should. White women, for their part, seem to have little interest in their husbands' occupations; many of them claim to get seasick easily. The rigid sexual division of labor practiced in the white community carries over into other areas of social life. Local men often go to the Canadian Legion clubhouse without their wives on week nights and Saturday afternoons, although Friday and Saturday evenings are reserved for partying with the ladies.

While Indian males in the productive age group are also absent from home for long periods during the fishing season, there are no explicit rules or sets of rationalizations associated with their behavior, perhaps because the economic activities of the sexes are not arbitrarily segregated. It was mentioned earlier that many of the women traveled on the seine boats with their husbands as cooks. Their familiarity with the work and intense concern with the outcome of fishing make them interested and sympathetic supporters.

Not all fishermen tie up their boats at the New Masset floats nor do they accept the conditions of the occupation that are promulgated there. The mosquito fleet is drawn up on the beach or anchored in shallow waters before the Indian village. Half of the Indian trolling fleet is moored at the Old Masset dock. This choice of moorage may be primarily one of convenience, but it gives physical expression to the different values placed on fishing by members of the various fleets.

In 1966 one could still say that the Haida identify themselves as fishermen. They find excitement and comradeship in the work, which impels them to leave well-paying jobs as loggers and laborers to join the fleet. The general expectation in the Indian village that a man will fish goads even the lazy ones into action. News of good catches is circulated, usually not by the individual concerned but by fish buyers at the cannery. This news, passed from household to household, stimulates others to greater effort. A man's performance is continuously

5. See also Jamieson and Gladstone 1950:8.

evaluated wherever other men gather. The "highliner" or top producer is congratulated, while poor fishermen provoke exasperation on the part of their relatives. These attitudes of approval and disapproval do not affect the older men as severely, although they may go through the motions of hanging a net and proclaiming their intention of going up-inlet for pinks. If the weather is bad or even moderately threatening, they may not make it, but face is saved. Men who in their productive years made good catches continue to receive esteem as "good fishermen" regardless of current performance.

The force of the expectation that "Haidas must go fishing" is shown by the fact that in 1965, 98 band members made fish and shellfish sales of at least $100 to the cannery (Table 3, col. B). Most of these were marginal producers: only 25 men—14 mosquito operators (Table 7), 8 trollers (Table 8), and 3 gillnetters—sold more than $1,000 worth of fish. Much of the fish caught never appears in the commercial market, but is intended for home consumption. In other words, the commercial and subsistence economy of the Haida overlap and both are served by the expectation that men will fish.

The fishermen of northern Graham Island do not form a solidary group. Within the specialized fleets they exercise strong social control over each other's behavior, but beyond these groups collective action is rare. Vic Hill, in his history of the Co-op movement in the fishing industry, refers to this behavior as "collective individualism" (1967:1). The failure of Masset fishermen to perceive an over-riding common interest as fish producers reflects in part the nature of their relationship with the Queen Charlotte Canners. The cannery was for decades not a monolithic business corporation but a community organization. Control remained in the hands of the founding family until 1966 when it was taken over by a large Vancouver-based company. The managers' pride in turning out a product of high quality was shared by all who had a part in producing crab or fish packed by the Queen Charlotte Canners— fishermen, shoreworkers, community. This strong commitment was based not only on affective bonds of loyalty and esteem, but also on economic self-interest. As a "shoestring operation," the company was constantly in need of financial resources to carry out necessary technological improvements. At one point shares were sold to members of the public, Indian and white. On another occasion fishermen themselves undertook to subsidize the operation of the cannery by accepting a lower-than-market price for their fish in exchange for a share in the ultimate profits for that season. Fishermen saw their self-interest served by cooperating with the cannery rather than by uniting against it (Hill 1967:173–81). It is not surprising, then, that efforts by organizers of the United Fishermen and Allied Workers Union to form a local chapter were not received with enthusiasm, although a few individuals regard themselves as union members.

A second factor in the fishermen's failure to organize as a group is found in their value orientations toward fishing. All fishermen support the value of high performance by rewarding the "highliner" with esteem. A second shared value is the importance placed on freedom of action. Local fishermen regard themselves as independent entrepreneurs. Unlike the large mainland fishing companies, the Queen Charlotte cannery does not own a fleet of fishing vessels to be leased annually to persons whose status is that of employee. Even so, the "independent" fisherman often has a client relationship with management. Boats bought or built by local people are usually financed through the cannery. All types of equipment including engines, nets, trolling gear, marine hardware, and so on, are purchased in this way. A percentage of earnings is deducted to pay for purchases and loans plus interest. The fisherman is obligated to sell his catches to the cannery, but he is free to fish when and where and as much as he chooses. He is also free to pay off his debt, ending the obligation. But although his independence from the cannery is often illusory and he submits to the disciplines of his specialized fleet, the fisherman, Indian and white, justifies his long, arduous and often dangerous labors on the grounds that he is his "own boss."

We began this chapter with a question about the nature and extent of the Indians' participation in the commercial economy. In fish production we have found that while band members own 62 percent of all boats engaged in commercial fishing (Table 4, col. A), they account for only 24 percent of fish sales to the cannery (Table 2, col. A). Compared with other fishermen, their investment in equipment is low. Of 45 Indian boats used in commercial fishing, 79 percent are valued at $2,000 or less. In contrast, 90 percent of fishing boats owned by other local people are worth more than $5,000. Difficulty in obtaining financing is often cited as the major reason for this disparity (Drucker 1958:124–25; Hawthorn 1958:116–18). Since boats of all sizes operated by Haidas have usually been built by their owners or kinsmen, they are not heavily mortgaged as are most white-owned boats. Nor are they equipped with the sophisticated electronic gadgets and powerful engines that symbolize the white fishermen's commitment to performance goals.

Average incomes of Haida fishermen are low. Mosquito fishermen in 1965 earned an average of $1,287, while the figure for trollers was $2,493. Two New Masset fishermen averaged $975 using mosquitos, while the average for trollers was $5,375. The gillnetters, the most typical white group, averaged $5,434.

Observing such contrasts in investment and income, certain policy-makers have concluded that Indians are discriminated against in fishing and that they can be enabled to "compete" with whites by the provision of financial assistance. It is a mistake, however, to assume that the difference between the gillnetter and the mosquito fisherman is only, or primarily, one of equipment. At least as important is the difference in meaning attached by whites and Haidas, respectively, to competitiveness and achievement in the economic sphere. For whites these values are supported by norms separating economic from domestic activities, the investment in expensive gear and gadgets, participation in dockside seminars, and so on. Of three band members owning vessels designed for gillnetting, only one subscribes to the means and goals of fishing as defined by whites.

To the majority of Haida fishermen, competition with whites on their own terms is irrelevant. The two cultural groups, after all, share only the physical environment and its material facilities. Since they belong to separate segments of Canadian society, the political, legal, and social statuses of their members are entirely different. The limiting conditions for each community reflect this fact. For the whites, earning a living may well be their most pressing concern, making economic performance the determinant of status and life-style. In the Indian community the physical survival of members is underwritten by the all-powerful government, which, during this century, extended its concern to every other social activity as well. For the Haidas the greatest value at the present time appears to be independence, on the community as well as personal level—the freedom to manage their own affairs, to practice their own culture, to preserve their own identity. Consequently they see competition in political rather than economic terms as we shall learn in analyzing militant action by cannery workers in the next section.

These dominant issues are naturally reflected in community attitudes toward fishing. In New Masset, fishing is not considered a prestigious occupation. Only 25 of the approximately 100 household heads were self-employed fishermen in 1966. Many of the businessmen, construction workers, loggers, Navy personnel, and teachers enjoyed average earnings well above figures cited in this chapter for fish producers of both cultural groups. With the exception of three very successful whites who own seine-crab boats and a large troller, fishermen enjoy little social esteem. There is great interest among landsmen, however, in the size of the catches and the performance of individuals, mixed with an expressed envy of the supposed ease with which fishermen can make a "fortune" or a "killing" in a few months and then lie about the rest of the year. Not only are community attitudes unsympathetic but, with the possible exception of sons, families of fishermen view their occupation simply as a source of income rather than as a way of life based upon long apprenticeship to the sea. Other fishermen are supportive, but one's own fleet is one's reference group. Standing in this group depends entirely upon performance on the fishing grounds.

In Haida Masset, fishing is considered not only a commendable occupation but an aspect of the Indians' self-image. Good fishermen receive approval from relatives and the community, but their accomplishments do not, in the absence of more important qualifications, entitle them to positions of leadership or high status. In contrast to New Masset, socioeconomic achievement is not directly related to the prestige system, which is based upon the support of traditional cultural values. Because of this, Indians can validate their status as fishermen by fishing. Whites, on the other hand, must excel in fish production in order to enjoy social esteem.

Fish Processing: The Cannery

The cannery is an organization based on three main role categories: management, supervisory and technical personnel, and workers. The manager at the time of this study was the grandson of one of the original founders of the business and so is a prominent member of a family which claims elite status in New Masset. Since control of the cannery passed into the hands of a large fishing company in 1966, the role of manager has become that of employee rather than policy-maker. The former owner-manager, who retired at the time of the change, was succeeded by his son, who enjoyed far less prestige and influence. Nevertheless, the strong loyalties developed between a paternalistic owner and his employees and suppliers had not entirely vanished.

The supervisory and technical staff consisted of an office manager and secretary, cannery and dock foreman, a floor lady and floor man. Recruitment to supervisory roles was not closed to persons of Indian background although nepotism prevailed. In 1965–66 the manager's wife served as bookkeeper and ran the office, assisted by a white secretary. The white cannery foreman was the brother-in-law of the manager. The floor lady in charge of all women workers was a white nurse married to a New Masset Indian who skippered a cannery boat. A Haida band member was dock foreman, while the floor man coordinating the work of men in the main plant was a New Masset Indian.

During the fishing season of 1965, 135 persons were employed in the cannery as shoreworkers. Men working on the dock under the supervision of the dock foreman are occupied with the buying of fish, the operating of ice-making and freezing equipment, and the trundling of loaded fish carts from the dock shed to the main plant. Women are employed in the dock shed to clean the salmon when fish is being processed. In the main plant the floor man coordinates the work of men who operate the cooking equipment, tend the brine tanks used in processing crabs and the scalding tanks used for clams. They also pack cans, haul freight and perform numerous other tasks. The majority of the women work on "the line," picking crab from the shell at a piece rate of 13 cents per pound. Some women examine crabmeat for shell fragments under ultraviolet light while others pack crab into cans and weigh them. Except for the piece workers, these jobs are rotated among the workers.

The cultural group membership of shoreworkers is summarized in Table 9. Of 70 women employed in crab processing in 1965, 52 were band members and 14 were Indian women living in New Masset. The only white women on the line were two young Navy wives and two women in their fifties.

Cannery jobs are eagerly sought after, particularly since there is rarely any other local source of employment for Indian women. Access to these jobs is determined by union seniority and by the size of the crew needed to process the fluctuating stocks of fish and shellfish. Not only does the workload vary with the success of the fishermen, but the crew needed to can fish is half that required for crab processing.

TABLE 9

CULTURAL GROUP MEMBERSHIP OF SHOREWORKERS, 1965

Workers	Male	Female	Total
Band members	35	52	87
	40%	60%	
	54%	74%	64%
New Masset Indians	13	14	27
	48%	52%	
	20%	20%	20%
Whites	17	4	21
	81%	19%	
	26%	6%	16%
Total	65	70	135
	48%	52%	100%

NOTE: First row percentages refer to sex; second row percentages referring to cultural group are to be read vertically.

The earnings of all shoreworkers are shown in Table 10. Comparison of average incomes of Indian and white workers appears to show considerable differences. The average income for Haidas, however, is depressed because of the practice of calling in additional workers from the village during peak periods. When a phenomenally large run of pinks occurred in August of 1966, the cannery was glutted with fish that had to be processed within hours. The plant operated from 7 o'clock in the morning until 11:30 at night for seven days of the week. All of the able-bodied women in both villages were called to work, as well as many high-school girls who had never been employed before. During this peak period many women doubled their usual earnings. As a rule, overtime work is not available and a uniform rate applies to all non piece-workers. In 1965 and 1966 the hourly rate was $1.93. For a 40-hour week, earnings averaged about $50 after deductions for income tax, unemployment insurance, Canada pension fund, and union dues.

Within the Haida contingent there is a considerable range in earnings as indicated by Table 11, which presents the income by age groups for female shoreworkers. There are three main wage categories with roughly a third of the women falling into each. Only two women had earnings in the fourth bracket (col.D). The average age for women in the lowest income group is 22 years (col.A); for women in the second bracket, 29 years (col.B); and for women in the third, 38 years (col. C). The average age for the two women earning more than $1,600 is 43. This pattern correlating age and earnings is explained by manage-

TABLE 10
EARNINGS OF SHOREWORKERS, 1965

Workers	Male	Female	Total
Haida Masset			
Band Members	35*	52	87
Total Earnings	$42,437	$41,842	$84,279
Average Earnings	$ 1,212	$ 805	$ 968
New Masset			
Indian Background	13	14	27
Total Earnings	$16,402	$12,688	$29,090
Average Earnings	$ 1,262	$ 906	$ 1,077
New Masset Whites	17	4	21
Total Earnings	$25,517	$ 3,936	$29,453
Average Earnings	$ 1,501	$ 984	$ 1,402

*Includes dock foreman.

ment's practice of calling older, experienced workers first, reinforced by the union rule of seniority. In terms of household status, 34 of the 44 women for whom these data are available were wives of household heads. The ten dependents of heads were casual workers, three of whom fell into the lowest income bracket and seven of whom were in the next category.

Cannery work imposes discipline on the workers, setting standards of performance that are enforced by threat of dismissal. Tardiness, absenteeism, and laxity are behaviors that provoke this sanction. The peer group of workers enforces different standards of behavior. The Indians feel that they have a vested interest in their jobs and the position of the few whites working in the cannery is not always comfortable. In this context, persons of Indian background living in New Masset align themselves with band members to form a group that includes 84 percent of the work force. As a solid bloc, they exercise strong control over all workers.

The Union. The union is an important factor in cannery organization

TABLE 11
INCOME FOR HAIDA FEMALE SHOREWORKERS,* 1965

Age	$1–5 A	$6–10 B	$11–15 C	$16–20 D	Total E
15–29	12	8	4	1	25
	48%	32%	16%	4%	
	80%	62%	29%	50%	57%
30–44	3	4	5		12
	25%	33%	42%		
	20%	30%	35%		27%
45–59			4	1	5
			80%	20%	
			29%	50%	11%
60–64		1	1		2
		50%	50%		
		8%	7%		5%
Total	15	13	14	2	44
	34%	30%	32%	4%	100%
Mean Age	22	29	38	43	32

*In hundreds of dollars.
NOTE: First row percentages refer to age category; second row percentages referring to income are to be read vertically.

since seniority not only governs access to employment but determines the relative status of workers. As a rule for ranking individuals in a specific context, seniority is a principle which the Haidas find congenial. An example of how this rule regulates relations between women was given by one of the older white workers who enjoyed high seniority herself. At the time she was in charge of the warehouse with six senior Haida women helping her. When a timekeeper was required, my informant was expected to appoint someone. She suggested to the women that they choose one of themselves for the job. They immediately began to discuss the question of who had the most seniority. Finally it was determined that Dorothy had started in June whereas Vivian had begun working in the cannery in August of the same year, 21 years ago. Only when the relative ranking of the two candidates was settled did the women consider the qualifications necessary for the job. Since Dorothy "did not write well," the task was finally assigned to Vivian after all.

One of the most jealously guarded privileges attached to seniority is the right to work overtime. However, working overtime means that a woman misses her bus trip after the shift and may have to spend part of her extra earnings for cab fare. When offered the job of washing up the sorting trays after the shift, the eligible Indian women declined because little money was involved. My informant, the 55-year-old white widow who reported on the selection of the timekeeper, lived just across the street from the cannery. When asked to wash up the trays she agreed, but the Indian women resented her usurpation of this privilege and protested bitterly to the union shop steward. She was warned by the steward, an Indian woman living in New Masset, not to continue this action. She also received three anonymous phone calls shaming her for "taking work away from people who need it." Since none of the Indian women wanted to work late, the task of washing up the trays fell upon the white floor lady. Naturally, she was not pleased with this solution but, as her status in the cannery organization was higher than any of the shoreworkers, the Indians were mollified.

There is no evidence that high seniority in the cannery carries any weight in the village ranking scale. The rule appears to function only as a means of regulating interrelations of participants in a limited sphere of action. It does help to create a solidary group which can be mobilized in the service of other goals. As we shall see, the shoreworkers discovered that the strike, even the threat to strike, placed in their hands a weapon which could be used in disciplining their own members as well as in exerting political pressure on whites.

The most important instrument in the Haidas' political education was the United Fishermen and Allied Workers Union. Drucker describes the way in which this union secured a foothold in Masset by intervening in a dispute between the Haidas and the Queen Charlotte Canners (1958:132). Although the cannery was not a cooperative, it had an agreement to can clams produced by the Masset Cooperative Association, 80 percent of whose members were Haidas (Hill 1967:152). The cannery had been operating in rented premises on the reserve. When the run-down condition of their plant forced the owners to think of constructing new facilities, they wanted to build on land they could own outright rather than on leased reserve land. The Haidas opposed the removal of the plant to New Masset three miles away on the grounds that it was too far for workers to walk. With their 80 percent majority in the clam co-op, the Indians successfully obstructed the move until the cannery, acting as a private company, bought property in New Masset and built the new facilities in 1950 (Hill 1967:179–80; Dalzell 1968:303). The women appealed to the Native Brotherhood for assistance, but this organization was not interested in the dispute. According to Drucker's account, the union business agent in Prince Rupert heard of the situation and came to Masset to volunteer his services. He conferred with the owner of the cannery and worked out an agreement whereby free bus service was provided for the workers. Then the union agent met with the women, telling them he could not sign the agreement unless they joined the union (1958:132). This expression of concern for their welfare, which contrasted with the cannery manager's apparent lack of sympathy, was very persuasive.

With a local chapter of shoreworkers established, the union took over wage negotiations with management, conducted periodic strike votes, and recruited Indian delegates to regional and provincial conventions. Indians were repeatedly assured of the union's concern with their grievances against management and against white society as a whole. Indeed, with union instruction, those grievances were crystallized and amplified until a role category, that of shoreworker, numerically dominated by Indians, was converted into a political group capable of paralyzing the economic life of New Masset. The Indians discovered this power gradually.

Political Action. In the spring of 1963 an event occurred which informants described as a "murder," that is, an intentional killing. Shock waves reverberated through the community; in my opinion, no lesser "crime" could have had such an impact. The case is mentioned here because of its crucial importance in the political awakening of the villagers. The person identified as "the killer" was a "mainlander," married to a local person. The victim was married to a sibling of the "killer's" spouse. The motive was said to be sexual jealousy. The police, of course, descended upon the scene, but could make no headway in their investigations. No one could be found to testify against the alleged killer, whom we will refer to by the pseudonym K. Green. Eventually the charges had to be dropped. But although the Haida wouldn't abandon K to the white man's law, they imposed severe informal sanctions. These took the form of verbal face-to-face abuse, avoidance, withholding of invitations to social events, pulling shades at K's approach, and so on.

The victim's spouse, who held a responsible position in the cannery, threatened to quit if K were rehired for that season. This ultimatum was supported by other Haida cannery workers with the implied threat that they would strike to back up their stand. The cannery manager bowed to this pressure. K was thus deprived of income, of status in the union seniority system, and of social interaction in the village. As a mainland Indian, K had no kinsmen to give support and comfort. When the victim's spouse remarried the sanctions were eased. K was permitted to work in the cannery the following summer, but was only gradually and partially readmitted to the social life of the community.

After the disciplining of K. Green, a more spectacular test of the shoreworkers' power was not long in coming. In October of 1963 a cannery truck taking workers home from their shift overturned. An Indian man who had been standing in the doorstep was pinned under the truck and later died of his injuries. According to informants who took an active part in events, about 30 women passengers were shaken up or injured. The women were taken to the Red Cross Hospital in New Masset, while those injured more seriously were flown to Prince Rupert or driven to the hospital in Queen Charlotte City. Doctors were flown in from several places, including the Indian hospital at Miller Bay. One Haida informant was incensed that the "Indian Service doctor came and not a bone specialist from Prince Rupert," claiming that this was evidence of second-class treatment for Indians. The union had sent a man from Prince Rupert immediately upon receiving a phone call notifying them of the accident.

In 1966 it was still impossible to obtain an objective account of what followed from any informant, white or Indian, although the bare facts can be outlined by comparing many statements. According to reports, the white assistant cannery manager, "Jim Black," who had been driving the truck, was convicted of negligence and fined $200. The Haidas were outraged, claiming that an Indian convicted of drunken driving was fined the same amount. They charged that $200 was too low a price for the life of an Indian and demanded that the assistant manager be dismissed as punishment. According to the account given by one of the leaders of the militant faction, "Nothing more was thought about the accident until the cannery opened the next April and we learned that the killer was still working there.'' Indignation mounted among the shoreworkers who appealed to the Native Brotherhood, which again refused to intervene. The union representative, hearing of the turmoil, was anxious to be of assistance. Acting upon his advice, the shoreworkers voted to strike to enforce their demand that the assistant manager be fired. The cannery manager refused "as a matter of principle." The principle in question apparently was the great difference between K. Green and "good old Jim," who was a veteran of World War II, a founder of the Masset Canadian Legion chapter, the husband of a teacher, and a popular member of the community.

Meetings were held in the Haida community hall where speakers from the cannery, the New Masset village council, local businessmen, and Indian moderates tried to persuade the Indians to abandon their strike. At other meetings in the village the union agent and Indian militants fortified the workers' righteous indignation. Informal leaders emerged, not within the union membership, but in the Indian community, galvanizing widespread resentment into political action, fanning long smouldering grievances against the whites. When the shoreworkers faltered in their resolve to hold out, they were goaded on by the militants.

In New Masset the wildcat strike, coming at the beginning of the fishing season of 1964, tied up fishing boats and was felt as a great hardship by all whose livelihood depended upon the cannery. The union agent tried to mobilize whites in support of the strike, emphasizing the worker-management dichotomy. White union members repudiated the strikers and the union agent. Even some of the Indian fishermen from Old Masset were opposed to the shoreworkers' action though few dared to stand and be counted. It is said that the Indian agent tried to break the strike by refusing relief funds to strikers. He was soon transferred to another agency, but whether the Indian Branch initiated his transfer or responded to Indian pressure is not clear. After two weeks of extremely bitter recriminations on both sides, the cannery manager capitulated. The shoreworkers went back to work, thinking that the matter was closed. The militant faction in the Indian community was jubilant. "We Indians always backed down before." The event is referred to by both Indians and whites as "the Revolution." It was recognized that the old working relationship between the villages had been destroyed. In a sense, relations had been reversed for now it was the whites who were suspicious and resentful.

The after-effects of the strike have ramified widely. A civil service job was found for Jim in Prince Rupert, but his friends bitterly resented his being forced out of the community. The cannery owner's wife, who had been active in running the company for many years and who considered herself a friend of the Haidas, refused to be concerned any longer. The owner himself, a paternal figure who had continued to operate a marginal business partly out of a sense of social responsibility, lost heart. The Parent Teachers Association in New Masset, which included both Haida and white members, was disbanded when the latter refused to have anything further to do with Indians. But the strike was only the climactic expression of an Indian discontent which was received by cannery management and other whites as a personal affront.

The Indians' relationship with cannery management had been a paternalistic one modeled on that with their Indian agent. Ownership of the business had remained in one family, the son inheriting the father's responsibilities toward the Indians along with the job. Sam Simpson, son of a founder of the business, described the post-missionary period extending from the early 1900s to the 1920s when "the Indians were so grateful for the help and guidance the White man had given." He said that the Indians were very reverent toward his father, leaned on him, and expected him to take care of them. When he died they placed a plaque in their church in his memory. The emotional bond was very strong on both sides of this economically oriented relationship. However, the paternalism and solicitude demanded of the manager did not reflect the fact that he had so much power over the Indians but that he had so little. Here the Indians dictated the terms of interaction since, in those days, the cannery could not function without the produce of the fishermen and the labor of the women.

The Indians were not equally dependent on the cannery because most of them were under contract to large fishing companies which extended credit to them during the winters. The clam-canning activities of the co-op eventually failed because the villagers would not dig clams during the winter when they could get credit elsewhere (Hill 1967:175–81). When they did accept employment with the Masset cannery, the price for their cooperation was an unending demonstration of concern from the incumbents of a role of high status and authority. It appears that management did not always understand that submissiveness and dependency were role-playing behavior. Even in 1962 the manager was still going down to the village on Monday mornings or on the day after a feast to muster a crew for the day's work.

By the time of my first visit to Masset in 1962 the Haidas' restlessness was being expressed in affirmative strike votes, white-baiting, and general tension between the villages. For some time various individuals, either more alienated or more aggressive, had been openly expressing their resentment of whites who, in turn, usually attributed their behavior to drunkenness. This group had been agitating about

Thomas Deasy (1857–1936), Indian agent at Masset from 1910 to 1924 (British Columbia Provincial Archives, no. 73294)

Section of plank road built by white settlers, early 1900s (British Columbia Provincial Archives, no. 41753)

Masset beach, 1880s (British Columbia Provincial Museum)

Mosquito boats drawn up on Masset beach, 1962

Houses on Masset Inlet, south of Mission Hill, 1962

White-style houses replaced long houses on main street by the turn of the century (Centennial Museum of Vancouver)

Charles Edenshaw memorial long house, Masset

Peter Hill's stone-moving, 1971 (from ''Those Born at Masset,'' Stearns and Stearns)

Guests at Peter Hill's memorial feast

Putative father's sister wiping Peter Hill's headstone, 1971

Children's dancing group waiting to perform at ''Tribute to the Living Haida'' festivities, 1980

Nursery school on Masset reserve, 1980

Haida carver at Masset

Cannery at New Masset

Storekeeping on New Masset docks, 1980

land claims, liquor rights, and a long list of other grievances. During the early 1960s their orientation became increasingly active, shifting from passive withdrawal to rebelliousness (Parsons 1951:257–59). At the same time, the majority of villagers, disillusioned and embittered by the government's change of attitudes, swung their support behind the militants. The emergence of an activist mood which mobilized the whole community placed a powerful political weapon in the hands of their leaders. It was not long before a new grievance helped to trigger the "Revolution."

This grievance may be described as a frustration of their expectations of solicitude from the whites. When the Good Friday earthquake of 1964 rocked Alaska, warnings of an expected tidal wave were radioed to all parts of the Pacific coast and residents were advised to remove themselves to high ground. Although the Masset villages are located at sea level, there are some slightly elevated places nearby. The preferred refuge was a high hill eight miles south of New Masset and eleven miles from the Haida village. This distance could only be traversed by car or truck and there were few vehicles in the village. Presumably most of the Indians remained at home. Many of the New Masset whites fled to "the hill"; later I heard some talk of an organized mass evacuation. Fortunately, the tidal wave did not strike Graham Island with any force although the waters rose and fell in an alarming manner. My Haida informant, who was the catalyst of the militant faction, was attending a union convention in Vancouver. When she returned and found that "the whites saved themselves without bothering to help the Indians," her indignation was boundless. It was only a week later that the cannery opened its spring season and the Indians learned that the man responsible for the fatal accident of the previous autumn was still employed there.

The Haidas were somewhat chastened by the violent reaction in New Masset to their "Revolution." When they realized they had "gone too far," they repudiated their militant leaders, some of whom sat on the band council. In the next election of councilors a new slate representing a moderate "pro-white" point of view was installed, probably in an attempt to placate their neighbors. That this election was a gesture is indicated by the fact that the community did not support the councilors once they were elected. Anti-Indian feeling in New Masset has only partially subsided in the years since the strike. In the viewpoint of many of the Indians, the results of the confrontation justified its costs. They had managed to demonstrate their strength both to the whites and to themselves, winning a political victory that has forever destroyed the sham of dependency in their relations with whites.

INTERPRETATION OF ECONOMIC ROLES

Given the seasonal nature of the economy of the Queen Charlotte Islands in 1965–66, it was not possible for the majority of Haidas to earn cash income on a year-round basis. Nor, given their inefficient equipment, the depleted stocks of fish, and government regulation of fishing practices, was it possible to earn enough money in this industry to support a family during the long winters. The Canadian government recognizes an obligation to provide financial assistance to indigent Indian families. At the same time, it encourages traditional subsistence activities by reserving certain salmon runs for Indian food-fishing. The Haidas' economic adaptation, then, combines the earning of cash income in fishing or wage work with food gathering and welfare payments. The people are neither economically self-sufficient nor dependent upon selling their labor in the market place.

Because of alternative sources of support, the Haidas enjoy some latitude in interpreting their roles in the commercial economy. Indians whose work is carried out in groups composed primarily of other Indians, such as the cannery line workers, are subject to cultural group control, which reinforces their sense of common identity and interest. As members of a solidary bloc within the cannery structure, shoreworkers have been able to adopt an aggressive posture, exercising coercive pressure against management in the service of their own self-interest. Under the direction of informal leaders, who have emerged not within their own ranks but in the Haida village, their self-interest is interpreted in political or social rather than in economic terms. Indeed, the politicization of utilitarian relations reflects the conflict within the village over the crucial issues of how to play the role of Indian and how to deal with whites. We return to this matter in chapter 8.

Fishermen are not only less subject to external supervision and control than shoreworkers, but are in a better position to benefit directly from their own industry. Even so, the majority of Haida fishermen are marginal producers, operating small boats that are used for subsistence fishing as well as for earning cash income. Indians may choose to "act like whites," accepting the role as it is defined in New Masset, by acquiring a suitable boat and becoming a member of the trolling or gillnetting fleets. The esteem granted to the single Indian highliner among the gillnetters suggests that no social barriers restrict the participation of band members. Even in the cannery, several achievement-oriented Haidas have occupied the supervisory roles of foreman and skipper of cannery boats. While their economic achievement in the white man's world is rewarded with approval, these individuals have not been recruited to positions of leadership or influence in their own community on the strength of this performance alone. Such positions, insofar as any were recognized in 1966, were awarded to those who perform traditional ceremonial roles in the feasting complex.[6]

Given the non-congruent prestige systems of the two communities, it is to be expected that those individuals who attempt to integrate economic roles in the white community and social roles in the Indian village will experience some role conflict. The cannery worker and marginal fisherman face no difficulty here since their economic roles are clearly subordinated to social roles. But political action undertaken by members of the Indian community against their white neighbors isolates the achievement-oriented individual who has attempted to "act white" on the job and Indian at home. In these circumstances, such men either stifle their ambitions and conform to the pattern set by the community, withdraw from active participation in community life while continuing to strive for economic achievement, or move down the road to become a sociological white, a New Masset Indian. As might be expected, then, we find considerable evidence of norm conflict in those institutions which are most vulnerable to external control.

Informants repeatedly stressed the importance of independence of action in commercial fishing and, as we shall see, in subsistence activities and other areas of social life as well. Individualism appears to be a value, fostered by the introduction of wage labor and resultant changes in social relations, which has suffused modern Haida culture. On the other hand we have found that this individualism is tempered by community pressure enforcing solidarity and conformity to norms and goals of the cultural group.

POLITICIZATION OF UTILITARIAN RELATIONS

At the beginning of this chapter we observed that the Haidas pursue other than purely economic goals in the intervillage context. In the confrontation that boiled up in the economic sphere, the local whites were a convenient target for the hostility engendered in the Haidas by their experiences with the dominant society. Largely through the intervention of external agencies, the Masset whites have lost the power to maintain asymmetrical relations with the Indians. The organization of a union local radically changed the management-worker relationship. It was with union instruction that the Haidas began to understand the implications of economic interdependence.

6. This situation has changed in the 1970s, due as much to the dying off of those schooled in "the old-fashioned ways" as to more direct involvement of younger adults in the management of band affairs.

The federal government's influence in redefining local relations has been felt in the integrated provincial school system which fosters new relationships between young people. To implement the achievement goals set for Indians in the economic realm, the Indian Affairs Branch offered to equip them to "compete" with the whites. This competition was to be carried out under the same paternalistic protection that has always been the reward for their special status. For example, attempts were made to induce business organizations locating in the Queen Charlotte Islands to practice preferential hiring of Indians. Boats built under the federally financed Indian Fishermen's Assistance Program were to be exempt from the license limitations imposed upon other commercial fishermen in 1968. Other "rights" of Indians as then interpreted included new houses at little or no cost to the recipient at a time when many local whites were not able to improve or replace their own housing because of prohibitive costs and interest rates. Early plans for a joint water system serving Haida Masset, New Masset, and the Navy base provided that the Indian and Navy facilities would be paid for from federal funds, while the incorporated village of New Masset would be forced to levy high assessments on its residents.

The inequities fostered by these externally imposed policies aggravate the tensions between the two villages. For many years the whites' attitude toward the Indians has been one of tolerance mixed with exasperation. Their expectations of Indians' economic performance reflect their own values of pioneering, independence, and self-reliance. They say it is "about time the Indians begin to think of themselves as Canadians." In response to the Haidas' aggressive behavior, many of the local whites express the opinion that reserves should be abolished and the Indians "made to stand on their own feet."

The Haidas, on the other hand, are aware of the sympathetic attitudes of the wider society and manipulate them in their dealings with local whites. Through the Indian Affairs Branch and other organizations that operate on provincial and regional levels, including the United Fishermen and Allied Workers' Union, the Native Brotherhood, and the Anglican Church, the Indians communicate with the larger public. The creation of a Haida art industry in the 1970s has focused the attention of a new and sympathetic audience on the community. The local whites who have no voice to speak for them to society-at-large find themselves labeled as bigots by outsiders.

In a situation where dominance relations have become unstable, the establishment of a new balance depends upon the outcome of competition. Behavior and expectations are being redefined by contention. There is lack of agreement about goals and appropriate performance as each side employs the weapons available to it. The whites interpreted the events of 1964 as an open contest for control of the shared institutions of cannery and school. The Haidas saw the contest as an opportunity for extracting from whites the admission that "Indian culture" is as valid as that of the whites. A frequent charge made in the tirades directed against local people is, "You Whites don't respect our culture." By demanding respect for "Indian culture," they have made the preservation of a distinctive identity a goal of political competition. It legitimates their claims to special rights and privileges, which are valued as evidence of the Indians' importance in the scheme of things. It is this notion of hereditary rights and status that most offends the achievement-oriented local whites and provokes their demand for abolition of reserves and the special privilege they allegedly represent. There is no evidence to suggest that they would welcome a "flood" of Indians into their own community should they succeed in striking down the ethnic boundary.

The Haida community has become achievement-oriented in an expressive sense. By this I mean that its solidary performances in "putting down whites" have become an intrinsic source of gratification. In this political competition with their neighbors, the Indians are attempting to redefine their status in the larger context. Implied here is an active rejection of the normative pattern which integrates the interaction of Indians and whites. That is, the Haida community has challenged the dominant-subordinate relation.

The eventual outcome of this challenge is still in doubt. The Haidas' competitive behavior takes place within a structural framework—the utilitarian sphere—which has been redefined as symmetrical. Nevertheless, control continues to be securely vested in the dominant sector. This was clearly shown when members of the Masset band challenged federal authority by dismantling a navigation beacon located on reserve land. In this case sanctions, including the threat of prosecutions, were swiftly applied. The development of political competition in the economic sphere, then, does not affect the Haidas' status as a subordinate enclave in Canadian society.

Chapter 5
The Family System

COMMUNITY LIFE is concerned with kinship and marriage, the domestic economy, hereditary chiefship, and ceremonial exchange. These institutions are distributed among the family, the bilateral circle, and the matrilineal network. Crosscutting these functionally specialized kin groupings are the five age grades. In this chapter we analyze the effects of social and economic change on the family system of the Masset Haida, taking up other inner-community institutions in subsequent chapters.

The family as defined here, following Levi-Strauss, is a social group originating in marriage, consisting of husband, wife, their children, and possibly other relatives, its members bound by legal, economic, religious and other rights and obligations, specific sexual regulations, and the exchange of affect (1956:267). Ideally the family is supported by formal legal, religious, and economic institutions, but where these are controlled by the external power structure, the norms and values they embody are antithetical to the traditional values of the cultural group. In these circumstances, the family is caught at the interface of two social systems where it bears the brunt of adaptive pressure.

The present family organization of the Masset Haida may be regarded as a response to prevailing social conditions. In chapter 1, we reviewed the way in which new economic opportunities and the pattern of seasonal migration reinforced the Haidas' perception of the conjugal bond as the most important social relationship. The joint responsibility of husband and wife for the maintenance of the domestic group precipitated changes in the idea system, emphasizing the economic independence of the conjugal pair from the larger kin group. The emergence of the nuclear family as the key social and economic unit represents a radical shift from the matrilaterally extended household shared, ideally, by brothers and nephews along with their wives and children.

In recent years the nuclear form has been giving way before another pattern, which also reflects adaptation to the possibilities of the social environment. Analysis of household composition data collected in Masset in 1966 reveals that while 40 percent of all households are comprised of two-generation nuclear families, one third are three generations in depth.

The development of the three-generation family may be viewed in large part as a consequence of the failure of many individuals to marry before producing children. Premarital children are assimilated into existing households. Since the earnings of household heads are insufficient to support such large families, government agencies have assumed the burden of financial assistance. This practice has far-reaching implications. Welfare assistance for the support of illegitimate children removes the necessity for their parents to marry and they remain in their respective natal homes. A striking feature of the Haida family system is the high proportion of adults 20 years and older who are living with parents (see Table 16). Some of these adult dependents, especially daughters, eventually marry and move out, often leaving their premarital children in the care of grandparents.

But if the three-generation family is the natural outgrowth of the sexual activities of unmarried children, it has quickly assumed additional social functions. The potential labor force provided by adult dependents enables heads of three-generation households to undertake more extensive social, economic, and ceremonial activities than can be carried out by nuclear families. This observation suggests that different forms of the family perform different functions for the social system.

Adjustments in the family system extend beyond the domestic grouping to the broader kinship network, which reflects, on a larger scale, relationships within the nuclear family. The households of senior couples and their married children form a narrow circle of continuously interacting kinsmen. This bilateral kindred, which I refer to in this volume as "linked households,"[1] performs many of the functions formerly carried out by the matrilineages. These include economic support of members' ceremonial activities, responsibility for aid in time of crisis, and sponsorship of public events of community interest or benefit. The independence as well as interdependence of each unit participating in the "bilateral circle" is recognized by obligations of reciprocal gift exchange between households.

Certain changes in the family system appear to be more or less deliberate attempts to cope with the social problems facing the community. The use of welfare as an alternative to parental responsibility

---

1. I prefer not to employ the term "bilateral kindred" as a label for closely related households because the Haidas do not formalize this unit. Nor do I wish to imply an ideological shift from a matrilateral to a bilateral model.

in providing for the material needs of children is one example (see chapter 7).

The way in which the Haidas themselves perceive family relations and the family system may be inferred from informants' verbal testimony and from observations of their behavior in a wide range of situations. The people apply the term "family" to all relationships of consanguinity and affinity. In Haida usage, as in our own, however, the primary meaning of "family" is a unit of parents and children. The Haidas extend the term to include any relatives who share a household whatever their genealogical relationship to each other.

In its second sense, family is used to refer to the bilaterally linked households of parents and married children. While members typically do not pool their efforts or resources in subsistence activities, these relationships are among the strongest bonds in community life for this is the group that provides economic support for the ceremonial feasting complex.

In its third meaning, family refers to the wider groupings of matrilineage and moiety, which are oriented to internal community action focusing on ceremonial exchange and rites of passage. The people's perception of all these relationships as family emphasizes the point that the nuclear unit, despite its economic independence, is not an isolate, but is embedded in overlapping networks of bilateral and matrilateral kinsmen.

HOUSEHOLD COMPOSITION

To understand structural changes in the Haida family system we shall analyze the composition of all households in the village at one point in time. The primary data for this study are provided by a household census, which pinpointed the whereabouts of every person ordinarily resident on the reserve for May 15, 1966. The terms "family" and "household" are not used interchangeably in this analysis.[2] Household refers to the coresidential group, whether its members are related or not; family refers to persons consanguineally or affinally related who live together. Related persons who are not coresident are referred to as kinsmen.

Using household composition data, we may delineate four family *forms* or structures of coresidential groupings based on relations of marriage and descent. Following Fortes (1958:3), Smith (1962:22), and others, it is assumed that in any social system there is only one family system. The various forms are not simply deviations from an ideal

2. For an able discussion of the conceptually distinct features of family, coresidence, and domestic functions, see Bender 1967. A recent review article is Yanagisako (1979).

type, but represent a sequence corresponding to phases in the life cycle of the head.[3] In terms of functions to be performed for the society, the most important factors to be considered are the presence or absence of a "conjugal pair," either married or consensual,[4] the number of generations, and the relationship of dependents to the head.

We shall see that each form of family carries out different, though overlapping, tasks. Although it is common practice to ascribe such functions as reproduction, childcare and socialization, economic activities, and affective support to the family, investigation reveals others which have decisive importance for the society. It may be said that the Haida family, as an element in a wider kinship network, contributes to cultural continuity through its sponsorship of ceremonial activities. Moreover, we shall see that the various tasks performed by the family do not receive equal emphasis at every phase of its development.

In May 1966 the resident population of 671 persons was distributed among 99 households. About 90 percent of the villagers lived in 79 households which included at least one conjugal pair. In only five of the 79 households were two couples found.

When conjugal units are classified according to number of generations, we find that six are one-generation households which include only the couple; 40 are two-generation households and 33 are comprised of three generations. In Table 12 are analyzed details of membership in these households: the average age of heads, average number of members, and total number of persons living in households of that type.

Twenty of the 99 households may be described as "nonconjugal" or "incomplete" since none of their members are at present living in a marital or consensual union. These households are formed either by the survivors of a marriage (ex-conjugal) or by unattached persons who share a dwelling or live alone. Characteristics of incomplete households are summarized in Table 13. We may note that these households are small with an average of 3.2 members (col. C) as compared with conjugally based households with an average of 7.7 members (Table 12, col. C). Furthermore, only 10 percent of villagers live in nonconju-

3. The concept of the developmental cycle of domestic groups so productively employed by Fortes (1958) has become an indispensable approach. I use his terminology to elucidate the structure of the Masset family system, but find it necessary to modify the sequence of phases.

4. In speaking of the organization of households where our interest is in the performance of the roles of husband and wife, father and mother, and the legal status of their union is immaterial, I shall use the term "conjugal" since I can find no other that will cover the situation better. When legal status is important, as in determining legitimacy of children or band membership, then marriage will be distinguished from common-law or consensual unions on the one hand and extraresidential mating on the other.

TABLE 12
Masset Households Based on Conjugal Pairs, May 1966

Household Composition	No. of House- holds A	Average Age of Head B	Average No. Members C	Total Members D
One-Generation (conjugal pair only)	6	65	2	12
Two-Generations Conjugal pair, own children	28	35	6.9	192
Conjugal pair, own, adopted children	7	33	7.6	53
Conjugal pair, adopted children	2	47	6	12
Conjugal pair, own, adopted children, siblings of couple	3	39	8	24
Sub Total	40	35.8	7	281
Three Generations Two conjugal pairs, children	5	58.6	12.6	63
Conjugal pair on junior generation	3	66	7.7	23
Conjugal pair on senior generation, parents of grandchildren present	18	57.9	10.6	191
Conjugal pair on senior generation, grandchildren, parents absent, own children	7	60.7	5.3	37
Sub Total	33	59.3	9.5	314
Total Conjugal Households	79	52.8	7.7	607

gal units. These findings are consistent with the characterization of households which include no conjugal pairs as incomplete or residual.

The status of household head is almost invariably assigned to a male if one is available. In 88 of 99 cases heads are, in fact, males. In 76 of the 79 conjugal households, the head belongs to the oldest generation present. Of these senior heads, 72 are married men while four are living common-law. In the other three conjugal households, the mar-

TABLE 13
NONCONJUGAL HOUSEHOLDS, MAY 1966

Household Composition	No. of House- holds A	Average Age of Head B	Average No. Members C	Total Members D
One-Generation				
Persons living alone	6	61	1	6
Adult relatives	5	52	2.8	14
Sub Total	11	57	1.8	20
Two Adjacent Generations				
Unwed Mother and children	1	38	7	7
Widow, own, adopted children	1	40	6	6
Sub Total	2	39	6.5	13
Three Generation Span				
One grandparent, grandchildren	4	73.4	3.5	14
Unmarried persons, children	3	74.3	5.7	17
Sub Total	7	73.8	4.6	31
Total Nonconjugal Households	20	61.3	3.2	64

ried pair is on the middle generation with a widowed parent—two males and one female—as head. Only in this one instance is a female the head of a household which includes a married pair. Here the widow lived alone in her own house until her son brought his bride and step-children to live with her. As head of a dependent nuclear family, he did not supersede his mother socially.

Of 20 nonconjugal households, half have male heads. Two widowers are raising grandchildren, while eight men live alone or share quarters with unmarried adult relatives. The circumstances of the 10 female heads may be examined: three women—single, unwed mother, and widowed—live alone. Two women—unwed mother and widowed—are raising children alone. Three widows are raising grandchildren in the absence of parents. One widow, referred to above, was joined by her son's newly acquired family. Two widows preside over households which include bachelor sons and daughter's children. The last item illustrates the point that marriage is a major criterion of sociological adulthood; bachelors are never pointed out as heads unless they live alone or with unmarried dependents. The presence of a woman as a household head is in itself evidence of a fragmentary family unit.

In certain respects all one-generation conjugal households found in Masset in 1966 were residual forms. With but one exception these were couples who had passed the reproductive period and whose children lived elsewhere. As Table 12 shows, the average age of these heads is 65 years (col. B). The youngest was a 45-year-old man living with a 22-year-old girl, but this relationship later dissolved and the girl married out of the band. No newly married couples were included among the one-generation households because, while setting up independent housekeeping is the ideal, it was seldom possible in 1966 because of the housing shortage. The one-generation conjugal household thus marks not the beginning but the end of the domestic cycle. In the majority of cases, however, households where children have reached adulthood do not enter a phase of dispersion of members to other households. On the contrary, they enter a phase of secondary expansion as grandchildren who are illegitimate or caught in broken marriages are added to the membership. This process is demonstrated by analyzing the composition of the three-generation households.

Three-Generation Households

The three-generation household in Masset is not the extended family of many other cultures, but represents a special adaptation to the social problems facing the community. Its importance is indicated by the fact that 33 percent of all households (Table 12, col. A) and 41 percent of those based on conjugal pairs fall into this category. Its composition is variable, including the head, usually a wife (30 cases) and unmarried children plus one or more of the following possibilities of secondary expansion:

1. The nuclear family of a child (8 units)
2. Single parent-child units composed of a child and grandchildren (24 units)
3. Grandchildren whose parents are absent (59 grandchildren)

In three of the 33 three-generation conjugal households the head is widowed and the conjugal pair is found on the middle generation. In five of 30 cases where the conjugal pair is on the senior generation, the household also includes the nuclear family of a son or daughter (Table 12, col. A). In these eight households which include a dependent nuclear family, the relationship of the linking member to the head is that of son in seven cases and daughter in one. Ages of the dependent husbands range from 28 to 41; both mean and median ages are 33 years.

One couple was newly married, while the others were parents of from two to eight children. These households were described as being "just like a duplex," meaning that each unit was independent economically. There is some justification for referring to these cases as "double households." With the accelerated housing program financed by the Indian Branch since 1966, dependent nuclear families have received high priority for new housing and are now able in most cases to set up housekeeping on their own. During the period of coresidence with parents, the junior conjugal pair acts independently; there is no pooling of resources and the head does not make decisions on behalf of junior married men. In every case, however, it is the senior man, married or not, who is pointed out as the household head.

While the pattern of temporary coresidence is typical for young married people, it is not characteristic of mating arrangements. During the 1960s it was very common for daughters to engage in casual mating for a period of years, residing at home with their children as dependent single parents.[5] In 1966, 24 units consisting of single parents and their children were incorporated in 21 of the 33 three-generation conjugal households. "Single parents" in this context refers to incomplete nuclear families in which marriage has not occurred or has been disrupted by death or separation.

The age and marital status of 22 female and two male single parents living in three-generation households is shown in Table 14. Eighteen of these dependents are unmarried daughters with a total of 35 children (col. A). These units are distributed among 13 households. Five of the

TABLE 14
AGE AND MARITAL STATUS OF DEPENDENT SINGLE PARENTS

Age	Unwed Daughter A	Formerly Married Daughter B	Separated Son C	Separated Son-in-law D
15–19	5			
20–24	9	1		
25–29	2			
30–34	2	1	1	
35–39				1
40–44		2		
Total	18	4	1	1

5. In the 1970s the pattern of premarital childbearing has become even more prevalent, beginning at earlier ages and involving a greater proportion of girls. But the average interval between first birth and marriage and the number of illegitimate children per mother may be decreasing. These matters are examined in chapter 6.

remaining six single parents are widowed and separated persons who have returned to their own parents' homes with 22 children (cols. B, C). It is noteworthy that while seven out of eight dependent married couples live with the husband's parents, the children of five formerly married daughters live with their mother's parents. In one case where the nuclear family of a daughter resided with her father, she left the village when she separated from her husband, leaving him and her four sons living in her father's house (col. D). Since the son-in-law was a member of another band he would not have been eligible for new housing allocated by the band council and would have had to leave the reserve if he moved out. One other separated man retained custody of his children, continuing to live with them in his parents' home (col. C), while his wife returned to her own parents. Female parent-child units are separate with respect to childcare, but are dependent economically.

The last type of secondary expansion is illustrated by 25 households, which include 59 grandchildren whose parents are dead, away from the reserve, or living in other households. These absent parents include 25 daughters, four sons and one grandson. In these cases the responsibility for childcare falls upon the older generation, although when adult children of the head remain at home they help to care for their nieces and nephews. This situation prevails in six three-generation families and in eight ex-conjugal households. In 11 of the 25 households more than one type of grandparent-grandchild relationship is found.

In analyzing the household composition of the Masset Haidas in 1966 we have identified four "types" or forms of organization:

1. The two generation nuclear family based on marriage and augmented by adopted children and, infrequently, adult relatives of the head's generation. This is the period of family development referred to as the phase of expansion (Fortes 1958:4–5).

2. An extended family formed when children acquire mates and produce grandchildren. Occasionally these mates become household members but more often the children and their mothers form dependent units within the household. During this period when Fortes' model would lead us to expect dispersion as the reproductive activities of the senior couple come to an end, we find a strong development of secondary expansion. This process slows as adult children depart, frequently leaving their premarital children behind.

3. The one-generation conjugal household where children have dispersed represents the process of replacement.

4. Where there is only one conjugal pair, the death of a spouse creates a residual type of family unit whose members may carry on alone, join an existing family, or keep house with survivors of another unit. Occasionally unattached persons live alone.

FUNCTIONAL SPECIALIZATION OF HOUSEHOLD TYPES

In order to discover whether there is evidence of functional specialization, these four phases of Haida family development are compared in Table 15. The 99 households are classified as conjugal (cols. A, B, C) or nonconjugal (cols. D, E), and grouped according to number of generations. Each of these structures is analyzed in terms of four variables: age of head, household size, earned income of heads, and participation in ceremonial life.

Comparison of mean age of heads and mean household size places each form in a logical sequence of development. Comparison of earnings of employed heads and feast scores of heads helps to identify the primary contribution of each form to the Haida social system. Two measures of central tendency, the mean and the median, are used. The standard deviation is included, although the variability on some points is so wide as to make the measure almost meaningless.

With respect to earnings, only persons with an income earned in the fishing industry in 1965 are included. Since 84 percent of all employed males were engaged in fishing or cannery work, the data are available for the majority of cases. No income data could be obtained for that 16 percent of workers employed in laboring, logging, or other occupations. Since only five men for whom information is missing, or 4 percent of the total, are over 39 years, the missing data do not jeopardize the conclusion that the heads of two-generation households are most active in the cash economy. The number of employed heads is shown for each household type.

For my analysis of ceremonial activities in chapter 9, I computed a feast score to measure participation in the community-wide ceremonies which mark marriage, burial, the erection of a headstone, and the assumption of an Indian name. These data are introduced here in anticipation of fuller discussion later. A score of 1.0 indicates no participation in the feasts, while scores ranging from 1.2 to 2.0 signify a marginal helping role in the ceremonies of kinsmen. Scores of 2.5 to 3.0 suggest regular attendance as guest or sponsorship and support of ceremonies honoring close kinsmen. Scores of 3.3 to 4.0 indicate that individuals took an active part in sponsoring or co-hosting feasts and perhaps received ritual payment for prescribed ceremonial services.

Comparison of the mean age of heads supports the postulate that each household type represents a phase of family development (Table 15). Paraphrasing Fortes (1958), the expanding phase is represented by the *two-generation household* comprised of the nuclear family headed by a married man whose mean age is 35.8 years (col. A). Nuclear families are large, including an average of seven members, five of

TABLE 15

COMPARISON OF HOUSEHOLD TYPES

Characteristics	Conjugal Households			Nonconjugal Households	
	Two-Generation A	Three-Generation B	One-Generation C	Two- & Three-Generation Ex-Conjugal* D	One Generation E
Number of Households	40	33	6	9	11
Age of Heads					
Mean	35.8	59.3	65	66.5	57
Median	34.5	60	65.5	71	52
S.D.	10	9.4	15.4	14.6	13.8
Total Number of Residents in Households					
Mean	281	314	12	44	20
Mean	7.0	9.5	2	5	1.8
Median	7.0	9.0	2	5	1.0
S.D.	2.5	4.1		1.5	1.0
Earnings of Employed Heads—Number	29	21	1	1	5
Mean	$1,940	$1,404	$1,514**	$251**	$2020
Median	$1,877	$913			$1496
S.D.	$1,194	$1,309			$1,655
Feast Score of Heads					
Mean	1.5	2.5	2.8	2.6	1.8
Median	1.2	3.0	3.0	3.0	1.6
S.D.	0.7	0.97	0.43	0.5	0.92

*Includes unwed mother.
**With only one case other measures not calculated.

whom are children. Heads of these units are the most active in the commercial economy with 72 percent employed in fishing or shorework, earning an average of $1,940. There is, however, wide variation in earnings from these sources as shown by the standard deviation. The level of participation in the feasting complex is very low. The mean of 1.5 indicates a marginal helping role in feasts sponsored by bilateral kinsmen. The great majority of heads in this category take no part at all as revealed by the median score of 1.2. The standard deviation is rather high, but is exceeded by the three-generation conjugal type (col. B) and the one-generation nonconjugal type (col. E). The relatively high earnings and low feast scores of two-generation family heads suggest different patterns of consumption as compared with older heads.

The mean age of heads of *three-generation conjugally based households* (col. B) is 59.3 years, placing them in the middle-age grade. By this stage of the head's life, his eldest daughters have reached child-bearing age and the household has entered the phase of secondary expansion. The three-generation household, along with the nuclear family, is actively involved in the processes of childrearing and socialization. Indeed, we may state that a major function carried out by conjugal households is the care of dependent children since only 7.6 percent of married heads, those living in a one-generation household, play no part in childrearing. The larger average size of the three-generation type, 9.5 members as compared with 7 for the two-generation form, is consistent with the presence of multiple mothers. The standard deviation, however, reveals that the three-generation form is more variable in size.

With respect to employment, 64 percent of three-generation heads are still actively engaged in the commercial fishery or in cannery work, but their income is well below that recorded for heads of two-generation units. The median income is half that for younger men. Within this category great variability in economic performance is indicated by the standard deviation. On the other hand, as we shall see later in the chapter and in chapter 7, this household type is most active in the subsistence economy. This statement rests upon observation and verbal testimony concerning the allocation of responsibilities to dependent adult children in these units, which makes it possible for the senior pair to spend considerable time in food-fishing and berry-picking.

The comparatively high feast scores earned by heads in this category support the statement later in this volume that by late middle-age many heads have begun to take an active part in the feasting complex. It is these persons who sponsor most of the feasts, drawing upon the labor and economic resources of their large households. As we shall see (in Table 45, col. F), three of the four persons who earned the highest score of 4.0 on the feast index fell into this age grade. The median score of 3.0 reflects a high level of participation as sponsors, helpers, and guests. The mean score of 2.5 may be interpreted as evidence of widespread support for traditional cultural practices among members in this category. The standard deviation is fairly high, however.

Heads of *one-generation households* which include only the conjugal pairs (col. C) have a mean age of 65 years, reflecting the fact that in Masset this type represents the phase of replacement. Only one head in this category, a 45-year-old fisherman, had any earned income. As a member of this class, he was atypical in every respect—his age, occupation, conjugal status as a single man temporarily cohabiting with a 22-year-old girl, and his feast score of 1.0. But, since he met the basic criterion as head of a one-generation "conjugal" unit, he was of necessity included in this group.

The one-generation conjugal household is the most active in ceremonial events as revealed by the mean score of 2.8. The median score of 3.0 reflects the fact that these persons participate primarily as guests or witnesses, regularly attending feasts sponsored by others. This statement is supported by observations discussed in chapter 9. The highest score of four points on the feast index was earned by only one head in this group, a man of high rank who was able to draw on the labor and financial resources of an unusually cohesive bilateral kin group. Other heads in the senior age grade can no longer rely on massive support from children and siblings living in separate households. Since they depend upon pensions and have no adult dependents to share the burden, their resources are inadequate to the sponsorship of major ceremonial events.

This pattern of feast participation tends to be continued by persons who become widowed (col. D). Heads of *two-* and *three-generation ex-conjugal households* have a mean feast score of 2.6 and median score of 3.0, signifying regular attendance at feasts as guests and helpers. The economic limitations described for heads of three-generation households apply even more stringently to these persons who are older as shown by the median age. The mean age is skewed by the inclusion of two female single heads of 38 and 40 years, who, incidentally, participate to some extent in feasts despite their young ages. This fact accounts for the relatively low variability in this behavior. These units are also concerned with childcare as is implicit in their structure of two and three generations' depth. Only one head had earnings, while the remainder depended upon pensions and welfare aid.

The *one-generation nonconjugal household* (col. E) is very heterogeneous in composition. This category includes six persons who live alone and 14 unmarried persons who share five other households. Heads tend to be middle-aged with a mean of 57.3 years. With respect to marital status, single, separated, and widowed persons, and unmarried mothers are represented. Employed persons comprise 45 percent of the category, but there is great variation in income. With the exception of a middle-aged spinster, feast participation is absent. On the other hand, many persons in this category participate in the "party life" of the reserve along with dependent adults affiliated with three-generation households (see chapter 6).

Our analysis has measured the relative contribution made by each of four household types in the performance of three major social tasks: (1) the care and socialization of children; (2) the economic support of members of the community; and (3) the support of ceremonial activities, which reinforce community identity and solidarity.

We have found that 83 percent of households, that is, all two- and three-generation households, whether conjugal or nonconjugal, are actively involved in childrearing. Most important, of course, are the conjugal forms. Comprising 74 percent of all households, they are responsible for 93 percent of the children. The significance of this fact lies in the provision of parents or surrogate parents for the great majority of children.

The extent of participation in the cash economy varies greatly both between and within categories. Heads of two-generation conjugal and one-generation nonconjugal forms (cols. A, E) are most active, although deviation from the mean is marked. Heads of three-generation conjugal households (col. B) are somewhat active, but their productivity as measured by income is significantly lower. One-generation conjugal (col. C) and two- and three-generation ex-conjugal households (col. D) are supported almost entirely by government aid in the form of pensions and welfare funds. Subsistence activities are of greatest importance to older heads who derive little or none of their economic support from the commercial economy.

Support of the feasting complex and, by inference, of the traditional value system shows an inverse relationship to participation in commercial activities. Two-generation conjugal and one-generation nonconjugal heads who are most active in the cash economy are least involved in the ceremonial life of the village, as revealed in Table 15. On the other hand, the rowdy element, referred to as the "hell-raisers," is recruited from these two categories and from the dependents of three-generation household heads (see chapter 6).

Among active supporters of the feasting complex, the nature of participation varies with age and household structure. Sponsorship and economic support of feasts is commonly associated with heads of three-generation households who are of late middle-age, have some earned cash income, and have large households which include adult children. Heads of one-generation conjugal (col. C) and three-generation ex-conjugal households (col. D) constitute the senior age group, which must witness and thereby validate status changes of other village members. This discussion anticipates the detailed analysis of ceremonial life undertaken in chapters 8 and 9.

HAIDA FAMILY STRUCTURE

Having established that the family in different stages of development performs different functions for the social system, we may now ask whether the data reveal any structural changes which may have transformed the basic nuclear form of the modern family into another type. So far we have based our analysis primarily on the presence or absence of a conjugal pair and the number of generations. The third variable used in this delineation of household structure has been implicit in the previous analysis. Table 16 summarizes relationships of dependents to heads. Here we learn that 69 percent of village residents are members of nuclear families—the head, his spouse, sons and daughters. An additional 28 percent of all household members are other dependent children whose genealogical connections to the head will be examined in a moment. The remaining 3 percent of dependents include nine spouses of children, two widowed mothers and a wife's mother, three brothers of the head and three of the wife, and three unrelated boarders.

Because of the patterns of non-marriage and of late marriage, to be analyzed in the next chapter, Haida households include a high proportion of adult children. Of 161 sons living at home, 18 percent are 20 years or older; of 129 daughters, 15 percent are 20 years or older (cols. D,F,H). Associated with this pattern of unmarried or separated adult children remaining at home is the presence of 33 children of sons and 99 children of daughters. In addition to these 132 grandchildren, 53 other children have been assimilated into various households. These are the offspring of wives, sisters, sons' wives, and grandchildren comprising 28 percent of the village population.

To summarize Haida household composition in 1966, only 30 percent of all households consist of parents and their own offspring, while 53 percent include adopted children, grandchildren, and other relatives. Adults, married and unmarried, make up the remaining 17 percent of households.

Expansion occurs primarily in descending generations. There is little

TABLE 16
RELATIONSHIPS BY AGE OF HOUSEHOLD MEMBERS

Relationship to Household Head	0-19		20-29		30-39		40-49		50-59		60-69		70-85		Total No. % of Total	
	A	B	C	D	E	F	G	H	I	J	K	L	M	N	O	P
Head	1	1%	15	15%	16	16%	18	18%	19	20%	15	15%	16	16%	99	15%
Mate			19	26%	15	20%	12	16%	13	17%	11	14%	5	6%	76	11%
Son	131	82%	16	10%	10	6%	4	2%							161	24%
Daughter	109	85%	17	12%	2	2%	1	1%							129	19%
Wife's child	21	64%	9	27%	3	9%									33	5%
Sister's child	6	100%													6	1%
Adopted child	7	78%	1	11%			1	11%							9	1.3%
Brother							2	67%			1	33%			3	0.4%
Wife's brother			2	67%	1	33%									3	0.4%
Mother													2	100%	2	0.3%
Wife's mother													1	100%	1	0.2%
Son's wife	1	15%	5	70%	1	15%									7	1%
Daughter's husband			1	50%	1	50%									2	0.3%
Son's child	32	97%	1	3%											33	5%
Daughter's child	98	99%	1	1%											99	15%
Son's step child	3	100%													3	0.4%
Great grand child	2	100%													2	0.3%
Boarders							1	33%	1	33%	1	33%			3	0.4%
Total per age group	411	61%	87	13%	49	7%	39	6%	33	5%	28	4%	24	4%	671	100%

inclination among the elderly to live with their children as dependents; pensions enable them to maintain their own dwellings. Only three widows live with their children, while eight are heads of their own households. Nor is there any strong tendency to lateral extension with adults living with married siblings. While six men reside with a brother or a sister's husband, the majority of unmarried adults live with parents, keep house alone, or share quarters with other unattached persons. The fractional percentages of these categories of dependents as shown in Table 16 (col. P) are ample evidence of these preferences.

One cause of expansion in the household is the assimilation of premarital grandchildren. A second is the formation of dependent nuclear units with the marriage of a child. Of nine coresident children-in-law, seven were sons' wives and two were daughters' husbands. Patrilocal residence thus appears to be the norm for dependent married couples. As has been mentioned, married men attempt to set up their own households as soon as housing is available, but in no case had this occurred before the birth of several children. There is a third source of expansion. Parties to disrupted marriages return to their paternal homes or leave the reserve. As we will observe in the next chapter, few separated or widowed persons form new cohabiting unions. From the standpoint of children, however, maternal grandparents are the most likely surrogate parents.[6]

From this analysis of household composition we may conclude that the development of the three-generation household does not constitute a fundamental change in the modern family system. The so-called "extended" household is typically a nuclear family, which incorporates grandchildren and other closely related dependent minors. This category includes 90 percent of all dependents who are not members of the nuclear family of the head. We may, therefore, describe the characteristic pattern of the modern Haida as a nuclear-core family based in the overwhelming majority of cases on a single conjugal pair.

Family Roles

The key roles isolated in our analysis of household structure are those of household head and dependents, husband-wife, parent-child, grandparent-grandchild, and siblings. The most crucial aspects of these relationships will be examined briefly.

The responsibilities attached to the role of household head include providing a cash income, carrying on subsistence fishing and food gathering, helping to socialize the children, giving aid to other families

6. Few illegitimate children have ever experienced any kind of relationship with paternal grandparents.

in times of crisis, participating in reciprocal gift exchange between households, honoring matrilateral kinsmen with feasts at life-cycle events, and dealing with the Indian agent. The head's capacity to carry out these duties depends upon his age and sex and upon the composition of his household. The division of labor in Haida society, however, is not rigid and wives are expected to help in all of these duties. A forceful woman may undertake to deal with the Indian agent, for example, even when she lets her husband take the lead in other matters. In 1966 the relationship with the agent was still a crucial one: not only did he administer the relief funds, which are a major source of family income, but he had to be consulted about housing, schooling, and other benefits.

All informants agreed that the man is the "leader" or "boss" of the household, but as one 14-year-old girl wrote in a home economics exam, "In some families it is the ladies who are the leaders. It usually depends upon who has the strongest tongue or rather who knows the most." When asked who makes the decisions, who has charge of the children, and who enforces the rules, the consensus was "both mother and father" or "husband and wife." Certainly Haida women are not submissive or dependent. They are expected to earn cash by working in the cannery and most of them do so at some time in their lives. In subsistence activities such as food-fishing and berry-picking they work as a team with their husbands. In addition to caring for the children, managing the household, and participating in every phase of the economy, women take the lead in community projects and in the political activities of the shoreworkers' union. Yet female informants would not agree with my remark that women seem to be the "boss" of the household.

The Conjugal Relationship. For both sexes marriage entails a drastic redefinition of roles. An unmarried man who has fathered children recognizes no responsibility to them or to their mothers. Economically, he is a free agent with the right to spend his earnings as he wishes. He is not required to contribute to the support of his family of orientation although he is expected to make generous gifts to parents and siblings. Since unmarried men commonly find employment in fishing, logging, and construction work away from the reserve, their status while living in the parental household, even for extended periods, is that of visitor and they are assigned no specific tasks.

Unmarried women enjoy no such freedom. Employment opportunities for young women living on the reserve are scarce since older women have first access to jobs in the cannery. In 1966 only one girl had a steady job clerking in the New Masset Co-op store. The few women who have learned vocational skills such as practical nursing and hairdressing have left the reserve permanently. Others with no such skills may drift off to the cities in search of employment, but those who do not enter common-law unions "outside" eventually return to the village. While they remain in the parental household they are expected to perform a large share of domestic chores. Unmarried mothers are fully responsible for the care of their own children and for younger siblings as well. When their parents sponsor feasts or support the ceremonies of others, it is the adult daughters who perform much of the cooking, cleaning, and serving. If parents wish to go out in the evening to feasts, club meetings, or other social events, it is the daughters who remain at home with the children. When middle-aged couples go food-fishing up the inlet, the daughters maintain the household in their absence. Their recreation consists in joining the "party life" of the reserve.

With marriage a man's freedom is restricted while a woman for the first time assumes a more independent role. Small wonder that marital relationships are turbulent in the early years. Many men continue to seek the company of the peer group, drinking, "running around," and beating their wives if they complain. Their participation in occupations such as fishing and logging, which require long absences from home, reinforces the pattern of male companionship during their twenties and thirties. As they grow older, men become less active in the work force until, by late middle-age, they seem to go about almost constantly in the company of their wives. By this age the stresses that buffet the marital relationship have been counterbalanced by the necessity for teamwork in carrying out household and community responsibilities. On the interpersonal level, the myth of the dominant male, so swaggeringly asserted during the early years of marriage, has become a transparent fiction affectionately propped up by the insistence of wives and children that "the man is the boss of the family."

For persons whose marriages do not survive these stresses there appears to be little public censure. Clearly, people's attitudes concerning the value of preserving marital relationships have changed. In the words of one middle-aged informant, "In the old days they wouldn't let a marriage break up. Now there is no law to force people to stay together. If a woman is mistreated she doesn't have to stay. In the old days she had to put up with it." I heard of no recent cases where family pressure was exerted to keep a couple together. On the contrary, many mothers are willing to take their daughters in when the latter have quarreled with or separated from their husbands. Even a woman without close relatives can always find temporary refuge in the home of a neighbor.

Parent-Child and Sibling Relations. In large families there is usually a great range in age between the oldest and youngest children of a marital pair. In three-generation households, mother and daughter often have infants of the same age. Fairly typical of this type is the family of William Barnes, who was 55 in 1966, and his 45-year-old wife Mary Ellen, whose living children include five daughters and three sons. At that time the household included eight children ranging from 3 to 19 years, Mary Ellen's 78-year-old mother, the boyfriend and two infants of the oldest resident daughter, and the premarital child of a married daughter. Two bachelor sons, 29 and 27 years old, also lived at home when they were not working away from the reserve.

All members of such households are mobilized as a work force in shopping, preparing meals, washing dishes, cleaning, preserving foods and playing the role of host. A visitor in the Barnes' household in 1966 observes that Mary Ellen does the shopping, accompanied by one or more of her older children. Her mother cooks the main dishes—the stews, chowders, and meats—but no longer bakes. Mary Ellen and two adolescent daughters bake cookies, cakes, and pies almost daily, and bread every other day. Since the water system had not yet been installed in the village, there is no sink. Dishes are washed in a dishpan on the big kitchen table and dried by several of the younger children. Cleaning with mop and broom is a chore performed by Mary Ellen and her daughters. With several small children in the household, clothes have to be washed three or more times each week, which means that water is hauled in buckets from the standpipe on the street and heated in boilers on the stove. The task of fetching water falls to the young boys and girls if they are home from school. Taking the big garbage cans down to the beach, emptying them, and washing them out is another chore assigned to boys. Sons also help their father cut wood for the stove in the living room; when they are older, they may go fishing with him.

Within the family grouping, as has been mentioned, the unmarried mother and her children constitute a separate unit, but only with respect to childcare. Grandmothers do not take care of their grandchildren when their daughters are present, though they may help out by washing diapers when the young women are working in the cannery. Young uncles and aunts play with the babies, scold and watch them, but if they cry or need attention, their mother is called. In the Barnes' household where there were seven "regulars" of 12 years and younger, there never seemed to be any quarreling among the children. This was true even when the eight children of the married daughters were visiting in the house.

There is always an older child or adult available to prepare a snack for a child or to comfort him. Rigorous schedules are not imposed for mealtimes or bedtimes. Babies are allowed to stay up until they become sleepy even though this may be midnight. As they drowse off on floor or sofa, someone, often their grandfather, carries them up to bed.

In two-generation households a woman with several small children and no adult relatives to help her finds that keeping house exhausts her time and energy. If she must work in the cannery, household tasks either fall upon older children or are neglected. Parents sometimes keep children home from school to watch younger siblings or to help with the work.

Parents express no preference for either boys or girls. Although women claim that they try to treat all of their children equally, girls frequently remark that "boys are treated like kings." They are believed to have more privileges and freedom with less work to do. This feeling stems at least in part from the fact that the burden of domestic tasks and child care falls upon girls.

If daughters have heavy household responsibilities, it appears that sons feel a different kind of obligation. It is not unusual for adult sons who are economically independent to make generous gifts to other members of the family, especially to parents and sisters. Gifts to parents include such items as television sets, washing machines, freezers, clothing, and large sums of cash to be spent for a holiday on the mainland. Instances were recorded of brothers buying clothing and household goods for sisters who were being married or were pregnant.

Mildred's oldest son had made a large contribution to the expenses of his youngest sister's elaborate wedding. At the time of my visit with his mother he had just bought "a lovely maternity outfit" for the same sister. Gift-giving is evidence of a close tie between brothers and sisters, which may be recognized at milestones of the life cycle—weddings, pregnancy, and death. Observance of this bond is not obligatory and Mildred's sons had not made any special gestures for the weddings of their other sisters; however, as Mildred said, "they were willing to treat their youngest sister royally for the first year." She explained that "brothers don't want people to look down on their sisters so they give them property to boost their standing. If a girl's family is afraid her husband's people won't accept her as an equal, they will give her property. Brothers-in-law of chiefs used to do this for their sisters." The brothers' behavior assumed greater significance in light of the fact that Mildred's daughter had married the son of a prominent lineage head. Other instances were recorded of brothers buying clothes and gifts for sisters. When Mary Ellen's daughter Rosalie lost an infant child in a house fire, her brothers bought the small white coffin, paid the funeral expenses, and donated $200 worth of clothing for the two surviving little girls.[7] Younger siblings also receive treats such as holiday trips to the mainland from older brothers. These gifts are not reciprocated in kind, but seem to be expected from relatively affluent members as a kind of payment for their place in the household.

Thus far we have discussed relations between family members as they concern cooperation in maintaining the household and in expressing affect through nurturant behavior and gift giving. Family solidarity is further enhanced by the sharing of pleasurable activities although household members tend to seek out others of their own ages for recreational pursuits. Various voluntary associations, which crosscut the kin groups, have been formed from time to time for special purposes. The feasts and parties which mark life-cycle events are adult affairs. Nevertheless, there are numerous occasions for sociability, which are observed by the family and related households. The most informal and frequent types consist of watching television and visiting. Friends of any member of the household may drop in to spend the evening. Refreshments are served and conversations go on until very late. In many cases mothers and married daughters visit almost daily. Young couples enjoy after-dinner coffee at the homes of parents or siblings. Often older relatives—siblings or cousins of grandparents—are included in the group. For special occasions, such as a child's birthday, outings are planned. Picnics and swimming at Pure Lake about 15 miles away are enjoyed when someone can be found to drive the family out and back for a small payment. Short trips in the family motorboat are a special treat for children who have no opportunity to go to fish camp or to leave the islands. Family holidays, such as Christmas, Easter, anniversaries, and the like, are celebrated with a big dinner at home.

In sum, relationships between adults and children of all ages appear to be very warm and affectionate. The bond between a child and its father may be especially close but in the absence of a father, grandfathers and uncles provide warm support. Since 93 percent of the children live in homes which include a conjugal pair, it is usually possible for a child to relate to a parent figure of each sex. In many cases where parents are absent, grandparents say that they have "adopted" their grandchildren. That is, they have assumed specifically parental responsibilities which are far more comprehensive than those of the grandparent role. Thus, the flexibility of family structure and its capacity to absorb extra members compensate to some extent for the

---

7. It is tempting to see the shadow of the mother's brother here, but I have not a shred of evidence that the Haidas share such a perception.

failure of many parents, married and unmarried, to perform their roles adequately.

The persistence of close affective ties between parents and children is expressed structurally in the linking of households, which has also been referred to as the bilateral circle. Links between siblings, who are apparently regarded as co-children of the same parents rather than as lineage mates, are strongest while at least one of the siblings remains in the parental household. After the death of their parents, interaction between married siblings living in separate households often diminishes to the point where we can no longer speak of the unity of the sibling group. We will find an illustration of this point when we discuss the lack of cooperation in his ceremonial activities by the siblings of Peter Jones (chapter 9). Where brothers and sisters are close, however, their relationship seems to endure, at least while the man remains unmarried.

Structural features of modern Haida family organization include an emphasis on the conjugal bond and the development of paternal authority. As a result of continuing changes in economic and social relations with Canadian society, a new pattern has emerged with the development of the three-generation family. Since its size and activities are not limited by the earning power and subsistence level of its members, the three-generation household must be seen as an adaptation to other economic possibilities, namely the provision of welfare funds and foster home payments by the external society. Because the contemporary "extended" family does not differ substantially from the simple nuclear family in the exercise of paternal authority, in rights and obligations of family members, and in its independence of action, we have described the modern family system as one based on a nuclear core.

Chapter 6
Marriage and Mating

IN PRECEDING CHAPTERS we have examined external political and economic relations to learn of their consequences for the structure of Haida society. We have analyzed their effects on the organization of the nuclear family, which has emerged as the basic social and economic unit, replacing the corporate matrilineage. In following chapters we enquire about the effects of these changes on what remains of Haida culture to see how the people carry on traditional behaviors that express traditional norms and values.

Here we will focus on the area of relationships where change has its greatest impact on the individual—in sex and marriage. We have already seen how the structure of the family responds to changes in mating behavior as to economic pressures and possibilities. Now we shall discover how sensitively mating behavior reflects social and economic conditions which are experienced by the individual in the quality of his contacts with the dominant society. Since these experiences are normally shared by all persons of similar ages, the grouping that acts as a source of attitudes is the age grade. The available data allow us to break the age grades, spanning roughly 15 years, into five-year cohorts, which are even more sensitive indicators. For in studying mating patterns we are not limited to narrative description of observed or reported behavior. Demographic analysis enables us to consider the whole population over an extended period of time during which we may observe and account for fluctuations in behavior.[1]

1. The demographic analysis presented in this volume is to be regarded as a preliminary report of a much more comprehensive study of the population history of the Masset Haida. For some topics, which it might be desirable to discuss, results are not yet available. In the interest of encouraging comparative work as well as of documenting my arguments, detailed data and methodological commentary are included in this chapter. For techniques of analysis Barclay (1958), Cox (1970), and McArthur (1961) were especially helpful. For ideas and methods of collecting and interpreting data I have drawn heavily upon the work of the Cambridge Group for the History of Population and Social

What we find in Masset in the 1960s and 1970s is a pattern which supports the contemporary norms of marrying for love and self-selection of spouses through dating. Since the dating complex entails mating behavior, the great majority of girls give birth to one or two children before marrying in their early twenties. Premarital children are usually left with the grandparents, contributing to the development of the three-generation family. This pattern contrasts sharply with the traditional institution of arranged, exogamous marriage. While this form is no longer supported by the social structure, the old normative ideas espoused by the elders are not entirely without force. Nor have the changes been as sweeping as the Haida themselves believe. For girls born between 1870 and 1959 we find remarkable continuity in such measures as age at first marriage, age at first birth, relative ages of spouses, completed family size, and what appears to be a persisting prohibition of lineage endogamy.

The unit of analysis must be the band, which is the closed, enduring corporate group. The village, which is the field of most intensive interaction and therefore the significant cultural group, is relatively flexible in composition, its membership fluctuating somewhat from season to season and from year to year. Were it not for the fact that the vital events of birth, death, and marriage are recorded for the band as a whole, it would be impossible to keep up with individuals when they are away from the reserve.[2]

MARITAL STATUS

Analysis of the family system in the last chapter emphasized the structural importance of marriage as the foundation of the major social grouping and as the criterion of adulthood for both males and females. Despite this importance, however, inspection of Table 17 shows us that a high proportion of Masset band members was not involved in marital relationships in 1966.

In a population of 967 persons there were 98 married pairs, 78 of whom lived on the reserve. That is, only 47 percent of men 20 years and older (col. B, last row) and 42 percent of women 15 years and over were married and living with a spouse (col. H). A further 10 percent of men (cols. C,D) and 16 percent of women (cols. I,J) were formerly married. Consensual unions, which are considered as a functional

Structure, especially Anderson (1971), Armstrong (1966), Eversley (1966), Glass and Eversley (1965), Laslett (1966, 1971, 1972), Wrigley (1966a, 1966b). An important work in this field is Hollingsworth (1969). A book that appeared after this chapter was written, but that would be very useful to anyone contemplating work in historical demography, is Macfarlane (1977).

2. The difference between "village" and "band" was explained on p. 17.

equivalent of marriage in our analysis of family structure, involved only 3 percent of men and 10 percent of women. Of considerable interest is the proportion of adults who were not married in 1966: 43 percent of men (col. A) and 42 percent of women (cols. F,G, last row). Half of these single women had never borne a child while the remainder were unwed mothers.

Consensual Unions

Because consensual unions are classified with formal marriages as "conjugal units" in this study and because considerable attention will be given to extraresidential mating, the frequencies of coresidential arrangements are tabulated in Table 18. Significantly, only about one quarter of formerly married women have entered common-law unions. The same is true of unwed mothers. Of the 23 cases of non-married but cohabiting women identified in Table 18 (col. A), only seven were living on the reserve. Seven other women lived with white men in New Masset, continuing to interact to some extent with relatives in the community. The other nine unions were established with non-Haidas in the cities.

Informants make a terminological distinction between legal marriage and unions where one partner "lives with" or "stays with" the other. Common-law arrangements do not seem to be a phase of an institutionalized sequence leading from dating to keeping house to marriage and the establishment of a family. It appears rather that couples intending to cohabit marry unless there is a legal impediment such as a living spouse. Of the seven common-law unions existing on the reserve in 1966, the female partners in four cases were separated from their spouses. Another case involved a widow whose husband had not been declared legally dead. In only two instances were both partners unmarried. In helping to compile household composition lists, middle-aged women remarked of these two latter cases, "Why don't they get married?" "It's about time they were getting married," and "It's funny they haven't gotten married yet." It seems likely that considerable social pressure is brought to bear against unmarried cohabiting pairs. Of the five cases where couples were not able to marry informants said, "It's just like they were married."

Age and Marriage

The significance of age at first marriage in demographic studies rests on the assumption that marriage performs the function of regulating sex activities or, at least, reproduction. A woman's age at first mar-

TABLE 17

AGE, SEX, AND MARITAL STATUS OF MASSET BAND MEMBERS, 1966

	Males					Females					
	Single	Married	Sep.	Wid.	Total	Single	Unwed Mothers	Married	Sep.	Wid.	Total
	A	B	C	D	E	F	G	H	I	J	K
0–4	103 100%				103 20%	96 100%					96 21%
5–9	105 100%				105 20%	78 100%					78 17%
10–14	54 100%				54 11%	51 100%					51 11%
15–19	39 100%				39 8%	36 77%	8 17%	3 6%			47 10%
20–24	34 94%	2 6%			36 7%	7 16%	19 40%	19 40%	1 2%	1 2%	47 10%
25–29	23 51%	21 47%	1 2%		45 9%	2 8%	5 19%	14 54%	3 11%	2 8%	26 6%
30–34	9 39%	10 44%	4 17%		23 4.5%	2 9.5%	7 33%	9 43%	1 5%	2 9.5%	21 5%
35–39	7 30%	14 61%	2 9%		23 4.5%	0	4 22%	8 45%	2 11%	4 22%	18 4%
40–44	3 20%	10 67%	2 13%		15 3%	0	3 19%	7 43%	3 19%	3 19%	16 3.5%
45–49	5 31%	7 44%	4 25%		16 3%	2 20%	0	7 70%	1 10%	0	10 2%
50–54	3 25%	8 67%	0	1 8%	12 2.3%	0	0	6 75%	1 12.5%	1 12.5%	8 1.8%
55–59	2 22%	6 67%	0	1 11%	9 2%	0	1 10%	8 80%	1 10%	0	10 2%

Age	A	B	C	D	E	F	G	H	I	J	K
60–64	1 / 10%	8 / 80%	0	1 / 10%	10 / 2%	0	0	11 / 92%	1 / 8%	0	12 / 3%
65–69	1 / 14%	4 / 58%	1 / 14%	1 / 14%	7 / 1.3%	0	0	2 / 67%	0	1 / 33%	3 / .6%
70–74	0	4 / 100%	0	0	4 / .8%	0	0	2 / 40%	1 / 20%	2 / 40%	5 / 1%
75–79	0	2 / 67%	0	1 / 33%	3 / .6%	0	1 / 14%	1 / 14%	0	5 / 72%	7 / 1.5%
80–84	1 / 25%	1 / 25%	1 / 25%	1 / 25%	4 / .8%	0	0	0	0	1 / 100%	1 / .2%
85–89	0	1 / 100%	0	0	1 / .2%	0	0	1 / 50%	0	1 / 50%	2 / .4%
Total	390 / 77%	98 / 19%	15 / 3%	6 / 1%	509 / 100%	274 / 60%	48 / 10%	98 / 22%	15 / 3%	23 / 5%	458 / 100%
% over 20 yrs (male); over 15 yrs (female)	43%	47%	7%	3%	100%	21%	21%	42%	6%	10%	100%

NOTE: Cols. A–D, F–J: percentages refer to marital status; cols. E and K: percentages refer to age group

TABLE 18
RESIDENTIAL ARRANGEMENTS BY MARITAL STATUS, MAY 1966

Female Band Members	Live with Mates		Do Not Live with Mates		Total
(15–86 years)	A	B	C	D	E
Single			49	100%	49
					21%
Married	98	100%			98
					42%
Separated	4	27%	11	73%	15
					6%
Widowed	6	26%	17	74%	23
					10%
Unwed Mothers	13	27%	35	73%	48
					21%
	121	52%	112	48%	233

riage, then, is a determinant of age at first birth and, in turn, of fertility: the longer a woman is married during the reproductive period, the more children she can be expected to produce. We have already discovered that in Masset the primary function of marriage is not the regulation of sexual activities but the establishment of a social and economic unit. As we have noted above, married status is the indicator of sociological adulthood for both males and females.

It may be inferred from Table 17 that the age at marriage is high for men. They seldom marry before the age of 25, while one third of all male band members over that age in 1966 were still single (cols. B, A).[3] In comparing men resident in the village with the larger band population we find almost identical proportions of married (46 and 47 percent respectively; see col. B, Table 19 and col. B, Table 17) and formerly married (9 and 10 percent; see col. C, Table 19 and cols. C, D, Table 17). Again, about a third of all men 25 years and older are single. However, 69 percent of villagers in the 25-29-year age group are or have been married (Table 19, cols. B, C), compared with 49 percent in the larger unit (Table 17, cols. B, C). Since the numbers of individuals involved are so small it makes more sense perhaps to state that 17 of the 21 married men 25–29 years (81 percent) live on the reserve while the remainder are permanently settled "away." On the other hand, 74

3. For a comparison of the ages at first marriage of males and females living in the village in 1966, see Stearns 1973:219. For comparative data for Indian and non-Indian populations of British Columbia, see Stanbury 1975:90–93.

percent of the single men in that age group were away temporarily or otherwise at the time of the household census in May 1966.

Table 17, which reveals that only 42 percent of female band members are married (col. H), deserves further scrutiny. When our perspective is narrowed to women in the reproductively active age group of 15–44, we find that only 34 percent are living with a spouse (calculated from

TABLE 19
MARITAL STATUS OF MALE VILLAGERS, 1966

Age	Never Married A	Married B	Formerly Married C	Total D
15–19	27			27
	100%			16%
20–24	18	1		19
	95%	5%		11%
25–29	8	17	1	26
	31%	65%	4%	15%
30–34	6	6	1	13
	46%	46%	8%	8%
35–39	4	10	2	16
	25%	63%	12%	9%
40–44	3	6	1	10
	30%	60%	10%	6%
45–49	5	6	2	13
	39%	46%	15%	8%
50–54	3	9		12
	25%	75%		7%
55–59	1	4	1	6
	17%	66%	17%	4%
60–64		9	1	10
		90%	10%	6%
65–69	1	4	2	7
	14%	58%	28%	4%
70–74		2		2
		100%		1%
75–79		2	1	3
		67%	33%	2%
80–86		2	2	4
		50%	50%	3%
Total	76	78	14	168
	45%	46%	9%	100%

NOTE: Cols. A–C: percentages refer to marital status.

col. H). An additional 13 percent were formerly married (from cols. I, J). Single women comprise 26 percent (col. F), while unwed mothers constitute 22 percent (col. G) of those 15 to 44.

When we analyze the five-year age-cohorts within the reproductive span we note that 6 percent of women 15–19 years are married (col. H) but 17 percent have borne illegitimate children (col. G). In the next cohort 44 percent are or have been married (cols. H, I, J) while 40 percent are unwed mothers (col. G). At this point there is a shift. Between the ages of 25 and 29 the proportion of ever-married women jumps to 73 percent while unmarried mothers fall to 19 percent. These data raise some interesting questions which will be dealt with at length in this chapter: What proportion of unwed mothers marry and at what ages? How many women who appear in this table as married gave birth to premarital children? More immediately, how are these categories distributed as to residence on or off the reserve?

To answer the last question first, Table 20 indicates that on the reserve the proportion of married women rises to 53 percent of adult females (col. C), although but 44 percent of those in the reproductively active range are married. From another perspective, 80 percent of married women 15 to 44 live in the community. On the other hand, about half the non-married are absent, including 55 percent of unwed mothers, 50 percent of the separated and widowed, and 55 percent of single women. In age, the female absentees parallel the males, most of them falling in the young adults grouping.

BIRTH STATUS

Obviously the most significant consequence of a situation where fewer than half of the adults are living with a spouse is a high rate of illegitimacy. If, when pregnancy results, the father can be identified, he may acknowledge paternity so that the child can be legally registered as a band member. This entails no social obligations to the child or its mother. Only when the parents are living in a common-law relationship does the man contribute to the child's support. Actually his acknowledgment of paternity is not required, for unless there is sufficient evidence that the father is not of Indian status, the child is automatically registered under its mother's band number. Occasionally an attachment will stabilize and the couple may live common-law until one or both reaches the legal age for marriage. This practice was more common in the past than at present. The process of legitimizing the birth of a child born before its parents marry is not automatic but has to be referred to the Indian Commissioner for action.

Data presented in Tables 21, 22, and 23 were drawn from the official birth register kept in the office of the Queen Charlotte Indian Agency, which I was permitted to consult during the summer of 1962 and the year 1965–66. Recorded in this register are the names of parents, their racial origin, band membership, birthplace, age and occupation, marital status, and place of residence at the time of birth. For the child, name, place and date of birth, sex, weight, and rank order of birth are

TABLE 20
MARITAL STATUS OF FEMALE VILLAGERS, 1966

Age	Never Married No Children A	Never Married Unwed Mothers B	Married C	Formerly Married D	Total E
15–19	21	4	3		28
	75%	14%	11%		19%
20–24	4	10	13	2	29
	14%	35%	45%	6%	20%
25–29	1	2	9	1	13
	8%	15%	69%	8%	9%
30–34		3	7	1	11
		27%	64%	9%	7.5%
35–39		1	7	1	9
		11%	78%	11%	6%
40–44		1	4	2	7
		14%	58%	28%	5%
45–49	1		7	1	9
	11%		78%	11%	6%
50–54			6		6
			100%		4.5%
55–59			8		8
			100%		5.5%
60–64			8		8
			100%		5.5%
65–69			2	1	3
			67%	33%	2%
70–74			2	4	6
			33%	67%	4%
75–79		1	1	4	6
		16%	16%	68%	4%
80–86			1	2	3
			33%	67%	2%
Total	27	22	78	19	146
	19%	15%	53%	13%	100%

NOTE: Percentages refer to marital status.

TABLE 21
ILLEGITIMATE BIRTHS IN MASSET BAND, 1920–64

Years of Birth	Total Births A	Illegitimate Births B	Ratio per 1000 Births C
1920–24	82	12	146
1925–29	77	10	129
1930–34	96	14	145
1935–39	108	22	203
1940–44	120	24	200
1945–49	127	30	236
1950–54	137	48	350
1955–59	171	52	304
1960–64	238	103	432
Total	1,156	315	Mean=272

given. For the mother, length of pregnancy and number of live births and living children are noted. This wealth of information makes possible the detailed analysis of reproductive behavior, which is drawn upon for this study. Little confidence can be placed in these records before 1917, and I was not able to gain access to them after 1966. Other, supplementary, sources were used as described in context.[4]

Table 21 summarizes births into the Masset band from 1920 through 1964; a ratio is computed to show the proportion of illegitimate births per 1,000 births (col. C). The most striking feature of this table is the dramatic increase in the rates since 1950. Illegitimate children accounted for 14 percent of all births in the 15 years between 1920–34, increasing to 21 percent in the next 15 years and 37 percent in the period 1950–64. In 1965, 52 percent of all births were illegitimate.

But Table 21 also reveals that, in spite of informant testimony to the contrary, there was a steady rate of illegitimacy in earlier decades. We saw in chapter 3 that up until World War II, ministers and Indian agents made strenuous efforts to regulate the mating activities of native people. Cohabitation without marriage was forbidden and prosecuted. In spite of their diligence, however, a few women living in stable

4. I have not yet reconstructed the total Masset population for the early years since this requires data on mortality as well as natality. Reliable death data have been exceedingly difficult to obtain. I cannot therefore offer any of the conventional crude rates at this time. Estimates of vital rates for the Canadian Indian population are presented in Romaniuk and Piché (1972) and Piché and George (1973). Stanbury discusses recent demographic trends for B.C. Indians (1975:82–106), describing vital rates on pp. 82–88; illegitimacy is considered on pp. 88–90.

TABLE 22

ILLEGITIMATE CHILDREN BORN IN COMMON-LAW UNIONS, 1959–66

Age of Mother at Time of Birth	Rank Order of Births										Total Births	
	1	2	3	4	5	6	7	8	9	10		
	A	B	C	D	E	F	G	H	I	J	K	L
15–19 years	2										2	4%
20–24	1	3	4	2	2						12	24%
25–29	2	1	1	4	3	2	2	1			16	32%
30–34				1	1	2	4	1	2		11	22%
35–39				2	1		1	1	1	3	9	18%
40–44												
Total	5	4	5	9	7	4	7	3	3	3	50	
	10%	8%	10%	18%	14%	8%	14%	6%	6%	6%	100%	

TABLE 23

ILLEGITIMATE CHILDREN BORN IN NON-RESIDENTIAL RELATIONSHIPS, 1959–66

Age of Mother at Time of Birth	Rank Order of Births									Total Births	
	1	2	3	4	5	6	7	8	9		
	A	B	C	D	E	F	G	H	I	J	K
14 years	1									1	1%
15–19	35	16	2							53	52%
20–24	6	8	7	6	2	1		1	1	32	32%
25–29		2			3		1	1		7	7%
30–34		1		1			1	1		4	4%
35–39									2	3	3%
40–44					1					1	1%
Total	42	27	9	7	6	2	2	3	3	101	
	42%	27%	9%	7%	5%	2%	2%	3%	3%	100%	

common-law unions regularly gave birth to technically illegitimate children. Occasionally young couples whose relatives opposed their marriage, especially when it violated the rule of exogamy, produced offspring before they were finally permitted to marry.

The rapid increase in illegitimacy in recent decades is associated with an important change in patterns of extramarital mating. The majority of illegitimate children are no longer born to women living in common-law relationships, but are the product of random mating in casual unions. This statement is supported by an analysis of marital status and residence of parents of children born during the years 1959 to 1966. During this period, 151 of 306 births, or 49 percent, were illegitimate.[5] Only one-third of these 151 children were born of a common-law union where they could expect to enjoy a stable relationship with a parent of each sex. The remaining two-thirds were born to young women still living at home with their parents. We have explained the emergence of the three-generation family as a response to this situation.

These two types of mating relationships of unwed mothers—common-law and nonresidential—are analyzed in Tables 22 and 23, in which the age of mothers is cross-tabulated with rank order of births. Since the data refer to births, some mothers are represented in the tables by more than one child. In the next section we shift our focus from births to mothers.

Table 22 summarizes data for children born of coresident parents. Only 10 percent are firstborn (col. A). Some young girls marry the father of their child, but many do not, as is indicated by the numbers of secondborn and later children of mothers in both categories. In Table 23, which is concerned with children born of casual or nonresidential mating relationships, 42 percent are firstborn (col. A), 27 percent secondborn (col. B), while roughly 31 percent are later children.

The tables show considerable differences in the ages of mothers in the two categories. Approximately 53 percent of all children of casual matings were born to girls 19 years or younger (col. K, Table 23) as compared to 4 percent for women in consensual unions (col. L, Table 22). The number of children produced in random mating decreases rapidly for women 25 and over, comprising only 15 percent of the total. On the other hand, 72 percent of children born to coresident parents have mothers 25 years of age and older.

Tables 22 and 23 reveal that several children of 6th, 7th, 8th, and 9th rank-order have been born to relatively young mothers (cols. F–I). The pattern of producing a child every year was noted for many women, married and unmarried, during the years covered by the tables.[6] But these tables, while they indicate the numbers of children concerned and cast some light on changes in the family system, provide few clues to the numbers of unwed mothers or to the prevalence of what I have described as a "pattern of premarital childbearing."

I have attributed this pattern to changes in mating behavior, which

5. My goal was always to obtain a 100 percent sample. As far as I could determine, this was the total number of births for these years.
6. Such matters as the spacing of births, age at last birth, and other aspects of reproductive behavior will be analyzed in the population history being prepared.

are described later in this chapter as the dating and "hell-raising" complexes. Another possibility which must not be overlooked is the physiological factor. Jane Underwood suggests that the increase in illegitimacy may reflect less a change in mating behavior than increased fecundity among younger cohorts of females. In this event "girls begin ovulating earlier, ovulate more regularly during the entire reproductive lifespan, resume ovulation after parturition more rapidly and continue ovulating to a later age" (personal communication). She finds support for this argument in Table 23 where 36 first-born illegitimate births are to girls 14–19 (plus two entered in Table 22). Sixteen second live births and two third live births are to girls 15–19. Data on girls born during the 1950s, not included in Tables 22 and 23, seem to confirm this trend (see p. 158). Additional support is provided by calculations of mean age at first birth for married and unmarried mothers born during the last hundred years (Table 25). Early returns for the oldest members of the 1960s' cohorts are inconclusive, but recent figures, received too late for inclusion in this study, indicate a continuing pattern of high illegitimacy and low age at first birth.

The studies of Rose Frisch link fecundity and nutrition in that "the onset and maintenance of regular menstrual function in the human female are each dependent on the maintenance of a minimum weight for height, apparently representing a critical fat storage" (1974; 1975:17).

Nancy Howell finds the link between nutrition and fecundity demonstrated by nonagriculturalists who are characterized by high age at menarche and low age at menopause (1976). In the Haida case some doubts may be entertained about the superiority of present levels of nutrition to the aboriginal situation. The description of food habits in the next chapter feeds these doubts.[7] An evaluation of physiological factors affecting fertility in Masset will be attempted in a future study. Meanwhile, we are warned that an explanation of reproductive behavior in social and cultural terms is incomplete.

For the present study it is possible, using birth and marriage records, to determine how many girls bear illegitimate children, the average age at first birth, and the average number of children per mother. It is a simple, if tedious, task to discover how many eventually marry and to compare their ages at first marriage with those whom I refer to, for convenience, as "virgin brides." But these methods give no indication of how many women never marry or bear children nor of those who are lost to the band through death and migration.

7. For a sophisticated analysis of nutritional levels for other B.C. and Canadian Indians, see Lee et al. 1971, and Canada, Dept. of National Health and Welfare 1975.

Cohort Reconstruction

To obtain some knowledge of these matters it was necessary to reconstruct the birth cohorts, to identify as far as possible every female born into the band during the last century. It is not as hopeless a task as might be supposed to obtain a reasonably, if not absolutely, complete record. Almost from the moment the missionaries set up housekeeping in the village they began to compile lists as well as official records of baptisms, marriages, and burials. When the Indian Department moved in, the kinds of events recorded multiplied many times. As a result, it is not only the persons with many descendants who can be traced, using genealogies. Many individuals who vanish from the record before the end of the century, leaving no close kin, can be recovered for the analysis. Of course, in the decades before 1885 we undoubtedly have only a portion of those born. Even today informants tend to forget or do not bother to mention persons who died young or left the reserve. On the other hand, anyone who took any active part in the community or who married, produced children, or died as a member of the band from the 1880s onward could not have escaped the notice of the record keepers or the recollections of their kinsmen.

Since there is no reliable count of the total population in the late nineteenth century, the cohort constructs must be built up from the histories of individuals. The first step in compiling individual histories was to sort persons according to year of birth and then to assemble all the materials available for each person—not only the official registrations, but any mention in the Indian agents' diaries, reports, and so on which place that person in a particular place at a particular time. In collating these, dates and relationships could be checked. Then, since my interest at this point is in the female population, the parents, siblings, and children of each woman were identified, a process which yielded linked sets of mother and daughters. For every female who married and/or gave birth, data were entered on a reproductive history form, which summarizes information on birth, death, and marriage, not only for the woman but for each of her spouses and all of her children.[8]

8. Age and marital status are areas where inconsistencies are most frequently found, though these are not numerous. Estimates of age on marriage records are usually very close to entries in baptismal records; however, these are probably not independent sources. An important independent check is the generation span. In compiling data on individuals from all the sources available, certain plausible attributions can be checked. Thus, children ascribed to a mother who has died as shown by headstone inscriptions, death records, or remarriage records can be identified and reassigned. The most frequent errors are those where a man or woman is given a birth year only twelve or so years earlier than his or her eldest child. In the case of women the reproductive span is a great landmark. I have used the age of sixteen as the onset of reproduction because, in early cases where the data are firm, birth seldom occurs before this. Very recently births to

TABLE 24
CÒHORT RECONSTRUCTION: FEMALE BIRTHS, 1885–1974

Birth-Year Cohorts	No. Born into Cohort A	Single B	Dead Before Marriage or Childbirth C	Unaccounted For D	Married and/or Mothers E
1885–89	41	?	41%	18%	41%
1890–94	41	?	41%	20%	39%
1895–99	47	?	15%	45%	40%
1900–04	31	?	23%	19%	58%
1905–09	42	?	17%	38%	45%
1910–14	39	3%	38%	23%	36%
1915–19	45	?	47%	9%	44%
1920–24	52	?	48%	9%	43%
1925–29	51	?	31%	8%	61%
1930–34	57	?	38%	19%	43%
1935–39	50	8%	30%	8%	54%
1940–44	59	9%	12%	10%	69%
1945–49	68	10%	21%		69%
1950–54	69	23%	12%	9%	56%
1955–59	92	46%	11%		43%
1960–64	107	94%	5%	1%	
1965–69	76	88%	8%	4%	
1970–74	67	92%	6%	2%	
Total	1,034	29.5%	21.5%	11%	38%

Thus, every child whose birth or existence was noted in church, agency, school, hospital, or other records has been entered on his mother's form and can be retrieved for a tabulation of birth-year cohorts. A card was made for every female birth noting name, mother's name and dates of her birth, birth of first child, first marriage, and death. In this way about 1,200 female births were tallied for the years 1850 to 1976. The process will be repeated for males later when my focus shifts from reproductive histories to other demographic questions.

The results of this exercise in cohort reconstruction are presented in Table 24. Because most of the data for women born before 1885 refer only to survivors—married women and mothers—early cohorts are not included here where our interest is in estimating the total number of

15-year-old girls have become more numerous. The age of 44 appears to mark the end of the reproductive period. An example of the method of handling these data appears in the text under the discussion of traditional marriage. My analysis of reproductive histories owes much to Wrigley 1966b.

female births. The category "Single" (col. B, Table 24) applies only to women who are known never to have married or borne children. Doubtful cases are entered in column D. Similarly, "Dead before Marriage or Childbirth" means known dead (col. C). Where death is presumed but no clear evidence exists, persons are allotted to column D. "Unaccounted for" also includes those who have become enfranchised or who are living elsewhere with no information available on their activities. Women in the latter category have played no part in community life or in band affairs and thus the lack of data does not affect the analysis. It is those persons classified in column E, Table 24, who are included in our study of marriage and motherhood. We turn to detailed examination of this segment of the population in Table 26.

Table 24 indicates, insofar as can be determined at present, the number of females born into each five-year cohort (col. A). A notable feature is the "baby boom," which occurred during the decade 1955–64. The sharp increase in the number of births (of which only the females are shown here), was accompanied by a gradual decrease in mean age at first birth among girls born from 1935 to 1949. The mean age was 19.4 for married women and 18.3 for unwed girls according to calculations made on Table 25. The impact on the family system of this sudden flood of babies, almost half of them illegitimate, was discussed in chapter 5. The psychological impact was also considerable. The general expectation was that the trend would continue and perhaps accelerate. Although no one, myself included, realized it at the time, the tide was already turning. The high point of 53 male and female births for one year was reached in 1963. When the total dropped to 29 in 1965 I suspected an error in the records, but exhaustive checking in the field revealed no unreported births.[9] In 1966, 26 males and females were born during the first six months of the year.

The apparent decline in the birth rate since 1963 is certainly not due to a rise in age at first birth, as Table 25 shows. The mean age at first birth for unmarried girls born in the 1950s has dropped to 17.5 and below (col. B). Of course, this mean will be raised somewhat when the remaining single girls in those cohorts bear children. It would be rash at this point to suggest that the age at first birth may soon begin to rise again. But it is noteworthy that none of the girls born in the 1960s had produced a child as of December 1976 although 34 had passed their fifteenth birthday and 16 their sixteenth. Of girls born in the 1950s, however, seven 16-year-olds, ten 15-year-olds, one 14-year-old and

9. Total male and female births for single years 1955–65: 30, 27, 40, 35, 39, 44, 44, 47, 53, 50, 29. My tabulations for 1966 ended in mid-year when the agency closed. I will return to this matter in another publication when I have been able to check recent data for completeness.

TABLE 25
AGE AT FIRST BIRTH FOR BRIDES AND UNWED MOTHERS, 1870–1959

Birth Cohort	Mean Age, Brides A	Mean Age, Unweds B	Mean Difference in Years C
1870–74	20.2	21.0	.8
1875–79	17.5	18.0	.5
1880–84	19.3	17.0	2.3
1885–89	20.4	19.3	1.1
1890–94	18.8	19.4	.6
1895–99	18.9	21.4	2.5
1900–04	22.1	20.3	1.8
1905–09	19.8	20.5	.7
1910–14	21.8	20.0	1.8
1915–19	21.3	20.2	1.1
1920–24	21.0	18.2	2.8
1925–29	19.9	19.4	.5
1930–34	*	19.1	*
1935–39	19.2	18.8	.4
1940–44	19.5	17.8	1.7
1945–49	19.5	18.3	1.2
1950–54	18.9	17.5	1.4
1955–59	18.0	17.1	.9
	19.7	19.0	.7

*Data insufficient to produce a valid result.

one 13-year-old had produced babies (i.e., 14 percent of the females in their cohorts surviving to 15 years). The social context for this behavior will be examined below.

If girls born in the 1950s were beginning childbearing at an earlier age, women of their mothers' generation were terminating their reproductive activities at a younger age as well. This point, which will be documented in a later study, is mentioned as the probable explanation for the declining numbers of births.

The essential point illustrated by Table 24 is that only 51 percent of girls born in the years 1895 to 1959 ever married or bore children. Leaving aside those born 1960 to 1974, most of whom have not reached reproductive ages, 26 percent of all females died before the age of 15. An undetermined number of those unaccounted for (col. D) would be added to these if the data were complete. The epidemics of 1918 and 1922 took a heavy toll of adolescents and adults, but congenital weaknesses, tuberculosis, and other respiratory diseases thinned the ranks of almost every cohort up to 1940. Only one third of the women who survived to become wives and mothers reached their fortieth year.

Marital Status at First Birth

Focusing now on the 51 percent of Masset females who have occupied the roles of wife and mother (col. E, Table 24), we may return to the questions raised earlier: What proportion of girls marry before childbearing and at what ages? How many become unwed mothers? How many of these later marry, and after how many children? How many unwed mothers never marry?

Table 26, which includes inmarrying women with survivors of birth cohorts, shows the relative proportions of "virgin brides" and unwed mothers. These data demonstrate the development of a strong pattern of premarital childbearing. We may use this term because, as we shall see in a moment, the great majority of unwed mothers eventually marry. The numbers of women who have premarital children have increased sharply in recent decades, exceeding the numbers of married mothers in all but one cohort since 1915 (cols. F, G). In the 1955 cohort, whose members were 17–21 years in 1976, 40 percent of all those surviving to 15 years had already given birth to illegitimate children. In the 1950 cohort, 43 percent of all girls aged 22–26 years had illegitimate children. When we omit single girls from the calculations, we find that a high percentage have become mothers before they have become wives—64 percent of the 1950 cohort and 82 percent of the 1955 group (col. G, Table 26). Virtually all of these births were the result of nonresidential mating associated with the dating complex. These girls were, of course, too young to be represented in Table 23, though the immediately preceding cohorts were not.

The dimensions of this pattern are sketched by data summarized in Table 27, where we may study the behavior of each cohort with respect to numbers of girls involved, mean age at first birth, and mean number of illegitimate children. Any conclusions about the behavior of the 1950–59 cohorts are tentative: 23 percent and 46 percent, respectively, were still single in December 1976 (col. B, Table 24). All the averages for these two groups will change as time goes on; however, the situation for all earlier cohorts has stabilized. The youngest members of the 1945–49 cohort were 27 years old in 1976, well beyond the mean ages at first birth and first marriage.

Table 27 shows that while the percentages of unmarried mothers have steadily increased over the period studied (col. B), other trends are not so decisive. Mean age at first birth remained below 20 years for

TABLE 26
MARITAL STATUS AT FIRST BIRTH, 1870–1959

Birth Cohorts	Born in	Married in	Total	Married Before Childbearing No.	% *	Unwed Mothers No.	% *
	A	B	C	D	E	F	G
1870–74	16	0	16	10	63%	6	37%
1875–79	10	0	10	8	80%	2	20%
1880–84	17		17	15	88%	2	12%
1885–89	17		17	12	70%	5	30%
1890–94	16		16	11	69%	5	31%
1895–99	19		19	14	74%	5	26%
1900–04	18	3	21	14	67%	7	33%
1905–09	19	2	21	13	62%	8	38%
1910–14	14	2	16	9	56%	7	44%
1915–19	20		20	9	45%	11	55%
1920–24	22	1	23	8	35%	15	65%
1925–29	31	6	37	20	54%	17	46%
1930–34	24	3	27	11	41%	16	59%
1935–39	27	9	36	15	42%	21	58%
1940–44	41	13	54	22	41%	32	59%
1945–49	47	7	54	26	48%	28	52%
1950–54	39	6	45	16	36%	29	64%
1955–59	39	1	40	7	18%	33	82%
	436	53	489	240	49%	249	51%

*Percentage of total wives and mothers

those born since 1920 (17.8–19.4 years) and also for those born between 1875 and 1894 (17.0–19.4; col. C). Significantly, the mean numbers of illegitimate children per mother are much higher during these periods than in the 25 years when the mean age at first birth was above 20 years (col. D, Table 27). The apparent exception, where a mean of 3.4 children is recorded for the 1895–99 cohort, reflects the case of one never-married woman who had seven children (cols. I, K). The mean number of illegitimate children for the other four unweds was one (col. H).

The correlation of relatively large numbers of illegitimate children with low age at first birth suggests a reformulation of the issue. It seems that there is little difference in sexual activities and childbearing experiences of married and unmarried females. In the next section, "Attitudes to Sex and Marriage," I shall describe the unrelenting pressures

TABLE 27

MARITAL HISTORIES OF UNWED MOTHERS, 1870–1959

Birth Cohort	Unwed Mothers				Married After Children				Never Married		
	No. A	% Adult Females B	Mean Age First Birth C	Mean Illegitimate Children D	No. E	% Unwed F	Mean Age First Marriage G	Mean Illegitimate Children H	No. I	% Unwed J	Mean Illegitimate Children K
1870–74	6	37%	21.0	nk	5	83%	24.0	2.8	1	17%	5
1875–79	2	20%	18.0	nk	2	100%	19.5	1.0	...	...	...
1880–84	2	12%	17.0	1.0	2	100%	17/nk	1.0	...	...	...
1885–89	5	30%	19.3	2.4	2	40%	21.5	1.5	3	60%	3
1890–94	5	31%	19.4	2.8	2	40%	19/64	5.5	3	60%	1
1895–99	5	26%	21.4	3.4	4	80%	24.3	1.0	1	20%	7
1900–04	7	33%	20.3	1.6	5	71%	22.7	1.4	2	29%	2.0
1905–09	8	38%	20.5	1.6	6	75%	19.8	1.6	2	25%	1.5
1910–14	7	44%	20.0	1.0	6	86%	21.6	1.0	1	14%	1.0
1915–19	11	55%	20.2	1.6	8	73%	23.6	1.4	3	27%	2.3
1920–24	15	65%	18.2	3.8	9	60%	20.3	1.6	6	40%	4.5
1925–29	17	46%	19.4	3.4	10	59%	24.4	3.5	7	41%	2.6
1930–34	16	59%	19.1	2.9	11	69%	23.0	1.9	5	31%	5.2
1935–39	21	58%	18.8	2.7	15	71%	21.4	2.1	6	29%	4.3
1940–44	32	59%	17.8	3.1	21	66%	20.7	1.8	11	34%	4.6
1945–49	28	52%	18.3	2.3	16	57%	21.3	2.4	12	43%	2.3
1950–54	29	64%	17.5	1.5	10	34%	18.7	1.2	19	66%	1.7
1955–59	33	82%	17.1	1.2	4	12%	18.7	1.3	29	88%	1.2
Total	249	51%	19.1	2.3	138	55%	21.6	1.8	111	45%	3.1

TABLE 28
AGES AT FIRST MARRIAGE AND FIRST BIRTH, 1870–1959

Birth-Year Cohorts	Mean Age First Marriage for Virgin Brides A	Mean Age First Birth for Unwed Mothers B	Mean Difference in Years C
1870–74	20.1	21.0	0.9
1875–79	17.4	18.0	0.6
1880–84	18.2	17.0	0.8
1885–89	18.1	19.3	1.2
1890–94	18.1	19.4	1.3
1895–99	17.6	21.4	3.8
1900–04	20.7	20.3	0.4
1905–09	19.3	20.5	1.2
1910–14	21.0	20.0	1.0
1915–19	20.0	20.2	0.2
1920–24	18.3	18.2	0.1
1925–29	18.5	19.4	0.9
1930–34	19.8	19.1	0.7
1935–39	19.2	18.8	0.4
1940–44	18.7	17.8	0.9
1945–49	18.9	18.3	0.6
1950–54	18.2	17.5	0.7
1955–59	17.3	17.1	0.2
	18.9	19.1	0.2

on young girls to engage in sexual relations. For this noncontracepting sector of the population,[10] their involvement in "dating" usually results in the early onset of a childbearing career, in or out of marriage.

Table 28 compares ages at first marriage for brides and first birth for unwed mothers. For the entire period 1870–1959, the mean age at first marriage for "virgin brides" is 18.9 years, fluctuating between 17 and 21 years (col. A, Table 28). The mean age at first birth for unmarried girls is fractionally higher, at 19.1 years (col. B, Table 28). Unmarried mothers tended to be slightly older until the 1910 cohort, exceeding 1.3 years difference only in one group (col. C). Since then mothers have generally been younger than brides, but the mean difference in ages is less than a year. Clearly, the high frequency of premarital childbearing

10. A few older women with several children had begun to use "the pill" by 1970; however, contraceptives were not available to the young girls who were most at risk. If there has been a recent lowering of the age of menarche, older generations could not have anticipated the pregnancies of their young daughters.

is not due to a cultural norm of delayed marriage. When asked about the ideal age at marriage, informants suggest 18 to 25 years for women. Inspection of mean ages at first marriage for unwed mothers shows that every cohort fits neatly within that range (col. G, Table 27). Leaving aside the 1950s cohorts for which data are incomplete, the mean age at first marriage for mothers is 22 years (calculated from col. G, Table 27).

What proportion of unwed mothers marry? Of those born 1870–1949, two-thirds had married by 1976 (col. F, Table 27). Of the other third (col. J), an as yet undetermined number died at young ages, often after a prolonged period of ill health. For example, all three of the never-married girls born 1890–94 died in their early twenties after each had given birth to one child (cols. I, K). For the first five decades, only four cases come to mind of women who remained technically single over several years, often as heads of their own households, entertaining whomever they wished. In several other cases where couples lived in common-law unions, one of the partners was married. A large proportion of unwed mothers born after 1920 never married, about half of them living consensually, while the others continued to mate extraresidentially, producing a high mean number of illegitimate children (cols. J, K, Table 27).

ATTITUDES TO SEX AND MARRIAGE

The social context of casual mating is the so-called "hell-raising" complex, which is symptomatic of the changes that have befallen the community in recent decades. Observers, including many of the Haidas themselves, interpret these changes as evidence of breakdown in the social order. Particularly disturbing to the old and middle-aged are the problems caused by the high rate of illegitimacy. Of course, attitudes to sexual behavior and marriage are but one aspect of the distinctive set of orientations that characterizes each of the five age grades. In periods of rapid social change each grade experiences different social and economic conditions, which profoundly affect its outlook and behavior.

The attitudes of the old people are still influenced by the norms inculcated in them as children about the turn of the century. In many cases their own marriages had been arranged by relatives even though the functional basis for the rule of exogamy disappeared with the emergence of the nuclear family. Elderly informants attributed the "bad behavior" and the instability of present-day marriages to the fact that the "old ways" are no longer heeded.

The people who comprised the middle-aged generation in 1966 were born between 1905 and 1920. They are often strongly oriented to the traditional culture, although most of them are by necessity still deeply involved in earning cash and in other activities that regularly bring them into contact with whites. Many of them had attended residential schools where they became acquainted with other natives and other customs. By the 1930s when younger members of this grade reached marrying age, many of the old cultural obligations had been reinterpreted, consistent with the economic and social importance assumed by the bilateral family. This change allowed for more freedom of choice, resulting in an emphasis on romantic attachments. Nevertheless, the authority of the old people was still respected in domestic and kin affairs.

The three younger age grades have experienced much greater exposure to white society. Standing at the fringes of their own as well as the dominant culture, they are vulnerable to conflicting demands for conformity. The parental generation, born roughly between 1920 and 1935, is active in the commercial economy and in relationships with Indian agents, school teachers, nurses, and other representatives of Canadian institutions. As children they grew up in a period which saw a great influx of outsiders into the area. Girls born into this grade were young single women during the war years when white servicemen and construction workers drove onto the reserve in trucks and carried the girls off to all-night parties (see chap. 3). The consequences for the 1920–29 cohorts are dramatically reflected in Table 27—a high percentage of never-married mothers (col. J), a high mean number of illegitimate children (cols. D, K), and for those who did marry, an extended interval between first birth and first marriage (cols. C, G).

Young adults born between 1935 and 1949 constitute the most heterogeneous age grade, including students, transient workers, and married persons. Children born into this grade were the first to attend the integrated provincial school in New Masset. Whether they continued here or were sent to the mainland for the completion of high school or vocational training, they were influenced by the wider youth-culture. Older members of this age grade sought employment, often leaving the reserve for temporary jobs. During much of this phase of the life cycle most individuals are engaged in dating behavior. For girls this brought involvement with a whole new generation of servicemen and construction workers. For some it meant a repetition of the experiences of their mothers' generation (cols. J, K, Table 27), while for others it led to marriage out of the band.

In 1966 children born after 1952 were 14 years old and younger. They comprised half the village population (cols. E, K, Table 17). Most of them attended the integrated school in New Masset where they came into daily contact with non-Haida children and teachers in a social environment which, at the time of this study, set up no barriers to interaction (see chap. 3). For this grade, however, the most important social relationships were provided not by the school but by members of their households and other relatives. The attitudes expressed by these children more closely resemble the values and opinions of parents and grandparents than those of older siblings who seek recognition in their own peer group.

Attitudes of School Girls

To examine these attitudes and to learn how they change as children grow older, I used my role as part-time teacher during the school year 1965–66 to conduct interviews, encourage discussions, and administer questionnaires to my classes. One home economics class was made up of four Indian and four white girls 14 years old. A second group included six Indian girls from 16 to 18 years who prepared the school lunch daily. For a third group of 25 high school girls, half of whom were white, I supervised a correspondence course in home economics. I also taught an eighth grade class in anthropology under the course title of "Guidance," and another in social studies which provided further opportunities for gathering texts.

A striking feature that emerges from these data is the extent to which the girls had internalized middleclass norms of the 1950s about love, marital fidelity, legitimacy, and the discipline of children. They criticized the behavior of married women who "run around," neglect their children, and "drink all the time." They enjoyed reading their home economics text, a glossy illustrated book titled "Your Home and You." It is clear that their written work was influenced by this reading. Essays about the rights and responsibilities of mother, father, and children in making a home did not reflect any household with which they had firsthand experience. However, the text did not deal with the most pressing problems and choices facing both white and Indian teenagers of Masset.

The issues of sexual behavior before marriage, the problems of the girl who becomes pregnant, the attitudes of the family and community, and the disposition of the baby were discussed informally. For the 14-year-olds these questions were still academic since none of them had begun dating, but their opinions were unequivocal and did not differ between Indian girls and white girls. There had obviously been a great deal of adult "lecturing" in the households of both villages. To summarize, sexual activity should definitely be postponed until after marriage because "The girl could get hurt" and "It is a big mistake and could ruin her life." One Indian girl felt that it was "all right if the couple is getting married anyway." This attitude seems to reflect the prevailing norms. But even older girls who were already dating insisted that "sex before marriage is wrong." One 14-year-old Indian girl remarked, "It's a girl's own fault if she gets pregnant because she shouldn't get so involved with a boy."

Asked what a girl does if she gets pregnant, the answers given by both older and younger girls of both villages were very similar: she usually gets married, may be forced to get married, or should get married. The white girls felt that the girl should marry the father of her child "only if she loves him" and that "It is pretty stupid to get married just to get out of a difficult situation." Two of the Indian girls pointed out that "The father is likely to be long gone." All mentioned "adoption" of the baby as a possible solution. While no one said as much, what "adoption" usually means in this society is turning the child over to its grandparents.

Concerning the attitudes of parents, the Indian girls thought that they would "be mad for awhile," but would usually try to protect the girl, perhaps by sending her to "a special home." I could learn of no cases where this had happened. "A home for unwed mothers" is an idea picked up from the surrounding culture but it is not a real alternative for village girls. If marriage occurs, parents "have to give their blessings whether they like it or not." White girls thought that parents should forgive the girl, even if they felt resentful and publicly disgraced.

The girls living in Old Masset seemed more apprehensive about community attitudes than girls in New Masset. The latter believed there was little disgrace, and that only temporary, in bearing an illegitimate child. They said, "The gossips would have a field day but would forget the girl as soon as there is someone new to pick on." According to one, "People just put another black mark against teenagers," and most agreed that "nobody ever forgets." Two of the Indian girls, on the other hand, thought that the disgrace would be extremely great, especially for a girl from 13 to 17 years if she does not marry (though not, apparently, for older women). All of the Indian girls in my classes had older sisters or other relatives who had been unwed mothers and they were probably intimidated by the family furore. This difference in perception of the consequences of premarital pregnancy may reflect the fact that the Indian community is more cohesive than New Masset and therefore negative sanctions are more effective. Younger girls are more sensitive to the disapproval of their elders since they have not yet been drawn into the peer group of older adolescents.

The attitudes of the girls' parents toward illegitimacy are ambivalent. Older Indian women whom I interviewed felt that perhaps one or two illegitimate children were "all right" but "five or six is disgraceful." The older girls spoke about beatings for skipping school, for crawling out of bedroom windows to join their friends, and for coming home late or drunk. The lectures about getting involved with boys make a deep impression on young girls as their replies to the questionnaires indicate. Parents are disturbed when unmarried daughters become pregnant, but after their initial reaction, they treat the premarital pregnancies of their daughters as the inevitable result of the dating process. They are more concerned that their daughters marry someone who is a good worker. Mildred was not upset by the fact that her daughter was pregnant by a feeble-minded boy, yet was anxious about the possibility that she might marry him when he was so obviously unable to support her. She discouraged another daughter from marrying the father of her two children because he showed no interest in getting a job. These examples illustrate the point that the function of marriage in modern Masset is less the legitimating of a sexual union and its offspring than the establishment of a viable economic and social unit.

Most of the sessions with the older girls of 16 to 18 years were completely unstructured. From 10 to 12 o'clock daily they met in the school kitchen to prepare lunch for sale to 70 or more children. Since my duty was only to supervise them, I spent the time in catching up on my lesson plans. While they peeled potatoes, boiled macaroni, or washed dishes they discussed the latest village gossip in detail, passing judgments. My presence was inconsequential to them. One of their discussions concerned the affair which a Haida married woman was carrying on with a white man. The girls felt that the woman in question treated her husband, also white, very badly. She was lazy and thought only of herself and what she was going to wear that night. The most notable point was their sharp criticism of the woman's infidelity.

Yet there is considerable ambivalence about the values of chastity and fidelity. When one of these girls became engaged to a Navy man who was transferred to Ottawa for a tour of duty, she was widely ridiculed in the community for believing he would return and marry her. She refused to date other men in the face of considerable pressure by would-be partners and even her family encouraged her "to get out of the house once in a while." That she was able to resist this kind of pressure for the entire year of her fiance's absence made her elaborate wedding a triumph of personal character.

The girls placed great emphasis on love in choosing a spouse, agreeing that young people should "play the field" so that they will be sure of "finding the right one." This may involve dating "half a dozen," "four or more," "quite a few," "maybe two and maybe twenty." As we have already noted, the ideal age for marriage was thought to be 18 to 25. Characteristics sought in a husband were "good character, good job, someone easy to get along with." Some girls thought that a couple should have common interests, while another wrote that "they don't have common interests in anything." Several echoed the sentiment in their textbook, "You need security as well as love to make a family and a home."

These 16- to 18-year-old girls were absorbed by the question of their own marriages and discussed this issue constantly. They agreed on the desirability of marrying white men because "they treat their wives much better." "Navy guys" are especially good prospects because their tours of duty take them to Ottawa, Halifax, Bermuda, Inuvik—away from Masset. White loggers are also favored because they earn high wages and take their wives away from the reserve. We shall see later how faithfully these attitudes reflect behavior.

The discrepancy between the girls' romantic daydreams and the available choices is illustrated by the case of a 16-year-old who announced in cooking class, "I'm old enough to get married—Dad said I could." She had been dating a 20-year-old boy who had just proposed. The girls discussed the pros and cons of this proposal for several days: one might as well get married—there was nothing else to do. On the other hand, after men get married they run around and think only about making money and drinking it up. Although there had been much talk of love in the abstract, the word was not mentioned in this concrete case. A short time later the girl announced her engagement and went to live in the household of her fiance's parents. The church wedding took place three months later, but even before this the other girls were pitying their friend because her "boyfriend" wouldn't let her go to dances or parties and beat her when he was drunk.

Throughout this discussion we have seen that young adolescent girls, both Indian and white, express textbook values concerning love and chastity that seem strangely out of step with the actual circumstances in which they live. Their hopes and dreams take on a poignant quality when we reflect that these 14-year-olds, born into the 1950s' cohort, would soon be caught up in the same net as their older sisters and mothers. For while they viewed dating as a means of recruitment to a marriage characterized by fidelity and affection, some participants regard it as an alternative to marriage, an end in itself. Many older men, for example, find that dating offers rich opportunities for the sexual exploitation of girls and women.

Dating and Mating

Although informants state that girls begin dating at the age of 13 and boys at 16, it is more accurate to say that young people become aware of the opposite sex at about this time. Boys and girls move about in clusters or pairs of the same age and sex, converging at "shows," basketball games, school dances, the local cafe, and the bowling alley. They share these interests until the girls are about 16 and the boys 19 or 20. By this time the girls have "rounded out," attracting the attention of older men. Many of them are recruited into the "party life" of the reserve which focuses on drinking and casual mating. Although these relationships usually do not involve "going steady," many girls probably enter them believing they will lead to marriage.

In other cases their initiation is more brutal. Outsiders commonly jeer at the idea of rape, making the familiar assumption that if a woman is attacked, she somehow invited it. However, there is little protection for women and girls. After a drinking party, for example, a man may enter a house and lie down in the bed of a young girl. If her parents are drunk or absent there may be no one to interfere; once this has happened she is fair game. The effects of such experiences are visible in that many girls of 16 and 17 years lose their sweetness and become "brass." In their parents' and grandparents' youth this term referred to women who brazenly did not lower their eyes when speaking to a man. Its connotations today are, of course, much wider. The bearing of illegitimate children is not in itself evidence of promiscuity, but after sexual abuse or the disruption of an affective relationship some girls become promiscuous. Although the practice is no longer allowed, in 1966 girls of 16, 17, and 18 would hang around the docks to welcome the fishermen when the fleet from other ports arrived in the spring. Younger sisters often joined older ones in promenading on the wharf whenever a fish patrol vessel, dredger, or freighter visited the harbor.

In general, single women are not conceded the right to refuse sexual advances, although if a couple is going steady their exclusive rights are recognized. Girls who marry their first boyfriend may escape the usual apprenticeship in the village dating system, which "marks" the girls as future targets. Some men apparently assume that if any woman's husband is away she is available. Older married women told of men coming to their houses at night when their husbands were out fishing, demanding entrance. Even girls who have married white men and reside in New Masset are plagued by former sex partners in their husbands' absence.

The undermining of norms supporting marriage and family is indicated by the breakdown of institutions regulating sex relations and providing for recruitment of spouses. As Goode observes in his analysis of changes in African family patterns, "A basic origin of high illegitimacy rates lies . . . in the failure of the kin to impose the normal social controls on young people and adults" (Goode 1963:185). The capacity of the family to regulate its own functioning depends upon adequate socialization and motivation of members. For reinforcement of the norms upon which its authority rests the family relies upon the support of formal institutions such as schools, police, courts, and Church. We saw in chapter 3 how agents of the external power structure not only sought to substitute their own moral standards for traditional values, but interfered with the performance of family functions. The undermining of marriage and family, then, is simply the echo in the domestic sphere of the destruction of traditional authority in political and legal spheres. The high rate of illegitimacy may be viewed as one symptom of the disruption caused by external interference in the affairs of the community. No less important are economic factors. Where the family is seen as the primary economic unit and the head has extensive obligations to kinsmen, many a dependent, chronically unemployed young man finds it difficult to assume these responsibilities. Furthermore, numerous disincentives are put in his way.

Hell-raising. The high level of sexual promiscuity is linked, symbolically and situationally, with drinking. An invitation to a drink is a sexual invitation when males and females are involved. Drink, meaning beer and wine, is only one element of the symbolic erotic complex of the modern Haida, though perhaps the most important one. Another element is "cooking," which signifies a common-law relationship. The term is used in this manner by older women who have been "housekeepers" or "cooked for" white men. The link between sex and fishing is less obvious out of context; however, the appearance of young, or old, Indian women on the docks is interpreted as an invitation to be invited to "go fishing."

This strong symbolic focus points to a set of patterned behaviors that may be referred to as "hell-raising." Using the "wild parties" which are the occasions for this behavior as a "pointer event" (Nadel 1951:99–100), a good case can be made for the existence of the institutionalized role of "hell-raiser." Occupants of this role include most of the unattached men in their late twenties to early forties. Most of the unwed mothers and single women who are not "going steady" or living common-law also participate in this group. Some married persons join in the partying as peripheral members although this interferes with the responsible discharge of family roles. Continuous efforts are made to recruit young schoolgirls. White men are often invited to "bring a bottle and join the party." Their activities are regarded as disruptive by other villagers. One old informant described the participants as "hell-raisers," while another deplored the widespread "hell-raising" behavior. Other persons used the term "that crowd" with an inflection and facial expressions indicating disgust.

Few if any adolescent boys take part in the group, nor do older persons who participate regularly in the ceremonial complex even when they are heavy drinkers. This raises the point that while the "hell-raisers" are not responsible for all the drinking, brawling, and promiscuous sex activity that occurs, they form an identifiable group which is the target for the blame and disapproval expressed by other villagers.

Several characteristics set the "hell-raisers" apart: the core members are either unmarried or separated from their spouses. They live alone or as dependents in their paternal households. They do not have stable cohabiting relationships, but mate randomly. The men, at least, do not assume financial or social responsibility for any children that result from their casual unions, while the women often assume that their parents will care for any illegitimate children. The men are able to spend the high wages earned in seasonal jobs as they wish, though as we mentioned in the last chapter, they do recognize family obligations. The fact that "hell-raising" has a distinct personnel suggests that it is an alternative pattern to marriage, a semi-deviant institution, which is disapproved but tolerated by other members of the community. Indeed, they can do little else. To a greater extent than other non-kin-based groupings, "hell-raising" is oriented to gratifying the basic needs of its participants though in a manner which creates serious and unresolved problems of social control. Its demographic consequences may be grasped by referring again to Tables 23 and 27.

The Gang. Dating activities of younger males are carried on within a different grouping, which may be described as a "gang." In 1966 its members included Indian boys of about 16 to 20 years and a few Indian girls of 15 to 18 who had not been recruited into the adult group. In the summer of 1969 several white girls and boys from New Masset, including the children of the so-called leading citizens, were participating in the group's activities. Indian boys explained that most girls from the reserve are "whores" and so they seek "steady" relationships with white girls. In 1966 no one could have anticipated the development of an intercultural social group among students, particularly in view of the local opposition to the Indian "invasion" of the school, mentioned in chapter 3. It will be recalled, however, that there was little evidence of discriminatory behavior or attitudes on the part of young people. It seems probable that a social group including members of both villages could not have emerged but for the integrative atmosphere of the provincial school.

Actually, in its composition and its activities, the gang may be seen as an extension of the "high school crowd." Its members are very much "tuned in" to the culture of their peers elsewhere, adopting the same dress, hair styles, musical taste, and social behavior. By 1969 several of the boys were able to buy or borrow cars, making it possible to hold parties far from parental surveillance. Naturally, this increased the anxiety of older people who were particularly concerned about the use of drugs. Several young people whom I had known as students in 1965–66 freely acknowledged that they used drugs—"grass, speed, LSD, everything." There was a certain amount of bravado in these claims for the speakers were fully appreciative of the shock value of such statements. Certainly some members of the group had experimented with drugs while at school in Vancouver and it is surprising that the practice did not reach Masset much earlier. Most adolescents, however, did not seem to know the jargon or technology of drug use, information which was readily available through official counter-drug programs as well as the "hippie" subculture in the cities. RCMP officers were very energetic in arresting suspected pushers, and adults of both villages were quick to report their suspicions to police.

Since 1970 there has been another great influx of transient construction workers and it is apparent that reliable sources of supply, of marijuana at least, have been established for those who want it. It is equally clear that neither members of the gang nor other Indians are the best customers. Nor does drinking appear to be as compulsive with members of the gang as with older people. Breaching the taboo in white society against sexual relationships between white girls and Indian boys was surely one of the major gratifications available to participants in the group. For Indian children who have been brought up in a community where extrafamily activities are oriented almost exclusively to the interests of the old, this new youth-centered behavior was far more satisfying than copying the "hell-raising" behavior of their elders. To the young people's surprise and perhaps disappointment, parental criticism has been subdued. Meanwhile, those Indian and white parents who could afford it were making arrangements to send adolescent children outside to school in a supposedly more wholesome environment.

The gang is age-specific in that its members belong to the younger half of the 15–29 grade. However, it is unlikely that as they grow older they will "graduate" into the hell-raising group whose members belong to the next oldest cohorts. These contrasting patterns reflect the unique experiences of the cohorts with members of the dominant society. While male and female participants in hell-raising do not marry each other (although a woman may find a husband outside the group), members of the gang tend to pair off and "go steady." These relationships have already resulted in several marriages.

In 1966 this pattern had not yet emerged though it may have been the bad dream that provoked so much hostility to the school in New Masset. Even now it involves a very small percentage of young people. On the other hand, the pattern of premarital childbearing by young girls continues apparently at an accelerating pace.

Courtship and Marriage "in the Old Days"

In the old days, insisted senior informants, there was none of this "bad behavior." A girl had an uncle "to walk around with her" when she went out with a young man. "People were still very strict. They would never stand for a baby being born before marriage. Only low people had babies without marriage." A daughter of a high-ranking family, a woman nearly 80 years old, told how she and her sister had been tied together back-to-back by their hair so that they could not sneak out at night. Other old people were also emphatic about the role of "no babies without marriage." Of course, accounts of virtue in earlier times are always suspect, reflecting ideal behavior. When actual behavior is inconsistent with this norm, it is ignored or rationalized. I had asked middle-aged informants how the community treated people like Louise and Margaret who, the records show, had several children without husbands. Mary Ellen answered, "It was just one of those things the village had to put up with." Of women who lived common-law it was said, "It's just like they were married."

Reference to Table 26 (cols. F, G) confirms that the incidence of illegitimacy was higher "in the old days" than informants care to admit. But, in considering the nature of premarital childbearing in the early decades, it is not meaningful to speak of illegitimacy. Before 1900 many couples lived together "according to Haida custom," in the missionary's words, often for many years until they were rounded up and married in church at a mass wedding. This event was usually arranged so that the ceremony might be performed by the visiting bishop. There seems to have been no resistance to this procedure. The ethical ideas and norms of Christianity penetrated deeply into the culture. Nor was this acceptance limited to those Christian practices compatible with a potlatching orientation: oratory, participation, vestments, and so on.

The idea of marriage as a sacrament was deeply internalized by the people as their verbal statements and reactions to events testify. I do not deny that the emphasis which the church attached to the marriage ceremony was consistent with the social importance of the marital union in traditional Haida society. Although children were automatically allocated to their mother's lineage, the establishment of the crucial ritual ties with father's matrilineage depended upon the formal recognition of a marital alliance.

Young people were prevailed upon by their elders to commence cohabitation with the blessings of the church. It should be noted here that during the late nineteenth and early twentieth centuries, wedding feasts and other festivities continued to be held during the winter when the people came home from the canneries and fish camps. But nature could not always wait for the ceremonial season. Betrothed girls who became pregnant were quickly married as we may infer from the high percentage of prenuptial conceptions. These are identified on women's reproductive history forms by an interval of less than nine months elapsing between marriage and first birth. The frequency of these cases is indicated by the short interval between mean age at first marriage and mean age at first birth (col. D, Table 29). Of course, this interpretation ignores the possibility that some of these births may have been premature.[11]

It must also be pointed out that many girls marry out of the band and their children are not included; indeed, data are usually not even available since they are no longer band members. Thus, mean age at first birth is calculated on a smaller population and this partly accounts for the short interval in some cases. For example, in the 1935–39 cohort where there is no difference in mean ages, 59 percent of the girls had married out (cols. B, C, Table 29; also cols. E, G, I, Table 32). In the 1930–34 cohort, 62 percent had married out and data for the remainder were so incomplete that no mean could be calculated. No judgment about the frequency of out-marriage for early cohorts can be made since such women would not be listed among the survivors who married and bore children for the band.

More conclusive statements about the frequency of prenuptial conceptions and premature births will be possible when analysis of the reproductive history forms is more advanced. It may be said meanwhile that the data in Table 29 confirm field observations that many brides are pregnant; usually this is a matter of engaged couples cohabiting.

In other cases, marriage followed childbirth within weeks or months. Some of these unions involved couples whose relatives' opposition to

11. I am indebted to Jane Underwood for drawing this possibility to my attention.

TABLE 29
AGE AT FIRST MARRIAGE AND FIRST BIRTH FOR BRIDES

Birth year Cohorts	No. A	Mean Age at First Marriage B	Mean Age at First Birth C	Mean Interval in Years D
1870–74	10	20.1	20.2	.1
1875–79	8	17.4	17.5	.1
1880–84	15	18.2	19.3	1.1
1885–89	12	18.1	20.4	2.3
1890–94	11	18.1	18.8	.7
1895–99	14	17.6	18.9	1.3
1900–04	14	20.7	22.1	1.4
1905–09	13	19.3	19.8	.5
1910–14	9	21.0	21.8	.8
1915–19	9	20.0	21.3	1.3
1920–24	8	18.3	20.0	1.7
1925–29	20	18.5	19.9	1.4
1930–34	11	19.8	*	*
1935–39	15	19.2	19.2	0
1940–44	22	18.7	19.5	.8
1945–49	26	18.9	19.5	.6
1950–54	16	18.2	18.9	.7
1955–59	7	17.3	18.0	.7
	240	18.8	19.7	.9

*Data insufficient to produce a valid result.

their marriage melted after the birth of a child. Usually, however, the interval between first birth and first marriage was much longer and might see the birth of additional children (cols. C, G, H, Table 27). What should not be lost sight of is the small number of individuals involved, even though they comprise up to a third or more of the girls becoming adults by 1920.

Just as the attitudes and behavior of younger generations can only be understood in their social context, so the old people must be seen against the backdrop of their time. The people who functioned as the elders of the village in 1966 were those born between 1880 and 1905. The oldest members of the community grew up at a time when ceremonial life was still vigorous, when the old arts and crafts were matters of household economy, and the social structure, despite the presence of the missionary, was comparatively unchanged. True, raids upon neighboring tribes had ceased and disease had carried off many victims. The most prominent shaman had become Dr. Kuday, a Christian convert. With the growing influence of Christianity, persons of highest rank were no longer interred in carved mortuary poles, but were buried in the new cemetery where crests carved in marble marked their graves. The last totem pole raising was held in 1890 on the occasion of a wedding. It was described by informants as a pitiful affair in terms of kinds and amounts of goods distributed.

While the people still depended largely on subsistence activities for their livelihood, such staples as flour, tea, molasses, cloth, and gunpowder were bought or traded at the Hudson's Bay Company store located on the little knoll where the Indian Day School later stood. Besides the missionary and his family, the only whites who resided permanently in the area were the Hudson's Bay man, a farmer, and a cattle rancher, along with their families. The first permanent white settlement in the area would not be founded until 1908. Meanwhile the Haidas continued to range over the whole coastline, which had recently become part of British Columbia and Canada.

Beneath the surface changes, the old norms and values were only slightly modified by changing conditions. The new Christian ethos, which asserted the equality of all men in the face of the rank structure, simply confirmed the Haida's opinion that "no one else was better" than he was and therefore he had as much right to compete for highest status as anyone. Old rivalries were not buried but diverted into new channels. The essential elements of the traditional marriage complex—arranged marriage, lineage and moiety exogamy, and the responsibilities of kinship—were strictly observed. Seventy years later people born during the nineteenth century were still espousing the norms and values instilled in them as children.

An Arrangement. In discussing marriage, the aspect that provoked the greatest interest among old people was the contrast in methods of spouse selection practiced today with those of "the old days," presumably during the youth of their parents. "In the old days when marriages were arranged, girls could be married off to an old man. If your grandmother died, they could make you replace her." One informant cited the case of an "aunty," who at the age of 10 or 11 was given to a man three times her age. "Her uncles made her go and stay with him but she pinned herself up in a blanket with safety pins and wouldn't let him come near her. But he was kind and one day after she'd been avoiding him, he came and told her that what her uncles were making her do was wrong. He said she could go back home to her mother and grow up. So she went home but a few years later her people did the same thing.

They made her marry an old man but he died eventually and then she picked her own man."

Aunty Emma was one of the persons whose marital and reproductive history could be reconstituted. By referring to her record we may not only illustrate a fairly typical case but may expand upon the narrative form of the informant's testimony.

On December 11, 1888, Emma was married to David Duan, a bachelor whose age is given as 38. Emma's age is recorded in the church register as 16, fairly young for a bride in those days but not extremely so. (See Table 29, col. B, for mean age at first marriage.) However, the whole point of the story told to me by Emma's sister's daughter was that her aunty had been a child bride. Further, Emma's eighth child was born in 1918 which would have made her 46 years old, late in comparison with other cases. Rarely does birth occur after the age of 44. If, on the other hand, Emma were 44 at the time of her last birth, she would have been born in 1874 and so 14 years old at the time of her first marriage. This makes more sense of the story. Very likely her "uncles," anticipating the missionary's disapproval of the marriage of such a young girl, gave her age as 16. Women, on the other hand, sympathetic with the emotional trauma of marriage to such an "old man," exaggerated her youth. This is a pattern that emerged in several other cases related to me—the bride was consistently 10 or 11 years old. The demographic data cast no light on the couple's post-marital residence, but there is no reason to doubt the story on this point. In any event, David Duan died a year after the wedding on December 28, 1889.

In January 1891 Emma, now 17, was married to Samuel Saikes, a bachelor 20 years old, not the "old man" of the story. There is no evidence of any children until January 1901 when a son Josiah was born; on his baptismal record is a note that he is Emma's second son. Her husband, Samuel, died in 1902 at the age of 31. In March 1905 Emma, now 31, married the man of her own choice, George Skilla, a bachelor about 38 years old. Her name is given in the marriage register as Emma Handford which suggests a period of coresidence with a white man. A year after her third marriage a son was born, but he survived only a year and ten months. Emma gave birth to five more children at the ages of 34, 37, 39, 41, and 44. Of these, three sons and a daughter died single at an average age of 19.5 years. Two sons—a bachelor and a widower—survive. Emma died in 1958 at the age of 84, surviving her third husband by 11 years.

Yet of this long and seemingly fruitful lifetime, the most vivid memory that Emma shared with her great-grandchildren was of her unhappiness and resentment at being forced to marry an old man while still a child. Nor was hers the only case. Women who have had this experience never seem to get over the feeling that they were betrayed and cheated. Evidently there is a great qualitative difference in the relationship of spouses of widely discrepant ages as compared with those of more nearly equivalent age. Women who must accept the authority of an older husband in their youth must often bear the burden of an infirm one in their mature years. They may never enjoy the companionship that characterizes the relationship of other couples in middle and later years.

Relative Ages of Spouses. The normative idea that spouses should be of roughly equivalent ages was frequently expressed by informants of all ages, including those who still supported the old ideas of arranged marriage and moiety exogamy. Ideally, the husband should be somewhat "but not too much" older.

To arrive at some idea of actual practice, the relative ages of spouses were computed in all cases where the data were available, for remarriages as well as first marriages. This information is frequently missing for outsiders, both male and female, who marry band members, but by far the majority is represented in Table 30.

The strength of the norm that the husband should be older excites no surprise in view of the same bias in Western culture, although the mean difference in ages is high (col. G). What is surprising is the great range

TABLE 30
RELATIVE AGES OF SPOUSES

Women's Birth Years	Husband's Relative Age						Mean Difference in Years	Range in Years
	Older Than Wife		Same Age As Wife		Younger Than Wife			
	A	B	C	D	E	F	G	H
1860–69	27	90%	1	3%	2	7%	6.1	−2: +33
1870–79	18	90%	1	5%	1	5%	8.2	−1: +23
1880–89	27	100%	0		0		6.4	+1: +23
1890–99	23	88%	1	4%	2	8%	7.5	−8: +20
1900–09	24	71%	3	9%	7	20%	3.4	−6: +12
1910–19	22	76%	0		7	24%	4.0	−6: +19
1920–29	29	83%	2	6%	4	11%	5.1	−10: +22
1930–39	32	82%	3	8%	4	10%	4.0	−7; +20
1940–49	56	90%	2	3%	4	7%	5.6	−3: +38
	258	86%	13	4%	31	10%	5.6	

in husbands' relative ages right down to the present (col. H). In most of the cases where the man is several years younger, he is the second husband of a widow, often a brother or other kinsman of the first spouse.[12]

The data on relative ages of spouses for the early period were gleaned from a record of 158 marriages performed in St. John's Anglican Church in Masset between the arrival of the missionary W. H. Collison in 1876 and 1907. This source also sheds light on other aspects of marriage.

Of the 158 weddings recorded, 56 were first marriages for both spouses and in 18 cases for one. Only 18 were new marriages of widowed persons. Many of the other weddings solemnized existing unions with offspring. In 57 cases the couples were described as "previously married according to Indian custom" and in 14 others they had "cohabited according to Indian custom."[13] The women who were marrying during the late 1870s and in the 1880s were those born about 1860 and earlier, before the keeping of birth records began. The mean of ages ascribed to "spinsters" marrying during these years was 19.9 years. This mean may be artificially high for reasons exemplified in the case of Aunty Emma. Girls born during the 1860s and 1870s were marrying during the 1890s, but in many cases the ceremony consecrated an existing relationship. Those born in the 1880s married at the turn of the century and in the decade before the establishment of the reserve in 1910. As Table 29 indicates, their mean age was about 18 years. Most, though not all, of the so-called unwed mothers of these early years, whose first births are tabulated in Table 25 (col. B), lived in these socially recognized unions which had not yet been solemnized by the clergyman. This was the old pattern of premarital childbearing.

Unfortunately there is a gap in the church records between 1907 and 1923. The marriage register kept by the Indian agent is incomplete until 1917 when the birth and death as well as marriage registrations become full and reliable. Wedding dates for most, if not all, of the girls born in the 1890s have been determined by field work and other kinds of records. Although the exact age at marriage is not available in every case, a reasonable average based on known cases is 18 years.

12. With a declining death rate and financial assistance to the aged, remarriage of the elderly became uncommon. Of 255 ever-married band members alive in 1966, 91 percent had married only once, 7 percent twice, while three persons had married three times. One woman had four husbands, while another had five (Stearns 1973:218). In the 1970s more liberal Canadian divorce laws have allowed younger people to escape from dead marriages. In addition, an increase in accidents and violent deaths of young people has created widows who may be inclined to remarry.

13. In computing ages at first marriage only new unions were included in Tables 26 and 29.

Exogamy

While there is no sense in which one can say that marriages are still arranged, relatives continue to take a keen interest in the selection of spouses. Young girls talked about how difficult it is to find a boy who is not related. When they found one they liked the old people would say, "You can't go out with him. He's your brother [or uncle]." The old people say, "The old way of Eagles marrying Ravens is all gone. Anybody marries anybody." One old gentleman, now deceased, worried about "all this marrying of relatives." Moiety exogamy was good because "it kept down the TB. Those old Haidas knew what they were doing when they wouldn't let close relatives marry." Clearly these old people were still thinking in terms of traditional kin categories. And while adolescents as well as their parents are intimidated by the criticism of the old, no informant would concede that moiety exogamy plays any part in marriage selection today.

Most middle-aged parents support the modern norms of marrying for love and the right of young people to choose their own spouses, although this right was not always conceded to them by their own parents. Mary Ellen Barnes, who was born in 1920 and married in 1937, said that her parents had a husband all picked out for her. The candidate was her "real" father's sister's son. However, she had already chosen a man of her own side. "The old people didn't like it and gave us a lot of trouble." It was two years before she and William were permitted to marry and by this time two children had been born to them, a fact that she did not mention in this context. In 1937 marrying within one's own moiety was considered scandalous and those who did so still feel defensive. They will often say with an embarrassed laugh that they "never saw ravens and eagles mate." Persons who "married right" say, "The old people don't look down on us." Mary Ellen's cousin Mildred married a "nephew" of her father's, again a father's sister's son. She loved him or else she wouldn't have married him, she said, but "it pleased her father's people very much." Clearly the normative power of the moiety-exogamous arranged marriage persisted long after its functional utility in linking corporate kin groups had eroded.

To determine when the prescriptions of moiety exogamy began to lose their force, we will examine the lineage affiliations of spouses. The lineage membership of females involved in 354 marriages was cross-tabulated with lineage or other group affiliations of husbands. In about 15 percent of the sample where these facts could not be determined for one or both spouses the marriage was not included. Data for women are arranged by ten-year birth cohorts. Using females as the reference point introduces a bias in that the percentage of out-marriage is higher than would be found if the analysis focused on the marital choices of males. The group affiliations of in-marrying wives will be considered in the discussion of contemporary choices (see Table 33).

Referring to Table 31 we find that down to the 1910 cohort, more than 60 percent of marriages were into the opposite moiety (col. D). This proportion would be much higher if the data for early decades were complete. With the marriages of girls born 1910–19 there is a shift, not to a more or less equal distribution between own moiety and other moiety as would be expected if the exogamic rule could simply be forgotten. On the contrary, for only two cohorts out of ten have marriages into own moiety exceeded 20 percent of the total (cols. B, C).

Moiety exogamy can only work in a closed social system of two categories, which can be stretched to accommodate outsiders as necessary. But since the late nineteenth century the categories have multiplied. Most important are "Other Indian" and "Non-Indian," though for our immediate purposes they may be subsumed in the category "Non-Haidas" (col. F). When non-Haida females marry Haida men they become members of the band but unless they are assigned to a lineage, their children belong to yet another category—descendants of a non-Haida ascendant (col. E; see chap. 8). This status is passed down the generations; its occupants stand outside the exogamic categories.

TABLE 31
MOIETY AFFILIATIONS OF SPOUSES (in percentages)

| Female Birth Cohorts | No. of Marriages A | Own Moiety | | Opposite Moiety D | Non-Haida Ascendant E | Non-Haida (out of band) F |
		Own Lineage B	Other Lineage C			
1860–69	24		12	88		
1870–79	20	10			90	
1880–89	31		26	65	3	6
1890–99	31	3	16	61		20
1900–09	35		11	63	3	23
1910–19	34	15	12	41	3	29
1920–29	39	2	13	41	8	36
1930–39	43	2	14	23	2	59
1940–49	66	1	14	14	12	59
1950–59	31	6		13	3	78
%	100%	4%	12%	43%	5%	36%
N	354	13	44	153	16	128

When Haida women marry non-Haidas they cease to be members of the band although there are frequent cases where their children, though not band members, marry back in. Their children do have lineage affiliations. Of girls born between 1910 and 1929, about a third married out (col. F). The rate increased to more than half of the girls born in the next two decades and to 78 percent for members of the 1950s cohort who have married thus far.

If we disregard out-marriage for a moment and consider moiety-exogamous unions as a proportion of band-endogamous marriages we may gain a better perspective:

	N	
1860–69	21	88%
1870–79	18	90%
1880–89	20	69%
1890–99	19	76%
1900–09	22	81%
1910–19	14	58%
1920–29	16	64%
1930–39	10	56%
1940–49	9	33%
1950–59	4	57%
	153	

Like other events studied statistically in this chapter, the percentage of moiety-exogamous marriages fluctuates in recent decades though the general trend is unmistakable. It would be difficult to argue that the rule of moiety exogamy has much force today. And yet if the old rules were bankrupt, we would expect all the recent cohorts to look like that of 1940–49, with its roughly equal distribution of cases among Other-Lineage-of Own-Moiety, Opposite Moiety, and Non-Haida Ascendants (cols. C, D, E, Table 31).

What Table 31 highlights most dramatically, however, is the strength of the norm of *lineage* exogamy. Only 13 breaches of this norm could be discovered for the last 100 years, about 4 percent of all known marriages. When these cases are computed as a percentage of band-endogamous marriages the results are as follows:

	N	
1860–69	...	0
1870–79	2	10%
1880–89	...	0
1890–99	1	4%
1900–09	...	0

1910–19	5	21%
1920–29	1	4%
1930–39	1	6%
1940–49	1	4%
1950–59	2	29%
	13	

These figures demonstrate the persisting effectiveness of proscriptions against marrying within one's own matrilineage. This is the negative aspect of exogamy—prohibition of marriage with matrilateral kinsmen, now more narrowly defined as lineage mates. As marriage into other lineages of own moiety becomes more common (but still only 12 percent, see col. C), the internal dichotomy is not abandoned but redrawn. This is clearly shown by Table 31. Since knowledge of lineage membership is almost entirely confined to the old (see chap. 8), the proscription is expressed by the formula, "You can't go out with him. He's your brother."

Traditionally, of course, exogamy was not simply a negative rule but a mechanism for establishing ceremonial interrelations. With the community's loss of self-sufficiency and increasing interaction, including intermarriage, with non-members, no attempt is now made to prescribe marriage partners. As we shall see in chapter 9 there has been a reinterpretation of ceremonial events and obligations consistent with the economic and social importance assumed by the bilateral family. This change allows for more freedom of choice in marriage, which results in the emphasis placed on romantic love.

But while the moiety can no longer be regarded as a category defining marriageability, its importance in regulating ceremonial interrelations in life-cycle events has been enhanced (see chaps. 8 and 9). Recruitment to these categories no longer depends upon matrilineal descent. Anyone who participates in ceremonial events, including an ethnographer, may be assigned a status that defines his or her relations with other participants. This is the manner in which outsiders were traditionally accommodated in the social system. Its decline may be attributed to the emergence of competing categories whose members are, unlike the ethnographer, disinterested in assimilation to the Masset Haida.

There is a demographic as well as a normative and functional aspect to this issue. If we refer to Tables 39 and 40, which classify village residents in 1966 by moiety, lineage, and age group, we may see how limited is the scope for lineage or even moiety exogamy today. Since these tables were computed to show the personnel available for ceremonial tasks within the village, they ignore off-reserve band members.

The inclusion of absent members, however, would not materially affect the point that the numbers of persons available for marriage in each lineage may be too few to support the practice of exogamy.

In the 15–29 age group, where most marriages occur, there are 32 male and 30 female Ravens and an almost identical number of Eagles. When divided among 11 lineages, each averages 5.8 males and 5.6 females in the young adults grade. In fact, however, the lineages are not equal in size. The largest, Tcetsgitinai, had a total of 101 members, while Stlinglanas, with which it traditionally exchanged wives, had 55. In the relevant age grade this amounts to 14 male and 7 female Tcetsgitinai and 4 male plus 7 female Stlinglanas. The once powerful STA-'stas are even weaker with only 3 males and 2 females of marrying age. Does this scarcity of potential spouses, coupled with a persisting norm of exogamy, persuade young people to marry out of the band?

Aram Yengoyan's studies of demographic and environmental influences on Australian section systems are instructive on this point (1968a; 1968b; 1972). Surveying various ecological zones of Australia, he establishes a correlation between the population parameter (population size, area, and density) and the presence of local group exogamy, moieties, 4-part sections or 8-part subsections. The method utilizes a model population pyramid for a generalized hunting-gathering group of 100. He derives a median population size for each form of social organization, which is then compared with, and supported by, empirical data. Using 25 eligible mates as his operational number, Yengoyan finds that with "only moiety restrictions, an ideal tribal size figure is approximately 262 which falls between the median range of 250–300" (1968b:259). A population of 530 persons can sustain a section system with a high statistical observance of the marriage rule. The empirically derived median for sections is 550–600.

Assuming for the sake of argument that these models are applicable to the Haida, at no time has the Masset population dwindled to a point where it could not support the prescribed rule of exogamy. (Band censuses tabulated 365 persons in the Masset band in 1912 and 360 in 1918). But the field of choice was far more restricted than the observance of moiety exogamy implies. Just as compelling was the rule of equal rank of spouses. High-ranking and geographically proximate lineages formed permanent relationships which included the exchange of women. The intermarrying of the Tcetsgitinai and Stlinglanas can be traced to their ancestral village of Yan, that of the STA'stas and Yakulanas at least to the period when they occupied Kiusta and North Island respectively. The extent to which the resulting pattern of bilateral cross-cousin marriage assumed prescriptive force is unclear. In any case, the observance of these various preferences and restrictions may have required a minimum population closer to that of a section system, that is, 530. The northern Haida fell below this number in the 1880s. However, the effects of population decline may have been more serious for the institutions of rank than for exogamy. We have noted instances in the 1930s where parents were still trying to marry their children to patrilateral or matrilateral cross-cousins.

The undermining of exogamy, I have suggested, owes as much to the taking root of new ideas of romantic love and free choice as to declining population. On the other hand, the elders' perception that the "right way" is still attainable but for the rebelliousness of youth gives this norm its persisting moral force.

OUT-MARRIAGE

Whatever the power of lingering traditions, the element of free choice fosters a different definition of the eligible partner. For several decades Haida women have experienced relationships of greater or lesser duration with white men. But the upsurge in marriage to non-Haidas coincides with the influx of construction workers, loggers, and Navy personnel to the islands since World War II. We recall that young girls frequently expressed a preference for white husbands— "Navy guys" and loggers—because "they treat their wives much better." Since many of the girls are very pretty, they easily succeed in attracting young white men. Further, some of the school girls who are highly motivated to "get out of Masset" have learned how to present themselves as attractively as girls outside. Their home economics textbook, which they had enjoyed more than any other prescribed reading, addressed itself to health, hygiene, nutrition, "charm," and similar topics. From the mail-order catalogues and magazines they absorbed information about clothing fashions and hair styles. Magazines aimed at the "teen" market also offer advice on "the dating game," "holding out for a husband," and other strategic matters.

The girl who wins the prize in these sweepstakes—a Navy man— enters upon a comfortable middleclass existence in standard housing with all the conveniences, travel with her husband to other stations in Canada and Bermuda, shopping at the Base Exchange, and other perquisites of service life. Although I was never able to learn of any negative reactions to these wives in clique-bound Navy circles, it may be significant that many of their husbands settle down in New Masset after their discharges. In contrast to the technical personnel who staff the Navy base, loggers and construction men are primarily of working class background. As the status and benefits they have to offer are less attractive, they are less desirable and in fact less frequently chosen as husbands.

For the young girl with no job skills, chances of marrying out are better if she remains at home. Usually girls who met and married white men in the cities were either students or women who had learned technical skills such as hairdressing or practical nursing. For the most part they maintain only tenuous ties with the reserve. These remarks do not apply, of course, to children raised away from the reserve by parents permanently settled outside. Older women, especially unwed mothers, are more successful in finding a husband if they leave the reserve. Considering the high proportion of unwed mothers who marry, even after several children, it would seem that premarital childbearing does not impair marriageability (col. F, Table 27). We remember, however, that young male members of the "gang" sought white girlfriends because "most of the girls on the reserve are whores." I cannot say whether they distinguish between the fact of motherhood and promiscuous behavior.

To determine the frequency of marriage to non-Haidas we refer to Table 32, which classifies husbands by cultural group membership. Band-endogamous marriages (cols. B, C, summarizing cols, B–E, Table 31) are distinguished from marriages with Indians of other tribes (cols. F, G) and non-Indians, mainly whites (cols. H, I). The category Enfranchised refers to persons of Haida background who are no longer band members (cols. D, E)[14]

The point Table 32 makes most emphatically is that of 338 known marriages during the last hundred years, 39 percent of the female spouses ceased to be members of the band and the community (cols. E, G, I). For several decades only a few individuals were concerned, though in such a small population they represented a substantial portion of potential wives and mothers.

Those few women of cohorts up to 1930 who married white men were usually of high-ranking families (col. H). They retained some of the romantic aura of the "Haida princess" enjoyed by several chiefs' daughters who had married professional men—geologists, surveyors, and so on—in the early days. Significantly, few members of the 1920–29 cohorts who were caught up in the wartime parties married

14. Table 32 does not purport to be a complete record of all marriages of Masset women. Only new unions listed in the church marriage register were tabulated. With a few well-documented exceptions involving chiefs' wives and others involving ex-slaves, pre-existent unions were village-endogamous. On the other hand, marriages of Masset women to outsiders which did not occur in St. John's Church were not recorded until the agency was established in 1910. Many females described as "unaccounted for" (col. D., Table 24) would have married out.

TABLE 32
CULTURAL GROUP MEMBERSHIP OF HUSBANDS

Birth Cohort	Marriages of In-Born Females	Masset Band Males		Exfranchised Haidas		Other Indians		Non-Indians	
	N	N	%	N	%	N	%	N	%
	A	B	C	D	E	F	G	H	I
1870–74	15	15	100%						
1875–79	10	10	100%						
1880–84	17	16	94%					1	6%
1885–89	14	12	86%	1	7%	1	7%		
1890–94	13	11	85%					2	15%
1895–99	18	14	78%			2	11%	2	11%
1900–04	17	15	88%			1	6%	1	6%
1905–09	18	12	66%			3	17%	3	17%
1910–14	13	9	69%			3	23%	1	8%
1915–19	21	14	67%	1	5%	4	19%	2	9%
1920–24	18	11	61%	2	11%	2	11%	3	17%
1925–29	24	17	71%	1	4%	2	8%	4	17%
1930–34	21	8	38%	1	5%	5	24%	7	33%
1935–39	22	9	41%	2	9%	5	23%	6	27%
1940–44	31	13	42%	1	3%	2	7%	15	48%
1945–49	35	14	40%			3	9%	18	51%
1950–54	20	4	20%	4	20%	3	15%	9	45%
1955–59	11	3	27%	1	9%	4	37%	3	27%
	338	207	61%	14	4%	40	12%	77	23%

whites. Many of them went on to "cook for" one or a succession of white men, usually those on lower rungs of the socioeconomic ladder. While this may seem an insecure position, many of these relationships are of long standing. As one middleclass male civil servant observed, "The Indian women know how to hang on to their men."

Beginning with the 1930s cohort, the proportion of out-marriage jumped from less than a third to almost two-thirds of all marriages (cols. E, G, I). These unions, contracted in the immediate postwar period, were almost evenly divided between whites and other Indians, including enfranchised Haidas. Of girls born 1940–54, however, almost half married white men. (It would be fruitful to explore the connection between this outflow of women and the hell-raising complex.)

Men are much less likely to marry out. Table 33 shows that only 14 percent of all wives are in-married women. These women are assigned to the cohorts of in-born women according to their own age. Haida men usually meet potential non-Haida spouses away from the reserve. The low incidence of in-marriage reflects the fact that only recently have the people begun to circulate freely in the larger society. There has been no pantribal social grouping equivalent to the spirit dancing ceremonies, which bring together Salish people from all over southwestern British Columbia and northwestern Washington. To be sure, the Haida have had long experience of residential schools, hospitals, seasonal cannery work, and fishing along the coast. Some of the intermarriage recorded in Table 33 reflects these kinds of contacts, although men who marry non-Haida women are often already settled outside. By far the greatest number of in-marrying women are other Indians: primarily Tsimshian, Kwakiutl, Alaskan Haida, Skidegate Haida, and daughters of enfranchised Haidas. Of the 23 percent who are white, few ever take up postmarital residence on the reserve. They are newcomers to the area, girls working in the cannery, and former wives of white men, but not longtime residents of New Masset.

TABLE 33
CULTURAL GROUP MEMBERSHIP OF IN-MARRYING WIVES

Birth Cohorts	In-Marrying Wives A	% of All Wives B	Enfranchised Massets		Other Indians		Non-Indians	
			N C	% D	N E	% F	N G	% H
1870–74								
1875–79								
1880–84								
1885–89								
1890–94								
1895–99								
1900–04	3	16%	1	33%	2	67%		
1905–09	2	11%			2	100%		
1910–14	2	13%	1	50%	1	50%		
1915–19								
1920–24	1	6%			1	100%		
1925–29	6	20%			4	66%	2	34%
1930–34	3	14%			1	33%	2	67%
1935–39	9	30%			7	78%	2	22%
1940–44	13	30%	4	31%	8	61%	1	8%
1945–49	7	17%	1	14%	4	58%	2	28%
1950–54	6	23%			3	50%	3	50%
1955–59	1	9%			1	100%		
Total	53	14%	7	13%	34	64%	12	23%

During the 1970s this picture has begun to change, largely as a consequence of that liberalizing of government policy which had such a devastating psychological impact in the short term. There is now much more social circulation as a consequence of integrational programs that bring natives of various cultural groups into contact with each other and with whites on an equal footing. Indian education programs in post-secondary institutions in British Columbia are one avenue. Museum training courses for Indian carvers are another. The belated recognition of Indian carving as a fine art form has created a rich and appreciative market for the output of a growing number of gifted native artists. These changes have stimulated a process of "consciousness-raising" with respect to the value of Indian culture. As Indian-ness becomes acceptable, even desirable, a political element enters into the selection of spouses. This conclusion is derived from interaction with native people; it is not deduced from the statistics, although statistical evidence has begun to accumulate. Marriage, like other demographic processes, is particularly sensitive to changes in the social climate. In Table 32 we see a shift taking place in the selection of husbands. The cohort of 1950–54 follows the trend of the previous decade when roughly half of all marriages were contracted with whites. For girls born 1955–59, 73 percent of all marriages are to Haidas, enfranchised Haidas, and other Indians while only about a quarter involve whites.

It would be risky to predict trends on the basis of such small numbers were it not for the almost militant statements one begins to hear about marriage with whites—white men, that is. The development of the "gang" and the recent occurrences of intermarriage of local white females and Haida males are even more powerful indicators of the extent of changed social conditions. One may speculate that as other Indians become more attractive to the girls, more white wives will become available to the young men. The men do not see these intercultural marriages as an avenue to more intensive participation in white society. On the contrary, the wives are required to renounce their "Hunky" ways and attitudes and become Indian.[15]

We have seen that many participants, observing the staggering increase in illegitimate births, the declining age of mothers, the high proportion of unmarried persons, and the disruptive patterns of mating, describe the social scene in terms of breakdown and disintegration. Even in this study I have spoken of the "breakdown of mechanisms" that should move individuals from one phase of the life cycle to

15. This ethnic slur, expressing the resentment felt by some in the larger community toward East European refugees who had allegedly "stolen jobs" from Canadians, has been applied by the young militants to all whites.

another (chapter 3). But in chapter 5, I analyzed the community's attempts to cope with the problems of illegitimacy by incorporating large numbers of dependent persons into existing households. This was interpreted as an adaptive, which is to say creative, response to economic opportunities.

In this chapter I have employed demographic analysis, attempting to be more precise in identifying crucial events and their consequences for the population. This approach, by extending the period of observation beyond the lifetime of any informant, reveals fluctuations in behavior over the long term. The different experiences that each cohort undergoes in conditions of rapid social change are reflected in the attitudes, values, and behavior of its members. Moreover, some cohorts are affected more drastically than others. By focusing upon events rather than long-term trends we may interpret changes in behavior as a short-term reaction by a cohort to its social experiences. With this perspective we are not crippled by the assumption of irreversible decline and thus are better able to appreciate the responsiveness of individual behavior to the social climate.

For example, girls born 1920–29, some of whom became the first "party girls" during the war, did not initiate a period of moral breakdown that has accelerated to the present. Rather, the conditions of that period were repeated as a new tide of transient workmen swept in during the late 1960s. And as institutions such as the three-generation family and the welfare program developed in response to these conditions, the behavior pattern in question—premarital childbearing—became institutionalized as well. Attitudes and expectations changed, the age of unwed mothers declined while the proportion of girls becoming mothers increased. Again, we are not looking at disintegration but adaptation.

Given this responsiveness of human behavior it is well to consider the nature of the social conditions which have such profound consequences. Great emphasis has been placed by the government on improving the economic conditions and prospects of the Indians. Surely the importance of employment, adequate housing, food, and clothing to the well-being of the people cannot be overestimated. But in reviewing the cohort histories, the factor which seems most critical for the concerns of this chapter is the nature of relationships with whites. There is already evidence that the integrational policies adopted by the government in education are beginning to have positive results. Intermarriage across the ethnic boundary is one indication of the Indians' growing ability to meet whites on equal terms.

Nevertheless, in marriage and family life as in other community institutions, traditional ideas persist though they are not supported by all sectors of the village population. Certain institutions which receive no expression in the present social structure, such as exogamy, are still advocated by the old people and exercise strong normative power. While the rule of moiety exogamy is usually ignored today, many of the middle-aged feel defensive about their breach of this basic regulation of old Haida culture. The suggestion that the rule has not lost all force receives further support from the fact that lineage endogamy rarely occurs. Competing norms, which receive their strongest support from the young and, to a certain extent, the middle-aged, seem to reflect the development of congruity with the normative system of the dominant society. Attitudes toward dating, marrying for love, and economic independence of the unmarried person and nuclear unit parallel those professed by white administrators and neighbors. Informants expressed the belief that "old fashioned" ideas concerning marriage and the family would be "all gone" in a generation. In the meantime the family, as a result of conservative selectivity in its internal adjustment, continues to support attenuated traditional relationships and behaviors.

Chapter 7
The Domestic Economy

IN 1966 the Masset Haidas exploited their physical environment almost entirely for food: fish and shellfish, berries, seaweed, and deer. Although the federal government regulates some aspects of food gathering and modern techniques of preservation have been adopted, traditional practices of food sharing and mutual aid are preserved.

Other aspects of the physical environment that were once important are now neglected. Hand logging to secure materials for houses, canoes, and totem poles has been discontinued along with the gathering of bark and roots for clothing and utensils. Wood is cut for fuel, but commercially milled lumber is used for house and boat building. A few old people continue furtively to collect herbs for pharmaceuticals, but all accept the medical services provided by the government. Clothing is purchased rather than made at home. The manufacturing of household utensils, baskets, and ceremonial objects had almost died away by 1966, although in more recent years a revival of these arts has occurred. In this chapter we shall consider various aspects of the domestic economy: household income, food gathering, store-bought goods, spending habits, and exchange as observed during the last year of the old administration.

HOUSEHOLD INCOME

In chapter 4, I analyzed occupations and incomes from the standpoint of the Indians' adaptation to the commercial economy. Now I will examine this data in the light of its implications for the household economy of the Haida in 1966.

Earnings from fishing and cannery employment flowing into the Haida village represented a per capita income of $304 per year. A better way of showing the importance of the commercial fishing industry to the family budget is to point out that of 99 households, only 13 received no income from the cannery. In many cases the sums were not significant. In three households, for example, earnings derived from sales of clams by children were less than $25 per household.

In 1965, 57 household heads earned at least $100 in cannery work or fishing while 34 wives of heads earned $100 or more as shoreworkers. The income of heads and wives and their combined income from the cannery is shown in Table 34. Since some of the heads supplemented their fishing income with wage work in other occupations, the figures given for men are to be considered minimum earnings; however, 1965, a poor year for the fishing industry, also saw few opportunities for winter employment. The earnings of women may be regarded as complete since no other employment was available to them. Not included in Table 34 are the earnings of other members of the household, although their incomes may have been considerable. In the discussion of family roles in chapter 5, it was pointed out that junior members of the family do not contribute cash for the maintenance of the household. There are one or two exceptions where the head of the house appropriated most or all of the earnings of his dependents, but the total income available to these households is not shown in the table.

A striking feature of Table 34 is the wide variation in cannery incomes of household heads in 1965. The unknown variable is the amount of other income that may have flowed into the households during the year. We must not assume, however, that heads with low incomes always had other employment. A few cases will illustrate this point.

TABLE 34
INCOME OF HEADS AND WIVES FROM FISHING, 1965

Income	Heads	Wives	Combined Family Income
$ 100–500	11	12	9
600–1,000	9	6	9
1,100–1,500	10	14	8
1,600–2,000	8	2	7
2,100–2,500	5		9
2,600–3,000	6		4
3,100–3,500	2		5
3,600–4,000	2		1
4,100–4,500	2		4
4,600–5,000			3
5,100–5,500	1		1
5,600–6,000	1		1
Total	57	34	61

Jim C., 64 years old, was head of a three-generation family which included his wife, two grandsons whose mother married out of the band, and the nuclear family of his 37-year-old son Bill. Jim, who sold a total of $226 worth of fish to the cannery in 1965, had no other employment. His wife's earnings were $579. His son Bill, father of eight children, earned $1,246 and his daughter-in-law earned $1,143. There was no pooling of funds by the two families sharing the same house.

Stu C., 66, was head of a three-generation household including his 58-year-old wife, three children of their own, and three adult children of his wife's previous marriage. Of these stepchildren, one 35-year-old man was separated from his wife who was in Vancouver and his five children who lived in Masset with their maternal grandmother. The other stepson was a 36-year-old bachelor. An unmarried 30-year-old stepdaughter and her five children also lived in the house. Stu used his outboard motorboat to jig for halibut and gillnet salmon, earning $1,669 for the four-month season of 1965. His wife's income was $1,575. The two stepsons earned $1,411 and $290, respectively, but again, this income was not pooled. Since no cannery earnings are recorded for the stepdaughter, it is likely that she spent the 1965 season elsewhere, leaving the children behind. Neither Stu nor his stepsons had other employment during 1965.

One case in which fish sales were incidental to a man's major occupation is that of Leonard D., 38-year-old father of nine children who described himself as a laborer. During 1965 he made fish sales totalling $17 while his wife earned $1,039 as a shoreworker. The combined income for that household in 1965 probably reached $4,000. In July 1966, Leonard quit his job to go fishing, selling $600 worth of salmon that month.

As indicated in Table 1 (chap. 4), six men combined fishing and logging in order to have a year-round income. One of these men was Glen L., a 31-year-old father of six children. During the 1965 fishing season he earned $2,111 fishing with a mosquito boat, while his wife earned $1,224, for a combined income of $3,335. He probably earned $1,500 in logging the following winter for a total income in the neighborhood of $5,000.

William Barnes was working as a carpenter during this year, bringing home $76 per week after deductions. There were no other earnings in this household which included 14 persons.

Although my data on other sources of income are incomplete, it is safe to say that the principal—and for the majority the only—occupation was that of fishing and cannery work. Data presented in Table 34 suggest that most of the Haida households depending on this source required additional economic support.

FINANCIAL ASSISTANCE

According to information provided by the Indian agent in May 1966, the Social Welfare Agency considered that an income of $180 per month, or $2,160 per year, was adequate for a family of seven in Masset. This estimate took account of the fact that village residents pay no rent or property tax and part of their food supply may be obtained from the environment. Table 34 shows that in 33 households, or 55 percent of those receiving at least part of their income from fishing and cannery work, the combined earnings of husband and wife were $2,000 or less. Most of the three-generation households are not self-supporting even during the productive season. In very few cases does income from fishing last until Christmas, but for those who have worked at least 15 weeks during the year, unemployment insurance is available.

A major source of income for the Masset Haidas in 1965–66 was government funds administered by the Indian agency. Pensions were paid to a total of about 30 aged, blind, and disabled persons. For persons 65 years and over, the federal government pension was $75 per month, supplemented by a $31 per month cost of living payment made by the province.

A monthly family allowance check is paid to mothers by the federal government for every child in Canada, including Indians and regardless of income. In 1966 this amounted to $6 for each child under 10 years and $8 for each child aged 10 to 16 years. The province also paid $45 per month for foster home care for each child who was not living with his own parents. Absent parents are not held accountable for their children's support. The foster care payment, plus the family allowance, supports the many children who are being raised by grandparents or others.

When the Indian agent serving in 1966 took up his post he found 39 cases where foster home payments were being made. Upon investigating he discovered that people had learned to manipulate the system by exchanging children so that each could collect the $45. When the agent insisted that all children be returned to their own parents and that only such placements as he authorized would receive foster home payments, the load was reduced to 16 cases.

It is no exaggeration to say that welfare payments are the economic foundation of the three-generation families and perhaps of many others. It was suggested in chapter 5 that the present family structure of the Masset Haida is, in part, an adaptation to the welfare program. In any case, the cost of the program is very high for this reserve where many large families have inadequate income or no opportunity for employment. During December of 1965 and January and February of 1966, welfare payments for Masset reserve exceeded $10,000 per month according to a clerk in the agency office. In March, with some people working again, the cost dropped to $6,000; the total was $79,917 for 1965–66.

The Indian agent naturally placed great emphasis on work and attempted to persuade employers and prospective employers to hire Indians. There was an arrangement with the cannery whereby the agent was notified of the earnings of all Indians. When the people came to him for relief he was able to refuse them if their earnings were adequate by welfare agency standards. In large households with many dependent children these standards were seldom met.

SUBSISTENCE ACTIVITIES

With a limited cash income at their disposal, many Haida families rely heavily on the food-gathering activities of their members. Of greatest importance is the spring and fall salmon fishery. The spring sockeye run and the late autumn dog salmon run have been reserved by the Department of Fisheries for Indian food-fishing. A permit is required, but this may be obtained by any band member from the Fisheries officer in New Masset. The object of the restriction is to prevent the sale of fish caught for domestic consumption.

Fishing

The sockeye season begins in the third week of April and includes all of May and the first week of June, closing before the commercial fishing season opens, normally on the second Sunday in June. When commercial fishing ends in mid-October the Indians return to the rivers for dog salmon fishing, which lasts until November. This fish is particularly suitable for smoking and in traditional times comprised the greater part of the winter food supply.

The size of the runs varies from year to year and from place to place, but never is there the abundance that the old people remembered as children. Data showing the number of fish caught in spring and fall fishing as reported to Fisheries officers during the period 1959 to 1970 are presented in Table 35. The table shows the number of permits issued in each year, the number of sockeye caught in spring fishing, and the number of dogs taken in the fall. The category "other fish" includes springs, pinks, and cohos taken in the nets during both seasons to give an annual total of all food fish. Some idea of the market value of these catches may be obtained when it is understood that sockeye, which average five pounds, enjoyed a steady price of about 38¢ per pound and dog salmon, which average nine pounds, sold for about 13¢ per pound during the period covered by Table 35.[1]

Considerable fluctuations in supply are shown: 1961, 1967, and 1968 were particularly poor years for sockeye; 1966 and 1967 were disastrous years for the dog salmon fishery. A poor run means hardship not only for persons relying on subsistence fishing but for commercial fishermen as well. In 1966 an average run of sockeye and the near failure of the dog salmon run were compensated for by a phenomenally large run of pinks, which boosted the cash income of almost everyone engaged in commercial fishing. Table 35 shows that in 1965 subsistence fishermen fared quite well although for commercial fishermen the season was very poor.

Different regulations and methods distinguish commercial from food-fishing even when carried on by the same individual using the same mosquito boat. The commercial fisherman using a net 200 fathoms long must fish in open water outside a boundary protecting the mouth of a river. The subsistence fisherman is permitted to set his 40-fathom net across the mouth of the river at spawning time, although he is required to leave one-third of the channel open to allow escapement upstream of some fish. In both cases fishing is allowed during a maximum of four days per week.

In the years since 1965 about one third of Haida householders have applied for food-fishing permits. Ages and occupations of the 34 persons holding permits in 1970 are shown in Table 36. Fourteen were commercial fishermen with an average age of 40. These men comprised 25 percent of the 56 band members holding commercial fishing licenses. Seven were wage earners including one carpenter, four laborers, and two janitors, with an average age of 49. Two salaried men with permits, both 33 years old, were employed by the band council as band manager and school liaison officer. Three unemployed men with an average age of 47 and eight pensioners, including two women, also held permits.

Of the 34 permit holders 28, including a 74-year-old widow, were household heads. The other woman was the 76-year-old wife of the enfeebled hereditary chief, and five men were sons of heads.

To sum up, food-fishing permit holders fall into all age categories, although but 6 percent are young adults. Thirty-eight percent are of the parental generation, 30 percent middle-aged, and 26 percent senior.

---

1. These were the prices paid to fishermen by fish-buyers for the companies. In 1980 they seem impossibly low but the reader is asked to consider them in the light of the gross earnings discussed in chapter 4 and other income data in this chapter. These data from the pre-inflation era make 1966 seem a remote time indeed.

TABLE 35
SPRING AND FALL FOOD-FISHING

Year	No. of Permits	Spring Fishing (Sockeye)	Fall Fishing (Dogs)	Other Fish (Coho, Pink) (Spring)
1959	40	9,856	415	205
1960	NA	13,500	500	253
1961	NA	2,500	2,000	566
1962	50	12,500	2,300	491
1963	NA	11,000	NA	NA
1964	NA	NA	NA	NA
1965	35	4,670	5,500	936
1966	35	4,600	100	85
1967	36	3,200	100	NA
1968	25	3,300	6,000	515
1969	30	5,000	2,500	325
1970	34	7,000	NA	NA

NA = not available.
SOURCE: Department of Fisheries Office, Masset, British Columbia

With regard to family status, 82 percent are household heads although only 34 percent of village households are represented. Forty-one percent are commercial fishermen, but they comprise only a quarter of that group. The point should be emphasized that these are persons who applied for food-fishing privileges; assessments of the relative importance of food-fishing to each group must take into account other factors.

It is true, of course, that while subsistence fishermen are not allowed to sell fish caught under a permit, commercial fishermen are free to keep some of their catch for home consumption. Consequently, the practice of home canning and freezing is undoubtedly more prevalent than these data suggest. Nevertheless, the distribution of fish caught in the rivers during the special food-fishing season is very unequal. There are two reasons for this: first, not all permit holders make a full-time job of subsistence fishing and, second, there is some evidence that traditional claims to the choicest fishing sites are still honored, although informants vehemently deny this.

Subsistence fishing and processing on the river banks is a time-consuming activity, carried out typically by a married couple working as a team. For 25 fish the preparation time from net to smokehouse is six hours. During the 48 hours or more that the fish hangs in the smokehouse over smouldering alder, the fire must be tended so that the proper amount of smoke is generated without too much heat. On the

TABLE 36
HOLDERS OF FOOD-FISHING PERMITS, 1970

Age	Commercial Fisherman	Wage Earner	Salaried	Unemployed	Pensioner	Total
Young adults 25–29	2					2 6%
Parental 30–44	7	3	2	1		13 38%
Middle-aged 45–49	5	4		1		10 30%
Senior 60–76				1	8	9 26%
Total	14 41%	7 21%	2 5%	3 9%	8 24%	34 100%

SOURCE: Department of Fisheries Office in Masset.

third or fourth day the strips of smoked salmon are packed into cans, sealed, and cooked in boilers for four hours. Fishing continues while previous catches are smoked, with an average production of 25 cans per day.

Going up-inlet to fish camp is considered a pleasant outing, for, although the work is strenuous, it is a break from the routine of a large household. During their childhood most of the middle-aged and senior persons were taken to camp with their parents to spend the spring and summer, a practice that caused the Indian agent and teachers great dismay. In the Barnes family, the grandmother and older daughters care for the younger children in their parents' absence. For seven weeks William and Mary Ellen camp on the river bank near other couples, coming back to the village in their mosquito boat once or twice to check on the family and replenish supplies.

When the fish run begins activity is intense. The nets, which are stretched across the river from shore to shore, are pulled in frequently and the fish picked. During the 30 minutes to an hour that the man is occupied with this task, his wife begins to clean the fish. When he has reset the net, he comes ashore to help her. To remove the slime, cut off the head, slit the belly removing the viscera, and fillet the fish requires about 5 minutes. The salmon are washed and then soaked in a brine solution for 30 minutes. After the fillets are rubbed with brown sugar, they are cut into strips and hung up in the smokehouse. When this task has been completed it is time to pull the net again and repeat the process.

When fresh fish are being canned, about 1½ hours are required to clean 25 fish and another 1½ hours to cut the fish into chunks and pack it into cans. The capacity of a boiler is about two dozen large cans, which must be boiled for four hours. Two batches can be processed in one day in addition to tending the net and the smokehouse.

Mary Ellen Barnes recorded in a notebook the number of sockeye salmon she and her husband caught during six weeks in the spring of 1967. During 27 days of actual fishing they caught 606 fish. I have reproduced the record in full (Table 37) in order to indicate the variation in size of catch from one day to another.

TABLE 37
SOCKEYE CAUGHT BY BARNES FAMILY, 1967

Date of Catch	No. of Fish
May 10	3
May 14–19	8
May 23	11
May 24	33
May 25	28
May 26	29
May 28	15
May 29	54
May 31	30
June 1	27
June 2	92
June 4	32
June 5	35
June 6	2
June 7	10
June 8	9
June 9	39
June 11	11
June 12	64
June 13	45
June 14	29
Total	606

The sockeye run began slowly with little profit for the first two weeks, but by the end of May, Mary Ellen and William were catching all the fish they could handle with their equipment. They arose early, attempting to process all fish on the day it was caught so as to maintain its firmness. On May 30 they had to suspend fishing in order to cope with the heavy catch of the previous day. On the second of June their daughter and son-in-law came up to camp and with their help 92 fish were caught, almost twice the number Mary Ellen and William were able to take by themselves. However, the capacity of their equipment could not be increased and again they were forced to suspend fishing the following day.

During the six week season they put up 400 2½-pound cans of salmon and 200 2-pound cans: 1,400 pounds of smoked and fresh canned salmon of the choicest quality. The nearest equivalent in commercially canned salmon sold for $1.19 per pound can in 1967, in Masset as well as in the cities. For their own use the Barnes required 300 2½-pound cans. With their large family two cans are used for a meal or one can for sandwiches. They gave 100 2½-pound cans to Mary Ellen's sister Clara who lives on the mainland and 100 2-pound cans to each of their two married daughters. Some of the salmon was not canned but brought back fresh and given to persons in the village who were unable to fish for themselves.

Subsistence fishing on a scale that will provide a winter food supply for a large family is a full-time job occupying two or more adults for the better part of two months. In a household where there are several children, the tasks of washing clothes, cleaning, preparing meals and so on also demand the full-time labor of at least one adult. In three-generation families where there are married or unmarried adults of the parental generation who can assume these duties, the senior members are free to carry on subsistence activities. Old people with only their own needs to meet are also able to engage in subsistence fishing with the aid of their children or grandchildren.

In two-generation families, however, where one or both parents are employed and there are small children to be cared for, extensive subsistence fishing is not possible. Many of the permit holders who are unable to get away to fish camp for extended periods travel up-inlet for a day or two of fishing, bringing their catch home to can. Even this was not possible for some of the women who were employed in the cannery processing crab during the spring sockeye fishing. These persons obtained their winter supply of salmon by purchasing the dented cans which the cannery could not ship to market.

The home freezer, which had been purchased by at least half the households by 1966, revolutionized food preservation. A wide variety of seasonal foods could be frozen for winter, thus reducing the need to can large quantities of fish. Even the largest freezers, however, cannot hold a winter's supply for a large family, and so it is the heads of the three-generation families, as well as the old unemployable people, who are most active in subsistence fishing and canning.

My observations that some families benefited more than others from subsistence fishing were confirmed by the Fisheries officer, who stated that "25 percent of the people get most of the fish." One man, he told me, caught 1,800 sockeye in the spring of 1970, or 26 percent of the 7,000 fish taken. Others, forced to take an upriver location behind a series of nets stretched from shore to shore, got nothing. One of these was the chief's wife who had gone fishing with her grandson.

For the Masset people, the most important sockeye river is the Yakoun, followed by the Ain and the Awun. For dog salmon, the Ain is the most important source although the Hancock River across the inlet from the village yielded rich harvests of dogs and cohos before it was overfished. The Yakoun, Ain, and Awun rivers, fed by freshwater lakes in the mountains, empty into the wide southern expansion of Masset Inlet, known locally as the "lake." In aboriginal times these rivers were the property of lineages. The Yakoungitinai, the Eagle people of the Yakoun, claimed this richest fishing site as their exclusive preserve. Other rivers and sections of coastline were claimed by other groups, but there were open stretches where anyone could fish without payment. Today, informants insisted, there was no private ownership of fishing sites. Extended discussions with the hereditary chief, with lineage heads and other old informants, pursued from one field season to the next, echoed with the refrain: "All that is gone now; that land is reserve land and belongs to all the Haidas." It was conceded that the family which first set its net in a particular place had the right to use it all season.

But to the Fisheries officer the chief's wife complained that she did not catch any fish because one man had taken the choicest section of the Yakoun and would let no one else fish near him. Moreover, she said, other people had not been able to catch any fish either and had given up. Nothing could be done. The man in question was the senior surviving member of the Yakoungitinai. And for the wife of the chief to whom he referred on ceremonial occasions as "my uncle," not one fish could be spared.

Houses and smokehouses are considered to be owned outright by individuals. In 1966 Mary Ellen inherited "a property" from a "cousin" of her father's who felt, at 73 years, that he was getting too old to go up-inlet to fish. The property, located on the Ain River, included two houses and two smokehouses. Following Haida custom,

Mary Ellen gave her "uncle" $50 in exchange for the "gift." She was very proud of her new holdings, which offered more comfort and convenience than camping on the boat. Her husband, William, had an interest in a second shack on another river.

As we observed in chapter 4, salmon fishing is not simply an economic activity, but the basic element in the Haidas' self-image. Just as the conviction that "Haidas must fish" drives men out to the fishing grounds in their small boats, so the idea that "Haidas must preserve a winter supply of fish" sends the traditionally-minded to camp on the riverbanks, tending their nets.

The set of traditionally oriented behaviors and ideas that surround salmon fishing do not apply to the halibut, which is the other economically important fish. Formerly the people were able to fish for halibut during most of the year but now the season, regulated by international treaty, begins in early May and is closed when the quota is reached. Indians jig for this large bottom-dwelling fish in their mosquito boats. If the storms frequent at this time of year keep the small boats on the beach on days when fishing is open, there is no opportunity to make up the lost time. Consequently, the returns on this type of fishing are very uncertain. William Barnes reported jigging for an entire day and catching nothing but dogfish, a type of small shark. On another day he caught 900 pounds of halibut in four hours. The catch may be sold to the cannery or kept for home consumption. The fish is still dried in the sun on racks leaning up against the houses, but much more is frozen and stored in the family freezer.

With the restriction of halibut fishing, the first fresh fish of spring is the eulachon. Since this species does not occur in the Charlottes, the Masset Haidas are still dependent on the Tsimshian for their supply of fresh eulachons and "grease." The eulachon run takes place in the Nass River on the mainland just after the spring thaw. One of the Masset fishermen made a trip to visit relatives on the Nass every spring in order to obtain a load of eulachons, which he sold to other villagers upon his return. When he had sold all he could at 50¢ per bucketful, he hauled the remainder to the village by truck and called people to help themselves. When he became too old to make the trip, this annual spring event ceased.

Other Food Gathering

Shellfish, which becomes available seasonally, is valued for the variety it lends to the diet. While crabs and razor clams are the object of extensive commercial activities, they are also harvested by individuals for home consumption. Fishermen or adolescents using outboard motorboats may easily set out a crab pot or two. Razor clams are dug on the wide, sweeping Tow Hill beach for sale to the cannery or for the table by men, women, adolescents, and children. After severe winter storms, family groups set out along the north beach to collect scallops which are thrown upon the shore in great quantities. After a "big feed" the surplus is frozen for future use.

Some traditional plant foods are still gathered by the people. Dulce, a black seaweed that grows on the rocks and is exposed at low tide, was formerly made into dried cakes and served with boiled fish or fresh clams and eulachon grease. Now the seaweed is carefully dried in the sun and put into jars "like tea leaves." Berry-picking is still important, although many berry patches have suffered the ravages of deer and cattle introduced to Graham Island by whites. The wild strawberries, which once grew so abundantly on the island, are no longer found; however, huckleberries, salmonberries, and raspberries are eagerly gathered.

Berry-picking is viewed as an outing to be shared by parents and children. In 1966, when few families owned a car, the head might hire a taxi to drop the group off along a roadside lined with berry bushes and to return for them several hours later. As with subsistence fishing, any surplus that cannot be eaten or stored is given away to persons unable to get their own. Unlike fishing, entire families are engaged in food gathering. Often children of nine or ten years who are ostensibly out playing will come home with a batch of fruit or shellfish tied up in their shirts. For this contribution they receive lavish praise.

The work of preserving food other than fish falls entirely upon the women of the household. Not only do they make jams and jellies of wild fruits but often they purchase crabapples, apricots, and peaches at the stores and preserve them in glass jars. No foods are being cultivated at present, although formerly gardens were made on the sites of ancient villages across the inlet and on the north coast. People speak of their crops of potatoes, turnips, cabbages, and carrots with nostalgia but say that it is no use to garden now because the cows and deer eat everything.

Formerly, an important source of food for some families was the "Indian cow." Cattle had been introduced to northern Graham Island almost a century ago. Some cattle were kept at the Hudson's Bay Company post at Masset. Several attempts were made by settlers to establish ranches in the area in the 1890s, but because of the difficulty of sending meat to market these ventures were financial failures (Dalzell 1968; Bass n.d.; O'Neill n.d.). During the 1960s a small herd of a dozen or so cattle of uncertain origin used to wander through the streets of New and Old Masset. These animals, owned by various

individuals in the Indian village, became emaciated during winter but in
spring when the lush grasses sprouted, they moved out to the fields and
soon fattened up. Before freezers were available in the village, cows
were slaughtered for the Christmas feasts. After they had eaten what
they could and canned several cases of meat, the hosts gave away large
quantities of fresh meat. Today much of the beef is simply frozen for
the family's own consumption.

Hunting is comparatively unimportant. Deer, which were introduced
to the Queen Charlotte Islands in 1916, multiplied so rapidly that for
many years hunting season was open all year. On summer evenings
these gentle animals came out of the forests to lick the salt from rocks
at low tide and to graze on the grass planted along the roadside by the
Department of Highways. While hunting is not important as a subsistence activity, a household head and an adult son or son-in-law occasionally go into the bush to bag two or three deer for the winter stores.
The meat is divided equally among the participants in the hunt.

Geese were once so numerous from August through the winter that
they could be counted on as a food supply. The Canada goose still
nests in the neighborhood but it is protected by federal statute. During
the open season from October to January the local flock migrates to
uninhabited parts of the island. Goose hunting is popular with both
whites and Indians for sport and food, but the contribution to the larder
is probably very small.

Store Goods

In this discussion of food gathering we have seen that household
members could obtain a substantial food supply from the environment.
To gain some idea of the amounts and kinds of foods that were purchased, I collected dietary records for two days from 20 girls in my
home economics classes. From discussions with friends and informants
about favorite foods and recipes and from analysis of menus served at
feasts, family meals, and snacks, it is possible to present a fairly accurate picture of food habits. These data do not justify discussion of
dietary deficiencies although the bad condition of the teeth of children
and adolescents suggests that grave deficiencies exist.[2] It is relevant to
note, however, that eggs, cheese and milk, citrus fruits, and leafy green
vegetables were not frequently mentioned in diet records and seldom
did I see them on dinner tables. Most of the eggs that are bought
probably go into cakes and pie fillings. Powdered and canned milk are
used on cereals and in coffee as well as in cooking. Babies are given

2. Nutritional studies of other Indian groups are reported in Lee 1971; Canada 1975.

canned milk in a bottle, but children are fed an adult diet at an early age. Milk is not used as a beverage except in cocoa. Far more popular with persons of all ages are coffee, tea, and "freshie," or Kool-Aid. A great amount of Coca Coca and other soft drinks is consumed. Large amounts of starch, fats and oils, and sugars are included in the diet.

In 1966 food was brought to Masset once a week by the Northland Navigation Company freighter from Vancouver and sold through two stores—the Co-op and "Kurt's," an old-fashioned general store. The Co-op stocks the same products as a city supermarket, including prepared bakery mixes, TV dinners, frozen vegetables, juices, and so on. The proprietor of Kurt's, now retired, had kept a store in Masset for more than 40 years. By offering charge accounts, free delivery, and 100-pound sizes in potatoes and flour, Kurt catered to the Indian trade. It was said that there was one price for whites and a lower one for Indians.

Food prices have always been high when compared with Vancouver prices. Then as now, merchants blamed this on the high cost of shipping. In 1966 such foods as cabbage, potatoes, turnips, onions, carrots, oranges, and apples were in good supply year round. More perishable foods such as lettuce, tomatoes, green peppers, celery, grapes, plums, peaches, strawberries, cherries, bananas, and melons were expensive and scarce. A day after the shipment arrived in Masset, most of the perishables were gone. Supplies of milk, bread and bakery goods were also exhausted days before the next boat arrived.[3]

It was not possible to determine what proportion of these goods were bought by Indians and local whites. It seems, however, that many long-time residents, accustomed to a more restricted selection of canned and preserved foods, had not yet developed a taste for the fresh greens and other vegetables that had recently become available.

When the freighter was delayed by storms or there was labor trouble on the Vancouver waterfront, as was the case in the winter of 1966, the food situation in Masset rapidly became critical. The Indians are not as dependent on the stores for their protein supply as the whites, and more Indian housewives than white bake their own bread. Otherwise, there seems to be little difference in food preferences. Although much fondness is expressed for "Indian foods," the people also enjoy and prepare "Chinese dinners" and Italian-style food. When I was in charge of the school lunch program in the provincial school, the Indian

3. These conditions are even more pronounced in 1980. Since the Northland Navigation Company has gone out of business, irregular and far more expensive barge service has replaced the weekly visit of the *Skeena Prince*. And since Kurt has retired as a general merchandiser, only the Co-op store is open to the public. The Navy establishment has its own restricted base exchange.

girls frequently prepared a fish and potato chowder similar to the Indian fish stew; however, the dish most often requested by students and cooks was my recipe for chili. Another favorite was meatloaf served with creamed potatoes. Carrot sticks, celery, and raisins were requested as garnishes, but I do not know whether these snacks were provided at home.

The Haidas, in common with whites in the area, are extremely fond of baked goods. One old informant said that when he was a boy, "They didn't know how to bake cakes." Now that dessert is the most elaborate part of any meal or feast, some baking probably occurs in most households every day. Cakes, pies, and cookies are consumed at meals and as snacks by family and guests. They are donated to hosts of a feast and contributed to fund-raising projects at school or in the community.

Staple foods purchased by Indian householders include potatoes, sugar, flour, butter, rice, mayonnaise, peanut butter, coffee, tea, Kool-Aid, and canned milk. Pickles, cocoa, canned fruit, canned soups, "store cookies," candy bars, and potato chips are regular items on a shopping list. Hamburger and pork chops are often served at family meals. Turkey, chicken, and ham, though very expensive, are served frequently at feasts and dinners. Such luxuries as a watermelon, which cost $3 in 1966, are eagerly bought when available and I found them to be suitable as gifts. In sum, the food bill, even for families putting up large amounts of their own supplies, is very high, requiring a sizeable cash income.

SPENDING HABITS

The discussion of diet suggests that a large proportion of family income is spent on groceries. No reliable figures on food expenditure could be obtained from the Indians for reasons having to do with eligibility for relief and drinking habits. White residents of New Masset were more willing to discuss the cost of food. Rather consistent estimates ranging from $275 to $300 per month for a family of five were obtained. Such families usually bought a side of beef from a local rancher, but obtained all other food supplies from the store. In contrast to the whites, Haida housewives bought potatoes and flour by the hundred-pound sack and canned goods and fruits by the case. Considering the lavish hospitality extended in the village, however, the expenditure for a family of ten must have reached $250 or more per month. Of course, this seems ridiculously low in 1980. In the light of household incomes tabulated in Table 34, it will be seen as a major expenditure.

For other purchases the catalogues of Eaton's and Simpson-Sears were the most important reference books used in either of the Masset villages. While clothing could be purchased from the local dry goods store or from the limited selection of work clothes at the Co-op and Kurt's, most individuals preferred to order from the catalogue. Household appliances, furniture, and equipment, even when ordered through local merchants, arrived on "boat day," adding to the excitement of that occasion.

Expenditures vary from household to household. Some families have well defined consumption goals where husbands and wives agree on projected purchases. Freezers, refrigerators, and TV sets have had high priority since the installation of electric service in 1964. In some households bathroom fixtures and kitchen sinks had been purchased and were stored in a corner in anticipation of the sewer installation.

Radios, phonographs, tape recorders and watches were purchased by young people earning money of their own. Fashionable clothing was a favored way of disposing of earnings by the young. Adolescent girls adopted calf boots and miniskirts as soon as they became available through the catalogues. At the end of the 1966 fishing season, which was exceptionally profitable, many late model secondhand cars and trucks were purchased. Many persons used the unexpected bonus earnings that year to take trips to the mainland to visit relatives or just to enjoy a vacation. In many households a major item of consumption is beer and wine.

It was not possible to obtain data concerning the number or value of savings accounts or insurance policies held by villagers. The most specific data on investments was that "quite a few" Haidas had shares in the credit union and Co-op. During the long lean winters many persons tried to cash in their shares but were discouraged from doing so by the managers of these organizations.

The spending habits of the Haidas resemble those described for the "shack people" of Springdale by Vidich and Bensman (1958:70). As a result of seasonal and yearly variation in income, consumption is not ordinarily planned far ahead. Little provision is made for ill-health or unemployment. Work and savings are de-emphasized in favor of immediate gratification and consumption. A high proportion of income is spent on recreation, drink, and holidays, while the more provident concentrate on acquiring home furnishings and clothing.

EXCHANGE

Within the community the needs of individuals are satisfied not only by their own efforts but by exchange of goods and services. Goldschmidt has postulated that the function of sharing or goods-circulation is universal although its expression varies with the environmental circumstances in which the society finds itself (1966:87–92). Although Masset does not exist on the brink of starvation, in at least two ways its economy resembles those of marginal food-gathering peoples. First, in a population depending for part of its subsistence on exploitation of the physical environment, there are individuals who are unable for some reason to gather their own food. In Masset these persons are pregnant and employed women and the old and handicapped. Second, the capacity of facilities for preserving and storing food are limited even though the Haida now make use of modern techniques of canning and freezing. With little extra effort, people are able to collect more fish, berries, and meat than they can immediately consume or conveniently store. As we have seen, however, Masset is not totally dependent on exploitation of the physical environment. Every household receives some cash income from participation in the commercial economy or government aid. This adaptation affects the kinds of institutional devices which carry out the function of sharing.

Another aspect of the social order relevant to patterns of exchange is the value system. Consistent with the high value placed on independence of action, the Haidas do not ordinarily *share* in the sense of pooling resources and collaborating in a single task. They give and receive.[4]

Informants insisted that no economic activities are undertaken cooperatively. "Every family gets its own," said Mildred in speaking of fish and berries. "Of course, people do things for each other," Mary Ellen added, almost as an afterthought. "But when you give something you always get paid back, maybe not in cash but in something they think you will like." Emphasizing reciprocity rather than cooperation has significant psychodynamic and sociological results. It underscores the identity and independence of the individual or household and reinforces the network of kinsmen, but does not override groups of narrow range to create a cohesive community. It tends to perpetuate the factionalism and competitiveness characteristic of the traditional village even though overt competition for status and prestige conflicts with the widely supported norm of "equality." Analysis of the Haida exchange system reveals how traditional ideas concerning the use of property as a means of handling interpersonal relations and of defining boundaries between groups are interpreted in the modern context.

In Haida Masset exchange takes the form of sharing, in which there

4. An exception to this generalization is found in the sponsorship of feasts where the host may call upon "close" lineage mates and members of bilaterally linked households for assistance without compensation (see chapter 9).

is ostensibly no expectation of return, and reciprocal gift exchange where the value of the gift is measured and remembered and the expectation of return is explicit. Sharing takes place within the household and in the community as a whole. Reciprocal gift exchange is carried on between households and on a community-wide basis.

Sharing

Within the primary social and economic unit of the household all members contribute their labor to the maintenance of the group. Responsibility for financial support of members falls upon the head who is expected to earn cash or obtain government aid and to carry on subsistence activities. It appears that membership in a household creates obligations beyond the sharing of work, which may be met by the presentation of gifts. In our discussion of family roles in chapter 5, we noted that while adult sons and daughters living at home do not pay room and board, it is customary for sons at least to make generous gifts to their parents and often to other members of the household.[5] The exchange of gifts between husband and wife does not appear to be a formal obligation. The giving of commercial greeting cards and small tokens on birthdays, anniversaries, Mother's Day, and so on seems to depend upon the warmth of the relationship between individuals.

On the community level, sharing pertains to the practice of giving away the surplus of one's own food-gathering activities to persons who cannot get their own supply. Several instances have been noted. Persons who slaughtered a cow for the Christmas feasts gave away fresh meat that could not be consumed or preserved. When the Barnes' were at fish camp they filled their supply of 600 cans and brought the excess fresh fish back to the village for distribution. Women who picked more berries than they could use gave some to relatives or friends. The fisherman who annually brought a cargo of eulachons from the Nass River sold what he could and hauled the remainder to the village where anyone who wished might help himself to the fish.

Traditionally, the disposal of food surpluses was an aspect of the prestige system, for when a chief "called the people in" to a feast, he received esteem for his wealth and generosity. During the 1960s "Indian foods" produced by subsistence activities were not served at the

5. While carrying out fieldwork in the fall of 1979, Marianne Bölscher lived with Emma Matthèws, widow of the late hereditary chief. She thus enjoyed a unique opportunity to observe transfers of cash within and between households. "Cash dealings take place under the table. The amounts depend on need, the kind of occasion, the amount available to the donor and his own economic status. It is a flexible scheme; contributions are expected and they raise the prestige of givers" (personal communication).

ceremonial feast, which featured "store-bought" foods exclusively. This reflects the fact that "surpluses" of wealth for ceremonial events are no longer obtained through the cooperative labor of the corporate lineage, but from the participation of individuals in the market system of the external society.[6]

It is not customary to sell food surpluses within the village. Commodities that are occasionally sold are those which would otherwise be bought at the store or made at home with store-bought ingredients.[7] These include bread, pastries, and "popsicles." Stove wood, which represents a store of labor expended in cutting and hauling it from the forest, is also sold by at least one man.

Food-sharing patterns are distinguished from selling and from reciprocal gift exchange in two ways. Fresh produce does not represent a store of wealth or labor to the extent that canned or smoked fish and cut wood do. Second, the emphasis is on giving to those who cannot get their own supplies and thus cannot be expected to return them. This consideration applies with particular force to the old and handicapped. It is quite likely that persons who are temporarily unable to participate in the food quest, such as employed and pregnant women, regard food gifts as an obligation to be repaid. I was not able to determine whether people felt constrained to return their own offerings to the specific persons who had helped them or whether they gave where the need was greatest. It is my impression that the latter is the case. However, the practice is carried out so informally that I could not learn what criteria influence "givers" in selecting specific recipients for their surplus goods, nor could I induce informants to speculate about this issue.[8] No one would concede that the traditional practice of making

6. An entirely new form of feast where the guests are nonlocal "friends of the Haida" had developed by the end of the 1970s. Here the sponsor is, for instance, a prominent native artist or the incoming "hereditary" chief, assisted by his own kin network, the band council, and a majority of Masset Haida residents. This latest cultural florescence, expressed in the renewed interest in dancing, carving, and other arts, is also reflected in the menu. At the four-day "Tribute to the Living Haida" held in Masset at the spring equinox (March 19–22, 1980), the major feast included such delicacies as smoked salmon, halibut, ghow (*k'ao*—herring roe on kelp), seal meat, dulce, and for dessert *djitl*, canned native berries. I cannot escape the conclusion that the people see all this as "show business." At the large family dinner held in Emma Matthews' house at Easter 1980, the menu was the familiar one of turkey, ham, mashed potatoes, dressing and gravy, carrots and peas, cranberry sauce, cole slaw, ice cream, and the usual pies and cakes.

7. By 1979, Marianne Bölscher reports, smoked salmon, eulachons, and other foods are occasionally sold (personal communication).

8. Marianne Bölscher, noting the sources of gifts flowing into the Matthews household in 1979, has observed that neighbors as well as kinsmen exchange food. In trying to understand why the chief councilor brought fish to Emma, she learned that his family used to live close by and he continues to honor this bond even though he has moved to the other side of the village (personal communication).

prestations to members of father's matrilineage is still observed or that this model guided their own "giving."[9] Informants apparently do not keep mental note of the many occasions when they "caught more than they could use and gave the rest away to the old people." As there are no verbalized rules for dividing the catch, it seems fair to state that food sharing in Masset is not systematic. Since the physical survival of all persons is minimally provided for by welfare and pensions, food sharing is a secondary rather than primary device for ensuring the food supply of the society's members.

A second type of sharing on a community-wide scale is the assistance offered to persons who have suffered some catastrophe. The most frequent occasion for such assistance is a house fire. Survivors of a fire are showered with gifts of money, food, clothing, furniture, and other goods.[10] In contrast to the ceremonial exchange system, it appears that no records are made of the source and size of these contributions. While no repayment is required, the appropriate gesture for recipients of community aid is to give a "thanking feast" to all who helped them. When the large old house of the hereditary chief burned down in 1962, the chief and his wife were assisted in reestablishing housekeeping in a small shack previously occupied by the chief's brother-in-law who had perished in the fire. The old couple was entirely dependent upon their government pensions and so could not repay the assistance they had received. It is clear that his indigence was a factor in limiting the chief's prestige since, as will be seen in chapter 8, he was criticized for not giving feasts as chiefs are expected to do.

Persons who are able to mobilize the necessary labor, money, and food to give a "thanking feast" may take advantage of this opportunity to improve their standing in the community. When Peter Jones' four-year-old grandson was lost overnight in the bush behind the village, scores of volunteers from the Indian village, New Masset, and the Navy base turned out to search for him. Several months later the Joneses rented the community hall and invited not only their fellow villagers but their white neighbors to a "thanking feast." A turkey dinner was served, speeches were made, and apples and oranges distributed as gifts. Few Haidas, however, are as meticulous in their observ-

9. This is an instance where the general applicability of personally observed norms is not recognized. When I sponsored a memorial feast for Peter Hill in 1971 and thereby validated my name in the Kun lanas lineage (see chapter 9), I received substantial donations not only from senior lineage mates but also from some of the young adults. Marianne Bölscher confirms that the obligation "to give" to members of one's own lineage is still compelling. Donations of $5 to $10 are expected for ceremonial events, but a $20 gift is still uncommon (personal communication).

10. Community assistance rendered to kinsmen of persons who die in fires follows the rules of the ceremonial exchange system which is analyzed in chapter 9.

ance of cultural norms as the middle-aged Joneses. Their care in re-
paying every obligation of either an economic or ceremonial nature,
their seizing of the opportunity to obtain an Indian name for Pete, and
their indispensable aid to the ethnographer in recording "Haida customs" belie their insistence that the prestige game is dead. In this
game, it is clear, one's performance in the exchange system is still of
crucial importance.

Reciprocal Gift Exchange

Reciprocity characterizes the exchange of goods between members
of linked households, reinforcing the network of relationships. The
circle of reciprocating gift givers includes those parents and married
children, siblings and more distant kin, and friends who collaborate in
supporting both the ceremonial exchange system and purely sociable
affairs. In Masset this unit is the most effective and least formalized
voluntary association. In few cases does the group include all eligible
participants, all married children or siblings, for example. On the contrary, several householders who are considered eccentric by my informants keep entirely to themselves, neither contributing to nor attending the social and ceremonial affairs of other families, including close
relatives. An extreme case is that of a man who bought headstones for
two dead sons, took the stones to the cemetery and placed them on the
graves, without giving a feast to the old people as required by
custom.[11]

The circulation of smoked and canned fish frequently entails reciprocal exchange. Earlier in this chapter we referred to the Barnes' practice of putting up 100 cans of salmon for each of their married daughters and one of Mary Ellen's sisters. Since the installation of electricity
in 1964, small electric appliances are often given in exchange for such
gifts. Prominently displayed on a shelf in Mary Ellen's kitchen is an
array of such articles, each representing the return for 100 cans of
salmon. A sister in Prince Rupert sent an electric frying pan, while
another sister in Vancouver gave a tabletop mixer. One daughter and
son-in-law presented an electric tea kettle, while the other daughter
and her husband gave an electric coffee pot. Clothing is sometimes
given. One Christmas Mary Ellen received a red wool dress and William a sport jacket from a non-relative in return for a gift of 100 cans of
fish. The dress was one size too large, but Mary Ellen wore it anyway,
explaining that to ask for a different size or to refuse to wear it would
signify lack of appreciation. On another occasion Mary Ellen's sister in

---

11. It was this same man who took the unusual step of appropriating the earnings of
his dependent adult children.

Vancouver sent her a pink suit trimmed with marabou feathers, also in return for a gift of fish.

Reciprocal exchange also operates on the community level, most notably in the ceremonial sphere where public payment is made for prescribed ritual services to kinsmen of the opposite moiety. This type of exchange, which is derived from potlatching and carried out in the context of the feast, is analyzed in chapter 9. A second form takes place at "parties" celebrating birthdays, wedding anniversaries, and other occasions not considered as life-cycle events. Middle-aged and older women or, alternatively, couples are invited to a social evening at the host's home. Here exchange involves the presentation of small gifts to the honored person in return for an invitation issued by a close relative of his. A very popular gift for such occasions has been bone china teacups, available in a wide range of patterns and prices. Many china cupboards in the village are filled with exquisite tea services which are used frequently in entertaining.

The idea of exchange extends to informal social interaction. Frequent visiting between households maintains a high intensity of contact. The people consider relatives at New Masset snobbish and unfriendly because they do not maintain this informal interaction even though they regularly attend feasts. I noticed a distinct coolness on the part of my closest Indian friends when other responsibilities such as teaching, housework, and record-keeping cut down on my regular visits throughout the village. When I returned to the field after the major part of my study was completed the chief's wife said, "You are losing all your friends in the village because you don't come to visit often enough." This expectation of continuous social interchange underlies the villagers' characterization of nonresident kin as "white men."

In studying the commercial and domestic economies as they functioned in 1966, we have found strong continuity in the nature of economic activity, in seasonal work patterns, and in the exploitation of traditional resource areas. Although other avenues of employment were, in principle, open to the Haidas, the majority of workers were still engaged in fishing and shorework. Earnings were supplemented or, in some cases, replaced by subsistence food gathering and government assistance, which freed the people from total dependence on the market.

Changes in the commercial economy since 1966 reflect conditions in the external field. After the cannery passed out of local hands in that year it served primarily as a remote fish-buying station for a succession of Vancouver-based corporations. Long the major industry on the northern Charlottes, it no longer offered employment to more than a few of the Indians. The federal government's salmon license limitation program, aimed at eliminating marginal producers, wiped out almost the entire Indian fishing fleet in Masset. "Only a few" still fish. Men seek employment as laborers when work is available, but usually it is not. With the Canadian economy in decline, little capital is pumped into peripheral areas such as the Queen Charlotte Islands. The band council is able to hire villagers for various community construction and improvement projects but its resources are limited. A growing number of individuals are engaging in the carving of gold, silver, and argillite for sale. A major new art form is the silk screen print, which finds a ready market in the cities.[12]

In the domestic sphere, food-gathering activities continue to be important although few men still own boats. Cultural persistence extends to cooperation by the family unit and patterns of exchange. Underlying these behaviors are traditional ideas concerning the uses of property and the meaning of wealth. Although "wealth" is still employed by some middle-aged and older persons to gain prestige in the hosting of lavish feasts, it has alternate uses. Many families prefer to spend their earnings on consumer goods, travel, or drink. With the exception of the latter, these expenditures also contribute to prestige. A second point is that since an emphasis on wealth is inconsistent with the need for welfare assistance, this central theme of old Haida culture does not receive explicit formulation in the value system. That people still think in these terms, however, is evident in their behavior. In chapter 9 we shall return to the subject of the ceremonial uses of wealth.

12. Bölscher (1977:9) describes the development of Haida art up to 1976. Other workers are studying the art industry. Margaret Blackman and Edward Hall are preparing a publication on this subject. Also see Stewart 1979 for the graphic work of Robert Davidson.

Chapter 8
The Matrilineal Model

THOUGH ALL that was left of the matrilineal structure in 1966 was the remnants of eleven lineages divided between the moieties, the matrilineal model continued to govern ceremonial relations and interactions within the community.[1] To be sure, it was only in the feasting complex that the lineage retained any of its former functions. Even here, however, where the linked households of the feast-sponsor assume the economic burden and the moiety classification of participants is emphasized, the central role of the lineage is submerged. It has become a shadow structure in which only the principal members are visible, even to other Haidas. Of its elaborate symbolic properties—the crests, songs, dances, myths, names, and titles—only the latter two are preserved. But the lineage principle still has meaning as a way of classifying village members, as a basis for allocating prestige symbols, and as a symbol itself of Haida identity.

TRADITIONAL KNOWLEDGE

In the face of the extensive social changes documented in preceding chapters, the people themselves underestimate the continuity of their way of life with old Haida culture. But although they see only change, their behavior on ceremonial occasions reveals the observance of traditional rules. My early efforts to understand the implicit structural framework within which these rules operate were confounded by informants' insistence that "All that is gone." Many persons expressed the opinion that my attempts to obtain data on kinship terminology, genealogies, and lineage affiliations were "a waste of time."

Old people who are primarily Haida speakers and who use English as

1. Unless otherwise indicated, the time frame of this chapter is 1966. Many of the people we meet here are gone by the late 1970s.

little as possible were reluctant to be interviewed when I called upon them. They protested that their English was poor, that they had forgotten too much, that "Everything is changed now." They were apprehensive about the question-and-answer routine and they were shy. When I interviewed middle-aged informants in their homes, these persons often referred my questions to older relatives in the household; however, much that was said was not translated. In view of the generally warm reception of my visits, I attributed this to impatience with the routine rather than to any desire to conceal information from me. Later I heard that "the old people" were pleased that someone was writing about the "old-fashioned ways." Their behavior when we met socially or on the street was friendly but still reticent. Occasionally when I was seated beside a senior guest at a feast or "party," I was able to obtain fragmentary data on participants and proceedings.

Half a dozen of the old people were fluent in English, accustomed to dealing with whites, and could become very expansive when the topic interested them. Vehement discussion was provoked by the subjects of rank and chiefship, but these issues appeared relevant to the speakers only in a historical perspective. Their interest was in setting the record straight regarding claims to high status made by certain individuals and they appeared to believe that my "book" was the means by which this aim might be accomplished.

Kinship Terminology

Kinship terminology was not a subject which stimulated much interest. I attempted, both in formal interview sessions with my most cooperative informants and in casual conversations with others, to elicit kin terms. Kinship terms used by English speakers include: mother, father, brother, sister, aunt, uncle, niece, nephew, cousin, grandson, and granddaughter. No terminological distinctions between maternal and paternal relatives are made in English. In other respects, however, the English term is not necessarily used with its English meaning. For example, sibling terms are extended to all children of parents' siblings. When sibling terms are extended to all members of the "tribe," i.e., lineage, the distinction between own and classificatory kin is expressed as "my own really sister," and "my sister Haida way." The term cousin is widely used but its referents are vague. From observation it appears that cousins are own-generation kin distantly related. Their children are nieces and nephews, as are the children of own siblings.

Parent terms are not extended unless adoption has occurred. Mother's sister is aunt. This term applies also to father's sister, to mother's brothers' wives and father's brothers' wives, and to grandparents' female siblings. Similarly, the term uncle applies to mother's brother, to father's brother, and to the husbands of "aunts." The term is also extended to the second ascending generation.

The single Haida word for grandchild is replaced by English terms recognizing sex differences. The Haida terms for grandfather and grandmother, which do not discriminate between paternal and maternal ascendants, are the only native kinship terms carried over into English. All Haidas use the old terms, pronouncing them as "chinny" and "nonny," for own grandparents and for other old people for whom they feel a special attachment.

Terminological merging of kin categories in translation does not necessarily reflect a shift in role content and obligations. For while the authority of mother's brother has certainly diminished, the ritual role of father's sister continues to be of great importance to the individual. That old people still think in traditional kin categories is illustrated by the frequently heard warning cited in chapter 6, "You can't go out with him because he's your brother [or uncle]." The old man who felt that "the old Haidas knew what they were doing when they didn't let close relatives marry" obviously did not consider first cousins in the opposite moiety as relatives. Haida speakers, including those who are bilingual, continue to use the Haida kinship vocabulary. While I have no data as to what terms may have become obsolete since Murdock's study (1934), it is clear that many distinctions obscured in English are preserved in the ceremonial context.

Genealogical Knowledge

In contrast to the recording of kin terms, the collection of genealogies was greeted with enthusiasm. After one middle-aged man took the pencil from my hand to draw his own kinship diagram, I made a practice of offering pencil and paper. While no older people accepted, many of those in their thirties and forties did. School children also appeared to enjoy the exercise when I administered questionnaires in my part-time role of school teacher.

The genealogical knowledge of most young and middle-aged persons was confined to parents' living siblings and to members of own and descending generations within a narrow span of bilateral kin. While living grandparents were treated as close relatives, their siblings often were not and consequently knowledge of them was scanty. Persons in the middle-aged and younger generations usually possessed slight knowledge of the membership of their own lineages. Those in their forties and fifties remembered being told by a parent or older relative that they belonged to a particular "tribe," that a certain man was their "uncle," and that they must always do what their uncles told them. They were also instructed that so and so was a "brother" or "sister" and was not to be dallied with. Even persons as active in the feasting complex as Ethel Jones, who was 46 at the time, had difficulty with questions concerning genealogies and lineage affiliations. In a few of the extended family groups there was a senior member who could give fairly complete genealogies for four to five generations of a limited segment of the population, usually their own and their father's matri-lineage. George Jones, for example, who was 82 when I interviewed him in 1962 could list his father's five brothers, their wives and children, and supply the lineage affiliations for in-marrying spouses. With the aid of these old informants I was able to construct partial genealogies for most of the old village groups that had relocated in Masset 100 or more years ago. What resulted were diagrams of four to five generations descended from a sibling set born roughly between 1850 and 1880. Where sibling sets representing known lineages were linked by marriage, the tracing of lineage affiliations and construction of kinship diagrams was a simple task. In many cases, however, genealogies included individuals without living kin, a consequence of the massive population losses of the last century. The greatest difficulty lay in identifying the lineage affiliations of lone females espoused to members of a sibling set. Informants could say only that so and so was a "cousin" of someone else or that "they had the same grandmother." The use of English kin terms obscured the distinctions necessary to trace matrilineal descent. Although I was occasionally able to obtain the Haida term for a given relationship, the informant usually professed ignorance of the precise links.

The kin diagrams based on informants' recollections were checked against the census, birth, marriage, and death records kept at the Agency office. Church records were also used in cross-checking relationships as described in chapter 6. Though gaps remain in the larger demographic picture, it has been possible to determine lineage affiliations, where they have been assigned, for all but nine persons living in Masset in 1966. These data are presented in Table 38. The lineage principle is employed here as a classificatory device, which means that these persons are potential and not necessarily active participants in ceremonial activities.

Three categories of persons cannot be classified as lineage members. Two unclassified Ravens are descendants of non-Haida Indian women whose clans were equated with the Raven moiety but who were never adopted into any lineage. Seven persons are non-Haidas who have married band members, while 71 persons are descendants of non-

Haida women who were not classified as to moiety or lineage. In chapter 6 it was noted that these people stand outside the exogamic rules.

The age and sex of members of the matrilineages of the Eagle and Raven moieties are presented in Tables 39 and 40, respectively. Here the small number of individuals in the ceremonially active age groups may be seen more clearly.

LINEAGE ORGANIZATION

Despite their small size and lack of solidarity the lineages remain an important unit of identification for the old people. It is possible to think

TABLE 38
LINEAGE AFFILIATIONS OF VILLAGE RESIDENTS, MAY 1966

Moiety, Lineage Number*	Lineage	No. of Persons	Percentage of Total Population
Eagles			
E1	K'awas (E 21a)	33	4.9%
E2	STA' stas (E 21)	12	1.8
E3	Djatlanas (E 18)	84	12.5
E4	Gitins (E 11, 12, 13, 14)	50	7.5
E5	Tcetsgitinai (E 17)	101	15.1
Total		280	41.9%
Ravens			
R1	Masset Yakulanas (R 19a)	44	6.6%
R2	Dadens Yakulanas (R 19)	71	10.6
R3	Stlinglanas (R 15)	55	8.2
R4	Kun lanas (R 14)	92	13.7
R5	Kiänushilai (R 17)	30	4.5
R6	Skidaqao (R 16)	10	1.5
	Unclassified	2	.1
Total		304	45.2%
	Non-Haida spouse	7	1.0%
	Non-Haida ascendant	71	10.6
	Not Known	9	1.3
Total		671	100%

*I have adopted Swanton's device of identifying lineages by a number preceded by E or R to designate moiety. Since many of the lineages he recorded have died out or amalgamated, I have assigned new numbers to extant groups. Swanton's designations appear in parentheses after the lineage name.

TABLE 39

Age and Sex of Eagle Lineage Members on Reserve, May 1966

Age Group	E1 K'awas N=33		E2 Sta'stas N=12		E3 Djatlanas N=84		E4 Gitins N=50		E5 Tcetsgitinai N=101		Total Eagles		
	M	F	M	F	M	F	M	F	M	F	M	F	T
Children 0–14	11	10	1		22	19	14	10	22	29	70	68	138
Young adults 15–29	2	6	3	2	10	9	3	7	14	7	32	31	63
Parental 30–44	1	2	2		5	4	5	1	6	5	19	12	31
Middle-aged 45–59		1	1	1	7	3	1	1	4	4	13	10	23
Senior 60–86			1	1	2	3	5	3	7	3	15	10	25
Total	14	19	8	4	46	38	28	22	53	48	149	131	280

TABLE 40
AGE AND SEX OF RAVEN LINEAGE MEMBERS ON RESERVE, MAY 1966

Age	R1 Masset Yakulanas N=44		R2 Dadens Yakulanas N=71		R3 Stlinglanas N=55		R4 Kun lanas N=92		R5 Kiänushilai N=30		R6 Skidaqao N=10		Total Ravens		
	M	F	M	F	M	F	M	F	M	F	M	F	M	F	T
Children 0–14	12	6	16	19	16	11	30	26	10	9	3	1	87	72	159
Young adults 15–29	8	4	7	5	4	7	10	9	1	4	2	1	32	30	62
Parental 30–44	2	1	9	4	3	1	5	3		2			19	11	30
Middle-aged 45–59	5	2	4		6	3		3	1	2	1	1	17	11	28
Senior 60–86	2	2	1	6	2	2	2	4	1			1	10*	15	25
Total	29	15	37	34	31	24	47	45	13	17	6	4	165	139	304

*Two additional Raven males in senior group are not assigned to any lineage, but are included in the total males.

of the senior age grade as a special interest group whose object is to practice and preserve the traditional culture by deploying an estate of names and titles owned by the lineages. With their power to bestow prestigious names and witness their validation, the old people can reward the aspirations of village members who still subscribe to neotraditional values. The passing on of names is a means of recruiting new members into the senior age group for, until they are so honored, middle-aged persons are not considered as *bona fide* members of lineages but as descendants or relatives of members. The middle-aged are, in fact, the persons who sponsor most of the feasts, accepting extensive obligations of reciprocity in exchange for the approval and recognition of the old people. Their active interest and participation are necessary to the survival of the institution.

A distinction must be made between persons who are ascribed membership in the matrilineal groupings on the basis of genealogical relationship and those who have validated their names, thus becoming principal members of the lineage. These names determine the lineage's internal organization of statuses and roles. When the incumbent of a high status name dies, the senior members of the lineage meet to select a successor, a procedure which may require hours of deliberation on successive evenings before consensus is reached. The candidate is usually the nearest matrilateral relative of the deceased. If this person already possesses a name, he may waive his right in favor of another, although there is no rule prohibiting an eligible person from assuming several names. The selection of Peter Jones to succeed his "maternal uncle" Joseph Edgars is an example of this kind of decision. Although any of Joseph's three younger brothers were eligible to claim the name they agreed, with consent of other members of the lineage, to designate Peter as heir. Since the name conveyed headship of the Stlinglanas lineage, the election of a 52-year-old man to a rank higher than that of senior lineage mates was a great honor. This gesture was especially meaningful because the name had previously belonged to Peter Jones' paternal grandfather, James Jones. Great prestige is attached to this form of inheritance.[2]

A name must be formally assumed by "giving a feast to the old people," a practice which is the modern equivalent of receiving names at a potlatch feast witnessed by lineages of the opposite moiety. Not everyone who is next in line can afford or cares to give a feast and so the name theoretically remains inactive. Nevertheless, several persons are acting as lineage heads without having performed this obligation and their legitimacy does not appear to be challenged.

2. See figure 6, chapter 9.

Relative ranking of names determines order of speaking at feasts. The hereditary town chief, Willie Matthews, is expected to give the opening speech at every feast, but, according to Ethel Jones, he sometimes waits for George Jones, head of the Tcetsgitinai "family" to speak. "When George speaks first he always apologizes for speaking before Willie." At other feasts I have heard senior members occasionally rise to speak, first apologizing for preceding the town chief. "When the Yakulanas give a feast they use Percy Brown right after Adam Bell." In this case, Adam is recognized as head of the Masset Yakulanas. Percy Brown, who was senior male member of the Alaskan Haida group absorbed by the Masset Yakulanas, ranked second in this lineage.

The name Sidaso, belonging to Henry Edenshaw, who headed the Dadens branch of Yakulanas, was passed to two maternal nephews—the eldest son of his eldest sister who is six years younger than the eldest son of his second sister. Since the younger man did not attend any of the feasts I observed in 1965–66 I was not able to learn who would have taken precedence in speaking.

When Peter Jones became head of the Stlinglanas, his wife Ethel noted that his lineage mate Willie Russ, who is his senior by 17 years, would not rise to speak until Peter had addressed the gathering. Sometimes, however, "When Pete feels it is too early in the feast for him to speak, he will nod to Willie to go ahead."

Only the senior set of lineage mates is visible on ceremonial occasions. Clearly, mutual obligations of matrilateral kin within the lineage have been greatly relaxed, probably because they cannot be enforced. On the other hand, role obligations linking members of different matrilineages remain crucial. Particularly important are the ritual responsibilities performed by father's sister. It is she who dresses the body at death, who wipes the tombstone when it is loaded on a truck to be taken to the cemetery and again when the stone is placed upon the grave. It is male cross-cousins who help with the body, dig the grave, and move the coffin. Later they will move the stone to the grave. When, as frequently happens today, the prescribed kinsman is not available, a person of the proper age and sex in the opposite moiety is asked to play the role.

In discussing the allocation of ritual roles, informants stressed that the "aunty" who wipes the stone must be of the "other side." Again, "people who bury you always belong to the other side." Informants appear to think of a network of kin roles bisected by the moiety division rather than in terms of contraposed lineages linked by obligations to male members' children. Under present conditions the first model is still workable while the second often is not. Emphasizing the moiety makes available a larger pool of relatives from which a substitute incumbent for a prescribed kin role may be drawn. Ethel Jones confirmed my conclusion that the moiety has assumed greater importance when she explained that she "didn't know the tribes of all the people because Raven and Eagle is more important now." Young people are often referred to by their elders as Ravens or Eagles. In identifying even the senior participants at feasts, informants would use moiety membership as a primary classification, which confirms that this is the most salient grouping today.

In view of the widespread lack of knowledge about traditional society among younger and middle-aged people, I sought to determine whether new criteria for classifying village members had been introduced. I wanted to know whether economic achievement, living standard, traditional versus acculturative orientation, or personal behavior such as drunkenness and promiscuity affected one's reputation or standing in the community. I prepared a "card game" by typing the name of each living adult member of the community on a small card, intending to ask informants to sort the cards into piles of "persons who have the same standing in the community." I was able to induce seven persons to play my card game: the hereditary chief and his wife, both in their seventies; a 59-year-old high-ranking woman; and four persons from undistinguished families—a man of 69 years, two men and one woman in their fifties.

Six persons interpreted the question as one concerning lineage membership. The four persons of undistinguished background, claiming insufficient knowledge of "families" and "tribes," were unable to assign the majority of cards to any group. I received one complete set of cards classified according to lineage membership by the chief and his wife who collaborated. They did not attempt to get through this task as rapidly as possible but, on the contrary, spent two hours bending over the dining room table, discussing individuals, working out genealogies aloud, assigning cards tentatively to one pile, shifting some of them after further reflection. It is significant that not even the chief and his wife could correctly identify the lineage membership of all adult Haidas, for when I subsequently attempted to use this set in compiling a roster of lineage members I found many errors.

The seventh player, the 59-year-old woman of high status, understood the question as one of rank. She sifted slowly through the cards, placing them in one pile, peering over her glasses at me from time to time. Finally she handed the cards to me saying that she was sorry but she could not do this. Her father had taught her that all people were equal and it was wrong to speak of some as higher than others.

Clearly the people do not feel that matrilineal kinship has been replaced by any other principle as a basis for classifying village members. At the same time, knowledge of lineage affiliations of co-villagers has become irrelevant to participation in activities which the lineage formerly dominated. Other groups are now involved in ceremonial events—the bilateral kindreds of the feast sponsors, the moiety, and the whole community. In analyzing the feasting complex in the next chapter, we shall ask what groups play what parts in the ceremonial exchange system.

Matrilineal Groupings

The five Eagle and six Raven lineages listed in Tables 38, 39, and 40 are those recognized in 1966. George Jones in 1962 recalled several subdivisions of these lineages, which were autonomous branches separated from the parent stock several generations ago. As these localized branches dwindled to a few members, their survivors merged. The Gitin lineage, E4, for example, now includes the S^eadjuga𝑙 lanas group of the hereditary chief, the Yakoungitinai and all other Eagles of Masset Inlet. Similarly, the Kun lanas group of Ravens, R4, includes the last survivors of the Yakoun River and Rose Spit Ravens.

Several of the groups are still identified with abandoned village sites. Thus the Stᴀ'stas, E2, and the K'awas, E1, are spoken of as "those people from Kiusta," while the Djatlanas, E3, and the Tcetsgitinai, E5, are "those people from Yan." These expressions do not, as I once imagined, reflect a merging of old-village kin groups in a reference group based on locality along the lines of modern Masset.

The K'awas and Stᴀ'stas lineages are grouped together by some informants since K'awas now has no recognized head. As Table 39 shows, the oldest male of this very small group is in the 30–44 age grade. Although the K'awas was an offshoot from the Stᴀ'stas many generations ago when they occupied Hiellen on the north beach, the heads of these two lineages were subsequently rivals for the ownership of Kiusta. By a lavish expenditure of wealth on housebuilding and potlatching, the Stᴀ'stas chief wrested the town chief's title from the K'awas who had colonized Kiusta. The sense of grievance over this unsuccessful competition was still being nurtured in 1962 by the last K'awas chief, Morris Marks.[3]

The fortunes of the Stᴀ'stas plummeted in turn. Their ambitious chief, Albert Edward Edenshaw, after winning Kiusta, later claimed to

---

3. The story of the K'awas lineage at Kiusta is analyzed in my paper, "Succession to Chiefship in Haida Society," which will appear in *The Tsimshian and Their Neighbors*, eds. Miller and Eastman (University of Washington Press, forthcoming).

be the "greatest chief of all the Haidas," superseding even Weah, town chief of Masset. It was part of the political game for chiefs to glorify themselves and the people treated such extravagant statements with scorn. So preposterous was Edenshaw's claim to be the great chief of Masset during Chief Weah's tenure that no one bothered to correct the white visitors who readily accepted it (Chittenden 1884; O'Neill n.d.). The present head of the small StA'stas group is an undistinguished man of much lower rank and far less prestige than two of the female members whose brother left the reserve years ago.

Two major branches of the Raven Yakulanas lineage remain. The head of the Masset Yakulanas, R1, who have "always" lived in this village, formerly occupied Mission Hill, which lies in the center of modern Masset. They have absorbed a small group originating in Alaska. The second major branch, the Dadens Yakulanas, R2, owned a village at North Island within sight of Kiusta which was then owned by the StA'stas. In fact, the town chief at Dadens was the son of Chief Edenshaw. By frequent intermarriage these two groups shared the reciprocal relationship of father's matrilineage. Although the prestige of the StA'stas has fallen with the death and migration of its ranking members, the Dadens Yakulanas still retained their high position in Haida society in 1966.

The Stlinglanas, R3, I was told, "had no village" but its branches, like the Kun lanas, lived in Masset Inlet, on the north beach and on the rocky west coast. In the 1960s there was no public acknowledgment of the fact that the Stlinglanas, as the amalgamation of surviving Rear Town People, R15, owned the old village of Yan across the inlet (Swanton 1909:87, 281 #89). Curiously, my informant was my close friend Peter Jones who had recently been elected head of this lineage in preference to several senior kinsmen (p. 224). Why did he conceal the momentous fact that with his assumption of the lineage headship he became the town chief of a major village? Perhaps it was because of the great prestige of two Eagle chiefs of Yan—his father, George Jones, head of the Tcetsgitinai, and Robert Davidson, head of the Djatlanas. It would have been impolitic for a relatively young man who had not previously been classified with the "high ranks" to claim precedence over such distinguished "subchiefs." Indeed, he probably could not have gotten away with it. But where assertiveness would have brought swift rejection, Peter Jones' modesty and dignity were rewarded with esteem.

The Skidaqao, R6, who are closely related to the Kiänushilai, R5, are often grouped with this lineage by informants. The Skidaqao, which numbered only ten in 1966, was one of the most powerful Haida groups in aboriginal times when it owned the village of Masset. When its ranking member, the town chief Sígai, designated his own son as his heir, the village passed into the hands of the Eagles. The event, which is considered remarkable by informants because it "broke the custom" of matrilineal succession, provided fuel for rivals who challenged the legitimacy of the contemporary hereditary chief. This chief, William Matthews, who described himself as "the fourth and last Weah," gave the following account of his predecessor's appointment.

Chiefship in Masset

Chief Sígai, the head chief of Masset, married the sister of Skil ta qá dju, who was the Eagle chief of a village called Sᶜuldju kun across Masset Inlet. "Our grandmother got a son, first born." He grew up with his uncle whom he expected to succeed as town chief of a village of perhaps 200 persons.

> There was a girl over on the west coast in Tian. She was the chief's daughter and was very pretty. Our grandmother's son from here got one of his father's servants to take him across the inlet in a canoe in the fall of the year. He walked on the beach way around to the west coast. When he got to Tian he stayed with relations from here. He stayed a whole year. He got married to the chief's daughter. After the marriage his father-in-law gave him a six fathom canoe, dried halibut, dried black cod, preserved fruit and two man-servants.[4] He came back here to his father's village.
>
> He was very popular with his father's tribe members. He got lots of property by hunting. His father made a big feast. He called people from Yan, Kayung, Hiellen, Sangan, all the towns around. When all the guests were here, the chief said, "I got a son. He's very popular here. He's a good hunter and has slaves of his own. I don't want him to be a common member of this village. I give him this village."

Other informants believed that Sígai's son had already assumed his uncle's place as chief of the Eagle lineage, Sᶜadjugaɫ lanas. After the great feast where he was named heir to his father, Skil ta qá dju moved across the inlet to Masset, bringing several households of kinsmen with him. Upon assuming his position he took the name of Weah, which had belonged to his father's father, a K'awas chief.

It is significant that although the title to the town "jumped clans," or in our terminology, moieties, Weah did not inherit the symbolic properties of his father's lineage. The name Sígai was passed down to matrilineal heirs. Nevertheless, Sígai's own prized crest, the grizzly bear, which is exclusive to the Raven moiety and nowhere is claimed by Eagles, was ascribed to Chief Weah by customary usage. This suggests that Weah was perceived as uniting the village. Swanton refers obliquely to this affair. He remarks of the Sᶜadjugaɫ Town People

4. A euphemism for slaves.

(whom he refers to as E14) that, "In former times it was considered a rather inferior division; but very recently its chief has become town chief of Masset, *by sufferance of the people, and owing to his personal popularity*" (1909:101, emphasis mine). In his list of towns the following entry appears for Masset: Family: Skidaqao (R16) recently given to the chief of the Sᵉadjugaɬ lanas (E14). Chief: Sígai (1909:281, item 87). Curiously, in his list of houses in principal towns, Swanton lists the house of Sígai as number 11 and "Wia" as number 13, but designates another, "Grisly bear house," belonging to another member of the R16 lineage, as the house of the town chief (1909:290). Further work may clarify this anomaly.

While the succession of a son to the highest political status in a matrilineal society may seem extraordinary, there was apparently no protest by Sígai's contemporaries. The appointment not only testifies to Chief Sígai's great prestige and power but suggests that there may have been more room for maneuver than conventional accounts allow. The appointment of Weah must have been acceptable since the candidate fully satisfied all the achieved and most of the ascribed qualifications for highest office. He was the son of a great chief in a society where chiefs' sons enjoyed high prestige and was, in addition, a town chief in his own right. He had married the daughter of an important town chief, had amassed wealth, had slaves, and was extremely popular with the people of the village.

In Tikopia the selection of a chief outside the senior branch was corrected by a return to that line in the next generation (Firth 1960). At Kloo, an important southern Haida village, the chiefship passed temporarily into the hands of a junior lineage, but reverted to the senior line when a successor became available (Swanton 1909:96–97). No such reversion occurred in Masset, which became the property of an Eagle lineage.

When Chief Weah died in 1883 without naming a successor, two candidates were put forward for the town chief's position. This case allows us to observe both the mode of *election* of a successor and the limitations of competition as an avenue to highest office. Weah's own family preferred his sister's son Harry, while the other subchiefs supported Paul Ridley, who was also a member of the Sᵉadjugaɬ lanas (E14). Paul was "prominent" in Masset, meaning that "he was a big man, polite, obliging, good-natured and wealthy" (Peter Hill, personal communication). Weah's immediate kinsmen considered Paul too distantly related, although he was a "blood relation of Weah's on his mother's side and a cousin of Harry's." For their part, the subchiefs of the lineage maintained that Harry wasn't wealthy enough to be town chief of Masset. At the potlatch held to decide the merits of the candidates, "The family produced things so Harry could prove that he was worthy. Harry couldn't do this for himself. Paul didn't need help." In the end, the sister's son was installed in the town chief's house, his opponent's wealth, display, and personal achievement notwithstanding. Peter Hill, who told me this version of the story, was Paul Ridley's paternal nephew (Stearns forthcoming).

Although it is difficult at this distance to assess the character of Harry Weah, it appears that his disappointing performance of the town chief's role downgraded this highest status in Haida society. Harry appears in the pages of the Indian agent's reports as an indigenous authority figure to be consulted about the designation of reserves, the location of the school, or a visit of the bishop. He was not prosperous and does not seem to have given any memorable feasts. His personal behavior in cohabiting with another man's wife was considered so unworthy by his contemporaries that he was excommunicated from the church. At feasts given by rivals he was deliberately slighted when the seat of honor and invitation to speak first were offered to someone of lesser rank. Much of the esteem reserved for persons of chiefly status and qualities was bestowed upon Henry Edenshaw, son of Albert Edward Edenshaw who had claimed to supersede Chief Weah. Nevertheless, claims to highest rank by Edenshaw's children and grandchildren on the basis of their paternal ancestor's achievements and pretensions were and are angrily rejected by other villagers. The implications of this case are considered further in my analysis of chiefship in Haida society (Stearns forthcoming).

When Harry Weah died in 1932 he was succeeded by his sister's son, Willie Matthews. According to some informants, Willie was not allowed to assume the high name of Weah because of objections by survivors of the K'awas lineage which originally owned the name.[5] Willie told me in 1962 that he had long ago adopted the name Skil ta qá dju which was one of Chief Weah's early titles. By this date he had firmly asserted his claim to be the "fourth and last Weah." Continuing opposition to his incumbency came from members of the Masset Yakulanas who have "always" lived in this village. Although they are not closely related to the Skidaqao who formerly owned the town, they claim to be the "real owners" of Masset. They pointed to George Spence, an unassuming middle-aged fisherman as the "real chief" since, as the oldest surviving male of the Skidaqao, he was nominally heir to the name of Sígai.

But while conflicting claims and rivalries between the highest rank-

5. Also Swanton 1909:290, item 13. The chief's widow insisted, in 1980, that the name owned by the K'awas was transcribed as Wiat. (Roger Wiat enters the demographic record as the second husband of Willie's mother, Kitty.)

ing families still reverberated in the 1960s, the majority of Masset
Haidas acknowledged the precedence of the hereditary chief whose
role retained symbolic significance for the entire community. It was he
who presided at ceremonial affairs within the village, although rivals
occasionally attempted to minimize his role when they were hosts. It
was the hereditary chief who represented the community in dealings
with whites. For example, he thanked the volunteer firemen from New
Masset and the Navy base for putting out a fire on the reserve. He
thanked the teachers in the New Masset school at the graduation dinner. He welcomed visiting dignitaries to the reserve and was invited to
participate in ceremonial occasions "outside." The latter two duties
were often shared with the chief councilor as the elected representative
of the people.

When asked whether he was trained to be a chief by his maternal
uncle with whom he had lived for many years, the chief's wife inter-
rupted, "No, that's how they did it in the old days." Willie, who was
born in 1887, added that he had learned by making speeches in the
villages, serving on the band council and "helping his people." His
performance of the chief's role was criticized by other villagers who
felt that he "caters too much to the whites and doesn't stand up to
them." Others complained that he never gave feasts, comparing him
unfavorably with the Davidson family whose large house was the scene
of frequent ceremonies.

In contrast to the Davidson family, which could mobilize eight
households including those of married daughters living in New Masset,
the chief had very limited resources. His household consisted of a wife,
a widowed daughter employed at the cannery and a great troop of
young grandchildren. Two other daughters married out of the band.
Being dependent on his old age pension, the chief had little to spare for
gift exchange. Since the ten middle-aged and senior members of the
Gitins lineage which he headed represented not a single descent group
but several branches of Masset Inlet Eagles, this group does not function as a solidary unit. Consequently the chief was unable to enlist the
aid of lineage mates who acknowledged his status but offered no material assistance. His inability to provide the feasts expected of a chief
limited his influence. Even so, the chief's great dignity and courtliness
of manner earned him the respect of villagers and outsiders.

In speaking of the role of the chief Willie said, "There is no respect
now for chiefs but it is what you make it by your own character and
reputation. You can build it up yourself today. If whites respect the
chief it is because of what he does." As a man who had served 48 years
on the band council including several terms as chief councilor, as
special constable, lay reader in the church, and active organizer in the

Native Brotherhood in Masset, the chief could claim to have met the expectations of community service attached to his role. In addition he was always called upon as counselor and comforter during the life crises of his people.

When discussion turned to the future, Willie repeated that he was the last Weah. He had no sister or sister's son, but his "cousin" has a "niece" living in Prince Rupert. "She has lots of children but they wouldn't come back to the village. They have homes and jobs. They are white men now." Willie had proposed that he give "the name" to his "grandson" but when this 20-year-old daughter's son of the opposite moiety was declared unsuitable by villagers, he dropped the idea.[6]

Although people insist that the role of chief is unimportant, their behavior frequently asserts the contrary. Traditionally the chief occupied the seat of highest honor and was the first to speak at feasts. In looking for evidence of treatment accorded the chief on ceremonial occasions I found that he occupies one of several such seats since both the head and foot of each of the long tables are places of honor. Others assigned to these seats are ranking old men representing the various lineages and, occasionally, the minister and the ethnographer. All persons so honored are expected to take part in the speechmaking following the meal. In this context then, the chief's position is not unique, although he clearly takes precedence as demonstrated by the fact that if others are called upon by hosts to speak before him they apologize for doing so.

One incident I witnessed indicates that even on non-ceremonial occasions the chief is treated with deference. The adult son of Peter Hill had drowned and about a dozen people gathered for a prayer service in the old agency residence where the bereaved father lived. When the prayers had been recited and the hymns sung, silence settled over the old house. Low pitched voices passed on a bit of news or spoke of plans for the funeral. During a lull in the talk there was a sudden loud rapping at the door. Startled, a few people jumped up but it was several moments before a man collected himself and crossed the room to open the door. In came the chief. There was a scraping of chairs as people rose quickly from their seats. The old ladies sitting on

6. When Hereditary Chief William Matthews died in February 1974, it was not clear who, if anyone, would succeed him. At a memorial service which I attended in August 1974, the chief's role as first speaker was filled by his *widow*. In 1976 the status of town chief was assumed by Oliver Adams, son of Alfred Adams and Selina Harris. Born in 1914, a member of the Eagle Gitins lineage, Oliver had lived in Prince Rupert for many years where he worked for the Indian Affairs Branch. His accession was marked by a lavish community feast, better described as a "media spectacular." Oliver Adams died in October 1979. It now appears that there are many candidates for the vacant office of hereditary town chief.

the sofa near Peter Hill moved aside. The minister reached for his coat,
but the chief rose from the sofa and detained him, thanking him for the
honor of his presence in the house of his uncle's son, a prominent chief
of Masset. He spoke in loud tones, though conversation had ceased.
Then he spoke at length in Haida. Only when he sat down did the
minister and a few of the old people leave. The old father repeated to
his kinsman the circumstances of his son's death and the speculation
that it was a heart attack and not a drowning. He spoke of the esteem
with which his son was remembered by outsiders. The chief nodded
sympathetically, looking discreetly at his watch from time to time. All
others in the room sat silently, seeming not to breathe, listening again
to the long tale in Haida. When it was finished all sat motionless for
several minutes. Finally the chief rose and came to me, as the only
white person remaining, to thank me for coming to console his relative
in his hour of pain. Then he hurried out. Later I asked a close friend,
who had earlier complained of the chief's poor performance, why
everyone had jumped up when Willie Matthews came in. She said
simply. "It is because he is our chief." But while the symbolic role of
the hereditary chief as representative of the Haida community is generally recognized, in the eyes of his rivals Willie Matthews was simply
the head of a weak and intrusive lineage whose members had no interest in maintaining his prestige.

Analysis of the internal organization of the lineage has shown how
slight are the prerogatives attached to names of high status. Indeed, the
lineage as a system of ranked statuses whose occupants enjoy differen-
tial access to symbolic properties has vanished. Only the status of
lineage head is distinguished although other "old men" who have received names and play active ceremonial roles are considered principal
members of the group. While prestige, reflected in the order of speaking at feasts, is attached to the position of head, comparatively little
attention is paid to the qualifications of candidates.

Some incumbents have been elected by a council of lineage elders,
but in other cases the senior male in the group is referred to as the
head. Little concern is shown over the fact that some so-called heads
have not validated their names in a feast. Nor have I ever heard any
expression of disapproval for this omission. In contrast, great concern
is shown over the qualifications and actions of instrumental leaders,
those who occupy political or association offices.

We have seen that with the loss of its corporate functions the lineage
has gradually diminished in size and importance. With changes in the
internal structure of the matrilineal descent group, interrelations of
groups have lost their competitive character. No longer does the potlatch or its present form, the life-cycle event, mediate the contest for

status and prestige between members of contraposed corporate groups. Nor, on the other hand, does it demonstrate consensus on social precedence. While lineage activities continue to express the traditional ideas of rank and matrilineal kinship, rank is no longer defined primarily with reference to the unilineal descent group. High status is still based on birth, but claims to social precedence are made by paternal as well as maternal descendants of chiefs. It should be noted, however, that the former claims are angrily rejected as illegitimate by the majority of villagers. And while the individual may earn prestige by the performance of traditional cultural behaviors and the support of traditional values, he is not thereby admitted to the "high ranks."

RANK

Traditionally, both ascriptive and achievement criteria were employed in the recruitment of persons to roles of high status. The Haidas had well-formulated expectations regarding the qualifications for chiefs, which included high birth, wealth, and personal qualities such as ambition, aggressiveness, and generosity (Swanton 1909:69; Niblack 1888:37, 250, 372). Their performance was continuously evaluated in these terms. Although the traditional system of status and authority has been discredited by the people as well as decapitated by the Canadian government, there is evidence of strong internal conflict between the norms of rank and "equality." This latter norm, which is often expressed as, "We are all brothers," "We are all equal," or "Nobody is better than I am," is supported by the economic independence of individuals. People deny the superiority of the "high ranks" and refuse to accept their leadership in political office, special interest groupings, and other community activities.

Yet many villagers, and particularly descendants of the old elite, retain a sense of the psychological importance of traditional rank relationships in the face of the fact that they are not really operational and, more important, are not honored by the external source of power with its "real" rank differences. This normative dissensus has serious implications for leadership and relations of authority.

Authority Roles

Norms of excellence and the sense of *noblesse oblige* were inculcated in many of those who are now senior members of the village. Not only the descendants of chiefs but the children of upwardly mobile individuals were imbued with a sense of responsibility for community welfare. Ethel Jones whose family is of "middle rank" said that her mother's brother instructed her not to refuse if people wanted her to do something or to serve in an office. Such "lecturing" by uncles was an important aspect of the socialization of many persons born as late as the 1920s.

Political office and the role of community leader have frequently, though not exclusively, been undertaken by persons of high rank. Often this expression of civic responsibility is interpreted by other villagers as a claim to authority on the basis of traditional rank. Leaders whose efforts are frustrated and resented become discouraged but claim they cannot find younger people to "take over." Voluntary associations collapse because of this tension and lack of support. The ideal of community service appears to have been internalized by a minority of villagers whose leadership is not acceptable to the majority. Or, perhaps it is simply the exercise of authority that is not acceptable.

Until recently an exception was made for authority enforced by coercion, such as that of the government. But while the people could not successfully challenge the authority of the Indian Branch and its agents, they could and did repudiate their band councilors. Villagers badgered councilors with charges of favoritism toward their own relatives, abused them verbally, and complained of a lack of leadership.

The political situation has long been complicated by an ideological issue. As "wards of the government" who have given up their autonomy and been "defrauded of lands and fish," some persons feel that they should "get everything they can" out of the government and white society. This militant position has had many spokesmen over the years. The moderate position, which stresses self-reliance, is also of long standing. Because its proponents are achievement-oriented and are often highly successful participants in the commercial economy, they are characterized as "pro-white." Members of both factions are elected as band councilors; the balance at any time is a good barometer of public opinion.

This factionalism does not merely subsume traditional rivalries. Between families of highest birth, status competition tends to be expressed in contests for the most prestigious association offices and for the reputation of most generous host. But political competition polarizes those of high birth and those of high ambition. There are few if any militants (as the term is used here) of high status. On the other hand, the militant faction provides an avenue for social mobility for new and younger leaders whose families were not active, or at least not successful, in traditional competition.

The people respect ability and select their councilors with this in mind. Those whose qualifications are most evident are persons of established prestige. This explains why councilors have so often been selected from among the "high ranks." In practice, they are also moderates whose views are acceptable to the Indian Affairs Branch. Once elected, however, these councilors may not represent public opinion, which then swings sharply against them. Disillusioned and sometimes embittered, they withdraw or threaten to withdraw from public service. They are replaced at the next election by militants who give voice to the community's resentments and hostilities. But the militants in turn find the role of councilor too circumscribed and they tend to take *ultra vires* action. Alternatively, the militants act as informal leaders with no institutionalized roles, mobilizing an aroused public opinion in opposition to the counsel of elected officials. They may seize the opportunity to assert leadership not only outside the formal framework but outside the community, as we observed in the cannery strike of 1964. In times of unstable intervillage relations, then, competition for status within the community is extended to political activity in the external field. But while the factions divide the villagers, they also focus attention on Indian–white relations. In the process, much of the bitterness aroused is channeled into political competition between the adjoining communities.

In 1966 the most prominent of the militant leaders was Mary Ellen Barnes. A woman of great energy, ambition, and civic spirit, she was motivated not only by the desire to gain prestige, but by a genuine concern for her people's welfare. She was in her mid-forties and the mother of 12 living children. While several Masset women have rendered outstanding community service over the years, few have chosen to engage in politics. Even Mary Ellen did not proceed with a frontal attack, but helped put her husband in positions of leadership and then stood beside him. When William was elected to the band council she attended all meetings where she supported and defended him from the floor. But the band council, hedged about by statutory limitations, offered little scope for effective political action.

The United Fishermen and Allied Workers Union was a more promising prospect. Although she no longer worked at the cannery, Mary Ellen managed to be elected, along with her husband, as a delegate to the union convention in Vancouver. In the second year of their participation the Masset delegation presented several resolutions promoting Indian welfare and the safety of fishermen. More important was the instruction in union organization and tactics which the Barnes' received in the study sessions, for, more than any other person, Mary Ellen Barnes was responsible for the wildcat strike of 1964. She became the spokesman for those in the community who felt angry and alienated. Described by New Masset whites as "the leading light of the

Revolution,'' she enjoyed an ascendant position in the village as long as the tide of anti-white feeling was rising. But when the object of the strike was attained, she bore the brunt of the white backlash. Sobered by the hostile reaction in New Masset, her supporters fell away and her prestige plummeted. The extent of her disgrace was vividly expressed in the fact that only 20 persons attended the elaborate wedding of her daughter later that season. A year later when I returned to spend my field year, she had been restored to the good graces of her fellows though not to a position of leadership.

The moderate who was elected chief councilor in the wake of the cannery strike was a 60-year-old man whose talents and civic-mindedness were praised by Indians and whites alike. He had served several terms on the band council, including a previous term as chief councilor. Because he had been employed by several government agencies and expressed liberal political views, he was considered pro-white. Although he was selected at this time as the person most able to smooth over the rift between the villages, his initiatives were not supported. While this man had a Haida grandmother, his father belonged to a chiefly family on the mainland. When the son married a high-ranking woman in Masset, he transferred to this band. The villagers claim that he is not, after all, a Haida, while he blames his troubles on the jealousy of persons descended from high-ranking families. He no longer takes any part in political life in the village.

His successor as chief councilor was a 42-year-old man of high-ranking family who worked as skipper of a cannery boat. His success in fishing was clearly demonstrated by his well-dressed family and by the large modern house which he built with his own earnings. He was selected for a leadership role because of his intelligence and ability, but lost support allegedly because of his pro-white leanings. As chief councilor he practiced a private form of government, holding closed council meetings in homes to avoid ''arguments.'' He had also withdrawn from active participation in village life although he is involved in the ceremonial affairs of his family.

The man who was chief councilor at the time of my first visit in 1962 and again in 1965 was a man of high rank, who earned his living as a skilled carpenter and boatwright. In office, he endeavored to forestall criticism by soliciting wide opinion before taking action. His attempts to establish consensus were often construed by both Indians and whites as an inability to make decisions. When his daughter was a member of my cooking class she expressed a vehement wish that her father would not be elected chief councilor again because of the blame and criticism he received during his previous terms. Another young girl added with uncharacteristic intensity that "Nobody will do anything but criticize." She went on to say that she wished the old men would run for council. "Young men are elected but they don't do anything. They are educated but they don't know anything. The old men never went to school but they know more."

Clearly, the "leadership vacuum" deplored by government officials and Haidas alike was not due to an absence of capable, committed persons as they imagined. One factor in the pattern of non-support of native authority figures is ambiguity in the qualifications for leadership which reflects the value conflicts inherited from traditional society. The criterion of high rank, though relevant in a ceremonial context is, in theory, rejected as the basis for instrumental leadership. In practice high-ranking persons have consistently been elected to office. Ability is recognized, but able men are frustrated rather than supported in office. Ideological position on the overriding question of how to deal with whites is important but public opinion on this issue fluctuates. It is difficult to assess the value placed on economic achievement. Certainly many of the councilors have been successful participants in the white economy. Many "achievers," however, have been disinterested in the internal affairs of the Indian community or have espoused values not shared by the majority of their fellows. Age is another factor of uncertain significance. Band councilors usually reflect a wide range of ages, including men in the productive age group from 30 to 45 as well as middle-aged and senior men who are less active in the marketplace. Of course, any given councilor will combine different values (in the mathematical sense) of these attributes, which makes it difficult to determine their relative importance.

A second aspect of the observed inability of many leaders to act effectively is the fact that no real power is attached to internal leadership roles. Villagers realize that ceremonial activity is a game that earns its participants no recognition or respect in the larger society where power is actually located. Informal leaders occasionally exercise power or influence, but it cannot be institutionalized. Band councilors, who occupy the only formal authority roles, are regarded as ineffectual by their constituents who take their requests and problems directly to the agent. Since the administrative role of the Indian agent on the reserve has been eliminated, band members chosen by the council now occupy the roles of band manager, welfare officer, community health worker, and home-school coordinator. If any real authority were attached to these roles we might expect to find a gradual change in villagers' atttitudes to native leaders.

Slave Descent

The gradual blurring of status differentiations within the community has not only undermined the position of the "high ranks" but improved that of persons of slave descent. In discussing rank with villagers in 1962 I was told that it was "wrong" to refer to the low-class or slave background of other Haidas because, "That is all over." "We are all equal now." "Descendants of those people still live here and it would make them feel bad." "It makes them feel low." "They threaten to commit suicide or leave here."

On one occasion when I had been working on historical materials in the Indian agency files at New Masset, I asked a man of high rank whom I encountered on the street who George Keetla was. He snorted and replied, "He was a slave. We're not supposed to talk about that anymore but here come two now," he said, indicating an old couple coming toward us. This kind of remark by a member of the "high ranks" indicates that the old attitudes have been softened but not eradicated. Still, the old habit of saying of a person whom one wanted to insult that he was descended from slaves has been replaced by the charge that he drinks.

I was also told by several informants that there was "a law against calling anyone a slave." People believe and state that "you can go to jail for calling somebody a slave." I combed through the agency papers available to me but could find no such by-law nor any reference to it. Neither the agent, the magistrate, nor anyone else in New Masset had ever heard of the alleged law. I consulted the Assistant Indian Commissioner for British Columbia with the same results. One of my informants, however, whom I will refer to as George Patterson, told me that in 1952 he had been "thrown in jail for three weeks for calling another man a slave."

It happened that an Indian youth of slave descent was appointed band constable. Said George, "He shouldn't have been." On one occasion when George was having a riotous party in his house, the Indian constable and a white provincial constable came to the door on a complaint from the neighbors. George reacted with rage, directing his anger at the Indian and shouting, "You dirty slave, you should be working for me. You should be put in a hole under the totem. Get out of my house," and so on. The provincial constable took charge, arrested George, and secured his conviction. According to agency records, George was charged under Section 110 of the Criminal Code, which makes it an offense to incite any Indian to commit an indictable offense, presumably by making a request or demand of an agent or servant of the government in a riotous, disorderly, or threatening manner or in a manner calculated to cause a breach of the peace as stipulated in Section 109a of the Criminal Code. George and others did not attribute his arrest and conviction to his riotous and disorderly behavior in obstructing a peace officer in the execution of his duty. They believed that he had been arrested and jailed because he called the Indian constable a slave. The incident made a profound impression on the people. Few of them would discuss slavery with me at all and then only in whispers. Not only does this example offer some insight into actual as opposed to normative attitudes, but it illustrates the process of reinterpretation of events involving agents of the dominant society in order to make them more meaningful in Haida terms.

An important milestone in the blurring of internal status barriers was the betrothal in 1948 of this same Indian constable to the daughter of one of the highest ranking households in the village. She is, in fact, the sister of the man who had told me that George Keetla was a slave. The old couple he had pointed out with contempt were close relatives of his own brother-in-law.

The community was shocked at the announcement of the betrothal and predicted that the bride's mother would never permit the wedding to take place. Preparations went forward. At the wedding feast the groom's father, who was very much esteemed in the village in spite of his low status, acted as "toastmaster." The bride's mother, a lady of great dignity, spoke to the guests saying, "Let there be no talk. I want these people to be happy. He is one of us." I believe that what happened here was that the status of the groom but not of his family was elevated to that of his bride. To all outward appearances this marriage has been very stable and successful. The man financed and built his own modern house and is skipper of a cannery boat with one of the highest incomes in the village. He is not active in village social life; his own relatives do not sponsor feasts nor does his wife take any prominent part in the ceremonial activities of her kin.

In subsequent field seasons, beginning in 1965 and continuing through 1974, no unsolicited reference was ever made to the slave background of a villager. This may simply reflect the fact that I was working with different informants; as my interests shifted from ethnohistorical research to an emphasis on contemporary social organization, I spent a larger proportion of my time with younger people. For these persons relative age is far more important as a principle governing role allocation and social participation than is hereditary status. In most cases they do not share the traditional knowledge nor do they take an active part in ceremonies where status and rank are recognized. On the other hand, the young and middle-aged participate in educational, economic, and political institutions where power is clearly vested in agents of the dominant society. From this perspective status competition in traditional terms is a charade. But although the rules and meaning of the prestige game have changed, relationships between the players are still defined by matrilineal kinship.

The discussion of household structure and family roles in chapter 5 has shown how fully institutionalized are patterns of paternal authority, conjugal teamwork, the autonomy of the nuclear unit, and the bilateral extension of kin ties. This fundamental shift from a matrilateral to a bilateral emphasis in the organization of primary kin groups has affected inheritance and the transmission of status. Changes in these institutions demonstrate the effects of direct intervention by the external society as well as the development of congruity with other "exposed" institutions, the family in particular. The transmission of property from father to children of both sexes is consistent with the bilateral model. This new pattern of inheritance is reinforced by government intervention for, as we noted in chapter 3, the Minister of Indian Affairs has power over testamentary matters concerning deceased band members. Nevertheless, there is a strong element of cultural continuity in these institutions. Since matrilineal descent still serves as a principle for classifying kin in wider contexts, traditional rules governing succession and inheritance are occasionally invoked. The resulting disputes over property may be interpreted as a conflict of norms, old and new. But if attention is shifted from the social system to the individual, these disputes illustrate the alternatives that may be manipulated for personal advantage.

The best-documented case concerns the claim of a man we shall call Elton Forrester to the house built by his mother's brother. His wife Myrtle cited this affair as an example of proper behavior for a nephew wishing to acquire his uncle's property. When his uncle Robert Hardesty died in 1941, Elton "fetched the body home from Rupert, paid for the coffin, bought the funeral clothing and all the rest." Immediately after the funeral he occupied the house, justifying his action on the grounds that he had paid $795 for burial expenses. Since he had had the foresight to keep all the receipts, probably anticipating a dispute, he felt that his claim was irrefutable. The house was also claimed by the uncle's "adopted son and daughter." Myrtle stressed that "they were adopted Indian way—no papers." Community opinion favored the adopted children since, after all, passing property down in the paternal line was "the new way of doing things." Although Elton and Myrtle received a great deal of unpleasant criticism, they refused to surrender possession of the house. The controversy simmered along for several years until finally the band council, which must approve transfers of lots, invited the disputants to present their claims. The Indian agent who attended the meeting forwarded the matter to Ottawa. In due time Elton was notified that "Ottawa had made its decision." The resolution passed by the band council in June of 1954 clarifies the details. When Robert Hardesty died, he left as his only heir his wife Fanny, a fact omitted from all verbal accounts of the case. When Fanny died in 1944 she left as her only heir her sister's son, "Henry Rogers," and it was this person who, according to Ottawa, was the rightful heir. If he would reimburse Elton for his expenditures for the funeral then he would inherit the house. We must note that Henry Rogers was not only the sister's son of Robert Hardesty's second wife, but the sister's son of Myrtle's mother. Since he already owned a house, he asked that the property be awarded to Elton, his "cousin's husband." The council agreed, but its resolution reflects its own interpretation of the facts:

"Whereas [Henry Rogers] is prepared to relinquish his right of succession to the only asset of the estate of [Robert Hardesty], the said lot . . . in favor of [Elton Forrester] in recognition of the wish expressed before his death by [Robert Hardesty] that his nephew [Elton] become his sole heir and in acknowledgement of expenditures incurred by [Elton Forrester] in caring for the remains of and erecting a memorial to [Robert Hardesty] and whereas this council can confirm the common knowledge of the Masset Band of Indians that the said [Elton Forrester] is recognized as heir of the said [Robert Hardesty] the transfer of the property is approved." In other words, the principle of matrilineal descent was invoked to explain the disposition of the case. At the outset Elton's claim based on traditional rules and behaviors was widely criticized and that of the "adopted" Hardesty children was supported by public opinion. The Indian Branch interpreted the case in the light of Canadian law, but its decision was rationalized by the band council as a vindication of custom. Verbal accounts of all parties entirely ignore the rights of the surviving spouse and the reasoning that led to the designation of Henry Rogers as the heir. Informants are more impressed by what they see as the rejection of the claim of the adopted children in favor of that of the maternal nephew.

Another case, described as "the same" by informants, involved the estate of Robert's brother, Jasper Hardesty. The house was claimed by the sister's son and by a man who described himself as an adopted son. Ottawa determined that the so-called adopted son was not a relative and the sister's son was the next of kin. This case too was interpreted by villagers as upholding the principle of matrilineal descent. It is significant that these disputes were stalemated for 13 years before the agent referred them to Ottawa for decision. This fact indicates that there are no mechanisms in the community for settling disputes between rival claimants. Even had informal means been available, there is a strong possibility that Ottawa might have reversed any such settlement, thus discrediting the native proceedings. Once a binding decision was imposed, however, the community was able to reinterpret the event in terms of its traditional idea system. As often happens when the external society intervenes in internal matters, the rules applied seemed ambiguous and arbitrary to the people. This ambiguity provides scope for alternative strategies.

Like inheritance, the transmission of status is subject to ambiguity as a result of the shift to bilaterality. The prestige attached to genealogical relationships to great chiefs is claimed by their children's children and other bilateral descendants. Two matriarchs who have been contending for several years for highest standing in the community are, respectively, daughter of the son and daughter of the maternal nephew of the prominent Eagle chief, Albert Edward Edenshaw. Each woman uses this relationship to support her claims. The privileges of rank, however, are not subject to bilateral distribution. Names and titles continue to be handed down to the oldest surviving male member of the lineage regardless of his rank. As we noted earlier the head of Edenshaw's lineage, the StA'stas, in 1966 was a man of low rank and little prestige who could trace no genealogical relationship to his predecessor. Occasionally a woman assumes her "uncle's" name, while in other cases the name is "forgotten."

The weakening of boundaries between overlapping bilateral and matrilateral kin groups reinforces a tendency toward congruity with the class structure of the outside world. An aspect of this shift is the separation of class standing from the ceremonial symbols of rank. These remain firmly attached to the lineage although much of their significance is lost. It has already been observed that with the devaluation of titles, some lineage heads do not trouble to validate their names, while upwardly mobile lower ranking persons may easily claim a name belonging to their matrilineal grouping. Although this action, legitimated by the provision of a feast to the old people, raises the prestige of the individual, he does not thereby enter the "high ranks" which are restricted to "descendants" of chiefs. It is noteworthy that these "descendants" include patrilateral as well as matrilateral kin (Stearns 1977).

The extent of change in Haida kinship and social organization can easily be overstated. The point that new forms emerge from preexisting ones is pertinent here (Goldschmidt 1959:133). The traditional importance of the conjugal bond, for example, is attested by Murdock's detailed description of the cooperation of spouses in hosting a potlatch (1936; also Swanton 1909:162). The ritual unity of husband and wife is demonstrated by the magic rites they performed before the husband went to war and by the strict taboos which his wife observed in his absence (Swanton 1909:54–56). The potential for bilateral organization which is suggested by these observations was suppressed by formal rules supporting a system of matrilineal descent groups. The links between uterine siblings and between mother's brother and sister's son were defined as pivotal social relationships superseding the marital relation and the father-child bond. That these rules governing group membership, succession, and inheritance were not inviolable even in traditional times is indicated by the instance, cited earlier in this chapter, where the town chief of Masset appointed his *son* to succeed him. When changes occurred in conditions permitting the existence of unilineal descent groups, particularly the institution of property and a median population density, the formal apparatus maintaining the matrilineal system gradually collapsed.

Simpler bilateral forms emerged in response to economic and demographic changes of the later nineteenth and early twentieth centuries. Changes also occurred in the distribution of social functions among groups of varying range and in interrelations between groups. In considering the functional specialization of kinship groups in the modern era we observed that matrilineal groupings are oriented to ceremonial, noneconomic aspects of behavior. They survive within the Haida community, protected by and reinforcing the ethnic boundary.

Chapter 9
The Ceremonial Exchange System

THE SYMBOLIC ACT at the core of the feasting complex and extending beyond it to every aspect of social life is exchange. Analysis of the ceremonial exchange system of the Masset Haidas will show how the continuity of matrilineal kinship patterns and obligations is maintained in the face of extensive changes in family organization. We shall see that traditional obligations involving public payment for ritual services performed for a kinsman by relatives of the opposite moiety are met by a group of closely related lineage mates, supported by members of their bilateral households and the senior age group of the village.

The cycle of exchange is renewed when an individual, announcing plans for a feast honoring a matrilineal kinsman, receives pledges of money, food, and labor. A heavy obligation is placed upon his close matrilateral kin who not only share the ceremonial duties of host but may be called upon for material assistance. The economic burden falls most heavily upon the host's own household, although linked households of married sons and daughters are expected to make significant contributions. Assisted by members of lineage mates' households, these bilateral relatives perform the duties of cooking, serving, and cleaning up after the feast. Other members of the community make small donations of money or gifts of food and merchandise to be distributed to the guests.

Invitations are issued to all members of the senior generation who witness the status-changes of individuals as representatives not of specific lineages but of all "families" in the village. The provision of food in such lavish quantities that it cannot be consumed at the feast itself but is taken home by the guests is considered as one form of return for their donations.

During the feast the host is assisted in ceremonial duties by lineage mates, who read off lists of donations received and ritual payments to be made, help to distribute gifts to all of the opposite moiety, and lead the singing. Speeches of tribute to the honored kinsman by senior members of the host's own moiety are followed by those of guests, who thank their hosts for ritual payments, gifts, and dinner. In this way the high value placed on the fulfillment of kinship obligations and on community solidarity is expressed. The feasting complex includes not only the culminating feast in which a change in status is publicly acknowledged but the full round of activities associated with life-cycle events. Occasions requiring ceremonial recognition are marriage, death, and name-taking.

Birth is not now nor was it in traditional times an important event in ceremonial life, although a pregnant woman was subject to dietary and behavioral taboos which recognized her special condition (Swanton 1909:47–48). The initial naming of an infant son was marked by a family observance and the giving of presents. Subsequent names acquired by an individual had status implications and were adopted during potlatches (Dawson 1880:131B). Today a baby shower patterned on white practices may be given for the expectant mother by members of the Girls' Auxiliary of the Anglican Church. Attempts by ministers to introduce Christian rituals, such as christening and confirmation, have not been widely supported.

The analysis of ceremonial events that follows is based upon my observation of about a dozen feasts during the years between 1965 and 1971. In six events attended during 1965–66 (two weddings, two stone-movings, one name-taking and one mourning feast), my relationship with the principals allowed me to obtain complete data on attendance, donations, ritual payments where applicable, and genealogical relationships between participants. With these data it is possible to determine first, what roles are played in the feast complex by each category of kinsmen and second, what proportion of village residents participate in ceremonial activities.

MARRIAGE RITES

Marriage, as a life-cycle event entailing irreversible status changes, receives ceremonial recognition by the community. Modern wedding celebrations entail several phases beginning with a kitchen shower given for the bride by the Girls' Auxiliary of the Anglican Church, "a social and inspirational group" of unmarried girls. The wedding ceremony itself is patterned on the white model even to the point of consulting the bridal counselor of a large department store by mail. White satin and lace bridal gowns, pastel bridesmaids' gowns, bouquets of plastic flowers, and engraved invitations are ordered from Vancouver. The couple is married in a brief afternoon church service attended by

members of the family and friends. Although there is no expressed
notion that an Indian ceremony as well as a "white wedding" should
be celebrated, the wedding feast is of more interest than the church
service to those who have been invited. The wedding dance held later
the same evening in the community hall is open to all villagers.

The wedding of Eli Abrahams' daughter and Adam Bell's son, which
took place in St. John's Anglican Church on a Saturday afternoon in
July, was typical[1] of other weddings witnessed in the village. The
church was festively decorated for the occasion with plastic flowers.
The bride, gowned and veiled in white, came in on her father's arm.
Attending her as matron of honor was the groom's brother's wife. The
bridesmaids and flowergirls included three sisters' children on the
bride's side and a brother's children on the groom's side. Three
brothers of the bride ushered guests to their seats.[2] The groom's family
occupied the first two pews on the left and the bride's family those on
the right. The middle section of the church was almost empty, but a
few older women sat in the last three rows.

After the short service the assembly sang a hymn while the new-
lywed couple signed the register in a side room. Then, while the wedding march was played on the organ, the young couple paraded down
the center aisle. Several minutes were spent in posing for pictures on
the front steps of the church before the wedding party climbed into
festooned cars for a triumphal tour of the Indian and white villages.

An optional element was the "cocktail party" held at the home of
the bride's father's mother's brother. Verbal invitations were extended
to close friends and kin who sat in the small livingroom while a larger,
informally dressed group of family and neighbors crowded into the
kitchen. The punch, consisting of a gallon of wine and a quart of
grapefruit juice, was quite sour and several guests asked for fruit juice
instead. Some persons who imbibe quite heavily on other occasions
abstained, feeling that drinking is not appropriate before a feast.

The wedding feast, held at the home of the bride's parents, was an
elaborate dinner party for about 60 guests. The living and dining room
furniture had been removed to make room for four long tables covered
with lace cloths, gleaming silverware, and bone china dishes lent by
relatives for the occasion. A huge wedding cake decorated with pink
and blue rosettes dominated the head table. It was not cut at the feast
but was taken to the wedding dance that evening and pieces of it were

1. In contrast to death rites, for example, the range of variation in weddings seems
narrow. If people marry at all they "do it right," "with all the trimmings." At the risk of
seeming facetious it may be noted that there is no such choice at death.

2. Genealogical relationships of persons playing ceremonial or helping roles in this
event are depicted in figure 4.

distributed to the hundreds of guests. On each of the four tables were several sponge cakes, lemon meringue pies, homemade rolls, pickles and olives, candy and cookies. At each place was a dish of jello, a tumbler for the ubiquitous Kool-aid, a teacup and saucer. Dinner plates were filled in the kitchen and passed along the rows of diners. Turkey with dressing, mashed potatoes, cranberry sauce, carrots and peas, and cole slaw is the standard fare at wedding feasts. Traditional "Indian foods" such as fish and "grease" were not served at feasts during the 1960s. Guests helped themselves to dessert from the varied selection on the tables. At the end of the feast all the food remaining on the tables was put into paper bags provided for the purpose and taken home by the guests. This custom, called "kokoł" is a vigorous survival of traditional customs.

At the head table sat the newlyweds and their attendants, including the five bridesmaids, two flowergirls, three ushers, the groom's brother who was best man and his wife, the matron of honor. Also seated here were the bride's father, mother's male parallel cousin, and the minister. Out-of-town relatives and several high-status village residents sat at the second table. The groom's parents sat at the third table with the parents of the matron of honor who are residents of New Masset. They were joined by other senior members of the community. The fourth table at the back of the room near the kitchen door was occupied by members of the family including the bride's mother who supervised the serving.

Although his genealogical relationship to any of the principals is remote, Peter Jones was called upon to serve as master of ceremonies. While he does not share lineage membership with any other major participant in this feast, his high status as head of the Raven Stlinglanas lineage may have determined his selection. To open the program Peter Jones called upon the best man to offer a toast to the newlyweds. A small amount of wine had been provided for this purpose although alcoholic beverages are not otherwise served at feasts. Peter Jones' next act was to read the names of 16 donors who had contributed $124 and 9 cakes to the bride's family.

A male parallel-cousin of the bride's mother spoke in Haida to "thank the people" for their attendance and then in English urged the couple to lead a Christian life and attend church. The head of the groom's lineage, who is also a sister's husband of the bride's father, read the list of donations offered by his kin group toward the wedding dance, which they were to sponsor.

The next speaker was the bride's father who spoke both in Haida and in English about his daughter's childhood and recommended that she be a good wife to her husband. The groom's father, called upon to speak next, treated the guests to some of the mildly ribald jests considered appropriate to such occasions. This tone was picked up by the next speaker, an elderly man referred to as a "grandfather" of the bride. Another "grandfather," a non-Haida who is husband of the hereditary chief's daughter and father of the groom's brother's wife, offered best wishes in English. Then Charlie Thompson, the father-in-law of the bride's sister and one of the oldest men in the village, spoke at length in Haida about other wedding parties.

At this point the bride's mother rose from her seat near the kitchen door and tearfully began to tell the guests how difficult it was to give up her last daughter, how she prayed for help and cried. She praised her child who had "taught Sunday School and followed the Lord's path even when her parents didn't set her a good example." She lamented the fact that one of her daughters couldn't make a go of her marriage. After reading aloud a "recipe for married happiness" cut from a magazine, she gave the clipping to her newly married daughter to hang on the wall of her home. With this she sat down and Peter Jones "opened the floor," as the people refer to the tacit invitation to persons wishing to speak.

The bride's father rose to acknowledge the gift of the wedding cake, followed by his brother who donated five dollars toward the expenses of the feast. The father's sister's husband, head of the groom's lineage, spoke. Then the bride's paternal grandmother got to her feet, suggesting a Haida dance. Turning her black coat inside out, she urged several of the old people to sing with her but they refused, acting embarrassed. Undeterred, the old woman put a scarf on her head, and shaking her cane, began singing a Haida song. After this unexpected performance, the bride's mother said a few words in Haida to the old people. Five more of the older relatives on both sides spoke briefly in Haida, offering thanks and best wishes. The minister was asked to close the feast with prayer. Since the bride's family had hosted the feast, the groom's family sponsored the wedding dance in the community hall.

The major factor governing the division of ceremonial responsibilities is the availability of space to accommodate the dinner guests. Up until the last decade or so the wedding feast was also held in the hall but the rising cost of extending such lavish hospitality has curtailed the practice. For the all-night wedding dance, an orchestra is engaged and sandwiches, cake, punch, and coffee provided. The hall is decorated with great numbers of balloons and paper streamers, which are cut down sometime after midnight, much to the delight of the hordes of children who swarm over the floor among the dancers. Highlighting the evening are the Grand Promenade and the cutting of the wedding cake. The dance is open to everyone in the Indian village,

New Masset, and the nearby Navy base; however, with worsening political relations between the two villages during the 1960s, few whites attended. A great deal of drinking occurs among some of the celebrants who go home or out to their cars for refreshment during the evening.

There is no honeymoon and seldom is a couple able to set up independent housekeeping at once, although this is the ideal. According to informants, the newlyweds take up residence with the parents of either one, depending, it is said, upon personal preference and the availability of space. In the analysis of household composition we saw that seven of eight dependent married pairs lived with the husband's father. Clearly the people's perception of what happens here differs from what actually happens. In this case, the bride explained that she was going to live with her mother-in-law because "she never had a daughter." For her part, the groom's mother was well pleased with her new daughter-in-law who brought her own housekeeping equipment, "even clothes pins," and took complete care of her husband.

Analysis of the Abrahams-Bell wedding raises several interesting points. A striking feature is the number of ceremonial roles played by young relatives as members of the wedding party. As shown in figure 4, which analyzes genealogical relationships of participants, four siblings of the nuptial pair and six children of siblings played ceremonial (as opposed to "helping") roles. Only one unrelated person of this age category, "a girl friend" of the bride, took an active part as a bridesmaid. On other occasions ceremonial participation is limited to the old and middle-aged.

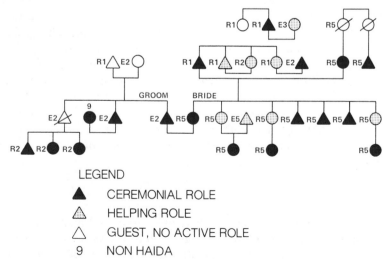

LEGEND

▲ CEREMONIAL ROLE
⬚ HELPING ROLE
△ GUEST, NO ACTIVE ROLE
9 NON HAIDA

Fig. 4. Host group of Abrahams-Bell wedding feast

On the parental generation it cannot be said that ceremonial roles were allocated on the basis of lineage affiliations, with two exceptions. The speaker announcing the donations to the dance hosted by the groom's kin group was head of the groom's lineage. On the other side, the bride's father and mother who were both Ravens must be considered co-hosts, with the bride's maternal "uncle" and lineage mate playing a supporting role. Their spokesman, Peter Jones, who, as we have noted, could trace no lineage or genealogical bond with any of these individuals, does not appear in figure 4. The groom's mother was present but took no active part in the wedding feast.

"Helping" roles at this feast were filled mainly by the bride's siblings and her father's siblings. In almost all cases, the spouses of persons playing either ceremonial or helping roles are also active participants. Peter Jones' wife, Ethel, for example, worked in the kitchen during the feast, along with several other guests unrelated to the hosts who "feel more comfortable in the kitchen than in the front room."

In several respects marriage ceremonies differ from death and name-taking rituals, probably because of the fact that in traditional times, marriage was not an occasion for potlatching. The lack of emphasis on lineage relations, which has been mentioned, reflects on the order of speaking in which bride's and groom's spokesmen alternate. In the absence of a potlatching orientation there is no gift distribution or ritual payment. These latter features characterize ceremonies in which changes of status are validated by the "witnessing" of the old people. In marriage ceremonies, the change of status is validated by the church service. It is likely that this fact accounts for the slight attention given to lineage membership of participants in the wedding feast. Bilateral kinship and friendship appear to be of greater significance here. Donations of money, food, and assistance are made and acknowledged as at other feasts. In the Abrahams-Bell case the wedding feast was sponsored by the bride's parents who are Ravens of different lineages, while the wedding dance was hosted by the groom's parents. Of the 16 contributors acknowledged at the feast, 14 are members of five Raven lineages as shown in Table 41. Gifts presented to the bridal pair were placed on a side table but were neither opened nor acknowledged during the feast.

DEATH RITES

Death receives the greatest ritual attention, mobilizing the entire community in support of the bereaved family. As late as the 1950s news of a death would bring people streaming out of their houses, setting up a wail that could be heard in the white village three miles

TABLE 41
DONATIONS TO WEDDING FEAST

Lineage	No. of Persons	Donation
R1 (groom's father's lineage)	4	$14 and 5 cakes
R2	1	2 and 4 cakes
R3 (master of ceremonies' lineage)	1	2
R4	5	20
R5 (bride's lineage)	3	75
E3	1	10
E5	1	1
Total Received	16	$124 and 9 cakes

away, or so it is said. This custom of keening or "wailing" is no longer practiced. Today the stereotyped speech for funerals and mourning feasts is, "We used to be afraid and sad when any of our people died. Now we know they are not dead but live in God."

The full set of death rites includes the following elements:

1. Tending the body
2. The wake or prayer service
3. The funeral in the church
4. Procession to the cemetery and burial
5. The mourning feast for the bereaved family after the burial
6. The thanking feast given by the family to those who helped with the funeral
7. A ceremony called "taking down headstone" or "stone-moving" in which a marble marker is placed on the grave, usually a year or more after burial
8. The "party" given the same night, which is the modern version of the funeral potlatch
9. The name-taking feast

These elements may be carried out as separate ceremonials or combined in various ways. Everyone, regardless of age, sex, or family status is accorded the first six rites, for, if his family's resources are inadequate, community support is always given. There is likewise no limitation on the raising of headstones other than the considerable expense involved. In traditional times, it has been noted (Swanton 1909:54; Dawson 1880:132–33B), rank determined the elaborateness of death observances. Today persons who possess or aspire to high status are still willing to commit their resources to the prestigious activity of erecting headstones and giving feasts, particularly if an Indian name is to be assumed.

The first step in the death observance is tending the body and preparing it for burial, a task assigned by custom to the father's sister. Male cross-cousins build the coffin although in recent years the people have preferred to purchase metal coffins through the hospital or the Indian Branch. For the funerals I witnessed during 1965–66 the coffins were made of wood and covered very carefully by the older women with whatever material was offered—a shower curtain, tablecloth, or chenille bedspread. After the body is released from the hospital where it was taken for the medical examination, it is escorted home by a procession of cars bearing relatives. When it has been dressed it is displayed in its former home. Various kinsmen keep watch through the night, visitors are received, and donations of money toward burial expenses are accepted. A prayer service and hymn singing may be conducted in the deceased's home on the night before the funeral.

The funeral in the church is attended by all who are able. Again, it is male cross-cousins who dig the grave and act as pallbearers. After the brief church service, the coffin is placed on the bed of a pickup truck, although formerly it was set upon a sledge and dragged the half-mile distance to the cemetery by members of the opposite moiety.[3] No longer required to pull the sledge, members of "the other side must walk down with the body." The role assigned to the opposite moiety is today performed by members of the Women's Auxiliary of the Anglican Church, which includes most of the senior women in the village. Relatives and friends also accompany the body on its last journey. A long procession slowly wends its way through the village, along the shore, through a tunnel of trees to the cemetery where another brief service is read.

Although traditionally no persons of different "clans" could lie together (Swanton 1909:52), today there seems to be no rule. New burials are made on the edges of the old cemetery with no attempt made to mark off family plots. Temporary wooden crosses are set up and the sandy mound is covered with wreaths of plastic roses, carnations, and daffodils. Before plastic blooms were available, crepe paper was used to make wreaths that were donated to the family.

After the burial a mourning feast is given to the bereaved family by relatives. Fifty or more persons may take part in the meal, which is followed by memorial speeches and hymn-singing. Other elements of the ceremonial complex are observed—the list of donations is read and the remaining food is taken home by guests. Mourning feasts are intensely affecting. On one such occasion, 25 of the 52 guests rose to speak in Haida, their voices barely audible over the subdued weeping.

3. This custom was "revived" in 1971 for the stone-moving for Peter Hill, as described later in this chapter.

They offered consolation to the family and referred to happier events in which the deceased had participated.

A month or more later, the family of the deceased gives a "thanking feast" to all who helped with the funeral. Payment of three, five, or ten dollars is made for such ritual services as helping to build the coffin, dig the grave, carry the coffin, and so on. The expenses of the feast are met partly by donations from the guests, many of whom will receive payment. All donations and services are noted, usually on loose sheets of paper, and this data is read off at feasts in public acknowledgment of a ritual debt.

Although the death observances of higher status persons are more elaborate, I have chosen more typical cases, which yet illustrate the basic elements of the death rites.

The funeral of Virginia Robinson,[4] who died in November 1970 at the age of 73, was described to me by her sister's daughter, Helen Cooper. Virginia, who had been hospitalized with high blood pressure and other symptoms of heart disease, sent for Helen when she realized that death was imminent. She had saved $300 from her monthly pension of $111, depositing this amount with the manager of the Co-op. Two days before she died, another pension check arrived. Helen consulted the band council about this and was issued a check in exchange for the pension check. With more than $400, she was able to plan the funeral as Virginia had instructed.

Before entering the hospital for the last time Virginia had packed her clothes in a blue suitcase. She asked that her father's sisters dress her for the burial, but insisted that no sweater or coat be put on her. Her blue angora sweater and her blue suitcase were to be given to her sister, Helen's mother. To Helen she gave a necklace which she had treasured.

During her last days in the hospital Virginia shared a room with her lifelong neighbor and lineage mate Jessica Wilcox, who was dying of cancer. The two women discussed the question of who would go first as casually, Helen said, as if they were planning a trip to town. Virginia awaited death with composure, her burial clothes packed, a tidy sum saved for her funeral, perhaps the first nestegg she had ever had, and detailed instructions given to her next of kin, knowing that she would be commemorated in age-old rites she had helped to observe for countless others.

When death finally came at one in the morning, the doctor called Helen from the hospital in Queen Charlotte City. The nurses dressed

4. In contrast to other names used in this historical account, Virginia Robinson, Libby Watkins, Jessica Wilcox, and Helen Cooper are pseudonyms, as are Agatha, Louella, Marie, and Hank.

Virginia in her own clothes and placed her in the "nice coffin," which
had been purchased for $203. When the body had been brought back to
Masset, Helen insisted that Virginia lie in her house for one last night
since she had liked to spend her time there as an old lonely widow. As
Virginia had no other surviving kinsmen the family had trouble finding
anyone to sit up with the body all night. Few persons attended the
funeral.

No mourning feast was given after the burial but about two months
later a "memorial feast," combining the elements of mourning and
thanking feasts, was held. Many donations were made. "The dollars
sure do count up," Helen remarked, saying that she was "able to buy
the meat, lots of cake mix, oranges, apples, everything that was needed
without being cheap." Ritual payments of $5 each were made to
Agatha and Louella, the father's sisters whom Virginia had specifically
wished to dress her. Since the nurses had put Virginia's funeral clothes
on her, the old ladies were asked to perform another service. It was
Agatha who opened the lid when the casket reached Helen's house and
Louella who closed it. The church was given $10, while the $25 donation from the band council was given to the driver of the truck who
hauled the casket to the cemetery. After all the bills were paid and gifts
made, $100 remained. Virginia had asked that if any money were left
over, even $5, it be kept for the funeral of her sister. It is likely,
however, that this money will later be spent on a headstone for Virginia.

In discussing the donations made to the expenses of Virginia's funeral and memorial feast, Helen noted that after years of donating to other
people's affairs, her "aunty" was finally repaid. With this allusion to
the reciprocal exchange system, I was prompted to ask what happened
in the case of someone who had not saved money for his funeral or who
had not participated in the exchange system. In reply Helen described
the death of her husband's sister Libby Watkins, who had died suddenly one day in June 1968.

Helen was about to leave the house to go shopping when her son
Benjamin came in to tell her that "Libby stopped breathing." He
didn't want to say that she died, Helen explained. Other relatives who
were on their way to the dead woman's house stopped by for her.
When they arrived, the reserve nurse was working over her but it was
too late. As soon as possible Helen asked her own son and Libby's
eldest son whether they had any money. "They didn't have a penny,
not a penny," she repeated. "They were paid the week before but had
blown it all, every penny."

There was some discussion about how to get the body to the hospital
for an autopsy. Finally it was wrapped in a blanket, put on a stretcher

borrowed from the nurse and taken to Queen Charlotte City in a neighbor's car. Helen took charge, sending the dead woman's son and husband to the hospital with her. "He looked dazed," she said of the husband. "He would just go join some party if he didn't go to the hospital," and she shook her head.

With the responsibility of making funeral arrangements thrust upon her, Helen worried about how to proceed when there was no money. Next morning, however, two members of the Women's Auxiliary went to every house in the village to collect donations, turning over $90 to Helen. Soon afterward Helen's sister Marie and her husband Hank who live on the mainland came to Masset for a visit. Hearing of the crisis, Hank donated $100 for the funeral of his wife's sister's husband's sister. Libby's stepmother donated a complete set of clothing for her to be buried in—"stockings, underwear, dress. All we had to buy her was a pretty sweater to wear over her dress. We were lucky to get a coffin at the hospital for $90. These are of grey metal and much better than the kind the people make."

Helen emphasized that all the services were donated with no repayment expected. The Pentecostal minister drove the family down to the hospital and back. He received $10 at the memorial feast to compensate him for gasoline. The persons who took the body to the hospital in their car and who drove the truck to the cemetery also expected no payment. "People are so good," Helen said of this treatment. In describing her sister-in-law she said, "She never went anywhere. She just stayed in the house all the time. They never went to a feast or gave anything to anybody. She never once came over to my house to see how we live."

So, although neither the dead woman nor her household had made any provision for emergencies nor contributions to other people's crises, the community rallied to give her a fine funeral and memorial dinner. Ironically, this memorial feast was one of the largest of recent history, attended by about 100 guests. Everyone who had made a donation to the funeral or who contributed to the feast was invited. "This is how we pay people back. Everyone who gives is invited."

I asked Helen whether everyone in the village received this kind of treatment or just the adults or old people. "Everyone," she said, "even little babies, although there wouldn't be such a large number of guests." Having attended several other funerals where family resources were slim—those of Peter Hill's son who fell from a dock and drowned, an epileptic adolescent who fell out of a rowboat and drowned, and of Helen's own granddaughter who had suffocated in a fire—I knew this to be true.

When I remarked that the old rules for burying people did not seem to be binding, Helen agreed that in Libby's case it was a good thing. If everyone hadn't pitched in and donated goods and services with no expectation of return, she didn't know how they would have managed.

In every case that I have record of, either a spouse or a matrilateral kinsman of middle-age is responsible for arranging the death rites. In the first case described here, Helen was a sister's daughter and lineage mate of Virginia. In the second, the dead woman was her husband's sister and lineage mate. In practice, it is Helen as the more forceful and efficient partner who assumes the burden of any obligations placed upon this family, regardless of whose kin may be involved.

Stone-moving

A year or more after the funeral, a marble headstone is ordered from Vancouver by close kin. Since the headstone cannot be taken to the cemetery until a feast is given, the marker may sit in the front yard of the deceased's former residence for many years. A ceremony called "taking down headstone" involves the actual moving and placing of the stone in the cemetery, an act which must be witnessed by the "other side." The Women's Auxiliary of the Church again acts as a functional equivalent of the moiety by "walking down with the stone." On the appointed day a procession assembles at the house formerly occupied by the deceased to accompany the stone to the cemetery where a prayer is read. This ceremony requires the services of male cross-cousins who load the stone on the truck and, at the end of its journey, set it in place on the grave. Father's sister wipes the stone before it is moved and again after it is in place.

The "party," which climaxes the stone-moving is sponsored either by the kin who have inherited the deceased's property (usually the son, daughter, or brother) or by the maternal heir who will assume the Indian name. The ceremony to be analyzed here honored Alfred Davidson, former head of the Djatlanas lineage of the Eagle moiety, who died in 1954. Its purpose was to repay the ritual debts incurred in the stone-moving and to validate the nephew's assumption of the name. Playing the role of host was his sister's son, Amos Williams, 58 years old, who was to take the name. Co-host was Alfred's younger brother Robert in whose house the "doing" was held. Amos' sister Hannah was co-hostess. Assisting Amos was Vic Adams, 42, Robert's son-in-law. Although an Eagle, he is affiliated not with the Djatlanas but with the Gitins lineage headed by the hereditary town chief. Of the relatively large Djatlanas lineage (Table 39) only three members played host roles in a major ceremonial. A fourth member of the Djatlanas, a "cousin" of Robert's, assisted in serving. It is worth emphasizing that even when this high ranking, strongly traditional family sponsored a feast, participation by other lineage mates was largely limited to attendance and donations.

The supporting staff, headed by Florence Davidson, Robert's wife and matriarch of the Dadens Yakulanas, was composed of households of the bilateral network. Five daughters and one son, their spouses and adolescent children assisted her. It was this strong economic base that allowed the Davidsons to play such a prominent part in the ceremonial life of the village. These relationships are shown in figure 5. Other helpers included the town chief's grandson who is a member of Florence's lineage. Participating only as guests were Florence's older son and his wife. Also conspicuous by her exclusion was Phoebe Marks, widow of Alfred Davidson, Sr., who attended but received no notice during the evening. Traditionally, the position of a widow at such an event would have been a peripheral one. There may be another explanation for this treatment on this occasion, however, since the "high ranks" were wont to slight those who did not measure up to their own standards in one way or another.

The "doing" or "party," as the people refer to an event where food is eaten from one's lap, was held in the large house owned by Robert Davidson. In the main room benches, sofas, and overstuffed chairs were ranged along the walls, in front of the hall doors, and against the deep freezer and china closet. Inside this outer U-shaped row of seats was a second parallel row of straightbacked chairs and benches. The center space was filled with chairs and benches placed in rows facing the west end of the room where a small clear area, impinged upon by

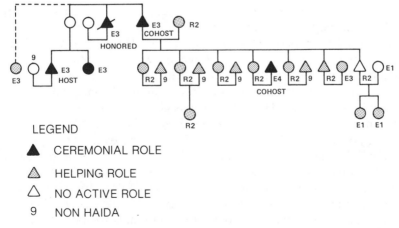

LEGEND

▲ CEREMONIAL ROLE

⨻ HELPING ROLE

△ NO ACTIVE ROLE

9 NON HAIDA

Fig. 5. Host group of Davidson stone-moving

additional chairs as the evening proceeded, functioned as a stage. As guests arrived they filled up the sides and rear of the room first. Close kin who had a part to play sat in the parlor or kitchen.

The evening opened with Hannah, sister's daughter of the honored deceased, passing down the narrow aisle between seats offering a basket of cigarettes. The hereditary chief, apparently at a signal from the host, began a speech of welcome. He spoke in Haida in a falsetto, punctuating his speech with elaborate gestures which drew much laughter. My close friend and informant Ethel Jones, who sat beside me translating and explaining throughout the evening, said that he thanked the people for coming, thanked the helpers, and thanked the nephew of the deceased who was responsible for putting up the stone to honor the memory of Alfred Davidson, Sr. There was a comical note regarding Reverend Collison, the first missionary to the Haidas who had arrived here in 1876, saying that the Indians would or should become like white men. "Now," said the chief in Haida with gestures, "we are all whites." The Indians roared.

Amos Williams as the maternal heir played the focal role of "master of ceremonies." It was he who attended to the details of seating, program arrangements, allocation of payments for ritual services, and introductions. At the conclusion of the town chief's speech Amos asked George Jones, 86-year-old head of the Tcetsgitinai, the other important Eagle lineage from Yan, if he would like to say a few words. George stood up, leaning forward slightly on his cane, and spoke for a long time in Haida about the honored deceased and old times. When he sat down there was a lull. Since Amos was busy in the other room, Robert Davidson, as co-host, rose and said something in Haida with the sense, "sit tight. There's a lot more yet."

Amos returned and thanked the "helpers," the Women's Auxiliary, and the guests. He spoke in English saying that his uncle had been dead a number of years and he had been forgotten. His name was not heard. Now that the stone was taken down he would be remembered and honored. Amos referred to his use of English and admitted that the old people criticized him for not speaking Haida. He said that he could "hear" every word of Haida but he was glad he spoke only English and he concentrated on the universal language. This was stated matter of factly, not defensively or defiantly. His speech over, Amos began to read off the amounts to be paid for ritual services. As he did so, Vic Adams, a member of the host group though not a lineage mate, passed envelopes to the persons named. "To Grace Wilson for wiping off the headstone before taking it to the graveyard, $5. To Isaac Edgars for helping with the stone, $5. To Archie Abrahams for taking the stone from New Masset dock to the reserve, $10. To Eli Abrahams for the use of his truck to bring the stone to the graveyard, $20. To the Women's Auxiliary for walking down with the stone, $27. To the church wardens for St. John's Church, $27 plus $3 donated by Mr. and Mrs. Robert Davidson for repairing the bell tower.''

The first two persons named, Grace Wilson and Isaac Edgars, are members of Alfred Davidson's father's matrilineage and thus fill prescribed ceremonial roles. Archie Abrahams and his maternal uncle Eli are members of another Raven lineage. Their payments, however, were made for the use of their trucks. The Women's Auxiliary representing the Raven moiety on this occasion received payment to be used in their charitable works. The "gift" to the church wardens was payment for the use of the church. The presidents of these groups and the individuals who received payment thanked the hosts for their "gifts" later in the evening when "the floor was open."

After the distribution of payments, Amos turned the floor over to Vic to read the lists of contributions to the ceremony. Before he began, Vic said, he would explain what had been said earlier for the benefit of those who didn't understand Haida, namely the minister and the anthropologist. He repeated the speakers' remarks about the things for which Alfred Davidson, Sr. was remembered. He had built the altar in the church. He had carved many fine pieces in argillite, and had built the 66-foot Haida canoe for the Seattle Exposition of 1908, a canoe which was sent to Ottawa instead. He had above all been a leader in the community. Then Vic read off the names of donors and the amounts of their gifts. Most persons donated small sums of money—one, two, three, or five dollars. The senior Davidsons gave $50 for the party and an unspecified sum for the headstone. Amos gave $95 for the stone and $20 for the party. Several persons contributed a half-dozen or a dozen head scarves, handkerchiefs, or towels. Someone gave a carton of cigarettes and several gave cartons of soda crackers, which have replaced the pilot biscuits distributed at feasts since late in the nineteenth century.

There was a bustle of excitement as the daughters of the family came into the dining room from the kitchen with piles of Japanese scarves over their arms, passing one to each woman guest. Other women distributed hand towels and handkerchiefs to the men. Everyone of both moities received, and people exclaimed over their gifts. Robert Davidson rose and spoke in Haida about the old ways of getting food and about the changes he has seen. Two of his small grandsons came in from the kitchen and solemnly passed paper napkins to the guests. There was much nodding of the old people about this; the performances of the very young are a matter of pride to the old.

Hannah Williams, who was a small wiry woman with thin white hair drawn back in a bun, began to tease her maternal uncle and the guests laughed. Robert countered by telling how he used to take care of Hannah when she was a baby. When she cried he would dip a crust of bread in molasses and give it to her to eat, he said, illustrating his anecdote with gestures. Hannah responded with other stories and finally began to sing, "Jesus Loves Me." The people joined in.

There was another stir as several of the daughters came into the room carrying stacks of paper plates. Each plate held two half sandwiches, one of crab salad, and the other of ham on homemade bread. The Danish son-in-law carried a huge bowl filled with bone china teacups, offering one to each guest. Dishes of pickles were carried round by the little boys. Large waxed brown bags were passed to the guests. The serving continued as each of the dozen women helpers carried round a tray or bowl filled with one kind of sweet—oatmeal cookies, unfrosted nutcake, date bars, and decorated cupcakes. Each person took one or more pieces from each tray or bowl and put them into his bag to take home. Two apples and a packet of soda crackers were issued to each guest. A large pot of coffee was carried by one of the sons-in-law, followed by granddaughters with cream and sugar in cut-glass pitchers. Additional gifts of fancy cakes made by the daughters and granddaughters of this large family were offered to the Ravens present.

Up to this point all the speakers had been Eagles, that is, members of the hosts' own moiety. Speeches by the "other side" were begun by Florence Davidson, sister-in-law of the honored deceased. Then Grace Wilson, father's sister to the Davidson brothers, addressed Robert while the guests smiled in anticipation. Her relationship gave her the right to ask him for a song, which he performed. The floor was open and the minister rose. He remarked that he liked to find something in the Bible applicable to these events of daily and community life because the Bible should be related to our lives in this manner. He spoke about the disappearance of Indian ways and language. He referred to the spending of so much money on tombstones, conceded that it was good to remember but implied that this kind of display could be carried too far. He approved the donation of money to the church instead of to individuals and said that it was a step in the right direction.[5]

Isaac Edgars was the next to rise and his speech was one of thanks for the money he had received. Joe Weir, a partly blind man of about 65, stood at his place. Although an Eagle, he was not related to the hosts and so did not appear on the formal program. His performance

5. Margaret Blackman suggests that the Haidas disarmed church opposition to potlatching by including the minister among recipients of cash awards at the feast (Blackman 1973:52).

was a mixture of stories, mimes, and hymns. He said something about the Women's Auxiliary of which his wife is president and called himself the B.A. or Boy's Auxiliary. The mime dealt with a raccoon hunt he had engaged in as a boy. The audience, which had laughed heartily, joined him in singing a robust revival hymn. Peter Jones next stood up with an announcement about the stone-moving to be held for Joe and Lena Edgars on the following Tuesday. He publicly invited the minister and me, which put the stamp of approval on my participation. This acknowledgment of my work required a speech of thanks and an anecdote. Adam Bell, head of the Masset Yakulanas, a Raven group, then rose and made some remarks in Haida teasing the Women's Auxiliary. He was followed by the president of that group who thanked the hosts for the donation. One of the church wardens acknowledged the gift for the repair of the bell tower. The head of the Dadens Yakulanas made a further donation to the feast expenses, followed by the closing speech of the hereditary chief. Then Amos Williams thanked everyone for coming and asked the minister to give the benediction. Sixty-three guests attended this affair and the close kin who "helped" numbered an additional 20 or more.

The stone-moving ceremony ended the cycle for Alfred Davidson, Sr., the honored deceased. Amos Williams, the sister's son said, "Now my uncle's name can be heard again." Referring to the list of death rites early in this chapter, we note that the first six elements were taken care of soon after death in 1954. The remaining three, which may be described as the rituals of rank, were combined in one event. The ceremonial transactions were straightforward. The maternal nephew had arranged for a headstone to be bought and moved to the cemetery, just as a century ago he would have organized the carving and raising of the mortuary pole. A senior lineage mate not only acted as co-host but contributed, through his own bilateral network, substantial economic support. Ritual payments were made to members of father's matrilineage who had performed prescribed services. Payment was made to the Women's Auxiliary for "walking down with the stone" as a surrogate for the Raven moiety members. Elaborate cakes were distributed to all Ravens present. Then, having fulfilled the obligations of rank and kinship, the nephew assumed his uncle's name.

Occasionally the name-taking may be a separate event. In an instance that will concern us here, the stone-moving and "party" elements were combined with mourning and thanking elements in one event sponsored by the surviving sibling group. The heir to the name, by consent of the siblings, was mother's sister's son. Confusingly, the people involved referred to the predecessor as the "maternal uncle," presumably because of an age difference of 15 years. This case was cited in chapter 8 as an example of the selection of an heir by a council of lineage elders. The memorial and stone-moving rites for Joseph Edgars are analyzed elsewhere (Stearns 1975:153–58; 1977:153–64). The name-taking feast hosted by Peter Jones shows us the minimal features of this event.

While Amos Williams could say, "Now my uncle's name can be heard again," for Peter Jones who had also acted as co-host and master of ceremonies at his "uncle's" stone-moving, there was yet another task. In order for him to be entitled to use his name, he had to "give a feast to the old people." The difference probably lay in the facts of purchase of the headstone. In the Davidson case, the nephew had paid the largest share. In the Edgars ceremony, credit for purchase of the headstones was not given. Although Peter Jones played a leading role in the program, it is unlikely that he was a major contributor to the purchase of the stone. His donation to the party was $10, two boxes of apples, and two dozen head scarves. His role as master of ceremonies was an aspect of his status as heir.

NAME-TAKING

The "name-taking feast" followed the general pattern of feasts, with a meal served to 72 people at the regular dinner hour. Peter and Ethel Jones, deciding to "hurry up and get it over with," scheduled the event less than two weeks after the Edgars stone-moving, thus evading the elaborate preparations usually made for such occasions. The feast was announced only 24 hours in advance; my own invitation was issued by telephone after midnight on the appointed day. Joe Edgars' father's sister, Emily Thompson, was called in to preside over the day-long preparation of the stew as custom required. It was her son Vic who "dished up," while Vic's wife and wife's sister helped to serve. The rest of the preparations were carried out by Peter's own large household. The distribution of host and "helping" roles in this event is shown in figure 6.

Peter's lineage mate Willie Russ acted as master of ceremonies, calling not upon senior members of his own side to speak first as was the practice at other events, but upon four senior Eagles in turn. The first speaker was Walter Samuels, an 84-year-old man belonging to father's matrilineage headed by George Jones. His long speech in Haida, as translated sketchily by Ethel Jones who sat beside me, dealt with the family history. The name Peter was validating had previously been held by his paternal grandfather, James Jones, and it was at the request of Peter's father that it was being returned to this family.

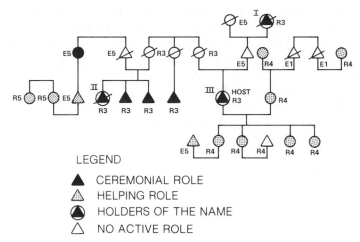

LEGEND

▲   CEREMONIAL ROLE
⬙   HELPING ROLE
◓   HOLDERS OF THE NAME
△   NO ACTIVE ROLE

Fig. 6. Host group of Peter Jones' name-taking feast

On this occasion the town chief was the second speaker. After paying tribute to earlier incumbents of the name, he related some humorous incidents that had occurred in his early married life. There was much gentle laughter at this.

George Jones, as third speaker, referred to the smokehouse at Ain Lake. With the assumption of his name, Peter became the fourth generation "boss" of the smokehouse. This appears to be a nonfunctional status with no specific rights or obligations attached, other than access to the facilities. Joe's brothers and son-in-law continued to have free use of the smokehouse. Robert Davidson, who followed George Jones, told a story about the Eagles. These two old gentlemen, each head of a large Eagle "tribe" from Yan, consistently received deferential treatment in the order of speaking.

The next speaker was Adam Bell, head of the Masset Yakulanas who gave thanks for the dinner and thanked the old people for their speeches. It was as a fellow Raven that he spoke for Peter. He also thanked the Edgars brothers for giving the name to Peter although he was young, only 52. "Whites don't care about giving names to each other," he said, "but Indians should keep on passing names down."

Joe Weir, a member of the town chief's lineage, said when called on that "a person feels like acting at an affair like this." He told one of his humorous stories, which provoked laughter.

Isaac Edgars, after thanking the people for helping Peter to take his elder brother's place, concluded with criticism of his own sisters for "drinking too much and not coming around to help when there is a doing like this." He remarked that if you have a gallon of wine, people are glad to help. Then, he chided Peter for not telling anyone about the feast in time for them to give assistance.

Peter took the floor and thanked the people for giving him the name. He also promised to inform Isaac in advance the next time something was planned. He then thanked his wife for preparing the feast. When she spoke later, Ethel remarked that this was the first time Peter had ever thanked her in public for cooking for him all these years.

Robert Davidson rose to thank Ethel for the meal because he had forgotten to do it when he spoke. Willie Russ thanked the people for their speeches and, after telling of an incident involving an old uncle, "opened the floor." Walter Samuels spoke again in Haida. It seems that many people thought it was a mistake for the Joneses not to have notified people in advance so that they might make donations. Ethel replied by saying that they thought it was their place to give the dinner on their own. The guests, to judge by their facial expressions and comments, were not convinced. Several other persons rose to give thanks for the meal, tell stories, make announcements and comments. There were no donations and, significantly, no gift distribution. But the requisite "feast to the old people" was given and the name legitimately assumed.

For the non-speaker of Haida there were no clues that this name was the high title of town chief of Yan. Nor did Ethel impart this information in her translations of the speeches. The Joneses' reticence in a matter so vitally affecting their own prestige seems odd—odd, that is, in the light of what the old ethnographies tell us about competitive potlatching and the behavior of chiefs. Elsewhere I have explored the limitations of potlatching as an avenue to high rank (Stearns forthcoming). My conclusions there about the Haidas' attitudes concerning proper behavior for chiefs are confirmed by Emma Matthews.

I had asked various informants whether Chief Matthews had given a feast when he took his uncle Harry Weah's place in 1932. No one remembered such a feast but as Ethel had remarked, "He must have given one." Finally in 1980, Marianne Bölscher had the opportunity to put this question to the chief's widow. "Yes," she said, they "put on a small feast. It didn't have to be a big one because he already had a chief's position and didn't have to promote himself" (personal communication). The value placed on dignity and moderation explains the disdain and resentment many people express toward the highly publicized "spectaculars" with which some villagers support their ambitions.

CEREMONIAL EXCHANGE

In analyzing the feasting complex as a ceremonial exchange system, it is necessary to determine what is exchanged by whom, what values are being expressed, and what proportion of villagers participate in this focal institution of Haida culture.

Traditionally, the host's own lineage supported his potlatches. Not only chiefs but lesser-ranking members could expect contributions of wealth, goods, and labor from a large group of lineage mates. The distribution of property to members of the opposite moiety drew a dichotomy between hosts and guests, emphasizing competitive relations between corporate lineages while acknowledging their ceremonial interdependence.

In the modern feast this dichotomy is blurred. In the words of one old informant, "In the old days only my own tribe would donate but now everyone gives." This tendency for the feast to become a community-wide event in which donations are made by all participants reflects changes in the social structure wherein the household has replaced the lineage as the basic social and economic unit and the village itself is the relevant corporate group.[6]

Villagers give to the host donations of money ranging from one or two dollars to five or ten, which is considered a large gift when made by someone who is not a close relative. The small size of these donations, representing the minimum necessary to maintain reciprocal exchange, reflects the economic impoverishment of the reserve in recent times. Food, especially cakes, sandwiches, soda crackers, and apples, and goods including aprons, hand towels, dish cloths, head scarves, and cigarettes are also donated for distribution at the feast. An essential contribution is their presence as witnesses to the status change of the host while the senior members of guest lineages offer speeches in tribute to the person being honored.

The host's kinsmen not only offer money, food, and goods but participate either as helpers in the preparation and serving of the feast or as co-hosts playing ceremonial roles.

For his part, the host, who is honoring a matrilineal kinsman and possibly assuming a name, fulfills the obligation of "giving a feast to the old people" by issuing invitations to all members of the senior age group who represent the community. He provides such a bountiful feast that guests cannot consume it all and must take home the remain-

6. In the 1970s it has become customary for the *band council* to make a contribution to any event of community significance. This may mean that the council is assuming the role of co-host on behalf of the whole community, since individuals are increasingly unable, or unwilling, to extend lavish hospitality. On the other hand, it may reflect the council's experience with government grants for specific enterprises.

der. He acknowledges the donations and labor that have been contributed and redistributes the goods to all members of the opposite moiety who are present and to his own as well if resources permit. Members
of the opposite moiety who have performed prescribed ritual services
for the host or his kinsman must be publicly paid in cash. Special gifts
such as bone china teacups are presented to senior members of the
opposite moiety.

Speeches are an important aspect of reciprocal exchange. The most
persistent theme running through these speeches is the offering of
thanks. Guests express their gratitude for the invitation to the feast, for
the meal and the gifts. Hosts thank guests for their presence, their
support, and their speeches. This reaffirmation of mutual indebtedness
is in sharp contrast to the traditional potlatch custom of exalting one's
own kin group at the expense of guests.

Most speakers regard the feasts as occasions for historical recollections, invoking the names of long-abandoned villages and the people
who lived in them. Their humorous anecdotes and tragic tales deal not
with mythical beings but with real people and actual happenings. They
appear to be collectively reconstructing their past and fitting the honored deceased into the company of long-dead Haidas. The feast is an
occasion for asserting the norms, the new myths: the norm of unity,
"We are all brothers"; the norm of equality, "We are all equal"; the
norm of cooperation, "Everybody helps." Warfare and slavery, which
are embarrassing to modern Haidas, did not exist.

Some of the speeches testify to an explicit awareness that their
rituals set them apart from whites and reinforce their cultural identity.
Reference was made to Adam Bell's remark, "Whites don't care about
giving names to each other but Indians should keep on passing names
down."

Feasts frequently take on the aspects of a town meeting. Speakers
take the opportunity to make announcements, to extend invitations to
another feast, or to voice an opinion on a matter of public interest. At
the wedding feast of the chief councilor's daughter, the hereditary chief
expressed his outrage that the British Columbia Ferry Corporation had
adopted the phrase "Route of the Haidas" for its new excursion trip
without asking permission of the Haidas for the use of their name. For
a time the wedding guests were absorbed in a heated discussion as to
how this injury might be redressed. It was finally decided to raise
money in the village to send the hereditary chief and chief councilor
with their wives, in whatever ceremonial regalia might be found in their
respective trunks, to Prince Rupert to greet the ferry on its arrival.
Having resolved to regard the "name stealing" as a compliment and to
lend their presence to the reception prepared for the vessel at the end

of its maiden voyage, the guests turned their attention again to toasting the bride and groom.

Rarely, mild censure is given when individuals do not live up to expectations. At Peter Jones' name-taking we saw that one of his matrilateral kinsmen concluded a long speech with criticism of his own sisters. The feast is not considered a forum for the airing of interpersonal grievances, however, and the sisters made no reply to these charges. Nor did Peter Jones himself protest when chided for not announcing in advance his plans to give a feast so that people might make donations and show proper behavior. For the fact is that Peter Jones, wishing to discharge the obligations connected with name-taking as quickly as possible and without incurring any further obligations, called only upon the father's sister of his predecessor for ritual assistance. The remaining labor of feast preparation was undertaken by his own large household and those of married daughters. Other relatives volunteered to serve the guests.

The life-cycle feasts have incorporated elements of Christian church observances: the presence of the minister, the benediction, the prayers, the hymn singing, the exclusion of alcoholic refreshment aside from the very small amount used symbolically in the nuptial toast. The minister's remarks at feasts reach a much wider audience than ever hears him preach in church. At the same time, groups with an avowedly religious purpose, such as the Church Army and the Pentecostals, find their meetings turned into social gatherings with the introduction of speeches, refreshments, and acknowledgments.

As the analysis of exchange indicates, the structure of relations supporting the ceremonial complex is no longer exclusively matrilineal. Although the people invoke a matrilineal model, a very narrow range of matrilateral kin are mobilized on any ceremonial occasion. In rituals purporting to meet traditional obligations, the role of host is usually played by a brother or maternal nephew. In recent times the actual sponsor of death rites and thanking feast may be the spouse, parent, or child, but ceremonial roles of co-hosts are still allocated to matrilateral kin of the deceased. The few lineage mates who perform the public roles of master of ceremonies, distributor of awards, and reader of donations are deeply involved in the planning of the feast. The full membership of the lineage is not called upon to share these duties. Indeed, few middle-aged persons could name all the members of their own lineages nor was this knowledge essential to participation in ceremonial activities.

Among the persons most active in the ten ceremonial events I witnessed during the period from September 1965 to July 1966 was Peter

Jones. He sponsored a mourning feast and his own name-taking feast, in addition to presiding as master of ceremonies over the Abrahams-Bell wedding feast and the stone-moving affair honoring his mother's sister's son. His prominence, however, was not based upon the support of a large and active matrilineage. The Stlinglanas which he heads was an aggregate of small sibling clusters totalling 19 persons 30 years and older living on-reserve in 1965–66. Peter Jones enjoys the active support of two out of five Edgars siblings and of Willie Russ, another parallel-cousin with no living siblings. Grace Wilson, born in 1908, is active not in the affairs of her own lineage but as father's sister to other groups. This is a role which her elder sister has refused to play. The remaining eleven lineage members neither volunteer nor are called upon for assistance. Even the sibling group is not always a unit of cooperation in ceremonial activities; Peter Jones received no support from his brother or three sisters.

While traditionally oriented persons still support the matrilineal model as an ideal, it has become ineffective as a principle of organization. It is not only that membership of the lineages has been so drastically reduced, but that surviving members no longer share the common interests and sense of identity that would mobilize them in common action. Changes in the social structure and in patterns of economic exploitation are reflected in the conduct of the feasting complex. Since the household has become the basic social and economic unit, the conjugal bond has been emphasized at the expense of matrilineal ties. The sponsorship of life-cycle events has become the responsibility of individuals who rely upon the instrumental help of their spouses and upon the expressive support of close matrilateral kin. "Close" refers here not to genealogical distance but to the strength of the bonds of friendship. Often these bonds are strongest between persons who belong to different lineages or even to opposite moieties. As a result of their mutual willingness to support the ceremonial enterprises of the other, the co-hosts of a single event may represent several kin groups. The planning of these events reveals the kind of interaction typical of the modern feasting complex.

Planning a Feast

While we have valuable reconstructions of Haida potlatches, descriptions of the preliminaries are comparatively scanty (Swanton 1909:167–68; Murdock 1936:3–4). Nor has there been any information available about present practice.

Although I had, over the years, participated in many feasts as a guest who made donations and received gifts and occasionally "helped" the hosts, I had never been privy to the planning of a ceremonial event. Indeed, as I look back on it, my curiosity about this aspect was allayed by such answers as "People ask you to do something," "People offer to do things," or "Everybody helps." Only when I set about giving a memorial feast myself did I discover that the procedures of planning a ceremony duplicate the formal structure of the climactic event. For the first time I was able to glimpse the well-synchronized mechanisms of feast-production set in motion by a proposal to honor a kinsman.

It may be useful to review the circumstances by which this came about. Ever since my first field trip to Masset in 1962, my teacher and warmest friend had been Peter Hill, born in 1890, and an elder of the Kun lanas lineage. He was not a high-ranking person. Although his father and father's brothers were "big men," he was not heir to any high names or titles in the maternal line. Consequently, there was little scope for his talents and abilities in the traditional sphere. His intellectual gifts, however, won him recognition from teachers at the Metlakatla Industrial School, which he attended in 1905, and from Bishop Ridley and other whites whom he met in his travels away from the Queen Charlottes. He was one of two persons selected by Agent Deasy to teach in the Indian Day School when white teachers could not be persuaded to stay. He was involved with Alfred Adams in the organization of the Native Brotherhood, served as a lay preacher for many years, and was elected to several terms as band councilor and chief councilor. To say that he took pride in the fact that he was several times chosen for special roles in preference to men of higher rank should not give the impression that he was a proud man. On the contrary, he enjoyed great esteem in the village as a wise and gentle-spirited person who stood outside the traditional rivalries. All of this made him an ideal informant.

When he died in April 1971 I felt a keen sense of personal loss. I had already been feeling great frustration because my sociological, historical, and demographic studies, though valid in their own terms, were not revealing the quality of life in the community that I had experienced and wanted to communicate. I deeply regretted that I had never been able to afford the equipment to record the voices and to make films of the old people.

I discussed this with my daughter who has not only spent time with me in the field but whose great ambition is to be a filmmaker. We began to consider how we might find some funds quickly to enable us to make film and sound recordings of the old people before their knowledge of old Haida culture was lost forever. At first we thought of a file of ethnographic reports on film and sound tape. But the medium makes its own demands for action and plot. And here the two ideas came together. I would express my gratitude to Peter Hill and to all the people of Masset by purchasing his headstone and giving a feast in his honor; and we would make our record of the people acting out their most meaningful traditions.[7] As it happened, I had been given a name in Peter Hill's lineage some time before this and I had known that the proper behavior was to give a feast "to make my name good." I had been enculturated to Haida ways well enough that this sense of obligation, lurking uneasily at the back of my mind, leapt forward to rationalize and legitimize my plans. The proposal made perfect sense to the Haidas though they gave me excessive credit for thinking of it.

Since the funeral and thanking feast had been given by Peter Hill's daughter Rose and her husband Alfred Davidson, it was to them that I turned for permission to donate the stone and food for a feast. In agreeing to the proposal, they assumed the heavy burden of co-hosts, although Rose is affiliated with the K'awas Eagle lineage E1 and Alfred is a Raven of the Dadens Yakulanas R2. As the most closely related member of the Kun lanas, R4, Ethel Jones was drawn immediately into the plans for her uncle's stone-moving along with her husband Peter, whom we know as head of the Stlinglanas, R3. As "close friends and cousins" of both couples, Eli and Emily Abrahams of Masset Yakulanas, R1, and Kianushilai, R5, respectively, were also recruited. This planning group, then, included members of one Eagle and five Raven lineages. By Haida standards they were middle-aged; the women's ages were 50, 57, and 62 years, while the men were 58, 59, and 60. At the "planning party," Peter Jones' lineage mate Willie Russ, R3, and wife Flora, E4, were prevailed upon to join.

To illustrate the extent of change in the composition of the host group, we may summarize the kin relationships to Peter Hill and lineage memberships of the principal planners:

Honored deceased, Peter Hill	R4
Daughter, Rose Davidson	E1
Daughter's husband, Alfred Davidson	R2
Wife's brother's daughter, Ethel Jones	R4
Husband of wi bro da, Peter Jones	R3
Lineage mate of husband of wi bro da, Willie Russ	R3
Wife of lineage mate, Flora Russ	E4
Mother's sister's son of wife's brother's daughter's husband, i.e. "cousin," Eli Abrahams	R1
Wife of "cousin," Emily Abrahams	R5
Ethnographer	R4

7. The initial grant for the filming of a Haida memorial feast was made by the Social Science Research Center of the University of Victoria. The laboratory phase of the project was supported by the Thea and Leon Koerner Foundation of Vancouver, B.C., and Simon Fraser University.

Ideally, lineage mates of the Kun lanas would be called upon to perform both instrumental and ceremonial roles; however, the resident membership of this group, which in 1966 included two men and seven women in the senior age grade, was reduced to one man and five women by 1971. Of these persons Charlie Thompson, then 85, was too weak to leave his house and a 68-year-old woman was hospitalized with a stroke. As one 58-year-old woman takes no part whatever in the feasting complex, the active members included only Ethel Jones, then 50, her mother Charlotte, 83, and a distant female relative 63-years-old. Clearly the assistance required to sponsor a stone-moving for Peter Hill could not be obtained from the matrilineage alone.

In this situation, close friends rallied to form the planning group just described. These are people who habitually act together, calling upon each other for assistance with their own celebrations. It may be recalled that Peter Jones acted as master of ceremonies at the wedding of Eli Abrahams' daughter, while Ethel helped Emily in the kitchen. Ethel had baked 30 lemon pies for the wedding feast of Rose and Alfred's daughter. Willie Russ had been the master of ceremonies at Peter Jones' name-taking. Most of these individuals were active in the memorial events for Joseph Edgars (Stearns 1975). It is difficult to know whether the closeness of this group is due to their ceremonial interdependence as moiety-mates or whether the affective ties of age-mates are the source of their cooperation.

The group had been mobilized immediately after my phone call to the Davidsons from Victoria proposing the feast and offering to bring some film and tape recorders to record it. When I arrived in Masset on a Friday afternoon I went immediately to visit with Alfred and Rose. After we had discussed the time, the place, the number of guests we could feed, and the money remaining from the funeral donations which could be used to buy property and make ritual payments, I was told that "the relatives" must be called together as soon as possible to hear the plans and give their approval. "Otherwise," Alfred said, "even if they are invited to the feast they feel hurt and left out." I was assured that they would let me know when the meeting would be held. Later this same afternoon when I paid a visit to Ethel Jones she indicated that the group had decided upon a buffet supper and asked my opinion of this proposal. When I admitted my disappointment that things were not to be done in the "old-fashioned way" with a "sit down" dinner in the hall, she agreed that that was best after all and she would see to it. On Monday Emily informed me that the planning meeting would be held at Alfred Davidson's house on Tuesday evening at 7:30. Only later did I learn of the supper held on Saturday night to plan the planning party and the meeting the next night to iron out the details, draw up the guest list, and discuss my preference for a sit-down dinner.

Interestingly, my role as sponsor and ostensible host did not require my presence at or even awareness of these preliminary meetings. I had hoped, even expected, to be involved in all the details but this was clearly naive. My role was to be a ceremonial one. While I had been exulting over the fact that for once I was not just the guest, the spectator, the real work was being done by my friends. I was coached in my duties by my co-hosts who impressed upon me the importance of not overlooking anyone whose status or relationship to the deceased entitled him to recognition and perhaps payment. I developed anxieties about my performance since I was daily confronted by the fact that my knowledge of the rules was very incomplete. I have since learned that such anxiety is a familiar companion to my Haida friends.

Rather than the informal gathering I had expected, the planning meeting resembled the culminating feast and in a sense was the climax of a series of consultations between various members of the community. When I arrived at the home of Alfred Davidson at about 7:45 on the appointed Tuesday, many of the guests were already seated on the sofas, easy chairs, and benches arranged along the walls. As the room filled up, more chairs were brought in. I was seated at the large oak dining table at the rear of the livingroom along with co-hosts for the proposed feast.

The hosts for this meeting, however, were Alfred and Rose Davidson, assisted by three daughters, 18, 23, and 28 years. All day these women, including the older two who were married with households of their own, had been cleaning and baking in preparation for the "party." Among the 24 guests were 18 Ravens of the senior generation. These persons, it developed, were the "relatives" whose approval for the proposed feast was sought. Accompanying them were six Eagle spouses.

The age distribution of guests is shown in Table 42. The two Raven participants younger than 45 included the 43-year-old daughter of a

TABLE 42
GUESTS AT PLANNING MEETING

Age Group	Raven Witnesses	Eagle Spouses
Younger than 45	2	1
45–59 (middle-aged)	1	1
60–90 (senior)	15	4
Total	18	6

member of the planning group and a 43-year-old man standing in for his hospitalized mother who is a member of R4, the matrilineage of Peter Hill. The single middle-aged Raven guest was Ethel Jones who has for the past decade been one of the youngest active participants in the feasting complex. As usual, participants who witness ceremonial events were concentrated in the senior age group.

The lineage distribution of guests is shown in Table 43. Representation at this meeting by five of the six Raven lineages reiterates the point that the moiety has become the significant reference group, whereas in earlier times only members of the sponsoring matrilineage would have been invited to the planning feast. The lineage membership of Eagles is relevant in this context only in that spouses jointly contribute money, food, goods, or labor to events in which one of them is involved.

TABLE 43
LINEAGE DISTRIBUTION OF GUESTS

R1	3	E1	
R2	6	E2	
R3	3	E3	3
R4	4	E4	1
R5	2	E5	2
R6			
Total	18		6

While no one in the village could have been unaware of the plans, the ostensible purpose of the meeting was to inform the old people that a stone-moving and feast honoring Peter Hill were to be held. The working agenda dealt with the time and place of the feast and the allocation of tasks. As was customary, speeches dominated the program. As host of the meeting and co-sponsor of the stone-moving, Alfred Davidson explained the history of the event in a long opening speech given entirely in Haida. After he had finished Ethel Jones rose rather quickly and spoke in Haida to her kinsmen, appending some remarks in English for my benefit. When she sat down, Alfred added the postscript that the feast was to make my name good. Fourteen persons spoke in turn, discussing the feast plans and the suitability of the community hall as compared with the nursery school as a location for the feast. With many speakers paying tribute to Peter Hill, the mood became melancholy. Some individuals made donations, others congratulated me in advance on assuming my Haida name and becoming a "real Indian." There was some excitement about the idea of reviving the old custom of pulling the headstone to the cemetery on a sledge. References to other places, other times crept into the discussion.[8]

The proposal to film the feast and record the speeches stimulated much interest and if there were any objections these were never revealed to me. In fact, as unsuccessful amateur photographers and recorders, many people were frustrated by their own failure to obtain good pictures and recordings of their celebrations.

Most of the senior women did not speak though they gave serious attention to others, and, when refreshments were served, visited among themselves. At this time a few guests volunteered to perform certain tasks. After conferring with his wife, Percy Brown offered to cook a turkey. Adam Bell, head of the Masset Yakulanas, offered to cook 100 pounds of potatoes. The wife of the hereditary chief, who was too ill to attend himself, volunteered to "do the carrots." Apparently senior women guests were not expected to help in the cooking although several of their daughters later offered to bake a few cake mixes or roast a turkey.

When most of the guests had departed a small group remained: Emily Abrahams, Peter and Ethel Jones, and Peter's lineage mate Willie Russ and his wife Flora. Many tasks were unassigned and it was clear that members of the co-hosts' households would have to perform them. The atmosphere was very warm and cordial. The discussion, carried on in English, returned to the "old-fashioned ways" which these people remembered as children. It had been Alfred's idea to build a sled to take the stone to the cemetery as they used to do long ago. A long rope would be attached and all of the opposite side would help to pull.

By considering each village household in turn, the names of all adult men and women of the other side were compiled. Two copies of the list were made, one for me to calculate ritual payments at the feast and one for the old man who would go to each house inviting its eligible members to the feast and instructing those who were expected to perform ritual duties. Although in recent times it has been customary to telephone invitations or to send written ones, for this occasion the planners decided to send Willie Russ in the old-fashioned way. This interest in reviving traditional customs has, incidentally, developed within the last few years. The cultural continuity revealed by analysis of feasts held in 1965–66 was not the result of any policy to preserve or resurrect old ways. At that time, as was observed in chapter 8, the people were

8. Through the kind offices of Lillian Pettviel, Haida speaker of Hydaburg, Alaska, and Seattle, and Carol Eastman and her students Robert Welsch and Daniel Vaughan of the University of Washington, these speeches have been translated and will be published.

convinced that "everything was changed," and little value was placed upon traditional knowledge by the great majority.

As the big day approached, the inevitable complications arose. Everyone else remained calm, knowing that "things always work out." Sure enough, when people who had promised to make certain contributions failed to follow through, help appeared from unexpected quarters. People who had never spoken to me before came forward to help with preparation of the food, cleaning of the hall, ushering, serving, and cleaning up.

The stone-moving took place on Saturday afternoon. Many persons, Ravens as well as Eagles, assembled at Alfred Davidson's house "to help pull" the sledge to the cemetery. But first the stone, which had been displayed in Alfred's front yard, was washed with a new floral-patterned hand towel by two honorary father's sisters of the Eagle side. The basin of soapy water was fetched by daughter's son, also representing the Eagle side. The placing of the stone and its props on the sledge was carried out by Willie Russ' two sons who acted as honorary cross-cousins.

The procession set off in a gay mood, its members more amused than self-conscious in the presence of the cameraman and the sound man who accompanied them. They seemed to enjoy the revival of an almost forgotten custom.[9] "In the old days" people would have come out of the houses along the route and piled blankets on the sledge as donations for redistribution. On this occasion, donations (though not blankets) had been given in advance. As the procession neared the cemetery, the mood became more somber. The harsh sound of the metal runners of the sledge scraping over gravel rose above the subdued voices. The double column moved out of the village, through the long tunnel of trees and across the old wooden bridge. The novelty was forgotten now for this was a journey often made. The sledge was dragged to a section of recent burials, of fresh-cut marble headstones with crisp lettering and scarcely faded plastic wreaths. The group reassembled at the grave to witness the placing of the stone and to sing, at Rose's request, "God Be with You Till We Meet Again." The thoughts of many sharing in this communal expression of grief and mutual support must have turned to others lying under stones weathered and overgrown. After the group dispersed, several persons remained behind to visit graves in other parts of the old cemetery.

The feast in the community hall that evening included all the elements of the contemporary ceremonial—the turkey dinner with provision for kokol; speeches of tribute to the deceased, reminiscences, and

---

9. Perhaps "revival" is the wrong word since the practice was not repeated.

thanks to guests, hosts and helpers; acknowledgment of donations; gift distribution and payment for ritual services. There was no dancing or singing of old songs; these practices, which have been enthusiastically revived in recent years, were not part of the rites of death in 1971.[10]

Extent of Participation

Given that the formal structure of the ceremonial exchange system has survived many social and cultural changes, what proportion of villagers actually participated in ceremonial activities?

The data, which permitted analysis of ceremonial roles played by each category of kinsmen (figs. 4–7), may also be used to determine what proportion of villagers in each age group participated in six ceremonial events held during 1965–66. The events for which I have complete data on attendance and sponsorship include two weddings, two stone-movings, one name-taking, and one mourning feast. Table 44 shows that of 313 persons between the ages of 15 and 86, 161, or 51 percent, took no part although they may have helped at other feasts that I did not attend (col. B).

The proposition that age is the basic factor determining participation in the feasting complex is well illustrated by these data. Eighty percent of young adults took no part, constituting 70 percent of non-participants (col. B). With the increasing social and family obligations assumed by members of the parental generation, only 43 percent remained uninvolved in feasting, forming 17 percent of non-participants (col. B). Among the middle-aged, 31 percent continued to avoid participation in ceremonies. In the senior age grade, however, only 6 percent were uninvolved.

While Table 44 offers no clue as to frequency of participation, it shows that 20 percent of young adults were involved in at least one event (col. A). Several of these persons played ceremonial roles in one or both weddings and a few helped to serve at family feasts. Fifty-seven percent of the parental generation participated, primarily as helpers. As 25 percent of all participants, their contribution was crucial. It was argued in chapter 5 that the responsibility for sponsoring and supporting the feasting complex is borne largely by the middle-aged. In Table 44 we see that 69 percent of this age group were involved, although they constituted only 25 percent of all participants. In the senior age grade, which is roughly the same size, 94 percent of members participated, forming 32 percent of the total.

Feast Scores. In order to measure the frequency and type of partic-

10. For the filmed record, see Stearns and Stearns 1978.

ipation and perhaps, indirectly, the strength of commitment to the values expressed in the feasting complex. I computed a feast score for the 313 persons between the ages of 15 and 86. Points were assigned according to type of participation in each of the six events and the total was divided by six:

Persons who did not participate	1
Persons who did not attend feast but received ritual payment	2
Persons who attended as a guest	3
Those who attended and received ritual payment	4
Those who participated as host or helper	5

The results for the 49 percent of the village population who participated are presented in Table 45. Scores of 1.5, 2.0, and 2.5 indicate a low degree of participation: "helping" at feasts given by own family groups or possibly attendance as guest at a family feast (cols. A, B, C). Scores in this range were found for 96 percent of young adults, 82 percent of parental generation, and 41 percent of the middle-aged. Only 16 percent of the senior grade fell in this low range.

TABLE 44

CEREMONIAL PARTICIPATION OF VILLAGE ADULTS

Age*	Participants A	Non-Participants B	Total Population C
Young adults	29	113	142
15–29	20%	80%	100%
	19%	70%	45%
Parental	37	28	65
30–44	57%	43%	100%
	24.5%	17%	21%
Middle-aged	37	17	54
45–59	69%	31%	100%
	24.5%	11%	17%
Senior	49	3	52
60–86	94%	6%	100%
	32%	2%	17%
Total	152	161	313
	49%	51%	100%
	100%	100%	100%

*Row percentages refer to participation; column percentages represent percent of population in age groups.

A score of 3.0 suggests that the individual attended all the feasts in
the role of guest; this interpretation is supported by the fact that 63
percent of persons with this score were members of the senior age
grade. The performance of ceremonial and helping roles at several
family feasts would yield this comparatively high score for younger
people. Twenty-four percent of the middle-aged, 13 percent of the
parental generation, and 4 percent of young adults have scores of 3.0
(col. D).

Scores of 3.5 and 4.0 indicate that individuals took an active part in
sponsoring or co-hosting events, or on the other hand received ritual
payment (cols. E, F). Among the middle-aged, 35 percent had earned
these high scores compared to 24 percent who earned the score of 3.0
and 41 percent who had low scores. Of the senior grade, 31 percent
earned high scores compared to 53 percent with the "spectator score"
of 3.0. With reference to the argument that the feasting complex is
supported by the middle-aged, it should be noted that three of the four
persons with the highest score of 4.0 were between 45 and 59 years.

By their regular attendance and performance of ceremonial and helping roles, 84 percent of the senior group and 59 percent of the middle-
aged (all those with scores of 3.0 or above) give active support to the

TABLE 45
Feast Scores of Ceremonial Participants

Age	1.5 A	2.0 B	2.5 C	3.0 D	3.5 E	4.0 F	Total G
Young adults	19	3	6	1			29
15–29	65%	10%	21%	4%			100%
	35%	30%	37.5%	3%			19%
Parental	20	4	6	5	2		37
30–44	54%	11%	17%	13%	5%		100%
	36%	40%	37.5%	12%	8%		24.5%
Middle-aged	10	2	3	9	10	3	37
45–59	27%	6%	8%	24%	27%	8%	100%
	18%	20%	19%	22%	38%	75%	24.5%
Senior	6	1	1	26	14	1	49
60–86	12%	2%	2%	53%	29%	2%	100%
	11%	10%	6%	63%	54%	25%	32%
Total	55	10	16	41	26	4	152
	36%	6%	11%	27%	17%	3%	100%

*Row percentages represent age group; column percentages represent scoreholders.

values underlying the feasting complex. The action patterns observed in the feast complex carry out distinctive cultural behaviors focusing on exchange. From a functionalist point of view, reciprocity reinforces a sense of unity, while the sense of identity is nurtured by the practice of a distinctive culture. The sharing of common action patterns entails a sense of responsibility for the fulfillment of obligations, thus creating solidarity among participants (Parsons 1951:41).

In analyzing change and continuity in the feasting complex we have seen that although this sphere of community action is relatively protected from external interference, the organization of participating groups has been affected by changes in other areas of social life. This reorganization illustrates the development of congruity between interlocking institutions within the Haida social system. It is in the composition of the host group and in the allocation of ritual duties to role equivalents that the modern feast most differs from the traditional potlatch. Since the matrilineage can no longer be mobilized as a unit, feasts are sponsored by individuals who wish to honor a matrilateral kinsman or to validate a change of status. Consistent with the value placed on individualism and independence in economic activity, it is the status and prestige of the individual host and his family that is celebrated in the feast. In his bid for prestige the individual is assisted by his spouse, his bilaterally linked households, and a small number of matrilateral relatives with whom he has close ties. This cooperation in feast preparation by persons belonging to opposite moieties helps to explain the suppression of traditional intermoiety competition in the feast and to nourish the current myth that "Everyone works together."

Adjustments in social relations are reflected also in the reallocation of ceremonial roles to equivalents. Thus the Women's Auxiliary, "standing in for the other side," walks down with the stone. Witnesses to changes in status represent the senior age group rather than opposing matrilineages. Ritual roles to be performed by members of father's matrilineage are assigned to a person of the proper age and sex in the opposite moiety if the prescribed kinsman is not available.

In content, the feasting complex reveals considerable continuity. The role behaviors which are emphasized are those of rank and kinship: (1) to obtain public recognition of life-cycle events such as marriage and death; (2) to give feasts thanking the people for ritual services; (3) to erect headstones honoring the memory of kinsmen; and (4) to pass on names and titles.

The compulsion these obligations exert upon traditionally oriented persons is suggested by comments of informants. Several persons were heard to say at a stone-moving ritual, "I should get my mother's stone this year." "I still haven't been able to get my father's stone after all these years." One middle-aged woman remarked with an embarrassed laugh, "If you don't give a feast for years and years you feel like your [deceased] loved one is hungry." Those who fulfill their ritual obligations are rewarded with esteem, while the self-aggrandizing aspects of rank are restrained. Name-taking, for example, appears to be a way of defining oneself as an Indian and of joining the senior age group, but it does not establish precedence in any but a ceremonial context.

These attempts to preserve traditional culture by reinterpretation and adjustment are not supported by all segments of the community. The people in Masset who carry on the feasting complex are, as we have seen, the old and, to a lesser extent, the middle-aged. The value patterns articulated in the feast by the senior age group on behalf of the whole cultural group are not shared by many of the younger members who are not recruited to active roles in ceremonial activities. They may be honored at a feast at marriage when their change of status is witnessed by the old people or they may take part in a wedding party. They are required to "help" when their family groups are hosts.

Until very recently no special effort was made within the community to keep the traditions alive among the young people. School children and their parents appeared to be totally ignorant of Haida history and myths. Their knowledge of Haida customs and language was fragmentary since enculturation in the neotraditional culture occurred in middle-age. As a consequence, there was a progressive deterioration of old patterns as each generation built upon a weaker foundation. It is to this situation that the people referred in their gloomy prediction that "the old-fashioned ways will be all gone in another generation." No one could then foresee the ebullient re-creation of Haida culture that would take place before a dozen years had passed.

Chapter 10
Conclusion

WHAT ARE the consequences of external control for Haida society and culture that could be identified in 1966, at the close of the Agency period?

We have seen that the Masset Haida were subjected to strict control by officials of boundary structures which mediated relations between the dominant and subordinate sectors of Canadian society. While the government's aims have shifted over time from a custodial to an integrative orientation, they have at all times been imposed upon the people unilaterally. The use of coercion to implement policies reflects the asymmetrical distribution of power which defines the compulsory system. Its inevitable result was the alienation of powerless lower participants. The forms in which alienation is expressed have also shifted over time from passivity and dependency to active opposition. At all periods, feelings of alienation have reinforced the boundaries which circumscribe the community.

The separation of white elites from the dependent group parallels the segregation of institutions of governance from those which meet psycho-biological needs of individuals. This is the condition I have described as structural discontinuity. External regulation of the political process has deprived the people of effective participation in the management of their own affairs. Decapitation of the traditional authority system has left them with no accepted criteria or scope for internal leadership and no formal machinery for defining and sanctioning disapproved behavior. This is not to suggest that political or sanctioning behavior does not occur within the village. My point is rather that the federal government's monopoly of the formal apparatus for carrying out these functions ensures that they are inadequately performed.

While it might control the formal political process, the government could not secure the villagers' approval for the new structure of the

council and the role of councilor with the coercive means that it employed. We noted in chapters 3 and 8 that band councilors received
little respect from their fellow villagers but were described as "yes
men" and "tools of the government." I have suggested that the people's refusal to back up their elected representatives is related to the
fact that little or no power was attached to their roles and they were
given little recognition by the external sources of power.

To some extent these considerations also affect traditional authority
figures who have been repudiated by the Haidas as well as superseded
by the government. No authority to exercise instrumental leadership or
to mediate disputes was granted to the hereditary chief nor did he try to
assume these functions. His role was symbolic and ceremonial. Even
in these respects, as we saw in chapter 8, his rivals were unwilling to
concede his precedence although the majority of villagers acknowledged the chief's high rank. Even less support is given to persons who
assume leadership of associations and *ad hoc* groupings, whether from
personal ambition or a sense of civic responsibility. In the case of
community leaders, other factors than their lack of recognition by
outsiders must be taken into account. First, ambiguity in the stated
qualifications for leadership leads to lack of consensus as to the legitimacy of candidates or incumbents. Second, there is an unwillingness
to accept the subordinate status implied in the role of follower or
supporter. As long as the potlatch was a viable institution it affirmed
the privileges of the hereditary "high ranks" and mediated claims
arising from the recognized right of individuals to compete for higher
status. So deeply rooted in the value system were rivalries between kin
groupings that they still channel relations within the village. The present "disorganized" state of the community, then, is due not only to
structural discontinuity resulting from external control but to the lingering influence of narrow, particularistic kin ties. In other words, modern political attitudes are influenced by the value conflicts inherited
from traditional society.

Had the people been granted more scope for independent action they
might have been able to reinterpret their political institutions as they
have adapted their economic, family, and ceremonial organizations to
meet changed conditions. It is clear that a major effect of Canadian
domination has been the stifling of the people's capacity to devise new
mechanisms of social integration, criteria of placement, and principles
of recruitment to positions of authority. Nevertheless, it must be recognized that the Indians are exercising political functions when they
exert pressure on members of white society. The most significant example cited in this study is the cannery strike of 1964, which forced the
dismissal of the man responsible for the death of a Haida shoreworker.

The capacity for collective action is also demonstrated by the community's attempts to enforce compliance with group norms. This is only possible, of course, where there is substantial consensus and we have seen that this is lacking in many areas of social life.

It appears that community pressure may be very effective in sanctioning expectations attached to roles of high status. For his poor performance of the town chief's role, for his poverty and "immorality," we recall that Harry Weah was slighted at feasts and later excommunicated from the church. The hereditary chief, William Matthews, was criticized for "catering to whites" and for failing to give feasts as a chief is expected to do. On those occasions when he presided at ceremonies or carried out other obligations of his role, however, he received great esteem.

In several instances the community has mobilized to inflict strong sanctions on persons whose actions injured group welfare or prestige. We have mentioned the case of K. Green who was deprived of employment in the cannery and of social interaction in the village as punishment for the "murder" of an affine. The cannery strike, which salved the pride of the Indian community, brought economic loss to many fishermen, shoreworkers, and merchants, provoking a hostile backlash in the white community. For this deterioration in their relationship with New Masset, the Haidas held the leader of the "Revolution" responsible, withdrawing their support and boycotting the wedding of her daughter.

While these normative controls may be effective in disciplining the isolated individual, they are completely inadequate to cope with the widespread disruptive behavior which is one symptom of community breakdown. In this situation native norms governing role behavior are not reinforced by the authority structure. Only informal sanctions are available to deal with deviance and where these are ineffective, disruptive behavior cannot be checked without recourse to external authorities. Nor can the application of a system of sanctions supported by the people's own moral and ethical code be expected when an Indian village must rely upon Anglo-Canadian police and courts. Too often the exercise of legal sanctions is distorted by the political polarization that develops between members of segregated cultural groups. The community's refusal to surrender K. Green to white justice illustrates this dilemma. As a result, one of the most important tasks of a social system—regulating the behavior of its members—cannot be performed by the community and is not adequately performed on its behalf by the dominant society. Drinking, for example, is widely condemned. Women firmly assert that they will not tolerate drinking in the house and that their husbands "know better than to come home drunk." This is wishful thinking. Wives flee from drunken husbands, parents are driven out of the house by a rampaging son, and children take refuge with neighbors to escape brawling parents.

We have been considering the ways in which structural discontinuity disrupts community functioning, leading to normative confusion and to an incapacity to establish consensus on behavioral norms among various segments of the population. From the standpoint of community action, the most significant segments are no longer the matrilineages, nor even the bilateral "kindreds," but the five age grades.

It is to be expected that members of these different age groupings share common values only on the most general level while their immediate goals and interests diverge widely. Such a divergence of interests is demonstrated by the three behavioral syndromes which we have referred to as the gang, the hell-raising complex, and the feasting complex. Each of these associations upholds different norms of personal conduct. But these norms are not considered as equally valid alternatives suited to the special interests of the age grades. "Hell-raising" is widely condemned as deviant and disruptive behavior. Informants describe "drinking, brawling, and running around" as "the cause" of community disorganization. Disapproval and anxiety about activities of the "gang" are expressed by parents and older relatives. Feelings of helplessness stemming from the realization that norms governing individual behavior cannot be enforced are summarized in the frequently heard statement, "The village is falling apart."

Yet if government intervention in political affairs and social control has had disastrous consequences, it has mitigated the impact of economic influences. In chapter 7 we described the kinds of government aid available to the people, pointing out the extent to which they have become dependent on welfare funds, family allowances, foster home payments, and pensions. We noted that the government has created a situation in which the market is not a decisive factor. Furthermore, the expectations held by Indian agents and employers, for example, are inconsistent, creating ambivalence in the performance of economic roles. For while achievement, high productivity, reliability and reinvestment of capital are emphasized in the commercial economy, the government has demanded dependency and conformity to the expectations of its agents. This inconsistency in demands made upon natives who participate in external institutions weakens the effectiveness of attempts to control the people's behavior and influence their idea system.

For the Haida, the impact of the market economy has not been as devastating as for many other matrilineal societies. They have retained a mixed economy based on the sale of produce and labor, subsistence activities, and "government handouts." They continue to exploit the physical environment for a significant portion of their food, preserving many of the relationships and behaviors associated with the food quest: the sharing of surpluses with persons who cannot get their own supply, cooperative labor by members of the household, and circulation of processed foods through reciprocal gift exchange between households.

As participants in the commercial economy, they have tended to specialize in fishing and shorework, occupations requiring no readjustment of the seasonal rhythm of social life, of work patterns, or of residence. They have adopted technological innovations to improve their efficiency, rejecting the behavioral complexes attached to them by white society. They have borrowed some techniques of social action, notably the strike, and share with whites certain values, especially those of independence and skill as expressed in high performance. But the majority have not internalized the economic ethos of Canadian society. Given their perception of fishing as the natural occupation for an Indian, individuals carry over into commercial activities attitudes characteristic of the domestic sphere, refusing to accept the definition of their vocation that is promulgated by the dominant society. But because the Indian community now carries on political competition in the economic sphere, those of their number who subscribe to the traditional Haida value of achievement experience considerable role conflict.

While structural discontinuity is a major source of strain and norm conflict, many of the changes we have observed in the communal system represent attempts to cope with its effects. Indeed, it is only where the Haidas have developed a partial congruity with the structures of the dominant society that we find any fit, any meshing between functionally interdependent subsystems.

As Canadian society consolidated its control over so many vital areas of Haida life, new forms of organization and new behavior patterns were implanted, requiring adjustments in supporting norms and values. Nowhere are their effects more visible than in the family system. The family, whose members now participate in external economic and educational institutions and receive medical and other services, has of necessity become articulated with institutions of the dominant sector. The development of congruity is expressed in the emergence of the nuclear unit, the emphasis on the conjugal bond, the shift to bilaterality in descent and in patterns of inheritance and in the extension of kinship ties.

As the basic economic unit, the family is involved in any enterpise concerned with production, consumption, and exchange. Its identity is underscored by the idea system which supports the individualism of the economically independent person and his mate, even where this "independence" is maintained by welfare funds and pensions. The contemporary family, based on a nuclear core, is embedded in overlapping networks of bilateral and matrilateral kinsmen. As we have seen, the households of senior parents, their married children, other relatives, and friends interact continuously. While they do not pool their efforts in subsistence activities, they share festive occasions and cooperate in providing economic support for ceremonial activities. Obligations of reciprocal gift exchange between households bind the members in a symmetrical relationship which recognizes the independence of each unit.

Because of the functional interdependence of social groups we find that externally stimulated change affects all institutions in a decapitated community. Much of its impact, however, is absorbed by the domestic family, permitting other inner-community institutions to maintain a greater degree of continuity with the past. We have devoted much attention to the ways in which kinship institutions differing in range and recruitment have specialized, carrying out complementary functions. We saw that while the nuclear family has become the coresidential, economically active grouping responsible for the physical survival, socialization, and affective support of its members, lineages and moieties continue to serve as models for ceremonial interaction, which reinforces the identity and integration of the cultural group. Thus we find that the impact of change on institutions peripherally concerned with economic functions is muted by processes of selection among available alternatives and by reinterpretation of events, rules, and relations in terms of a traditional idea system.

The emphasis on the individual rather than the group as the basic unit of the matrilateral network is reflected, of course, in ceremonial behaviors. No longer do corporate matrilineages confront each other in the potlatch, mobilizing the resources of their members in competitive display. Rather, stress is placed upon fulfilling obligations to matrilateral relatives with a "feast to the old people," which earns prestige for the host and his family. It seems clear, however, that the "kindreds" are engaged in covert competition to provide the most lavish feast. Here there is no contraposition of groups in terms of formal rules but simply the assertion by rival "families" of their wealth and importance. But although the relationships of participants differ from the old model, for the community the functional result of the life-cycle ritual is very similar to that of the potlatch. By pursuing their rivalries in the context of the feast, carrying out traditional behaviors which express traditional values, individuals are contributing to the continuity of the old culture.

Gift exchange is another traditional pattern acted out by a majority of modern Haidas. The transfer of goods, which is referred to by the people as "gift giving," continues to bind members of groups on every level of the native social system: family, linked households, community. Within the family this includes obligatory gifts made by adult children to their parents and voluntary gifts from brothers to sisters. The native concept of gift exchange subsumes the sharing of surplus foods with persons who are unable to get their own and the offering of mutual aid in times of crisis. Reciprocal gift exchange takes place between households comprising the bilateral network and occasionally includes unrelated or matrilineally related persons with whom affective ties are shared. When parties are held to honor an individual on a birthday, anniversary, or any other occasion not classified as a ritual event, invited guests present the honoree with gifts. In the ceremonial context where exchange receives its most formal expression, the hosts receive "donations" from members of the community who are, in return, invited to the feast. The distribution of cash and goods at the feast includes payments for ritual services performed by members of the opposite moiety, obligatory gifts to members of the opposite moiety for witnessing the event, voluntary gifts to members of one's own side, and voluntary "special" gifts to senior members of the other side. The functions served by this continuous exchange are the traditional ones of defining and symbolizing one's membership in the group and reaffirming and reinforcing crucial social relationships.

The Masset case demonstrates that a decapitated native community can maintain cultural continuity in those areas of social life that are relatively protected from external interference. I have suggested that this continuity in behavior reflects the persistence of a set of ideas derived from a distinctive framework of perceptions and assumptions that comprise the Haida world-view. The persistence of these ideas is possible because, behind the ethnic boundary, the cultural group continues to exist as a separate territorial unit, a corporate band possessing an inalienable estate of lands and moneys, in a familiar habitat where the traditional economic adaptation is still viable. Certain institutions operating entirely within the community are relatively autonomous. Given the community's isolation from the mainstream of Canadian culture, these institutions lie beyond the effective control of external agencies. Further, they emphasize noneconomic aspects of behavior or, if present, economic elements are subordinated to other values. This finding points back to Goldschmidt's postulate that while economic institutions are particularly vulnerable to change, those oriented to non-economic goals are more resistant (1959:107). The most important examples are matrilineal kinship, hereditary chiefship, life-cycle rituals, and gift exchange.

Even in those institutions which have undergone radical change in adaptation to external pressure, some traditional principles such as ranking and exogamy retain strong normative power for some participants, although they receive little or no expression in the present social structure.

We have identified three basic mechanisms by which the continuity of Haida culture is maintained:

First, traditional behaviors, including exchange of property, observance of life-cycle events, and honoring of matrilateral kinsmen, are carried out by a significant proportion of community members, thus expressing and reinforcing old Haida norms and values.

Second, social relations are redefined and prescribed behaviors are reallocated when traditional structures charged with certain activities no longer function. For example, the Women's Auxiliary of the Church substitutes for the other moiety in "walking down" to the cemetery with the body and later with the headstone. The senior age group replaces opposing matrilineages by acting as witnesses at feasts where a status change is to be validated. If a father's sister is not available, prescribed ritual obligations are assigned to another woman of the opposite moiety. And a last example, where formerly only the members of the deceased's own lineage contributed to his funeral expenses, now the whole community "donates." By the redefinition of social relations, traditional behaviors are preserved in spite of extensive structural changes.

Third, events are reinterpreted to make sense in terms of the Haidas' own system of ideas. We have observed several cases where whites have intervened in internal affairs, imposing rules based on unfamiliar assumptions. We recall that the resolution by "Ottawa" of two disputes over property was considered a triumph for matrilineal rules of inheritance. The jailing of a man for disorderly behavior and interference with a police officer was perceived as punishment for calling the constable a slave.

Although I have argued that traditional institutions may persist in relatively protected areas of social life, I am not suggesting that continuity is passive—that societies change at points of pressure and remain static in "untouched" areas. My analysis has shown that no area of Haida culture has escaped the effects of external intervention. Rather, the preservation of cultural continuity is the result of conscious action, as illustrated by the reinterpretation of events and the reallocation of roles. However, cultural continuity does not depend solely upon the tenacity with which the people cling to traditional ideas.

The persistence of modified traditional behavior is possible only when it continues to serve felt needs without conflicting with adaptations to changes in social and natural environments. The culture patterns described in this volume meet these conditions: the practice of exchange; the extensive complex of behavior surrounding the burial of the dead, the honoring of their memory, the changing of status; the belief that "Haidas must fish—it's in their blood." Other patterns fade, though they are not necessarily forgotten, when they no longer have any functional basis as, for example, the rule of exogamy and the practice of arranging marriages to ensure that spouses are of equal rank and of the proper group.

Culture patterns change more radically when they are incompatible with structural changes resulting from external pressure. With the shifting of functions from one structure to another, submerged principles of organization become dominant. The replacement of the corporate matrilineage by the nuclear family as the basic social and economic unit emphasized the conjugal relation at the expense of matrilineal bonds. But insofar as the latter do not conflict with new adaptations they continue to be important.

In the ideological sphere, too, the people retain traditional elements which, superficially, appear to be inconsistent with adaptive changes. The high value placed on individualism and economic independence does not rule out the observance of traditional exchange and cooperation in ceremonial events. And while the values of independence and individualism imply equality in relations between members of the cultural group, the idea of rank is not totally eclipsed. For ranking formed a basic dimension of the Haida perception of society. Gradually this value has been transmuted to the analogous principle of seniority, which recognizes a finely graded series of statuses based on age. Although the elderly have always enjoyed respect in Haida society, their position was formerly overshadowed by the "high ranks." We have seen that the hereditary chief and lineage heads continue to receive great prestige, at least in the context of the feast where they are called upon to speak in order. On the other hand, age, as a more egalitarian principle than order of birth, is consistent with other changes in values. Consequently, the prestige of all senior members of the village, and particularly those who take part in ceremonial activities, is elevated. This fact probably accounts for the observed tendency of the middle-aged to become more "traditional" as they grow older.

Despite their individualism, the people find the union rule of seniority a congenial principle. In political affairs, however, the majority reject the right of other Haidas to exercise authority. Perceiving that all Indians share a subordinate position in Canadian society, they ascribe equal status to all members of the community, insisting "We are all the same," and "Nobody is better than me." With the repudiation of ranking, competition for status is also suppressed. But although the ceremonial feast has been stripped of the potlatch elements of overt competition, the values it celebrates are those of rank and kinship. As we have just observed, the hereditary chief, lineage heads, and descendants of chiefs receive deference and precedence in speaking. Wealth is another example of a traditional value which is suppressed because of its inconsistency with the people's need for welfare and pensions. Still, at the feasts individuals are rewarded with prestige for lavish expenditures in the provision of food and gifts of money.

The analysis has shown that in the Haida case the primary mechanism of change is not innovation but selectivity among available alternatives. Their adaptive strategy has favored a shift in emphasis from one set of traditionally dominant ideas to others implicit in the culture rather than wholesale adoption of new behavior and ideas. And, clearly, ideas which have ostensibly been suppressed do not cease to exist simply because they receive little or no expression in the social structure. On the contrary, they remain in the consciousness of culture-bearers as standards of behavior and as alternatives, to flare up sporadically in conflict between vested interests. This conclusion substantiates Barth's point that what is critical for social change is not innovation but institutionalization. "The main constraints on change will thus be found in the system, not in the range of ideas for innovation, and these constraints are effective in the phase of institutionalization" (Barth 1967:668).

I have referred to Gough's hypothesis that the replacement of matrilineal descent groups by nuclear units enmeshed in bilateral networks results in the eventual disappearance of traditional culture (1961). Implicit in this view is the assumption, frequently encountered in the literature, that structures determine functions, that cultural behavior expressed and supported by traditional systems of relations is no longer carried out when those systems change. This study refutes that conclusion. The Masset Haida case testifies to the durability and resiliency of that cultural system of ideas, perceptions, and techniques, which, by redefining social relations, finds new structures for its expression.

Epilogue

RETURNING to the village at "potlatch" time, the visitor is swept up in the euphoria of a people playing their most accomplished role, that of host. The whole community has mobilized to greet the guests who have been arriving by plane. Invited to participate in a "Tribute to the Living Haida," Indians have come from Ketchikan and Hydaburg, Alaska, and from Prince Rupert and Port Edward in northern British Columbia. Others have flown in from Vancouver, Victoria, and Seattle. They are billeted with relatives, many meeting their kinsmen for the first time. People have driven up from Skidegate and students have returned from university. Artists of other Indian nations have also come to attend the festivities.

White friends are welcomed, too: anthropologists, art dealers, teachers, students, and neighbors. Wandering through the village, browsing in the new gift shops, crowding the bar at the Singing Surf in New Masset are colleagues one usually sees only at exhibition openings and conferences in the cities.

The visitor, dropping in for tea, is put to work. There are schedules to keep—supper in the long house at 5:30, Indian dancing in the community hall at 7:00 P.M., and, on Friday, the main feast with traditional foods, speeches, and performances by all the visiting dance groups. My old friends Ethel Jones and Grace Wilson, who play the new role of honorary "nonnies" for the village, have been rehearsing the "tiny tots" who go through their paces in a swirl of miniature button blankets.

The visitor, returning after a long absence, may wonder whether everything has changed, or nothing. This spectacular event—held at the spring equinox in 1980, sponsored by the best-known Masset Haida artist, supported by the band council and by the labor and donations of the entire community, feasting and entertaining hundreds of nonlocal

Indians and whites for several days—seems to contrast sharply with
the life-cycle rituals of the 1960s. What has happened?

This book has described the limited forms of expression available to
the people under the constraints of the compulsory system. It appears
in retrospect that repressive government control had stifled artistic as
well as political creativity by devaluing native culture and undermining
the people's pride and self-esteem. We have seen how the Haidas were
involved, unwillingly but inescapably, with government agents who
settled in their midst and interfered with their most intimate activities.

Girded by their resentment, the people resisted enculturation to the
new norms and values. What they exchanged for the paternalistic concern of their agents was submissiveness and dependency. This accom-
modation cost them heavily in psychic energy and self respect, but it
could not extinguish learned patterns and perceptual frameworks. Nor
did the pressure to change affect everyone equally. High-status persons in particular—*those who knew who they were*—found ways to
assert themselves and to earn recognition and rewards. Others could
use these same means to express their aspirations and to achieve higher status. In these families, the seeds of new growth were nurtured.

In Hilary Stewart's warm portrait, *Robert Davidson: Haida Printmaker* (1979), we see the young Davidson working quietly to develop
his talents as an artist, seeking out the work of the great Haida carvers
of the past, moving easily between the village and the larger world.
With the high-status person's characteristic sense of responsibility for
the village, he carved the first totem pole to be raised in Masset in eight
decades. This pole raising in August 1969 was the first of the "media
events" which large numbers of outsiders were invited to attend,
and the proceedings were recorded for television. Although the prominent roles were played by members of the Davidson family, the entire
community, following the pattern established in the life-cycle rituals,
contributed substantial support. While this affair undoubtedly helped
to rekindle interest in old songs, dances, and crafts, it was not yet time
for looking to the past. The challenges lay in the present.

By the time the agency had closed in 1966, it appeared that federal
administration had rendered the Indian people incapable of managing
their own affairs. At this point, responsibility for the community's
welfare fell upon its elected councilors. The frustration, the anger, the
problems of the agency period remained, but the people had found
their voice. They had discovered a means of uniting the community in
the politics of confrontation. Their grievances were articulated in the
charge, "You whites don't respect our culture." Leadership remained,

for a time, in the hands of the militants. Confrontations with outsiders, including the restrictive research contract of 1974, represented attempts to redefine relations with whites, to wring from them the expressive rewards of recognition and respect. The message was, "We are in control."

They were not in control. Decisions were being made in Ottawa by the departments of national defense and fisheries that would profoundly alter the social context and prospects of the Masset Haidas. Even in grappling with the social and economic problems of the reserve, native officials enjoyed little autonomy. The Indian Act was still in force and the band depended upon federal financial support.

Nevertheless, the new roles of band-manager, legal assistance counselor, home-school coordinator, community health worker, and so on allowed the Haidas to take charge of their own affairs. With little experience or training they grew into their jobs, relishing the opportunity to "make our own mistakes," as one woman put it. Nor were they prepared to accept the loss of their cultural heritage. The first demonstration of their resolve was the installation in November 1976 of Oliver Adams as Chief Gala, assuming the office of hereditary town chief left vacant by the death of William Matthews in 1974. The festivities of this second "media event" were enlivened by the performances of Haida dancers in button blankets and traditional headdresses.

By the late 1970s the work of Haida artists had received wide acclaim. Many villagers, inspired by the achievements of Robert Davidson and Bill Reid, were interested in carving. In the execution of the house front commemorating his great grandfather Charles Edenshaw, Robert carried out a training program for apprentices in the village. Including those who were self-taught or had been trained elsewhere, the Masset Haidas numbered about thirty working artists. Looking back to the traditional idiom for inspiration as well as motifs intensified their interest in other areas of Haida culture. This heightened awareness found expression in the construction and dedication of the new long house. It stands on the shore beyond reach of the tide, close to the site where Albert Edwards' house used to be, and long before that, the great planked houses of "White Slope Town." Its magnificent carved front overlooks the beach that could launch two score war canoes . . . Although the project was financed by government grants, Robert's central role in its design and execution allowed the Davidson family to play host, with the assistance of the band council and the community. Multitudes of guests converged on Masset for the dedication of the house front and the feasting, speeches, and entertainment.

Community support of a media event visibly reinforces group solidarity, uniting the people in an enterprise that is a source of pride to all. Moreover, a major ceremony enhances the prestige of its organizers, a point which is not lost on other villagers.

The domination by a single family of an event expressing a cultural pattern of reciprocal exchange between coordinate groups seemed anomalous to some of the participants. In the weeks following the dedication, meetings were held to discuss reviving the lineages so that traditional rules governing potlatches might be observed. It was too late. Those born in the nineteenth century are all but gone; today's elders are the survivors of that middle-aged cohort whose members "didn't know the tribes of all the people" fifteen years ago. What they had hoped to restore was the structure that persisted, attenuated and perhaps unrecognized, in the life-cycle rituals of the 1960s.

With knowledge of the old ways fading and young people assuming leadership, the prestige of high-ranking families had been diminishing. Beneath their pride in the accomplishments of Robert Davidson as a fellow townsman and their delight in the lavish spectacle, many villagers viewed the "Tribute to the Living Haida" as a reassertion of the old values of rank and kinship and perhaps as a claim to the vacant town chiefship. Given this interpretation, those who contributed to the community undertaking were advancing the status of a rival family both within and beyond the village. To allow the rituals of rank to be adjudicated in the media event, where the whole village acts as host, would be to turn over to the guests—nonlocal Indians and whites—the potlatch functions of witnessing and validating status claims. The Haidas have always honored achievement in the outside world, but they have never permitted this kind of prestige to be translated into internal authority.

Though the media event is referred to as a "potlatch," its structure is different. It establishes a new kind of relationship with outsiders, incorporating them in the ceremonial exchange system. The service the guests perform for their hosts is not the legitimating of individual status changes, which would be viewed as intolerable interference. What they are validating is Haida culture itself. This arrangement does not obliterate social boundaries, but formalizes in an unexpected way the recognition and approval that Haidas have long sought from whites. What we see, then, is another shift in the mechanisms maintaining the boundary. We recall that, during the 1960s the community was perceived by its members as poorly integrated: "the village is falling apart." The old forms of cultural integration had weakened but the people found new ways of reinforcing the ethnic boundary by political action. In 1980 the militant voices are subdued. Confrontation has been replaced by ceremonial exchange. These alternate modes of relating to whites are oriented to the same expressive needs, the same cultural goal—earning respect for Haida culture.

By the week after the "Tribute" most of the visitors have gone. Bitter March winds scour empty streets. There is time to visit the cemetery where I am surprised to see row after row of new headstones, placed here since we brought Peter Hill's stone down in 1971. I have looked in vain for so many other friends, not just the old but the young and middle-aged. Here they are, their names inscribed on black marble tablets. In the excitement of the past week it has been easy to forget about the deaths, and the grief and despair that follow.

March is traditionally time to begin work on the boats and to ready the gear for the opening of fishing season, but the beach is idle. Only eight band members still own boats, although others may work as crewmen. This situation is the direct result of fisheries department policies, as I shall show in a separate paper. The cannery has become no more than a fish-buying station for a large Vancouver company, employing only a handful of workers. For most persons, the decline in traditional employment is not balanced by new occupational opportunities. The art industry, however, provides income as well as recognition for some of the better craftsmen. A few individuals have found permanent jobs in minor capacities at the armed forces installation, though by no means in the numbers anticipated when the facility was in the planning stages.

The old social and economic interdependence of the Masset villages has disappeared. This is partly due to the changed character of New Masset, with its expanded population and its reliance on the military base. Equally important, the geographical isolation of the Charlottes no longer impedes communication with the mainland for either Indians or whites.

In the government sphere, the boundary structures remain but their primary function is to provide services. In some areas, such as medical care and educational facilities, there has been great improvement in the last decade. The old task of mediating relations between Indians and the larger society has been minimized. This is true even of that village-based boundary structure, the band council. In interviews with former fishermen in spring 1980, I found little interest in a proposal to vest nontransferable fishing licenses in the band, to be administered by the council. Several men maintained that the council does not represent their interests. These fishermen want to receive licenses as individuals and to apply for boat loans "just like anybody else." To many native people, Indian intermediaries are no more acceptable than white.

Even in depressed economic circumstances, then, we see that surge

of independence and pride that is the most remarkable achievement of
the last decade. It is difficult now, in the aftermath of the "Tribute," to
realize how recently this change has come about. Only fifteen years
ago my gratitude at being allowed to participate in a feast was met by
the people's disbelief that a white person would want to. Nine years
ago, during the filming of Peter Hill's memorial feast, the hereditary
chief acknowledged the gift of the tombstone, saying, "It's a miracle.
It's something we never thought could happen." I found these effusive
speeches embarrassing but attributed them to customary etiquette. As
an integral part of the ceremony, the thanking speeches could not be
deleted from the film without implying that the people "didn't know
how to behave." In showing "Those Born at Masset" to a class recently, I suddenly realized that the chief's remarks help to measure the
distance the people have come. In the 1960s many of them could not
understand what an anthropologist would find to study in Masset, but
by 1971 Ethel Jones could say: "Now we understand why an educated
person comes into a reserve to learn our customs." Within the decade
great numbers of people have come to Masset to help the Haidas to
celebrate their identity and to demonstrate the expansion of their
world.

Bibliography

Anderson, Michael
    1971   *Family Structure in Nineteenth Century Lancashire*. London:
           Cambridge University Press.
Armstrong, W. A.
    1966   "Social Structure From Early Census Returns." In *An Intro-
           duction to English Historical Demography*, E. A. Wrigley,
           ed., pp. 209–37. London: Weidenfeld and Nicolson.
Balandier, Georges
    1970   *Political Anthropology*. New York: Vintage Books.
Barclay, George W.
    1958   *Techniques of Population Analysis*. New York: John Wiley
           and Sons.
Barth Fredrik
    1967   "On the Study of Social Change." *American Anthropologist*
           69:661–69.
    1969   "Introduction." In *Ethnic Groups and Boundaries*, Fredrik
           Barth, ed. Boston: Little, Brown and Company.
Bass, Martha Washington O'Neill
    n.d.   "A Tale of Northern British Columbia from Cariboo to Cas-
           siar." Unpublished typescript in British Columbia Provincial
           Archives, Victoria.
Bender, Donald R.
    1967   "A Refinement of the Concept of Household: Families, Co-
           Residence and Domestic Functions." *American Anthropol-
           ogist* 69:493–504.
Bennett, John W.
    1967   "Microcosm-Macrocosm Relationships in North American
           Agrarian Society." *American Anthropologist* 69:441–54.
Blackman, Margaret B.
    1973   "Totems to Tombstones: Culture Change as Viewed through

the Haida Mortuary Complex, 1877–1971." *Ethnology* 12:47–56.

Bölscher, Marianne
1977 "Aspekte der Gegenwartigen Kultur der Masset—Haida." M.A. thesis, University of Göttingen.

Braroe, Niels Winther
1965 "Reciprocal Exploitation in an Indian-White Community." *Southwestern Journal of Anthropology* 21:166–78.
1975 *Indian and White: Self Image and Interaction in a Canadian Plains Community*. Stanford: Stanford University Press.

British Columbia, Department of Agriculture
1965 *Climate of British Columbia, Tables of Temperature, Precipitation, and Sunshine*. Report for 1965. Victoria: Queen's Printer.

Calder, James A., and Roy L. Taylor
1968 *Flora of the Queen Charlotte Islands*. Part I: *Systematics of the Vascular Plants*. Ottawa: Queen's Printer.

Canada, Department of Citizenship and Immigration
1951 *The Indian Act*. Ottawa: Queen's Printer.

Canada, Department of National Health and Welfare (Nutrition Canada)
1975 *The Indian Survey Report*.

Canada, Joint Committee of the Senate and the House of Commons on Indian Affairs
1961 Minutes of Proceedings and Evidence. No. 8. 2 May 1961 and 3 May 1961. Ottawa: Queen's Printer.

Canada, Indian Affairs and Northern Development
1969 Statement of the Government of Canada on Indian Policy. Presented to the First Session of the Twenty-eighth Parliament by the Honourable Jean Chretien, Minister of Indian Affairs and Northern Development ("White Paper").

Canada (Statistics Canada)
1977 *Perspective Canada II. A Compendium of Social Statistics*. Ottawa: Information Canada.

Canadian Corrections Association
1967 *Indians and the Law*.

Carl, Clifford G.
1963 *Guide to Marine Life of British Columbia*. Handbook No. 21. British Columbia Provincial Museum. Victoria: Queen's Printer.
1964 *Some Common Marine Fishes of British Columbia*. Handbook No. 23. British Columbia Provincial Museum. Victoria: Queen's Printer.

Chittenden, Newton H.
  1884 *Official Report of the Exploration of the Queen Charlotte Islands for the Government of British Columbia*. Victoria: Queen's Printer.
Collison, William Henry
  1915 *In the Wake of the War Canoe*. London: Seeley.
Colson, Elizabeth
  1953 *The Makah Indians: A Study of An Indian Tribe in Modern American Society*. Manchester: Manchester University Press.
Cox, Peter R.
  1970 *Demography*. 4th ed. London: Cambridge University Press.
Dalzell, Kathleen E.
  1968 *The Queen Charlotte Islands, 1774–1966*. Terrace, B.C.: C. M. Adam.
Dawson, George M.
  1880 "On the Haida Indians of the Queen Charlotte Islands." Report of Progress for 1878–79 of the Geological Survey of Canada. Montreal.
Deans, James
  1891 "Carved Columns or Totem Posts of the Haidas." *American Antiquarian and Oriental Journal* 13:282–87.
Dixon, George
  1789 *A Voyage Round the World*. London: J. Stockdale and G. Goulding.
Drucker, Philip
  1958 *The Native Brotherhoods: Modern Intertribal Organizations on the Northwest Coast*. Smithsonian Institution: Bureau of American Ethnology Bulletin No. 168. Washington, D.C.: Government Printing Office.
Duff, Wilson
  1964 *The Indian History of British Columbia*. Vol. 1: *The Impact of the White Man*. Anthropology in British Columbia Memoir No. 5. British Columbia Provincial Museum. Victoria: Queen's Printer.
Edgerton, Robert
  1971 *The Individual in Cultural Adaptation*. Berkeley and Los Angeles: University of California Press.
Ells, R. W.
  1906 "Report on Graham Island, British Columbia." Geological Survey of Canada. Ottawa: King's Printer.

Epstein, A. L.
 1962–3 "The Economy of Modern Matupit: Continuity and Change on the Gazelle Peninsula, New Britain." *Oceania* 33:182–215.
Etzioni, Amitai
 1961 *A Comparative Analysis of Complex Organizations, on Power, Involvement and Their Correlates.* New York: Free Press.
Eversley, D. E. C.
 1966 "Exploitation of Anglican Parish Registers by Aggregative Analysis." In *An Introduction to English Historical Demography*, E. A. Wrigley, ed., pp. 44–95. London: Weidenfeld and Nicolson.
Fields, D. B., and W. T. Stanbury
 1970 *The Economic Impact of the Public Sector upon the Indians of British Columbia: An Examination of the Incidence of Taxation and Expenditure on Three Levels of Government.* Vancouver: University of British Columbia Press.
Firth, Raymond
 1960 "Succession to Chieftainship in Tikopia." *Oceania* 30:161–80.
Fisher, Robin
 1977 *Contact and Conflict: Indian-European Relations in British Columbia, 1774–1890.* Vancouver: University of British Columbia Press.
Fortes, Meyer
 1958 "Introduction." In *The Developmental Cycle of Domestic Groups*, Jack Goody, ed. Cambridge: Cambridge University Press.
Frisch, Rose E.
 1974 "A Method of Prediction of the Age of Menarche from Height and Weight at Ages through 13 Years." *Pediatrics* 53:384–90.
 1975 "Demographic Implications of the Biological Determinants of Female Fecundity." *Social Biology* 22:17–22.
Frisch, Rose E., and R. Revelle
 1971 "Height and Weight At Menarche and a Hypothesis of Menarche." *Archives of Disease in Childhood* 46:695–701.
Gladstone, Percy
 1953 "Native Indians and the Fishing Industry." *Canadian Journal of Economics and Political Science* 19:20–34.
Gladstone, Percy, and Stuart M. Jamieson
 1950 "Unionism in the Fishing Industry of British Columbia." *Canadian Journal of Economics and Political Science* 16:146–71.

Glass, D. V., and D. E. C. Eversley
  1965 *Population in History, Essays in Historical Demography.*
        Chicago: Aldine.
Goldschmidt, Walter R.
  1959 *Man's Way.* New York: Holt, Rinehart and Winston.
  1966 *Comparative Functionalism.* Berkeley and Los Angeles: University of California Press.
  1971 "Independence as an Element in Pastoral Social Systems."
        Anthropological Quarterly 44:132–42.
Goode, W. J.
  1963 *World Revolution and Family Patterns.* New York: Free Press.
Gough, Barry M.
  1971 *The Royal Navy and the Northwest Coast of North America 1810–1914.* Vancouver: University of British Columbia Press.
Gough, Kathleen
  1961 "The Modern Disintegration of Matrilineal Descent Groups."
        In *Matrilineal Kinship*, David M. Schneider and Kathleen Gough, eds. Berkeley and Los Angeles: University of California Press.
Gregson, Harry
  1970 *A History of Victoria, 1842–1970.* Vancouver, B.C.: J. J. Douglas Ltd.
Hawthorn, H. B.; C. S. Belshaw; and S. M. Jamieson
  1958 *The Indians of British Columbia.* Toronto: University of Toronto Press.
Hawthorn, H. B., ed.
  1966 *A Survey of the Contemporary Indians of Canada.* Part I. Ottawa: Queen's Printer.
  1967 *A Survey of the Contemporary Indians of Canada.* Part II. Ottawa: Queen's Printer.
Hill, A. V.
  1967 *Tides of Change: A Story of Fishermen's Co-operatives in British Columbia.* Prince Rupert: Prince Rupert Fishermen's Co-operative Association.
Hollingsworth, T. H.
  1969 *Historical Demography.* Ithaca: Cornell University Press.
Howell, Nancy
  1976 "Toward a Uniformitarian Theory of Human Paleodemography." *Journal of Human Evolution* 5:25–40.
Jamieson, Stuart M., and Percy Gladstone
  1950 "Unionism in the Fishing Industry of British Columbia."

   Canadian Journal of Economics and Political Science
   16:1–11.
Keyes, Charles F.
 1976 "Towards a New Formulation of the Concept of Ethnic
   Group." *Ethnicity* 3:202–13.
Knight, Rolf
 1978 *Indians at Work. An Informal History of Native Indian*
   Labour in British Columbia, 1858–1930. Vancouver: New
   Star Books.
Laslett, Peter
 1966 "The Study of Social Structure from Listings of Inhabi-
   tants." In *An Introduction to English Historical Demogra-*
   phy, E. A. Wrigley, ed., pp. 160–208. London: Weidenfeld
   and Nicolson.
 1971 *The World We Have Lost.* 2d ed. London: Methuen.
Laslett, Peter, ed.
 1972 *Household and Family in Past Time.* London: Cambridge
   University Press.
La Violette, F. E.
 1961 *The Struggle for Survival.* Toronto: University of Toronto
   Press.
Lee, Melvin; Braxton M. Alfred; J. A. Birkbeck; D. D. Indrajit; G. S.
 Myers; R. G. Reyburn; and Anne Carrow
 1971 *Nutritional Status of British Columbia Indian Populations. I.*
   Ahousat and Anaham Reserves. Vancouver: University of
   British Columbia, School of Home Economics.
Levi-Strauss, Claude
 1956 "The Family." In *Man, Culture and Society*, Harry L. Sha-
   piro, ed. New York: Oxford University Press.
Lyons, Cicely
 1969 *Salmon: Our Heritage.* Vancouver: Mitchell Press.
Macfarlane, Alan
 1977 *Reconstructing Historical Communities.* Cambridge: Cambridge University Press.
McArthur, Norma
 1961 *Introducing Population Statistics.* Melbourne: Oxford University Press.
McTaggart Cowan, Ian, and Charles J. Guiget
 1965 *The Mammals of British Columbia.* Handbook No. 11. British
   Columbia Provincial Museum. Victoria: Queen's Printer.
Merton, Robert K.
 1957 *Social Theory and Social Structure.* New York: Free Press.

Murdock, George Peter
　1934　"Kinship and Social Behavior Among the Haida." *American Anthropologist* 36:355–85.
　1936　*Rank and Potlatch Among the Haida.* Yale University Publications in Anthropology No. 13. New Haven: Yale University Press.
Nadel, S. F.
　1951　*The Foundations of Social Anthropology.* New York: Free Press.
　1957　*The Theory of Social Structure.* London: Cohen and West.
Niblack, A. P.
　1888　*The Coast Indians of Southern Alaska and Northern British Columbia.* Report of the U.S. National Museum for 1888. Washington, D.C.: Smithsonian Institution.
O'Neill, Wiggs
　n.d.　"My Memories of a Lifetime in British Columbia." Unpublished typescript in British Columbia Provincial Archives. Victoria.
Parsons, Talcott
　1951　*The Social System.* New York: Free Press.
Peake, Frank A.
　1959　*The Anglican Church of British Columbia.* Vancouver: Mitchell Press.
Piché, Victor, and M. V. George
　1973　"Estimates of Vital Rates for the Canadian Indians, 1960–1970." *Demography* 10:367–82.
Quayle, D. B.
　1960　*The Intertidal Bivalves of British Columbia*, Handbook No. 17. British Columbia Provincial Museum. Victoria: Queen's Printer.
Romaniuk, A., and Victor Piché
　1972　"Natality Estimates for the Canadian Indians by Stable Population Models, 1900–1969." *Canadian Journal of Sociology and Anthropology* 9:1–20.
Roquefeuil, Camille D.
　1823　*A Voyage Round the World Between the Years 1816–1819 in the Ship* Le Bordelais. London: Sir Richard Phillips and Co.
Smith, M. G.
　1962　*West Indian Family Structure.* Seattle: University of Washington Press.
Stanbury, W. T.
　1975　*Success and Failure: Indians in Urban Society.* Vancouver: University of British Columbia Press.

Stearns, Mary Lee
  1973 "Culture in Custody, Adaptation in a Canadian Indian Com-
         munity," Ph.D. dissertation, University of California, Los
         Angeles.
  1975 "Life Cycle Rituals of the Modern Haida." In *Contributions
         to Canadian Ethnology*, David Brez Carlisle, ed., pp. 129–69.
         Mercury Series. Ottawa: National Museum of Man.
  1977 "The Reorganization of Ceremonial Relations in Haida Socie-
         ty." *Arctic Anthropology* 14:54–63.
forthcoming "Succession to Chiefship in Haida Society." In *The Tsim-
         shian and Their Neighbors*, Jay Miller and Carol Eastman,
         eds., Seattle: University of Washington Press.
Stearns, Mary Lee, and Eileen Stearns
  1978 "Those Born at Masset, A Haida Stonemoving and Feast."
         Film, 16 mm. Toronto: International Telefilms Enterprises.
Stewart, Hilary
  1979 *Robert Davidson: Haida Printmaker*. Vancouver: Douglas
         and McIntyre; Seattle: University of Washington Press.
Swanton, John R.
  1908 *Haida Texts: Masset Dialect*. Leiden: E. J. Brill.
  1909 *Contributions to the Ethnology of the Haida*. Memoirs of the
         American Museum of Natural History, vol. 8, part 1. New
         York.
  1911 *Haida Texts and Myths: Skidegate Dialect*. Bureau of Amer-
         ican Ethnology, Bulletin 29. Washington, D.C.: Smithsonian
         Institution.
Turner, Nancy J.
  1975 *Food Plants of British Columbia Indians*, Part I: *Coastal
         Peoples*. Handbook No. 34. British Columbia Provincial
         Museum. Victoria: Provincial Museum.
Vancouver Sun
  1979 "Band seeks $40 million damages" and "Widow defends
         dead Indian agent," September 19.
         "Indian fight against Ottawa closely watched" and "1950s
         Indian agent 'a tyrant'," September 22.
Van den Brink, J. H.
  1974 *The Haida Indians: Cultural Change Mainly between
         1876–1970*. Leiden: E. J. Brill.
Vidich, Arthur J., and Joseph Bensman
  1958 *Small Town in Mass Society*. New Jersey: Princeton Uni-
         versity Press.

Wike, Joyce
    1947   "The Effects of the Maritime Fur Trade on Northwest Coast Indian Society." Ph.D. dissertation, Columbia University.
    1958   "Problems in Fur Trade Analysis: The Northwest Coast." *American Anthropologist* 60:1086–1101.
Wrigley, E. A., ed.
    1966a *An Introduction to English Historical Demography from the Sixteenth to the Nineteenth Century.* London: Weidenfeld and Nicolson.
    1966b "Family Reconstitution." In *An Introduction to English Historical Demography*, E. A. Wrigley, ed., pp. 96–159. London: Weidenfeld and Nicolson.
Yanagisako, Sylvia J.
    1979   "Family and Household: The Analysis of Domestic Groups." *Annual Review of Anthropology* 8:161–205.
Yengoyan, Aram A.
    1968a "Demographic and Ecological Influences on Aboriginal Australian Marriage Sections." In *Man the Hunter*, R. Lee and I. Devore, eds., pp. 185–99. Chicago, Aldine.
    1968b "Australian Section Systems: Demographic Components and Interactional Similarities with the Kung Bushman." In *Proceedings of the VIIIth International Congress of Anthropological and Ethnological Sciences* 3:256–60. Tokyo.
    1972   "Biological and Demographic Components in Aboriginal Australian Socio-Economic Organization." *Oceania* 43:85–95.

Index